Natural Resources in Early Modern Economies of Knowledge

Episteme in Bewegung

Beiträge zu einer transdisziplinären Wissensgeschichte

Herausgegeben von Gyburg Uhlmann
im Auftrag des Sonderforschungsbereichs 980
„Episteme in Bewegung.
Wissenstransfer von der Alten Welt
bis in die Frühe Neuzeit"

Band 40

2025
Harrassowitz Verlag · Wiesbaden

Natural Resources in Early Modern Economies of Knowledge

Edited by
Pietro Daniel Omodeo and Helge Wendt

2025
Harrassowitz Verlag · Wiesbaden

Die Reihe „Episteme in Bewegung“ umfasst wissensgeschichtliche Forschungen mit einem systematischen oder historischen Schwerpunkt in der europäischen und nicht-europäischen Vormoderne. Sie fördert transdisziplinäre Beiträge, die sich mit Fragen der Genese und Dynamik von Wissensbeständen befassen, und trägt dadurch zur Etablierung vormoderner Wissensforschung als einer eigenständigen Forschungsperspektive bei.
Publiziert werden Beiträge, die im Umkreis des an der Freien Universität Berlin angesiedelten Sonderforschungsbereichs 980 „Episteme in Bewegung. Wissenstransfer von der Alten Welt bis in die Frühe Neuzeit“ entstanden sind.

Gefördert durch die Deutsche Forschungsgemeinschaft (DFG) –
Projektnummer 191249397 – SFB 980.

Abbildung auf dem Umschlag:
Athanasius Kircher, *Mundus subterraneus, in XII libros digestus*, Bd. 1, Amsterdam 1678, S. 254.
Universitätsbibliothek Heidelberg, O 2526 A Gross RES::1–2,
https://doi.org/10.11588/diglit.7650#0297.

Bibliografische Information der Deutschen Nationalbibliothek
Die Deutsche Nationalbibliothek verzeichnet diese Publikation in der Deutschen Nationalbibliografie; detaillierte bibliografische Daten sind im Internet über https://www.dnb.de/ abrufbar.

Informationen zum Verlagsprogramm finden Sie unter
https://www.harrassowitz-verlag.de

Verlegt durch Otto Harrassowitz GmbH & Co. KG, Wiesbaden 2025
Kreuzberger Ring 7c–d, 65205 Wiesbaden, produktsicherheit.verlag@harrassowitz.de
Gedruckt auf alterungsbeständigem Papier.
Druck und Verarbeitung: Memminger MedienCentrum AG
Printed in Germany

ISSN 2365-5666
eISSN 2701-2522
DOI 10.13173/2365-5666

ISBN 978-3-447-12369-3
eISBN 978-3-447-39668-4
DOI 10.13173/9783447123693

Preface

Andrew James Johnston and Gyburg Uhlmann

Since its inception in July 2012, the Collaborative Research Centre (CRC) 980 "Episteme in Motion. Transfer of Knowledge from the Ancient World to the Early Modern Period", based at the Freie Universität Berlin, has been engaging with processes of knowledge change in premodern European and non-European cultures.

The project aims at a fundamentally new approach to the historiography of knowledge in premodern cultures. Modern scholars have frequently described premodern knowledge as static and stable, bound by tradition and highly dependent on authority, and this is a view that was often held within premodern cultures themselves.

More often than not, modern approaches to the history of premodern knowledge have been informed by historiographical notions such as 'rupture' or 'revolution', as well as by concepts of periodization explicitly or implicitly linked to a master narrative of progress.

Frequently, only a limited capacity for epistemic change and, what is more, only a limited ability to reflect on shifts in knowledge were attributed to premodern cultures, just as they were denied most forms of historical consciousness, and especially so with respect to knowledge change. In contrast, the CRC 980 seeks to demonstrate that premodern processes of knowledge change were characterised by constant flux, as well as by constant self-reflexion. These epistemic shifts and reflexions were subject to their very own dynamics, and played out in patterns that were much more complex than traditional accounts of knowledge change would have us believe.

In order to describe and conceptualise these processes of epistemic change, the CRC 980 has developed a notion of 'episteme' which encompasses 'knowledge' as well as 'scholarship' and 'science', defining knowledge as the 'knowledge of something', and thus as knowledge which stakes a claim to validity. Such claims to validity are not necessarily expressed in terms of explicit reflexion, however – rather, they constitute themselves, and are reflected, in particular practices, institutions and modes of representation, as well as in specific aesthetic and performative strategies.

In addition to this, the CRC 980 deploys a specially adapted notion of 'transfer' centred on the re-contextualisation of knowledge. Here, transfer is not understood as a mere movement from A to B, but rather in terms of intricately entangled processes of exchange that stay in motion through iteration even if, at first

DOI: 10.13173/9783447123693.V

glance, they appear to remain in a state of stasis. In fact, actions ostensibly geared towards the transmission, fixation, canonisation and codification of a certain level of knowledge prove particularly conducive to constant epistemic change.

In collaboration with the publishing house Harrassowitz the CRC has initiated the series "Episteme in Motion. Contributions to a Transdisciplinary History of Knowledge" with a view to showcase the project's research results and to render them accessible to a wider scholarly audience. The volumes published in this series represent the full scope of collaborating academic disciplines, ranging from ancient oriental studies to medieval studies, and from Korean studies to Arabistics. While some of the volumes are the product of interdisciplinary cooperation, other monographs and discipline-specific edited collections document the findings of individual sub-projects.

What all volumes in the series have in common is the fact that they conceive of the history of premodern knowledge as a research area capable of providing insights that are of fundamental interest to scholars of modernity as well.

Contents

DOI: 10.13173/9783447123693.VII

Introduction: Natural Resources in Early Modern Economies of Knowledge

Pietro Daniel Omodeo and Helge Wendt

In the foreword and introduction to *A Discovery of Subterraneall Treasure*, from 1639, the English man of letters Gabriel Plattes expressed a widespread teleological vision about the precious elements that were waiting to be discovered and extracted from the depths of the earth:

> I being from my Child-hood a strict observer of the great losse that came to this Country, partly through ignorance, and partly through negligence, in raysing that benefit out of the superficiall, and subterraneall Treasures of the Earth, ordained of GOD (no doubt) for the releese and sustenance of mens livings ; thought that I could not bee better employed, then to advertise the World thereof, and to Divulge my knowledge, and experience in these affaires for the common profit ; deeming my selfe obliged thereunto ; for that it hath pleased GOD to give a large blessing to my long labours, and Charges spent in these and such like affaires.[1]

In this manner, Plattes expressed two main ideas that merit our attention as an entry point into widespread conceptions about resources and their value in the early modern world: the providential, divine origin of natural resources, and the advantage to human societies of using and exploiting them to improve living conditions. Plattes clearly thought of terrestrial (subterranean) treasures in relation to their use-value, and not in relation to pricing and the circulation of commodities. In this sense, his outlook was not framed by the monetary sense of values and wealth dictated by classical economic analysis and ideology, even though capitalist economic processes had by then been underway for some time.[2] Yet, at the same time, Plattes had a solely instrumental view of the laboring people who would physically make the extraction possible and work the precious resources to craft artisanal products. The theological perspective thus obscured not

1 Gabriel Plattes, *A Discovery of Subterraneall Treasure, viz. Of all manner of Mines and Mineralls, from the Gold to the Coale; with plaine Directions and Rules for the finding of them in all Kingdomes and Countries*, London 1639.

2 On which we limit ourselves to mention, among the classics on this subject: Fernand Braudel, *Civilization and Capitalism 15th–18th Century*, vol. I: *The Structure of Everyday Life*, London 1985; and Giovanni Arrighi, *The Long Twentieth Century: Money, Power, and the Origins of Our Times*, London 1994.

DOI: 10.13173/9783447123693.001

only the commercial dimension of mining, but also its exploitative and extractive dimensions as well. The divine and the natural occupied center-stage in his account, a signal that in Plattes's time, in contrast the average perception today, the value of resources was not keyed to a monetary standard.

Whatever the difficulties and consequences of the removal of natural resources from their natural site, Plattes argued that humans had a right to the enjoyment of these materials; that was the providential goal of nature rooted in Christian anthropocentrism. In the mid-17th century, Plattes also highlighted a fundamental problem of modern economies of knowledge: in the metallurgical sector, finding, mining, melting, and refinement were knowledge-dependent operations. Wealth was an epistemic output. Besides the treasures hidden in the belly of the earth and brought to light by mining activity, Plattes considered other elements, materials, and substances that are worked upon by human societies. Indeed, the management and transformation of materialities for useful goals also encompassed activities aimed at controlling water for agriculture, transportation, farming, fishing, and other uses, part of a broad and very differentiated range of human practices. These practices connected natural processes and societal agency, a dialectics between humans and the elements that foreshadows the planet-wide reflexivity of the Anthropocene.[3]

Terrestrial and aquatic resources are the center of investigation in the present volume. We focus on two resource groups: water in urban and planetary contexts, and mineral and metallic resources in mining contexts. The knowledge connected to these contexts ranged from fishing to ichthyology, tidal and water-current observation, hydrology, extraction, proto-geology, classification, and the history of the Earth. We address the multi-layered episteme of resource-related knowledge from the 16th to the late 18th century, arguing for the inter-relatedness of management, practice (including labor and technology uses), and theoretical knowledge. The contributions to the volume address both the use of resources and their conceptualization as parts of "nature", a concept that was constantly redefined depending on the ecological roots of economic activities and the kind of resource that was being exploited and valued.

Evidently the wide range of material and intellectual activities produced anthropogenic side-effects that Plattes and his contemporaries could not fully address, although proto-ecological conceptions were already arising. From the vantage point of our current knowledge of these anthropogenic impacts on broad ecologies (and the Anthropocene awareness of humans as a *geological force*), we can infer how actors of the early modern period provoked an irreversible process of environmental alterations that have now reached planetary breadth and geo-

---

3 We use the term dialectics to refer to complex natural-cultural processes in line with emergent uses in hydrosociology, on which see Jamie Linton, *What is Water? The History of a Modern Abstraction*, Chicago 2010.

logical depth.[4] Deforestation, water diversion, mining, cultivation, and fishing techniques have triggered changes in landscape, hydrology, and biodiversity, for instance. In addition, non-sustainable activities have affected ecosystems in irreversible ways and have shaped mentalities that favor exploitation and depletion, in line with the emergent capitalist economy and industrial production.[5] Behavioral path-dependencies can be detected in the application of ever newer technologies to the exploitation of resources. In the sphere of fuel use, for example, the metallurgical complex that evolved from using charcoal to the employment of coal and petroleum is related to a wide range of consumer objects that have satisfied basic needs for centuries.[6]

This volume also looks at the close relationship between resource exploitation, early capitalism, and new scientific knowledge. The "knowledge economy" of early modernity inextricably connected societal and natural processes to each other, but at the same time obscured this connection at a philosophical level of reflection. From the 17th century onward, dominant worldviews considered societies and their environments to be external to each other. The establishment of an incommensurable opposition between active subjectivity and passive objectivity had a functional role in justifying concrete socio-environmental processes which – quite the opposite to the supposed separation of nature and culture – were metabolizing environments at accelerating speed. This widened the gulf between economic growth and natural cycles to the point of creating what has been termed a "metabolic rift".[7] The logic of growth and accumulation of capital, on the one hand, and the regenerative capacities of nature, on the other, created imbalances that lie at the origin of an unprecedented environmental crisis today.

While philosophical speculations often erased the materiality of culture, early modern science engaged with natural processes in various ways. Different

4 Matt Edgeworth et al. "Diachronous beginnings of the Anthropocene: The lower bounding surface of anthropogenic deposits", in: *The Anthropocene Review* 2/1 (2015), pp. 33–58, https://doi.org/10.1177/2053019614565394; Marina Fischer-Kowalski and Daniel Hausknost, "Large Scale Societal Transitions in the Past", in: *WWW for Europe. Working Paper* 55 (2014); Sverker Sörlin and Erik Isberg, "Synchronizing Earthly Timescales: Ice, Pollen, and the Making of Proto-Anthropocene Knowledge in the North Atlantic Region", in: *Annals of the American Association of Geographers* 111/3 (2021), pp. 717–728, https://doi.org/10.1080/24694452.2020.1823809.

5 Tina Asmussen, "Arm, nützlich, giftig und verheissungsvoll: Eine Ressourcengeschichte von Blei in der Frühen Neuzeit", in: *Ferrum* 92 (2022), pp. 18–26. See also Helge Wendt, *Kohlezeit: Eine Global- und Wissensgeschichte (1500–1900)*, Frankfurt/New York 2022.

6 Paul Warde, *Energy Consumption in England and Wales, 1560–2000*, Naples 2007; Sheilagh Ogilvie, "Consumption, Social Capital, and the 'Industrious Revolution' in Early Modern Germany", in: *The Journal of Economic History* 70/2 (2010), pp. 287–325, https://doi.org/10.1017/S002205071000029X; Frank Trentmann, "Introduction", in: *The Oxford Handbook of the History of Consumption*, ed. Frank Trentmann, Oxford 2012, pp. 1–21.

7 John Bellamy Foster, "Marx's Theory of Metabolic Rift: Classical Foundations for Environmental Sociology", in: *American Journal of Sociology* 105/2 (1999), pp. 366–405; Kohei Saito, "Marx in the Anthropocene: Value, Metabolic Rift, and the Non-Cartesian Dualism", in: *Zeitschrift für kritische Sozialtheorie und Philosophie* 4/1–2 (2017), pp. 276–295.

codifications were shaped by local, epistemological, and social contexts and their respective resources.[8] The epistemic structures were constituted by a great variety of interconnected factors, as the material basis, the ecological conditions, activities intervening in the natural world, the technology employed, knowledge or science available and employable to different groups of actors, societal values, religion and mentalities that we here term "economies of knowledge". This concept is primarily used to refer to the cultural development of societies at the crossroads of social history, economic history, and environmental history.[9] Environmental history, especially, helps us understand the consequences of human knowledge and actions for non-human spaces and beings. Economic history looks at evolving interests in materials and natural processes for the sake of trade and exchange, including in relation to matters that were regarded as worthless or were taken for granted. Social history in the broad sense considers the relation between evolving social formations and the resources that are available and are necessary for their existence. Hence, we here mobilize the concept of economies of knowledge in order to connect different branches of historical research and to look at evolving social and geographical spaces of knowledge circulation and transfer.

Activities related to ecosystems and intervention aimed at exploiting and transforming natural settings link resource management to broader vistas on nature. Past knowledge economies bear witness to early, effective, and irreversible interventions in nature. These have recently been described as the Anthropocene condition, considering the accelerating effects of large-scale application of technology to industry in the 20th century. We regard the transformations of materials, spaces, and habitats that occurred in the early modern period as part of a larger process of systematization of practices, domination, and epistemology: a sort of "Protoanthropocene".[10] Wherever large-scale complex societies emerged – in Europe, Asia, the Americas, and Africa – the human impact considered in this volume grew out of local adaptations to regional and meta-regional anthropogenic footprints. Local solutions then served as models that were adapted in other places. Or, in some cases, they were regarded as models for development, representing common or even universally valid ways of using, exploiting, or understanding a given resource. These kinds of local specificities and their entanglement with other settings, spaces, and places will be presented in the chapters of this book.

8 To define a material-focused economy of knowledge, Anne Eusterschulte has emphasized that different social, technical, economic, media, and political conditions are entangled with the materials that they either depend upon or deal with. See Anne Eusterschulte, "Epistemische Materialität", in: *Logbuch Wissensgeschichte*, eds. Mira Becker-Sawatzky et al., Wiesbaden 2024 (Episteme in Bewegung 36), pp. 209–210.

9 Anne Eusterschulte and Andrew James Johnston, "Vorrede", in *Logbuch Wissensgeschichte*, eds. Mira Becker-Sawatzky et al., pp. 1–23.

10 Helge Wendt, "Epilogue: The Iberian Way into the Anthropocene", in: *The Globalization of Knowledge in the Iberian Colonial World*, ed. Helge Wendt, Berlin 2016, pp. 297–314; Sörlin and Isberg, "Synchronizing Earthly Timescales".

Knowledge economies of resources include spaces of communication in which knowledge about the resources was spread in many conceivable respects. Within multi-local spaces, societies further developed forms of knowledge and action that impacted on environments and their imbalances.[11] This publication focuses on the early modern period, which forms part of the era preceeding the semi-official onset of the Anthropocene – commonly dated either to the Industrial Revolution or to the post-1950 Great Acceleration.[12] While the chapters concentrate on water and water-related resources, as well as mining and extracted materials, the scope could be extended to encompass broader human impacts on soils and biodiversity, including activities such as deforestation, agriculture, and landscape management. Water and mined materials were present in most parts of Europe and played an important role in shaping European societies. They were objects of economic competition, legal processes, textual production, and abstract knowledge – thus, together forming an economy of knowledge.

Recent years have seen a proliferation of perspectives that relate the early modern period to the Anthropocene. In *The Shock of the Anthropocene*, Christophe Bonneuil and Jean-Baptiste Fressoz have shown how changes in the perception of nature during the Enlightenment had long-term consequences for how Europeans treated nature in the industrial age.[13] However, it is essential to understand and analyze the early modern period in its own right, as neither industrialization nor the Anthropocene should be regarded as inevitable consequences of earlier developments. In this regard, Thomas Leinkauf, among others, has analyzed earlier shifts in the natural philosophy of the 16th century. He notes that nature either replaced the figure of God in a transcendental sense or became an almost tangible mechanism that could be dissected, analyzed, and studied.[14] This latter manner of conceiving nature gave way to more standardized epistemes that have gravitated around the constituency of modern science, as Jürgen Renn emphasizes in *The Evolution of Knowledge*. In the early modern period, these new forms of knowledge expanded, sometimes by force, to other places; and in a more intense

11 Gian Battista Vai, *The Origins of Geology in Italy*, Boulder 2006; Martin Guntau, "The Rise of Geology as a Science in Germany around 1800", in: *Geological Society, London. Special Publications* 317/1 (2009), pp. 163–177, https://doi.org/10.1144/SP317.9; Simon J. Knell, "The Road to Smith: How the Geological Society Came to Possess English Geology", in: *The Making of the Geological Society of London*, ed. Cherry L.E. Lewis and Simon J. Knell, London 2009, pp. 1–47.

12 There have been many controversies over the beginning of the Anthropocene. For some historiographic considerations see Pietro Daniel Omodeo, "History of Science and History of the Earth in the Anthropocene", in: *Physis* 57 (2022), pp. 171–188.

13 Christophe Bonneuil and Jean-Baptiste Fressoz, *The Shock of the Anthropocene: The Earth, History, and Us*, London 2016.

14 Thomas Leinkauf, "Der Naturbegriff in der Frühen Neuzeit", in: *Der Naturbegriff in der Frühen Neuzeit*, ed. Thomas Leinkauf, Tübingen 2005, pp. 17–18, https://doi.org/10.1515/9783110942552.1.

way than before the European economies of knowledge communicated in colonially asymmetrical ways with other regions of the world.[15]

Fundamental changes affecting even the most abstract forms of knowledge occurred through their constant interplay with fields of practice. Within more practical areas of activity, such as forestry, alchemy, mining, or fishing, some important transformations occurred in the way a resource was conceived and treated. Martin Knoll has shown that from the 16th century onwards the representation of 'socionatural spaces' went hand in hand with the use of land and its resources.[16] Flows of energy and goods were dynamic, as were the imagination of, access to, and forms of exploiting territories, materials, waters, and living resources.[17] In these relations, an important role was always played by the means (communicative and technological) that mediated between societies and ecosystems,[18] as a part of knowledge economies, which both dynamized and stabilized knowledge.[19]

In this twofold dynamic, the 16th century already witnessed a profound transformation of energy regimes with the development of new milling technologies and the substitution of wood by coal or peat in some European regions.[20] Regarding the introduction of coal into regional energy systems, Marina Fischer-Kowalski and Daniel Hausknost note that the early industrialization 'starts in the 16th century, pretty much at the same time when the humanities date the start of the modern age, and well over 100 years before Newcomen invents the steam engine.'[21] Coal, then, was a new material that gave rise to new forms of use, in a time in which protoindustrial developments were still propelled by water in places in which this element flowed in abundance, for instance in northern Italy.[22]

New uses of materials, artefacts, and resources were linked to new technologies and technical processes. Here, too, the medialization of knowledge contributed to its dissemination beyond the immediate social environment of its origin. Knowledge about unfamiliar goods or practices found its way into different

15 Jürgen Renn, *The Evolution of Knowledge. Rethinking Science for the Anthropocene*, Princeton/Oxford 2020, pp. 13.

16 Martin Knoll, *Die Natur der menschlichen Welt: Siedlung, Territorium und Umwelt in der historisch-topografischen Literatur der Frühen Neuzeit*, Bielefeld 2013, pp. 18–20.

17 Rolf Peter Sieferle, "The Energy System. A Basic Concept of Environmental History", in: *The Silent Countdown: Essays in European Environmental History*, ed. Peter Brimblecome and Christian Pfister, Berlin 1990, p. 10.

18 Stephen Yeager, Fiona Somerset and Daniel T. Kline, "Preface: Media Before 1800", in: *Old Media and the Medieval Concept. Media Ecologies Before Early Modernity*, eds. Thora Brylowe and Stephen Yeager, Montreal 2021, p. xii.

19 Eusterschulte, "Epistemische Materialität", pp. 196–98.

20 Paolo Malanima, "The Energy Basis for Early Modern Growth, 1650–1820", in: *Early Modern Capitalism. Economic and Social Change in Europe 1400–1800*, ed. Maarten Prak, London 2000, pp. 49–66.

21 Fischer-Kowalski and Hausknost, "Large Scale Societal Transitions in the Past", p. 37.

22 Deborah Howard, *Proto-industrial architecture of the Veneto in the age of Palladio*, Roma 2021.

socio-epistemic settings, as did material objects that traveled and spread.[23] Thus, the spatial scope of an economy of knowledge expanded and the adaptation of these received epistemological items (or *episteme*) into the global socio-epistemic context began. As with any innovation, the adapted *episteme* transformed the socio-epistemic context and with it the socio-natural settings. New forms of practice caused the transformation of landscapes, demanded new technological objects, and produced side effects and by-products. The transfer of knowledge thus accelerated ecological alterations and changes in production, reproduction, and consumption patterns.

Yet, microscale changes in early modernity are hardly comparable to those of the industrial and the post-industrial societies, because the human community was much smaller and the technical tools less powerful. They had less impact on climate, rarely erased species, and rarely made land uninhabitable. Thus, the anthropogenic effects of early modern technologies could affect human and animal bodies, could pollute water and air, and damage biodiversity and the habitats of certain species, but the effects were mostly localized, although they can be traced in wider geographical spaces with modern measurement techniques.[24] New construction works, such as ponds, artificially created by a dam, or ditches, could be used for multiple purposes, such as water milling, laundry, or fishing. New species of animals could live within this water and plants could grow around such a pond. This new technological infrastructure was fed by water that had previously flowed naturally, certainly in a different way and in a different environment. New technical infrastructures thus had a twofold aspect, both transforming natural landscapes and also enabling the emergence of new ecologies. The cases of early modern hydrology in Venice and the Netherlands are paradigmatic of a shift in intensity and amplitude in their geographic impact.[25] They can be regarded as liminal cases connecting small-scale environmental changes to large geomorphological and ecological transformations.

It was in the early modern period that remarkable developments in the relationship between humans and "nature" were set in motion. The changes of landscapes into infrastructure or of natural objects into resources brought about profound socioeconomic and epistemological transformations. European societ-

23 Jürgen Renn, "Survey: The Place of Local Knowledge in the Global Community", in: *The Globalization of Knowledge in History*, ed. Jürgen Renn, Berlin 2012, https://doi.org/10.34663/9783945561232-20; Kathleen E. Kennedy, "Naming the Coconut and (De)Colonizing the Middle Ages", in: *Digital Philology: A Journal of Medieval Cultures* 11/1 (2021), pp. 61–85, https://doi.org/10.1353/dph.2022.0006.

24 Tina Asmussen and Pamela O. Long, "Introduction: The Cultural and Material Worlds of Mining in Early Modern Europe", in: *Renaissance Studies* 34/1 (2020), pp. 8–30, https://doi.org/10.1111/rest.12581; Franz Mauelshagen, *Geschichte des Klimas: Von der Steinzeit bis zur Gegenwart*, Munich 2023; Ran Segev, *Sacred Habitat: Nature and Catholicism in the Early Modern Spanish Atlantic*, University Park, PA 2023.

25 Salvatore Ciriacono, *Building on Water: Venice, Holland and the Construction of the European Landscape in Early Modern Times*, New York 2006.

ies began to appropriate minerals and gradually transformed them into commodities. Through innovation and dynamics of consumption, it was less an individual appreciation than, rather, a consideration of them as mass goods that turned them into exploitable objects, depriving them of their character as active beings, which was still being defended in the treatises of alchemy.[26] These resources were involved in infrastructures of knowledge exchange between scholars, laymen and practitioners, officials, princes, artisans, and workers. The knowledge economy was a field composed of many parts: a wide range of human actors and of material components, natural environments and infrastructures, ecologies and technical apparatuses, all interacting in asymmetrical ways. Only the learned could write in 'higher' cultural forms that often required the mastery of Latin, mathematics, or concepts from natural philosophy, but vernacular forms of knowledge dissemination did emerge, too: illiterate actors appear indirectly as transmitters of knowledge, as practitioners in certain fields, as knowledgeable persons, in the representations by those who wrote. The same happened with objects, animals, or materials, because they were carriers of knowledge and were included in the written testimonies without being asked. In these writings, materials and objects appear in the forms in which humans conceived them, often from the perspective of use, exploitation, and utility.

In the first chapter of this volume, Pietro Daniel Omodeo and Justas Patkauskas articulate a heuristic concept of knowledge economy that connects the ecological, socio-economic, and epistemological axes on the basis of considerations concerning the multiple functions of water knowledge in Venice, especially in early modernity. Water and its management have always been crucial to the material reproduction of Venice from its origins in the Middle Ages. Yet, institutions and codified forms of knowledge became increasingly important quite late in the city's history, in early modern times, when appointed water officers developed scientific, technological, and social methods of managing the waters. Venice's hydrological reproduction regime, it is argued, fostered the consolidation of a water-knowledge economy that could rest on a large socio-epistemological basis. Its knowledge bearers were many, ranging from fishermen to water officers, proto-scientists and politicians. It involved multilateral republican governance. It also rested on constant monitoring of the material conditions of the water body of the lagoon, its riverine system, and societal behaviors. Indeed, Venice's knowledge economy of water integrated epistemic and societal components in such a manner that the resulting knowledge can be regarded as a true "common", a kind of "dispersed collective intelligence" in the service of the maintenance and flourishing of the water-city and the composition of its various interests, even competing ones.

26 Simon Brandl, *Mystik und Magie im Frühparacelsismus: Erkundungen um Alexander von Suchtens Traktat 'De tribus facultatibus'*, Berlin/Boston 2021.

In the second chapter, Ovanes Akopyan and Pietro Daniel Omodeo present a rare document of the hydraulic and cosmological culture of early modern Venice, a text on tides by the most prominent Renaissance water officer of Venice, Cristoforo Sabbadino. The authors also offer a transcription of a significant section of the manuscript, which they interpret in light of the water economy of early modernity, the institutional and cultural settings of Venice, and Renaissance natural debates on tides in general.

In his contribution to this volume, Omar Rodríguez Camarena considers the water knowledge economy of a locality that was often regarded, in early modernity, as the American twin city of Venice: Tenochtitlán, that is, the Aztec capital of Mexico. Although it was in an elevated location encircled by mountains, it stood in a lagoon which resembled that of Venice not only in its environmental conditions but also in its watery lifestyle. Yet, unlike in the Italian case, the Hispanic colonizers considered the management of the waters of the lake to be an overwhelming challenge, which rested too heavily on indigenous knowledge. In a long process of social and ecological reorganization of forces and relations among the people and the waters of the Watershed of Mexico, major engineering projects were set in motion in early modernity. They would eventually mark the development of Tenochtitlán into Mexico City, an urban setting that could be expanded through massive land reclamation and water diversions. Rodríguez Camarena's chapter explores the conditions and controversies that set this historical process of socio-ecological transformation in motion, which had significant negative impacts on the surrounding communities and the environment. Today, this model exhibits its limits, as water scarcity is threatening the Valley of Mexico. Therefore, it is important to recover historical alternatives of hydropolitics that can help us imagine alternative options to face current environmental problems. As he argues, in order to explain this process, it is necessary to situate it not only within the cross-cultural clash of European and American cultures and natures, but also within early globalization and the beginning of the modern world, including its colonial practices. The emergence of the Ibero-American world implied not only a mixture of cultures, but also of "natures", developing together in terms of human and material resources.

With a focus on the political discourses on water scarcity, Alexander Schunka shows the importance of water management in central European territories, taking the example of the efforts of the Thuringian territory of the Duchy of Saxe-Gotha and the Mark Brandenburg to bring clean water to the people, to transform natural watercourses into a useful resource. In this chapter focused on the 17th century, Schunka draws his understanding of political considerations, technical solutions, and social conflicts in relation to water from the source-based diagnosis of an actual or perceived water shortage. Thus, saving this scarce resource became one of the ways to deal with water in Gotha, giving the authorities a new lever of power. In Brandenburg, the building of canals to increase the number of usable waterways also implied an extension of power mechanisms to compel the local population and to change the regional landscape.

Practical knowledge comes to the fore in Florike Egmond's contribution. She analyzes the so-called 'Fishbook' of the Dutch marine expert Adriaen Coenen, who recorded whales, herring, and other animals of the sea, described their different habitats and fishing methods, and opened up a world full of fantasy. Coenen's images and writings reveal an economy of knowledge in which different human actors, climates, and animals interacted and provided valuable information. Egmond's chapter shows the connection between water and its resources, situated knowledge and its circulation, media and content. She also draws attention to the fact that ecological changes, perceived already in the early 16th century, were linked to human activities. Coenen's depiction of fish and other marine animals as resources implied a call for conservation, moderation, and recognition of local knowledge.

Local knowledge is also part of Barbara Orland's contribution, focusing on the Upper Rhine region rather than the sea. Here, the economy of knowledge is built by fishermen on the one hand and by erudite writers on the other. By identifying authors and fishermen, Orland achieves a socially profound insight into the processes of knowledge formation from the 17th to the 19th century. In this way, she is able to trace changes of knowledge based on terminology, as well as the changes in fish populations related to overfishing and the transformation of different habitats. As Orland points out, the economy of knowledge of fishing in the Upper Rhine Valley can best be described through the perspective of the long-term establishment of terminology and the entanglement of different actors and groups of actors.

Another comprehensive economy of knowledge about fishing is revealed in Aina Trias Verbeeck's contribution on the fishery manuscripts of the French official François Le Masson du Parc. During his lifetime, this mid-18th century civil servant and expert in fish and fisheries collected a great amount of information on fishing practices and fish taxonomies in Europe and beyond. He linked a large number of places with different local epistemic traditions, in order to give a centralized account appropriate to the centralized political and administrative project of French politics. Trias Verbeeck discovers a European network of knowledge exchange between experts, and a personal network of Le Masson du Parc and the fishermen of the French coasts.

Water was not only an important source of energy in mining but was itself a source of minerals, as Helge Wendt shows in his contribution. The idea of the usefulness of some types of water in this sense is clearly evident in the writings of the 16th-century naturalist Georgius Agricola. Wendt reconstructs the argumentation of how and why minerals were to be found in water, and the techniques by which these could be acquired. The knowledge economy consisted of transforming water into a solid matter, of different metallurgical techniques, and of the transfer of knowledge from Antiquity to the Renaissance and from different European regions into Saxony. In addition, Agricola addresses the technical question of winning minerals from water in relation to legal, social, political, and economic issues.

In his chapter, Francesco Luzzini deals with early modern interconnections between hydrology and mining knowledge based on the work by the Italian metallurgist and minter Vannoccio Biringuccio, *De la Pirotechnia* (1540). In this early companion on mines, Biringuccio connected water and ore generation following a widespread Renaissance notion, according to which mineral ores were formed by the combination and condensation of moist and dry vapors produced underground by solar heat. In agreement with this model, the differences in the seven classical metals – gold, silver, copper, tin, lead, iron, and mercury – were generally assumed to be the result of the influence of celestial bodies on different proportions of the two *essential constituents* of these vapors: sulfur and mercury. Biringuccio was one of the earliest practitioners to openly question this interpretation in a published text. His engagement was shaped largely – though not solely – by his direct experience in mining contexts. As Biringuccio wrote in his treatise *De la Pirotechnia* ('On Pyrotechnics'), he could not believe sulfur or quicksilver to be the essential constituents of all metals, as he never observed metallic ores grow near sulfur or mercury ores. As the following decades would show, these and other remarks were harbingers of a conceptual turn in the study of the mineral world, a change where alchemical and classical knowledge, empirical evidence, and natural philosophy interacted in different yet substantial ways and led to new understandings of the role of water in mineral processes.

Joshua Hillman shows that practical knowledge played a role even in the circles of London's Royal Society of Science, with Robert Boyle at the center of knowledge transfer. Hillman reveals a deep commercial interest in mining behind Boyle's philosophical works. The philosopher, chemist, and naturalist gained knowledge directly from the mines, either through his own research or by communicating with miners. Although it is difficult to identify individual miners, a network of places, people, and minerals emerges that is situated within a European network of knowledge exchange between scholars, as well as the institutional setting of the Royal Society. The identification of resources – both their geological location and their quality – was the goal of Boyle's inquiries, which underlines the importance of the economic aspect of Boyle's economy of mining knowledge.

To sum up, the contributions to this volume especially deal with two resource groups, water and extracted minerals, investigate their societal and cultural contexts and explore their practical and cognitive dimensions. The practical dimension comprises labor, for instance mining, fishing, engineering, while the cognitive dimension concerns the codification and transmission of knowledge, both vernacular and scientific. The authors of the various chapters shed light on the multiple strata of knowledge (from natural history to proto-geology, metallurgy, alchemy, early hydrology, ichthyology, tidal theories, natural philosophy and cosmology) that emerged from and contributed to the material and immaterial knowledge economy of early modernity. The volume interjects the current debate on natural resources, including water, plants and wood, which has gained much attention in the history of knowledge and science. Our investigations connect theoretical questions stemming from global history of knowledge and the Anthropocene perspective on human geological agency with approaches derived from microhistory. While practical knowledge of resources often was local or localized knowledge, economic and political relations fostered exchanges of knowledge that were variable in space and distance. In this local-global perspective, this volume presents case-studies of the past forms of observation, management, exploitation and conceptualization of nature and its resources: the management of water in its various facets and according to sometimes conflicting uses, from transportation to fishing; mining that enabled the utilization of metallic and other subterranean materials and gave insights into important subterranean phenomena. The role of water as a natural good was certainly related to religious accounts about the direct causality of human behavior, nature's responses and providence. Those big pictures of anthropogenic agencies are here contrasted and related to forms of everyday practice, with practices of legal and scientific codification and with institutional interactions of spheres of knowledge, as in administration of water and mining resources. This volume also contributes to the ongoing eco-social debates in Science and Technology Studies by offering a historical and epistemic perspectivation that connects the history of knowledge with environmental history.

This publication is especially linked to institutional and research contexts that the editors would like to acknowledge. Our work would have not been possible without the support of the CRC 980 "Episteme in Motion" at the Freie Universität Berlin. We the editors of this volume had the chance to collaborate within this research framework, more specifically in the context of the subproject B06 "Dimensions of Knowledge Oikonomies: Theory and Practice in Premodern Mining and Cosmology" based at the Max Planck Institute for the History of Science, Berlin and led by Jürgen Renn, to whom we also wish to extend our gratitude.

We are also thankful to the following contexts and projects that offered us unvaluable occasions of research, exchange and conversation about the questions and topics of this volume: the Max Planck Institute of Geoanthropology, Jena; the UNESCO Chair Water Heritage and Sustainable Development at Ca' Foscari University of Venice; the FARE project *EarlyGeoPraxis* (Grant of the Italian Ministry of University and Research, no. R184WNSTWH); the Max Planck Partner Group *The Water City* (Venice and Jena); and THE NEW INSTITUTE Centre for Environmental Humanities (NICHE) in Venice. We would also like to express our sincere gratitude to Orla Mulholland, who carefully reviewed several contributions and helped shape the many subtle details that make this volume what it is. Our thanks also go to Julia Guthmüller at Harrassowitz Verlag for her patience and the outstanding work she has done throughout the process. Finally, our heartfelt appreciation goes to our long-time colleagues Sofie Mörchen and Katrin

Wächter, whose tireless dedication and meticulous commitment have been invaluable to the completion of this volume.

Reference List

Arrighi, Giovanni, *The Long Twentieth Century: Money, Power, and the Origins of Our Times*, London 1994.

Asmussen, Tina, "Arm, nützlich, giftig und verheissungsvoll: Eine Ressourcengeschichte von Blei in der Frühen Neuzeit", in: *Ferrum* 92 (2022), pp. 18–26.

Asmussen, Tina and Pamela O. Long, "Introduction: The Cultural and Material Worlds of Mining in Early Modern Europe", in: *Renaissance Studies* 34/1 (2020), pp. 8–30, https://doi.org/10.1111/rest.12581.

Bonneuil, Christophe and Jean-Baptiste Fressoz, *The Shock of the Anthropocene: The Earth, History, and Us*, London 2016.

Brandl, Simon, *Mystik und Magie im Frühparacelsismus: Erkundungen um Alexander von Suchtens Traktat 'De tribus facultatibus'*, Berlin/Boston 2021.

Braudel, Fernand, *Civilization and Capitalism 15th–18th Century*, Vol. I: *The Structure of Everyday Life*, London 1985.

Ciriacono, Salvatore, *Building on Water: Venice, Holland and the Construction of the European Landscape in Early Modern Times*, New York 2006.

Edgeworth, Matt, et al. "Diachronous beginnings of the Anthropocene: The lower bounding surface of anthropogenic deposits", in: *The Anthropocene Review* 2/1 (2015), pp. 33–58, https://doi.org/10.1177/2053019614565394.

Eusterschulte, Anne, "Epistemische Materialität", in: *Logbuch Wissensgeschichte*, eds. Mira Becker-Sawatzky, Şirin Dadas, Anne Eusterschulte, Kristiane Hasselmann, Andrew James Johnston, Falk Quenstedt, Claudia Reufer, Hanna-Zoe Trauer, Christian Vogel, Katrin Wächter and Helge Wendt, Wiesbaden 2024 (Episteme in Bewegung 36), pp. 189–213.

Eusterschulte, Anne and Andrew James Johnston, "Vorrede", in: *Logbuch Wissensgeschichte*, eds. Mira Becker-Sawatzky et al., Wiesbaden 2024 (Episteme in Bewegung 36), pp. 1–23.

Fischer-Kowalski, Marina and Daniel Hausknost, "Large Scale Societal Transitions in the Past", in: *WWW for Europe. Working Paper* 55 (2014).

Foster, John Bellamy, "Marx's Theory of Metabolic Rift: Classical Foundations for Environmental Sociology", in: *American Journal of Sociology* 105/2 (1999), pp. 366–405.

Guntau, Martin, "The Rise of Geology as a Science in Germany around 1800", in: *Geological Society, London. Special Publications* 317/1 (2009), pp. 163–177, https://doi.org/10.1144/SP317.9.

Howard, Deborah, *Proto-industrial architecture of the Veneto in the age of Palladio*, Roma 2021.

Kennedy, Kathleen E., "Naming the Coconut and (De)Colonizing the Middle Ages", in: *Digital Philology: A Journal of Medieval Cultures* 11/1 (2021), pp. 61–85, https://doi.org/10.1353/dph.2022.0006.

Knell, Simon J., "The Road to Smith: How the Geological Society Came to Possess English Geology", in: *The Making of the Geological Society of London*, eds. Cherry L. E. Lewis and Simon J. Knell, London 2009, pp. 1–47.

Knoll, Martin, *Die Natur der menschlichen Welt: Siedlung, Territorium und Umwelt in der historisch-topografischen Literatur der Frühen Neuzeit*, Bielefeld 2013.

Leinkauf, Thomas, "Der Naturbegriff in der Frühen Neuzeit", in: *Der Naturbegriff in der Frühen Neuzeit*, ed. Thomas Leinkauf, Tübingen 2005, pp. 1–20, https://doi.org/10.1515/9783110942552.1.

Linton, Jamie, *What is Water? The History of a Modern Abstraction*, Chicago 2010.

Malanima, Paolo, "The Energy Basis for Early Modern Growth, 1650–1820", in: *Early Modern Capitalism. Economic and Social Change in Europe 1400–1800*, ed. Maarten Prak, London 2000, pp. 49–66.

Mauelshagen, Franz, *Geschichte des Klimas: Von der Steinzeit bis zur Gegenwart*, Munich 2023.

Ogilvie, Sheilagh, "Consumption, Social Capital, and the 'Industrious Revolution' in Early Modern Germany", in: *The Journal of Economic History* 70/2 (2010), pp. 287–325, https://doi.org/10.1017/S002205071000029X.

Omodeo, Pietro Daniel, "History of Science and History of the Earth in the Anthropocene", in: *Physis* 57 (2022), pp. 171–188.

Plattes, Gabriel, *A Discovery of Subterraneall Treasure*, London 1639.

Renn, Jürgen, *The Evolution of Knowledge. Rethinking Science for the Anthropocene*, Princeton/Oxford 2020.

Renn, Jürgen, "Survey: The Place of Local Knowledge in the Global Community", in: *The Globalization of Knowledge in History*, ed. Jürgen Renn, Berlin 2012, https://doi.org/10.34663/9783945561232-20.

Saito, Kohei, "Marx in the Anthropocene: Value, Metabolic Rift, and the Non-Cartesian Dualism", in: *Zeitschrift für kritische Sozialtheorie und Philosophie* 4/1–2 (2017), pp. 276–295.

Segev, Ran, *Sacred Habitat: Nature and Catholicism in the Early Modern Spanish Atlantic*, University Park, PA 2023.

Sieferle, Rolf Peter, "The Energy System. A Basic Concept of Environmental History", in: *The Silent Countdown: Essays in European Environmental History*, eds. Peter Brimblecome and Christian Pfister, Berlin 1990, pp. 9–12.

Sörlin, Sverker and Erik Isberg, "Synchronizing Earthly Timescales: Ice, Pollen, and the Making of Proto-Anthropocene Knowledge in the North Atlantic Region", in: *Annals of the American Association of Geographers* 111/3 (2021), pp. 717–728, https://doi.org/10.1080/24694452.2020.1823809.

Trentmann, Frank, "Introduction", in: *The Oxford Handbook of the History of Consumption*, ed. Frank Trentmann, Oxford 2012, pp. 1–21.

Vai, Gian Battista, *The Origins of Geology in Italy*, Boulder 2006.

Warde, Paul, *Energy Consumption in England and Wales, 1560–2000*, Naples 2007.

Wendt, Helge, *Kohlezeit: Eine Global- und Wissensgeschichte (1500–1900)*, Frankfurt am Main 2022.

Wendt, Helge, "Epilogue: The Iberian Way into the Anthropocene", in: *The Globalization of Knowledge in The Iberian Colonial World*, ed. Helge Wendt, Berlin 2016, pp. 297–314.

Yeager, Stephen, Fiona Somerset and Daniel T. Kline, "Preface: Media Before 1800", in: *Old Media and the Medieval Concept. Media Ecologies Before Early Modernity*, eds. Thora Brylowe and Stephen Yeager, Montreal 2021, pp. xi–xiv.

Water Knowledge Economy in Early Modern Venice

Pietro Daniel Omodeo and Justas Patkauskas

1 Introduction

In this essay, we consider the connections between nature, economy, and knowledge in early modern Venice from the perspective of political epistemology. To this end, we follow the example of historical epistemologists who interfused philosophical and historical investigations (e. g., Ludwik Fleck, Georges Canguilhem, and Hans-Jörg Rheinberger).[1] However, whereas historical epistemology investigates the genesis, verification, and application of knowledge, particularly science, political epistemology expands the inquiry by considering the interests and agendas underpinning knowledge structures.[2] Therefore, the methodology of political epistemology is post-foundational:[3] instead of presuming *necessary* transcendental grounds for epistemic structures, we can only assume *contingent* foundations subject to social struggles. This does not mean that everything goes but rather that the objectivity of knowledge is conditional and its universality is a task to be accomplished, like a promise that must be constantly restated and fulfilled anew. It also suggests that conditions of epistemic production can, and often do, change, which means that knowledge is neither intrinsically emancipatory nor inevitably embedded with oppressive forces; instead, its orientation depends on socio-political framing.

To contribute to the field of political epistemology, we would like to expand its methodological toolkit by proposing the following two analytic concepts: sufficient abstraction and conditional objectivity. We believe that this conceptual pair can help navigate the dichotomy between scientism and relativism, or between a technocratic epistemology that assumes direct access to subject-independent reality and radical constructivism that postulates only minimal or no reality beyond what society makes of the world. To achieve this objective, in the following

1 See Dominique Lecourt, *L'épistémologie historique de Gaston Bachelard*, Paris 1969; Hans Jörg Rheinberger, *Historische Epistemologie zur Einführung*, Hamburg 2007; Gerardo Ienna, Pietro Daniel Omodeo and Massimiliano Badino, *Epistemologia storica: Correnti, temi e problemi*, Roma 2022.

2 Pietro Daniel Omodeo, *Political Epistemology: The Problem of Ideology in Science Studies*, Cham 2019.

3 Oliver Marchart, *Post-foundational Political Thought: Political Difference in Nancy, Lefort, Badiou and Laclau*, Edinburgh 2007.

DOI: 10.13173/9783447123693.015

discussion, we alternate between conceptual development and historical explorations of early modern water management in Venice.

Our historical case study concerns the Lagoon of Venice and draws on archival material produced by the water officers, who, from the sixteenth century onwards, were in charge of the surveillance, maintenance, and transformation of the Venetian water bodies in the service of the political and economic interests of the insular city's ruling mercantile class. They belonged to an institution called *Collegio delle acque,* which can be literally translated as 'Water College' or, more freely, as 'Water Office'. This institution was composed of approximately 45 people, the most important of whom were the *savi alle acque* ('water sages' or, in more modern parlance, 'water experts') and *esecutori alle acque* ('water executors').[4] In *De origine, situ et magistratibus urbis Venetae* (On the Origin, Site, and Magistrates of the City of Venice), Venetian historian Marin Sanudo (1466–1536) considered the *savi* to be the most important persons within the Water Office:

> The water sages are three; they stay for two years; meet at Rialto; are chosen through an election by the Senate; are mostly patricians with the title of 'Pregadi' [Senators]; receive no stipend and attend the Senate without voting. They ensure that the waters flow properly and that the rivers do not silt up with earth [*interrano*]. They moreover [control] that nobody appropriates the common waters [*le acque del Commun*].[5] They are free, whenever they like, to request from the Senatorial Council to undertake those measures that they consider [to be necessary] in relation to the waters.[6]

The water officers collected information, mapped the territory, and interacted with political institutions, civil society, and corporations, including fishermen communities, in order to safeguard the lagoon and implement lasting transfor-

4 Archivio di Stato di Venezia (ASV), *Savi ed esecutori alle acque,* Atti, Folder 238, "Elezioni del Collegio Eccellentissimo delle acque 1564–1792."

5 There is some ambiguity about the expression 'le acque del Commun', which we decided to render as 'the common waters'. First, the term 'Commun' may refer to the Commune of Venice, in which case Sanudo would be talking about water understood as the property of the Commune. Then, this expression could also designate 'waters of the commons' understood as a public resource available for social use. Finally, it is also possible that Sanudo was referring to water as a common good of the Venetian political community in the broad sense. Given that the context of the document does not allow for a clear decision to be made regarding Sanudo's intended meaning, we chose a neutral translation, but the ambiguity of this expression should be noted. We would like to thank Erasmo Castellani for his invaluable insights into this matter.

6 Marin Sanudo, *De origine, situ et magistratibus urbis Venetae, ovvero, La Città di Venetia (1493–1530),* Venice 2011, pp. 109–110: "Savii sora le Acque sono tre, stanno do anni, sentano a Rialto, si ellezze per elettion in Pregadi [il Senato veneziano], ut plurimum patritii che hanno titolo di Pregadi, non hanno alcun salario ma vanno in Pregadi non mettando ballotta [senza diritto di voto], ut supra; attendino a far che l'acque habbino il suo corso et che le fiumare non atterrino; anchora, che niun non toglia le acque del Commun. Et è in sua libertà, ogni volta li piace, dimandar il Conseio d'i Pregadi per far quelle provision a loro paresseno sopra il fatto delle acque."

mations of its geography. As part of their epistemic practices, the water officers consulted multiple knowledge bearers, which points to the existence of a complex knowledge economy centered on Venetian water management. For instance, the material we found in the State Archive of Venice included hydrological assessments by Padua professors[7] in the seventeenth century and records of interactions between water officers and local fishermen concerning the state of the lagoon in the seventeenth century. These documents exhibit tensions among reputed intellectuals (particularly mathematicians in the hybrid sense of the word in the Renaissance[8]), state officials, and the popular strata, indicating the contested and shifting grounds of knowledge-making, along with the limited validity of epistemic claims premised on notions of unbounded objectivity. In this multidimensional epistemological setting, water emerged as a mediated resource whose use and preservation depended on a kind of *composite hydraulic intelligence* consisting of socio-cultural dialectical relations between societal groups and their distinct but interconnected epistemic practices.

2 Theoretical Description: Material Base

In order to survive, persevere, and flourish, every society must reproduce its material base.[9] Speaking schematically, an adequate understanding of the material base of society needs to consider at least three fundamental dimensions: production, reproduction, and knowledge. Each dimension involves specific natural, technical, and cultural factors, along with the 'forces' capable of mobilizing them for societal purposes. In the tradition of historical materialism, to emphasize the significance of the active, mobilizing component, production and reproduction have been referred to as 'forces of production' and 'forces of reproduction'. Although we partly subscribe to this tradition, given the limited attention paid to the knowledge dimension of production and reproduction within classical Marxist thought,[10] we draw on historical epistemology and the concept of the knowledge economy to address the epistemic dimension of the material base.

The *forces of production* include various means of production, such as raw materials, tools, and machines, as well as forms of social organization, such as the division of labor, the pooling of stock, and the distribution of things. In other words, the forces of production are not merely natural and physical but also social and cultural. In addition, by themselves, without people to use and put them

7 ASV, *Savi ed esecutori alle acque*, Atti, Folder 123, f. 296.

8 See, among others, Jens Høyrup, "Practitioners – School Teachers – 'Mathematicians': The Divisions of Pre-Modern Mathematics and Its Actors", in: *Writing and Rewriting the History of Science 1900–2000* (Les Treilles, 5–11 September 2003).

9 Stephen Gudeman, "Community and Economy: Economy's Base", in: *A Handbook of Economic Anthropology, Second Edition* (3rd edition), ed. James G. Carrier, Cheltenham 2012, pp. 45–56.

10 See "Foreword" by Marcello Cini in Giovanni Ciccotti, Marcello Cini, Michelangelo De Maria, Giovanni Jona-Lasinio, *The Bee and the Architect: Scientific Paradigms and Historical Materialism*, Venice 2024.

to work, all these means of production would remain largely inert and useless. For means of production to be active and contribute to the material base – that is, for means of production to become forces of production proper – they require labor. Therefore, we can only speak of the forces of production when various means of production, whether natural or social, are put to work by human labor.

The significance of human work for the forces of production, and thus for the replenishment and expansion of the material base, means that the reproduction of human beings is a chief component of the material base. However, contrary to popular biopolitics, such reproduction is never a matter of mere procreation and biology. Instead, it involves a whole range of social institutions (e. g., family, guilds, academies) with cultural and historical foundations. Other means of reproduction can include 'subsistence farming, fishing and gathering, domestic work, gardening, teaching, nursing, healthcare, waste collecting and recycling'.[11] The totality of all these means and those who work them constitutes the *forces of reproduction.*

In this analytic vocabulary of the forces of production and reproduction, which is partially inspired by Marxist historical materialism, it may appear as if the interactions between people and things, between labor and means, and between society, culture, and nature happen immediately, with minimal epistemic mediation. However, even in the most basic situation of worker and tool, the relationship between the two is never immediately given and involves multiple dynamic gaps that require constant negotiation. For instance, is this tool functional or inadequate? Is it a means of oppression or emancipation? Is the worker a revolutionary or reactionary subject? In other words, both the worker and the tool need to have meaning and *make sense* – on their own and in relation to each other. This meaning is always created because it is historically conditioned; no means or forces of production and reproduction possess a default, fixed sense. Rather, what they mean is the result of a contested process that involves language, communication, and knowledge – in other words, societal epistemology. We could say that without the various abstractions needed to make sense of all the components of the material base, we would be baseless and impoverished even when surrounded by the greatest stock of things. To account for this epistemic mediation of the relationships between the various forces and their subcomponents, we must consider the *knowledge economy* as an intrinsic part of society's material base.

In the context of historical epistemology and Anthropocene studies, the concept of the knowledge economy was discussed by Jürgen Renn,[12] who drew on the longue durée historical epistemology research performed at the Max Planck Institute for the History of Science. According to Renn,

11 Stefania Barca, *Forces of Reproduction: Notes for a Counter-Hegemonic Anthropocene*, Cambridge 2020, p. 6.
12 Jürgen Renn, *The Evolution of Knowledge*, Princeton 2020.

> Every society has its own "knowledge economy." It comprises the ensemble of its social institutions and processes producing and reproducing the knowledge at its disposal, and, in particular, the knowledge on which its reproduction as a society relies.[13]

We could say that a society's knowledge economy provides the epistemic circuits that loop together the various forces and dimensions of the material base. Without a knowledge economy, the different components involved in the reproduction of the material base would remain little more than disparate entities with nothing in common. It is the epistemic circulation enabled by the knowledge economy that ultimately makes the material base make sense. But what is it that circulates across these circuits and loops of the knowledge economy? What is the epistemic medium that can be produced, exchanged, and modified within the knowledge economy?

For Renn, whose theory connects Jean Piaget's individual development of cognition and Peter Damerow's societal dynamics of representation,[14] the basic unit of the knowledge economy is *abstraction*. At the individual level, abstractions are developed from individual experience: as people interact with their environments, they generate internal cognitions that facilitate ecosystemic manipulation. From the very outset, knowledge is imprinted with a practical, utilitarian dimension. Such individual cognitions can become externally represented, for example, by using signs and symbols. It is only with the development of external representations, which make possible the sharing and exchange of codified experience, that a society can be said to have a knowledge *structure*. Through reflection, these first-order abstractions can be modified and become the basis of further, second-order abstractions and more elaborate knowledge structures. At a certain point, when a society develops not only external representations and knowledge structures but also institutions for the formal reproduction and transmission of selected abstractions, that society can be said to have a knowledge economy. In addition, 'scientific knowledge first emerged in complex societies that created social spaces for exploring knowledge independently from immediate practical purposes'.[15] Therefore, although the foundations of knowledge are largely practical, whereby knowledge production is a means of problem-solving, science becomes possible only when at least a certain part of knowledge production is 'released' from immediate practical and utilitarian concerns.

With the concept of the knowledge economy, the complexity of the material base is evident. A society's material base is not merely an inventory of the various forces and their means, locked in immediate relations of production and repro-

13 Ibid., p. 7.

14 See, e. g., Peter Damerow, *Abstraction and Representation: Essays on the Cultural Evolution of Thinking*, Dordrecht 1995.

15 Renn, *Evolution of Knowledge*, p. 15.

duction. It also includes the epistemic practices needed to generate the abstractions necessary to represent and make sense of the base and its content. (In fact, the material base is itself an abstraction – an advanced-order representation for making sense of the complex processual and collective character of the self-reproduction of society.) Such abstractions are never organic in the sense of deriving from the experiences of individuals in direct contact with society and nature; instead, they are byproducts of the knowledge economy and its institutions, which mediate society to itself and its members. In short, one could say that, in order to understand the full complexity of societal reproduction, a robust historical-epistemological materialism is required that takes into account the strongly epistemic dimension of the material base.

However, even with the addition of the knowledge economy, the schematic description offered above contains several limitations, such as the absence of governance considerations, the idealization of epistemology as homogenous and without contradiction, and a bias toward radical constructivism (which overprivileges the cultural in relation to the natural). Later on, we will address each of these issues on the basis of our case study, to whose description we now turn.

3 Case Overview: Water-Knowledge Economy in Early Modern Venice

Given that a full reconstruction of a society's knowledge economy would be an exceptionally demanding task, one way in which its structure can be approximated involves identifying and describing the relevant 'knowledge bearers', as externalist historian of science Edgar Zilsel would have called them.[16] To this end, our case study is built primarily using the institutional documents preserved in the Venice State Archive, but always with a mind toward another implicit source of information, namely, the geomorphology of the Venetian Lagoon.

On the one hand, the Archive is a monument of this water city's knowledge economy in the longue durée. Since the sixteenth century, the Republic of Venice kept extensive records of the institutional day-to-day activities involved in the running of the city and its territories. Despite the political upheaval after the fall of the Republic at the end of the eighteenth century, which resulted in a dispersal of archival material, and several disastrous fires, significant records have survived and can be publicly accessed at the Venice State Archive. If one considers the great amount of documentation related to water assessments and hydrological projects therein, the existence of a well-developed water-knowledge economy in the Republic becomes evident. This is not surprising given that the very existence of Venice, physically and politically, rested on the balancing of its relationship with the surrounding waters, which constituted a significant part of its material base. Moreover, as the lagoon was part of a complex hydrographic system, water management was not limited to Venice, some islands, the lagoon

16 Edgar Zilsel, "The Sociological Roots of Science", in: *Social Studies of Science* 30/6 (2000), pp. 935–939.

canals, and the costal lines. Rather, it had to address the entire hydrographic basin from the Alpine water catchment to the Adriatic Sea. For instance, to tame and control the waters and preserve the lagoon, rivers in the entire Veneto region were constantly engineered and diverted.[17]

In addition to archival evidence, there is another relevant information source that needs to be mentioned: geography itself. We follow the insight of Fernand Braudel and the Annales School that waters and territories (even the Mediterranean basin!) are the archives of their own histories.[18] In the case of Venice, the geomorphology of its lagoon is a natural–artificial entity. Countless interventions have been necessary to preserve the lagoon's water body against adverse environmental factors. The fifteenth-century initiator of Venetian hydrology, Marco Cornaro (not to be confused with Alvise Cornaro, to whom he was not related), compared them to enemies fiercely attacking the lagoon: 'Day and night, twenty rivers carry land into this lagoon of ours, besieging the city and surrounding it with land.'[19] For Marco Cornaro and all those who, after him, acted to preserve Venice's maritime nature, it was necessary to progressively divert rivers and their sediments toward the open sea, outside of the lagoon. A long-lasting process of modern interventions made it possible to avoid embankment and shoaling, thus ensuring the survival of the lagoon, but this happened at the cost of other geographical areas sacrificed in favor of a maritime vision of Venice and its future.

The written and natural archives of early modern Venice reveal at least three broad groups of 'knowledge bearers' who participated in, and sometimes clashed over, the city's reproduction of its hydrological material base along with its water-knowledge economy: reputed experts, state officials, and the popular strata. Among the experts, the most celebrated person of Renaissance Venice was Cristoforo Sabbadino, who advocated the preservation of the Venetian lagoon. For him, the lagoon served as a natural defense, the liquid walls upon which the 'serenity' of the Republic rested. Furthermore, the same water that protected the city also connected it with the rest of the world, as Venetian harbors were at the center of a broad Mediterranean and international mercantile network, from which the urban classes benefitted in particular. Sabbadino argued that only salty water – the kind coming from the sea – could protect Venice and its lagoon from the noxious effects of tributary rivers. Among other documents, his letter from 16 May 1552, which is preserved in the State Archive of Venice, considers the efforts to mark

17 Salvatore Ciriacono, *Building on Water: Venice, Holland and the Construction of the European Landscape in Early Modern Times*, New York 2006.

18 Fernand Braudel, *The Mediterranean and the Mediterranean World in The Age of Philip II*, transl. Sian Reynolds, New York 1972; Pietro Daniel Omodeo, "History of Science and History of the Earth in the Anthropocene", in: *Physis* 57 (2022a), pp. 171–188.

19 Marco Cornaro, *Scritture sulla Laguna*, ed. G. Pavanello, in: *Antichi scrittori d'idraulica veneta*, Vol. 1, Venezia 1919, p. 143: "XX fiumare […] dì et nocte mena terreno in questa nostra laguna […] assediando la citade e lasciandole fra terra."

the boundaries of the lagoon. In the letter, Sabbadino emphasizes the advantages of river diversions:

> The benefits are countless and most certain. Some of them here follow. The lagoon will all be salty, from one end to the other: [it will] all [be made of] living water, and sea, in great quantity. […] Fresh water, dominated by salty water, will be fully weakened and will not produce the bad effects that occur when it overcomes salty water. Venice, Mestre, and all the localities will be transformed into a most perfect sea. The localities dominated only by salty water will be distanced from firm land. The canals and mudflats which, due to the continuous presence of the freshwater lagoon, have lost their depth, and those that still remain and are hardened, will become deep and low again.[20]

The success of Sabbadino's campaign to link the future of the Venetian material base to the preservation of the lagoon is evident in nineteenth-century sources celebrating the hydrological past of Venice. For example, Pietro Paleocapa, the most renowned Italian hydraulic engineer of his time, wrote a historical pamphlet attacking Benedetto Castelli and all those who, in ancient and recent times, argued that the rivers should be allowed to flow freely into the lagoon. In his words,

> One ought to consult people who are knowledgeable in science and art. If they examine today's situation with an unbiased spirit, they will all agree on the following assertion: The ruin of Venice is a necessary consequence of the introduction of the rivers into the lagoon.

Regarding the mainland, it shall be clear that the disorders which can be observed in the water system follow from other causes than the diversions of the rivers, and require different remedies [than bringing the rivers back into the lagoon] to be resolved! Otherwise, bringing the rivers back to their old riverbeds would be not only useless but even dangerous.[21]

---

20 ASV, *Savi ed esecutori alle acque*, Atti, Folder 124, "Scritture diverse circa l'allontanar l'acqua dolce dalla Laguna 1505–1620", f. 38*r*: "Gli benifitii veramente serano innumerabili e certissimi: et in parte sono questi. La laguna serà da un capo all'altro tutta salsa tutta di acqua viva e mare et tanta […] il dulce superato dal salso serà del tutto mortificado né opererà il cativo efetto ch'egli fa superando il salso. Si redurrà Venetia, Mestre et tutte le contrade in perfettissimo mare. Le contrade dominate solamente dal salso se discostaranno dal terren fermo. Gli Canali et Velme che per il continuar quasi sempre di laguna dolce hanno perso gli fondi et quelli che sono restati se sono induriti, si farano denuo profondi e bassi […]."

21 Pietro Paleocapa, *Esame delle opinioni di Benedetto Casteli e di Alfonso Borelli sulle Lagune di Venezia*, Venezia 1819, pp. 96–97: "Bisogna consultare le persone dotte nella scienza e nell'arte. Le quali con animo spassionato esaminando le cose tali quali sono ai dì nostri, tutte di comune accordo discenderanno in questa sentenza: la rovina di Venezia essere necessaria conseguenza della introduzione dei fiumi nella laguna. E quanto alle cose di Terraferma si riconoscerà che da altre cagioni che non sono le deviazioni dei fiumi dipende il disordine che si scorge nel sistema delle acque, e ad altri rimedi! si vuole quindi ricorrere per ristorarlo.

What was still a heated debate in the sixteenth century – Sabbadino's vision of preserving the lagoon was opposed by agrarian landowners, who preferred investments in land reclamation over hydraulic projects – had become, three centuries later, a self-evident presupposition. Past controversies to do with the lagoon were resolved and sedimented, over an extended period of time, into a strong path-dependency whereby the preservation of the lagoon was largely depoliticized into a truism. For Paleocapa, it was not necessary to acknowledge the political motivations behind the long history of the hydraulic reengineering of the Venetian waterscape. Instead, he could invoke dispassionate expertise and common sense, further signaling the successful depoliticization of what had been, in historical actuality, a contentious political decision. As we elaborate in this essay, the hydrological 'destiny' of Venice was not fait accompli; instead, it was an outcome of protracted political and epistemic clashes. At the same time, the very need for Paleocapa's nineteenth-century pamphlet shows that the matter of river diversion was not entirely settled among engineering elites even at the dawn of modernity.

Whereas renowned intellectuals and engineers concerned themselves with the 'grand' planning of Venetian hydromorphology, the innumerable day-to-day activities involved in overseeing and handling water-related issues were the duty of the water officers, particularly the executors. Although the Water Office was led by a specific kind of practitioners – technicians concerned with water management, planning, and control – the documentation that they collected concerned various social groups (or 'socio-epistemic' communities). In fact, the water officers mediated between different sectors of society, along with their needs and perspectives related to the water bodies of Venice. However, the overarching knowledge economy that the water officers tapped into was more than a mere aggregate of individual and group interests. It was an interconnected, dynamic structure premised on a multiplicity of experiences, situations, and abstractions. The archival material reveals water knowledge derived from practice, labor, technical skills, university erudition, and mathematical expertise – to only mention some of the identifiable sources of epistemic know-how. Moreover, the Water Office was in direct contact with both political institutions and working people (e. g., fishermen and peasants), all of whom were concerned with the 'public waters' of the lagoon. From an epistemological viewpoint, the water officers positioned themselves at the nodal points of this distributed structure, codifying and bringing together the different forms of knowledge dispersed across the knowledge economy: the situated and proto-experimental knowledge of those working with and on water, the practical arts that flourished in the late Middle Ages and the Renaissance (especially practical mathematics), and the emergent sciences of the classical age of Galileo. Their interest was not merely academic; the water officers

Senza dei quali anche il rimettere i fiumi negli antichi loro alvei sarebbe opera non solo inutile ma perniciosa."

leveraged their intermediary position to put the various abstractions to work in maintaining and transforming the Venetian water bodies as needed.

Finally, in addition to the grand planners and the water officers, there were also those who worked on the lagoon and the related rivers, both for their own sustenance and for the implementation of state-mandated modifications of Venetian hydromorphology. They were a host of laboring people, such as the peasants who dug canals, the fishermen who policed the waters to prevent abuses (e. g., illegal fishing, the usage of prohibited nets, or the construction of barriers that could hinder the flow of water), and the contractors who transported mud and sediment away from the places of extraction. Although their voices are seldom directly present in archival material, the various kinds of workers surface through interviews, bills, letters of protest, defenses, reported conversations by the water executors, and the like. For instance, there is a folder on inspections of the southern area of the lagoon close to Chioggia by *esecutore* Zuane Garzoni in 1611–1612 and his efforts to improve the local situation. The concerned territory had been radically reengineered for the diversion of the Brenta river in 1610. Garzoni temporarily moved his residence to Codevigo in May 1611, a place close to the area to be supervised. In particular, he was there to direct excavations aimed at letting salty water enter parts of the so-called 'dead lagoon' (*laguna morta*). In his reports (in the form of epistles) to the *savi alle acque*, he mentioned enrolling local peasants for the manual work of canal digging.[22] The labor of these anonymous people was instrumental to the goals set by water technicians, such as Garzoni, and the political elite.[23]

Some laborers are prominent in the documents of the water officers, such as the fishermen, particularly those of the San Nicolò community.[24] They surveilled the territory and, on many occasions, denounced abuses and illegal activities that could damage their fishing and the lagoon – for example, the construction of blockages (*grisiuole*) that hindered the flow of water streams and the free navigation of public waters. Among others, a letter of denunciation from 12 August 1610 is preserved in the archive. In the letter, the head of the fishermen community of San Nicolò (the *Gastaldo*) protests against illicit constructions. To solve this incident, the officers referred to a similar case from the past. More specifically, they referenced a condemnation, dated 31 August 1569, of a certain Iseppo Gatto, who

22 ASV, *Savi ed esecutori alle acque*, Atti, Folder 130, "Tagli nelle Barene della Laguna morta 1611–1612", f. 2*r*.

23 See Pietro Daniel Omodeo, "The Invisible Fisherman: The Economy of Water Knowledge in Early-modern Venice", in: *Ichthyology in Context (1500–1880)*, eds. Paul J. Smith and Florike Egmond, Leiden 2023, pp. 362–391.

24 Roberto Zago, *I Nicolotti: Storia di una comunità di pescatori a Venezia nell'età moderna* (Padova 1982); Solène Rivoal, "Agir en être collectif: L'État, la communauté des Nicolotti et l'approvisionnement de Venise à l'époque moderne", in: *Tracés: Revue de Sciences humaines* 29 (2015), pp. 65–84; Solène Rivoal, *Les marchés de la mer : Une histoire sociale et environnementale de Venise au XVIII*e *siècle*, Roma 2022.

constructed a blockage in the lagoon. The text of the sixteenth century condemnation reads as follows:

> Iseppo Gatto is condemned in the following manner: that before leaving prison he must pay [...] 30 ducats of which will be applied to the excavation of the lagoon, and another third shall be allocated to the denouncer. In fact, Iseppo is obliged to completely remove all the impediments of reeds made by him, as ascertained in the present trial against him. The term is within the next ten days. Otherwise, he will be banished from Venice and the district for five continuous years, in addition to the mentioned pecuniary penalty, as in any case the impediments of reeds are to be removed completely at his own expense. He shall also pay the costs of this trial. Let this sentence be in the usual and customary places.[25]

Another group of people involved in the maintenance work were those responsible for the transportation of sediments and mud from excavation sites. They must have been small entrepreneurs contracted and paid on the basis of invoices in which they listed the costs of their work (e. g., the number of trips and the quantity of the materials they transported and discharged).[26]

4 Analysis

Despite its usefulness as a heuristic tool that provides an analytic entry point for scrutinizing the material and epistemic composition of a society, the schematic description of society's material base and its three dimensions (i. e., forces of production, forces of reproduction, and the knowledge economy) offered earlier has certain shortcomings. As with all schematic descriptions, it is highly general and requires a greater degree of particularization, which we hope to accomplish by drawing on our historical case study. More specifically, the schema suffers from the following three issues that may lead to a distorted understanding of societal reproduction: an absence of a governance dimension, which may give the impression that societies run 'organically'; an apparently homogenous knowledge economy, which hides the tensions and contradictions involved in knowledge-making; and a bias toward radical constructivism, which makes it seem as if societies reproduce their material bases without natural and objective

25 ASV, *Savi ed esecutori alle acque*, Atti, Folder 121, "Deposizioni de' Periti ed altro circa la Laguna, conterminazione sua medisima, etc. 1582–1670", f. 328*r*: "Iseppo Gatto sii condannato in questo modo che inanti, che l'uscisca di pregione et debbba pagar [...] 30 ducati de quali siano applicati alla cavatione della laguna, et l'altro terzo sia del denunziante, essendo obbligato lui Iseppo far cavar, et del tutto rimover tutti; et cadauni impedimenti per lui fatti di Grisiole, come consta nel presente processo contra de lui formato in termine de giorni X prossimi altramente sii, et s'intende esser bandito de Venetia, et del destretto per anni cinque continui, oltra la pena pecuniaria soprascritta, dovendosi anco in tal caso a tutte sue spese de lui, et intermessati [?] far cavar l'impedimentisudetti di esse Grisiole, et debba pagar le spese del presente processo, et la presente condanason sii pubblicata alli luochi soliti, et consueti."

26 ASV, *Savi ed esecutori alle acque*, Atti, Folder 129, "Escavazioni nella Laguna 1520–1688."

constraints. In this section, we draw on our historical case study to show how the perspective of political epistemology can help overcome these limitations.

4.1 Problem 1: The Question of Governance

In our schematic description of the material base, which draws on the discourses of political economy, economic anthropology, and historical epistemology, the notion of governance is conspicuously absent. It may appear, therefore, as if the material base is reproduced 'organically' – that is, in direct response to natural conditions and societal, perhaps even biological, needs. From the perspective of political epistemology, this is never the case – whatever the origin of any need, its sense is epistemologically mediated, and its satisfaction is conditioned by political institutions, whose direction leaves its formative mark on all three dimensions (i. e., production, reproduction, and knowledge) of the material base. One could say that across the different dimensions of society's material base, governance can be detected as a shaping infra-power that semi-passively channels states of affairs toward certain outcomes and semi-actively intervenes to resolve conflicts over directionality. Such shaping is rarely 'fully' passive or 'fully' active; instead, the multiplicity of political agency, both top-down and bottom-up, generally involves many processes of adjustment. In fact, one expression of differences in power concerns precisely who will have to adjust the most. Although these power differences often become most obvious in moments of crisis and reform, when large-scale modifications are effectuated, they are also present in everyday administration.

With the above discussion in mind, we pose the following research question, which we will address on the basis of the historical case study:

> **RQ1.** What is the connection between governance and the knowledge economy, and how are the relations between various knowledge bearers articulated in connection with the material base?

4.1.1 Involved Governance in Early Modern Venice

The records maintained by the water officers are one means for understanding the epistemic governance of water in the reproduction of the Venetian material base in the early modern period. It was through the institutional and epistemic activity of the water officers that transformative 'forces' could mobilize apt means for the maintenance and development of the lagoon and, thereby, of society. Clearly, knowledge alone does not move things. Among the forces to consider, the most important one is, of course, labor: the peasants who dug the canals, the boat people who transported the waste, the fishermen who moved across the waters and oversaw the territory. At the same time, those who work do not labor aimlessly and arbitrarily. Rather, they operated within the institutional framework instituted by Venice and represented by water officers. In this sense, the latter were the embodiment of epistemic governance. Their knowledge-informed and knowledge-producing actions were possible because political-economic 'powers' – the ruling institutions of Venice – made decisions which set priorities and directed money toward the achievement of goals that were economic and political in their essence. In addition, these powers could exert coercion and control (e. g., policing and establishing punishments for transgressions). Nonetheless, as the discussion below will show, the epistemic governance performed by the water officers cannot be reduced to the overarching political imprint received from the ruling class; the Water Office also had its own operating logic and social function.

The overall agenda behind the actions of the water officers ought to be stressed once more. They served a vision of Venice and its interests that coincided with those of the ruling elite. The lagoon was its main defense against external aggression and its primary means for external expansion, both mercantile and geopolitical. In terms of political organization, the republican form of rule at the time did not correspond with modern representative democracy and was quite mixed: As far as internal politics was concerned, the Republic of Venice functioned as an oligarchy, while in governing subjected territories, it exhibited characteristics of feudal power and social relations. Finally, the treatment of faraway maritime territories was based on constant negotiations that can be called imperialistic.[27] To add further complexity to this already composite picture, Giovanni Arrighi argued that Venice was 'an enclave of capitalist rule within the medieval system' – an exemplary instance of capitalist governance practices that marked the path for future world hegemonies.[28]

Interestingly, and perhaps unsurprisingly, an investigation of the Venetian water-knowledge economy complicates the vision of Venice resulting from Arrighi's geopolitical perspective focused on international politico-economic relations over long periods of time. As mentioned earlier, there is no doubt that the water officers followed the general agenda of the mercantile elite. Nonetheless, the social reproduction of the material base was not subject to direct capitalist organization, as would occur in the ideal case of a fully developed capitalist mode of production, nor was the knowledge economy dominated by centralized institutions dedicated to the needs of industrial production. In fact, many concerns related to social reproduction, such as food security, were under public authority and were removed from laissez-faire arrangements favoring private interests. In a sense, Venetian capitalist geopolitics, along with some capitalist characteristics in manufacture, coexisted with a largely non-capitalist arrangement of society's reproduction.

The central axis of this reproduction, and of the associated knowledge economy, was water management, which was persistently non-capitalist even though

27 Erasmo Castellani, *Negotiating Sovereignty through Petitions in the Early Modern Mediterranean: Patterns of Political Expression in the Venetian Stato da Mar*, PhD dissertation, Duke University 2021; Clémence Revest, "Ciceronianismo e ideale repubblicano nell'età dell'espansione veneziana in Terraferma", in: *Storica* 82 (2023), pp. 17–63.

28 Giovanni Arrighi, *The Long Twentieth Century: Money, Power, and the Origins of Our Times*, London 1994, p. 37.

it was ultimately subjected to the interests of the ruling oligarchy. Sabbadino stressed that when it comes to water bodies, individual interests and interventions should be avoided. In this respect, he named three kinds of people whom he considered to be most responsible for the negative alterations of the lagoon:

> If one well considers the damage that humans inflicted on this lagoon, one will notice that it is no lesser than that inflicted by the rivers and the sea. There are three types of men who caused this great evil: first, the *signori* and the powerful people; second, the engineers; and third, private people pursuing their own advantage.[29]

A similar ethos of caring for the lagoon existed among the water officers. Whereas non-regulated actions, or abuses, could severely damage the lagoon (or transform it in directions that were not considered desirable), the water officers sought to skillfully maintain a balance of natural forces, namely, a balance between freshwater and saline water, to guarantee the health of the water body.[30] Furthermore, the lagoon and the rivers carried 'living waters' (*acque vive*) that could degenerate into 'dead' – stagnant, swampy, unhealthy – waters.[31] This degeneration had to be avoided by all means. The water officers thus saw their own interventions as a healing practice within a kind of medical art of waterscape physicians. In this context, the water officers often presented the lagoon as a living organism and its imbalances as sickness. For the treatment of 'diseases' such as embankments, shoaling, and stagnation, various 'cures' were implemented. Marco Cornaro explicitly called for measures (*provisioni*) aimed at 'prolonging the life of this sick lady', the lady in question being the lagoon itself, which Cornaro referred to in the feminine ('prolungar la vita a questa inferma').

In general, we find that despite Venetian oligarchy's geopolitics with a capitalist disposition, the reproduction of the material conditions of Venice, particularly when it comes to water bodies, was a complex affair involving multiple socio-epistemic groups and layers of organization. Contrary to reductive biopolitics, this reproduction cannot be simplified to a binary conflict between exploitative elites and their institutional servants, concerned only with extraction and appropriation, and the virtuous poor, who valiantly struggle to preserve the environment in pristine conditions. Instead, the knowledge-economy of Venice, particularly from the perspective of the mediating water officers, shows that many kinds of

29 Cristoforo Sabbadino, *Discorsi sopra la laguna*, ed. Roberto Cessi, Venezia 1930, p. 31: "Chi bene considera la ruina, che hano data gli homeni a questa laguna, non la giudicarà minor di quella, che le ha data gli fiumi et il mare. Tre conditione de homeni sono state, che ha causato questo grandissimo male. Gli primi sono stati gli signori et homeni potenti, gli secondi li inzegneri, gli terzi li particulari per il bene proprio."

30 Francesco Luzzini, "The Floating Price of Beauty: Water and Land Management in Venice Through the Centuries", in: *Venice and the Anthropocene: An Ecocritical Guide*, eds. Cristina Baldacci, Shaul Bassi, Lucio De Capitani and Pietro Daniel Omodeo, Venice 2022, pp. 29–32.

31 Cornaro, *Scritture sulla Laguna*, p. 147.

actors participated in the care, as well as the exploitation, of the lagoon. Local communities, such as fishermen's guilds, played a proactive role, but the interventions of public regulators, both practical and juridical, were a constant feature of the societal reproductive process.

A case in point is fishing, a practice whose regulation underwent strict legislation. This is witnessed by the many documents on this topic preserved in the Venetian archive. Throughout the centuries, orders were issued to hinder overfishing and facilitate the use of nets that allowed young fish to escape catchment and grow. As early as 1314, an edict was issued that set the tone of fishing regulations until the end of Venetian rule:

> It is ordered that no fisherman should dare to catch young fish with a net until the feast of Saint Peter [June 29] [...]
> If someone catches any fish, he should throw them back into the water and should not dare sell them or let anyone else sell them [...]
> If someone contravenes this [order], he will forfeit his equipment and pay a fine, which will be more or less [steep] depending on the judges' decision.[32]

Moreover, the effective management of water was the premise for maintaining public health. Stagnant waters were considered dangerous sources of infection. By contrast, flowing (especially salty) waters, currents, and tides provided fundamental 'ecosystemic services' (in today's parlance related to 'natural capital'[33]) by regularly cleansing the water body of the lagoon. A case of mismanagement that required the intervention of water officers occurred in 1618. According to archival documentation, on April 30, they inspected the monastery of St. Maffio (St. Matthew) on the island of Mazzorbo. The reason for their visit was the spreading of a lethal disease: the nuns of the monastery were dying from an infection that, supposedly, derived from pestilential airs which, in turn, depended on water conditions. Eight nuns had perished within just a few days, while others were sick and dying. The officers inspected the location and the canalization to discover that the cause of the sickness was a lack of water flow in a place where garbage was disposed of. As the report reads, this place was a pit in an orchard close to

32 ASV, *Compilazione leggi Pesca*, f. 516*r*: "Ordinatum fuit quod nullus piscator a modo usque ad festum Sancti Petri [29 giugno] sit ausus capere pisces vaninos cum tractis ... Et si quis ceperit eos debeat eos proiicere in aquam, et non sit ausus eos vendere, nec vendi facere. Item si quis fecerit, vel facere fieri voluerit tracturos de nocte debeat accipere [...] Item quod nullus audeat ire ad tratturos pedem per palludos. Item, si quis vult ponere cucullos, vel sorborarcios in aqua, debeat ispos ponere de vero in prima campana et in mane ante tercias ipsos debet elevare: et si quis contra haec omnia [...] fuerit debeat perdere ipsas artes, et insuper solvat bannus intergum, et plus et minus ad voluntatem Dominorum Iustis."

33 For a criticism of the financialization of the Earth and the commodification of natural processes that is connected with current discourses on 'natural capital', see John Bellamy Foster, "Nature as a Mode of Accumulation: Capitalism and the Financialization of the Earth", in: *Monthly Review* 73/10 (2022), pp. 1–24.

the monastery. The problem was twofold. Previously, the pit had been connected to a canal and would be cleansed by the tidal motions of the waters, but the connection had become obstructed. Due to the obstruction, there was no water flow and no cleansing, hence the occurrence of bad airs. The officers' diagnosis and the restoration of the canal's regular flow, as well as their instructions about the disposal of waste, evidence that their role as water experts also concerned public-health issues. Indeed, the document includes considerations about the more general problem, which was not limited to that single case. As the officers argued, Mazzorbo and other nearby areas, such as Torcello, were too often infected. For this reason, local children rarely reached adulthood, and people did not generally grow old. In their opinion, the main cause of such insalubrity was the constant inflow of riverine freshwater and the accumulation of sediments brought by the rivers Marzenego, Dese, Zero, and Sile, the mouths of which were in that area of the lagoon.[34] This analysis reinforced the argument in favor of river diversions. In addition to other considerations that we have already mentioned, the officers regarded the ban on rivers from the lagoon and the exclusive preservation of salty water as an issue of public health.

In the case of Venice and its lagoon life, the three dimensions of the material base (i. e., production, reproduction, and knowledge) were mutually interdependent to the point where production and reproduction were difficult to separate, while vital knowledge-making was dispersed across multiple social strata. The relatively clear divisions that would emerge during the early industrial and Fordist phases of capitalist development were not yet present. Moreover, governance functioned as an infra-power that sutured the material base together in a manner that was involved rather than distant. The water officers participated in quotidian situations of production and reproduction, as well as canvassed various knowledge bearers to ascertain the status of the lagoon. In saying this, we have no intention of romanticizing the Venetian form of rule, which was indeed oligarchic, feudal-imperial, and early-capitalist. Nonetheless, an examination of societal reproduction and the knowledge economy in early modern Venice shows that the governance of the material base was not a direct reflection of its capitalist geopolitics, even as this base constituted the foundation upon which the Venetian geopolitical exploits rested. Rather, public institutions actively intervened in restraining private interests to maintain the water commons. Nor was this involved kind of governance a natural outgrowth of organic relationships between communities and their environmental settings. Instead, water management was subject to extensive epistemic mediation that combined top-down imperatives, bottom-up know-how, and 'diagonal' contributions from various knowledge-making institutions.

34 ASV, *Savi ed esecutori alle acque*, Atti, Folder 121, f. 371*r*.

4.2 Problem 2: Homogenous Knowledge Society

Despite its usefulness in bringing out the epistemic dimension of the material base, Renn's conception of the knowledge society does not expand on the political and contested process of abstraction development. If we agree that foundational abstractions are representations of social experience, then we must ask whose experiences are considered valuable enough to be included in the structures and institutions of the knowledge economy. For Renn, knowledge is largely defined by its problem-solving capacity, and within his so-called 'evolutionary account of knowledge',[35] it would seem that abstractions are selected by a kind of principle of epistemological efficacy, or rather the survival of the most useful abstractions that allow for the best solutions to societal problems within a certain historical horizon. However, this principle, taken in isolation, is not satisfactory because utility itself is a historical concept and leads to the same question: Useful to whom and for what purpose? Unless one posits some sort of natural or transcendental foundation for human society, there is no escaping that all foundational categories, such as utility and human nature, are open to struggle. The settlement of such foundational categories is thus a political rather than a natural question.

As a result, we can assume that at any moment in a given society, there are competing abstractions for representing various events and phenomena, including issues related to the reproduction of the material base. Therefore, one should expect different socio-epistemic groups to have at their disposal distinct and even incompatible sets of abstractions; in that case, the selection criteria by which certain abstractions are endowed with general validity become less a question of evolution and more a matter of hegemony. In other words, the sufficiency of a particular abstraction to represent the general interest depends on political as much as epistemic grounds. Consequently, we pose the following research question regarding the problem of *sufficient abstraction*:

> **RQ2.** In the case of competing abstractions in response to a common problem, how does one abstraction become selected as a *sufficient* solution from among the various candidates?

4.2.1 Competing Abstractions in Early Modern Venice

Sources indicate conflicting uses of water in early modern Venice. At the level of everyday economic usage, conflicts existed over attempts by individuals to employ parts of the embanked lagoon for cultivation, to have cattle grazing on the sand marshes, or to build some form of barrier for fish farming. Such private practices were severely reprimanded by water officers in the name of higher public interests. In many ways, water constituted a regulated common, and certain forms of overtly private uses of water were not accepted. Thus, recurring conflicts occurred between the authorities and various social groups. In addition, agricul-

35 Renn, *Evolution of Knowledge*, p. 18.

tural, navigational, and other mainland interests were a source of strife because the regulation of waterways was geared toward maintaining Venice's insularity at the expense of other programs. This created tensions between the mercantile elites, who lived in the city's center, and the landowners, whose primary interests were in the mainland.

After the fifteenth century, particularly after Venice's conquest of Padua, an attentive study of the territory and the control of the hydrological system became a political and theoretical possibility. The river Brenta, which connected the two cities, was at the center of several reengineering projects. In 1428, the Brenta river mouth was first redirected to the locality of Fusina, in front of the main islands of the city of Venice. In 1432, the Brenta broke its banks but no remedy was undertaken. As Marco Cornaro reports, the air became unhealthy, and fevers spread. A committee of *savi* accompanied by engineers was appointed to assess the situation and propose solutions. Despite their unanimous opinion that the Brenta river mouth should be diverted elsewhere, away from its position at the center of the lagoon, discussions continued. There were differing opinions about the necessary intervention and opposing interests, especially because the Brenta served as a transportation route to Padua and as a source of drinking water for Venice. Some discontent was starting to spread, as Cornaro wrote: 'The land cried out' (*la terra gridava*).[36]

Marco Cornaro, who was highly reputed on these matters, was involved in the assessment of the situation. In 1457, he himself would be appointed 'water sage'. Since the 1440s, he had already interacted with the people of the area, the 'villani', and with the engineers (*li inzegneri*), whose opinions he recorded and from whom he gathered valuable information. Engineers feature prominently in his *Della laguna*. Equally present are 'those from San Nicolò' (*quelli da San Nicolò*), that is, the most important fishing community. The latter expressed their opposition to having the Brenta river mouth at Fusina, reported on the alterations of the lagoon following the river's diversions, and gave their opinion when the new course of the river was agreed upon. Such attention to the territory and its people, interests, and divergent opinions, along with mediation, is exemplary of the involved kind of governance and knowledge-building described earlier. It was a systemic approach in terms of understanding the environment and society in their mutual interrelationship. Although social conflicts (and differences in abstractions) could not be solved through such participatory practices of decision-making and assessment, they could certainly be tamed.

In the sixteenth century, Venice witnessed controversies over water that went beyond quotidian economics and concerned highly distinct, and even mutually exclusive, societal visions of the material base. The best-known controversy was the opposition between Sabbadino, defender of the maritime interests of Venice and thus of the preservation of its lagoon at all costs, and Alvise Cornaro, defend-

36 Cornaro, *Scritture sulla Laguna*, p. 89

er of agricultural interests, who favored the transformation of the lagoon into land. This could be understood as a conflict between hydrology and agriculture. Both visions needed to be supported by large economic investments and interventions for the transformation of the territory, but in opposite directions: land reclamation against lagoon preservation, mainly through canal maintenance against river diversion. A material base organized around the agricultural use of Venetian waters would have drastically changed the future of the city – and it is difficult not to assume that this was one of the reasons why the hydrological vision prevailed, given that the ruling oligarchy was significantly more prone to endorsing actions that maintained the status quo rather than challenged it. Nonetheless, the hydrological approach to water management and the preservation of the lagoon was not a predestined outcome without its own struggle.

In this clash, which was equally political and practical, and which entailed radically opposed understandings of the material base, theological arguments were mobilized in addition to more pragmatic concerns. Alvise Cornaro invoked God's will to argue for the pious nature of work in the fields, wherefore the landowner who made the soil productive had a divine mission that also secured the peasants' salvation through labor.[37] He presented himself as the embodiment of such a divine mission of land stewardship, among others, in an autobiographic letter to erudite Padua philosopher Sperone Speroni (Codevigo, 2 April 1542):

> I have acquired [my wealth] by the best and most praiseworthy means, namely, by means of holy agriculture; and not by means of arms and efforts and harm to others; nor by means of crossing the seas with infinite danger to life, or by other means full of adversities. Hence, only by one praiseworthy means have I acquired it [the wealth], always spending much, not renouncing expenses, nor any pleasures that are proper to a gentleman; things that have escaped those who have no possessions but wish to have them. In spite of these ample expenses, I have accumulated it, building a temple to God (and to myself), and at my own expense I donated to God a people, which I brought into the world. For I have driven out the bad air from this village [villa][38] where children could not be raised. By freeing it from the waters, I brought forth an infinite people. Moreover, by enriching myself, I have enriched many of my factors and many of my servants [...].[39]

37 Giuseppe Fiocco, *Alvise Cornaro, il suo tempo e le sue opera*, Vicenza 1965, p. 83.

38 There may be some ambiguity regarding the term 'villa'. On the one hand, given Alvise Cornaro's reference to saving a people, the simple translation of 'village' seems appropriate. On the other hand, a villa was also an agricultural estate characterized by quasi-colonial power relations between landowners and peasants (see Reinhard Bentmann and Michael Müller, *Die Villa als Herrschaftsarchitektur: Versuch einer kunst- und sozialgeschichtlichen Analyse*, Frankfurt am Main 1971. We would like to thank Meital Shai for her invaluable insights regarding the translation of this quotation.

39 Alvise Cornaro, *Discorsi intorno alla vita sobria: edizione ricca di aggiunte*, Venezia 1826, pp. 108–109: "La ho acquistata [la roba, la ricchezza] con il migliore mezzo e più laudevole di ogni

Sabbadino had a different idea of divine Providence. Contrary to Alvise Cornaro, he argued that Venice's location as a city-island protected by its own waters was inscribed in God's benign design. As one reads in his *Discorsi sopra la Laguna di Venezia*,

> Before the lagoon located between the Tagliamento and the Brenta, which was our lagoon, was divided, God decided to create a city, which would be a support and a pillar for the faith in his son, Jesus Christ, our God and Lord. And He placed there a people, who without tyranny governed themselves in a republican form and had known no other God but Lord Jesus Christ. Thus, through the Holy Spirit he inspired some people, who had fled to other cities, to found on the islands of Rialto, in this lagoon, this noble city of Venice, giving it the name which before was that of the whole province. This happened on March 25 of the year 421 after the birth of our Lord Jesus Christ.[40]

In the case of a struggle that could not be immediately won using political and economics abstractions – after all, the 'rational' arguments of the agriculturalists were just as plausible as those of the hydrologists – it was possible to continue on the grounds of theology. In both cases, however, all epistemic weapons were marshaled to lend additional weight to the proposed visions regarding water usage and the future of the Venetian material base.

The manner in which protagonists of Renaissance territory politics, such as Sabbadino and Alvise Cornaro, called upon God and Nature to support their positions stands in stark contrast to the way in which common people were reprimanded for venturing into similar 'overabstractions'. This double standard emerges from a set of interviews with local fishermen conducted by the water officers after the diversion of the Brenta river in 1610. When Gastaldo Domeni-

altro, ch'è il mezzo della santa agricoltura; e non con mezzo di arme e sforzi e danni d'altrui; né con mezzo di passare i mari con infiniti pericoli della vita, ovvero con altri mezzi pieni di contrari; sicché con uno modo solo laudabile io la ho acquistato, e con uno sempre largo spendere, non lasciando spese, né sollazzi appartenenti a gentiluomo; cose che sono sfuggite a chi non ha roba, e la vuol fare. E pur con tal largo spendere io la ho fatta e con uno edificare ad Iddio (e del mio) tempio, ed a mie spese dando, e ad esso Iddio populo, il quale ho fatto venire al mondo, per aver discacciato io il mal aere che era in questa villa, dove non si poteva allevare figliuoli, e liberandola dalle acque, ho fatto nascere infinito populo; ed ho, facendo la roba, fatti ricchi molti miei fattori, e molti miei servitori […]."

40 Sabbadino, *Discorsi sopra la laguna*, p. 21: "Prima che laguna, situata tra il Tagliamento e il Brenta, che era la laguna nostra, si dividesse, parse al signor Dio, di creare una cittade, la qual fosse il sustentavulo e la colona de la fede de il suo figliolo misser Jesu Cristo Dio, e Signor nostro, et in quella colocarli un populo, il quale senza tirannia si reggesse a Republica, e non havesse conosciuto altro Dio, che esso signor Jesu Cristo; e cosi cum il Spirito Santo inspirò alcuni populi, fugiti in altre cittadi, a dover in le insule de Rivoalto, poste in essa laguna, dar principio a questa alma città di Venetia, dandole il nome della provincia: et fo nelli anni del signor nostro messer Jesu Cristo, dopo la sua incarantione, quatro cento e venti uno, alli venticinque dì de il mese di martio."

co Papacica, the head of the fishermen community of San Nicolò, criticized the diversion by arguing that it was achieved against God's will, the water officers countered that 'the river Brenta did not naturally end where we used to have it, but it had been artificially brought there'[41] (Omodeo 2022c). In fact, arguments based on nature were not better received – the officers reprimanded sixty-four-year-old fisherman Nadalin Gritti for his skeptical attitude concerning the limited power of human beings in relation to the forces of nature.[42]

It seems, at least judging by these sources, that arguments from nature and providence could be legitimately employed by the authorities or higher positioned individuals but not by the common people. Such arguments, in turn, served the former as further ideological bulwarks for their visions of territory and society.

In addition to incompatible visions for the material base among the elites, as well as the differing standards for legitimation discourses among social strata, the hegemonic classes were not in agreement about the best means for managing the waters. Such disagreements could go as far as to question the sufficiency of the foundational abstractions about the functioning of the lagoon's hydrology. A case in point was the contrast between Galilean hydrologist Benedetto Castelli on the one hand and Venetian senators and water officers on the other.[43] In the context of the diminution of the lagoon's water depth in the sixteenth and seventeenth centuries (for reasons that are unclear even now[44]), various opinions circulated that can be simplified to two main positions: excessive riverine sedimentation or decreasing water levels. Some thought that the Brenta diversion was the cause of the lowering of water levels due to the inflow of a lesser quantity of water. Although this opinion could easily be rejected by arguing that the water level in the lagoon was the same as the sea level (since a lagoon is not a lake), it found a strong advocate in Castelli. On the basis of his newly discovered computation methods for the measurement of running waters, he calculated the quantity of the water that had been diverted together with the Brenta and demonstrated, by methods derived from physical-mathematical principles, that bringing the water of Brenta back to the lagoon would be sufficient to raise the water level enough to secure its navigability.

Although Castelli could boast of using innovative methods to compute flows, they rested on abstractions that neglected basic environmental aspects, such as the

41 ASV, *Savi ed esecutori alle acque*, Folder 123, f. 11*r*. Gastaldo's words are as follows: "In my opinion, Brenta should be brought back where it used to be, because God made it like that, and we should let it be."

42 Ibid., f. 15*r*.

43 For a detailed discussion, see Pietro Daniel Omodeo, Sebastiano Trevisani and Babu D. Senthil, "Benedetto Castelli's Considerations on the Lagoon of Venice: Mathematical Expertise and Hydro-Geomorphological Transformations in Seventeenth-Century Venice", in: *Earth Sciences History* 39/2 (2020), pp. 420–446.

44 On the climatic reasons for costal and riverine alterations and the historiographic and scientific debates on the so-called Little Ice Age, see Franco Cazzola, *Uomini e fiumi: Per una storia idraulica ed agrarian della bassa pianura del Po (1450–1620)*, Roma 2021, ch. 6, pp. 155–180.

connection between the lagoon and the Adriatic Sea as well as the sedimentation problem. Therefore, his opponents accused him of ignoring elementary facts that were well known to water officers, such as interdependencies between rivers, sedimentation, tides, water flows, canalization, and aquatic life. Whereas the water officers, just like the fishermen community, used vitalistic and medical metaphors to talk about the *living waters* of the lagoon body, Castelli's abstractions rested on a proto-mechanical model. According to this model, interdependencies did not count because the solution depended exclusively on the variables that could be isolated, quantified, and (as it were) mathematically modeled. For him, water became an abstract entity, just like the lagoon. It was extracted from its environmental conditions (e. g., hydrogeological interconnections and tides) and qualitative components (e. g., turbidity) along with all biological and societal factors.

For the water officers, such environmental and social dimensions went hand-in-hand with a partially mathematical understanding of the lagoon, but they never reduced water to a mathematical abstraction. To be sure, the *savi* made large use of mathematics and computation techniques. However, these never turned into abstractions that would eclipse other forms of knowing. Instead, mathematics remained an instrument of intervention and governance to support the general management of Venice's water economy – for instance, in the calculation of costs and materials to be extracted and transported; in the prediction of natural events, such as soli-lunar influences on tides and flows; and in mapping. This could not have been further from the position of Castelli and his followers (among whom Paleocapa especially criticized Giovanni Alfonso Borelli), for whom water became a quantity to be handled without consideration of individuals and environments.

All of these tensions and contradictions – between competing visions for the material base, between distinct manners of employing theological arguments to defend mutually exclusive positions, and even between different standards among social strata for the use of said arguments, as well as differences over foundational science – indicate that a society's knowledge economy is never homogenous, and that the abstractions that are deemed sufficient for political action are not necessarily so chosen due to their epistemic efficacy. Instead, sufficiency is often suffused with the interests of the ruling class, and those abstractions are prioritized that are most useful to rulers. Nonetheless, having contested homogenous epistemology, we should not replace it with the uniformity of power. As demonstrated by the controversies among renowned engineers, and by the 'talking back' of the fishermen to the water officers, just as the knowledge economy is a field of contention, so is power challenged both from below and at the same level. Moreover, specifically in the case of the Republic of Venice in early modernity, an involved rather than distant form of water governance was aligned with a more epistemically inclusive practice of knowledge-making which resisted top-down mathematical abstractions that considered water a mere computational quantity devoid of geopraxiological embeddedness.

4.3 Problem 3: Constructivist Bias

When considering the natural–cultural nexus, there is a historiographical tendency to focus on the social side while treating the natural factor in the most generic terms only.[45] Furthermore, with the addition of the knowledge economy, it may appear as if society develops its abstractions in a self-reflexive loop, whereby one abstraction substitutes another, and the natural world only contributes in the infamous 'last instance', which, as we know, never quite arrives.[46] There is a very real possibility, in other words, of escaping biological and physicalist determinism only to be roped into a bad infinity of cultural immanence. However, there are constant irruptions of objectivity into the circuits of abstraction that interrupt the smooth cultural circuit of the knowledge economy and which function as reminders of a world that exceeds the cultural-epistemic boundaries of society.

We can identify several forms of objectivity in the reproduction of the material base. To begin with, societal reproduction is invariably connected with resources, which, even if they receive their function from the social side of the natural-cultural nexus,[47] exist in specific geographical locations, such as in valleys surrounded by mountains, at the bottom of the sea, in deserts with no rainfall, and so on. Given that all resources must be worked, their geographical locations pose problems that society must overcome by drawing on the various components of the material base. Geographical objectivity confronts the materiality of the various forces that make up the societal base, which provokes an objectifying question: Are the forces of the material base capable of tackling this resource in this geography? The initial encounter of mutual objectification – of geography and society – leads to further questions: Who will work the resource extraction? How many resources can be spent to obtain new ones? In what way will this location be integrated with other links in the production chain? Such increasingly complex considerations produce a strong need for *planning*, which not only highlights the importance of governance and knowledge in the reproduction of the material base but also constitutes the second moment of objectivity, insofar as objectivity involves supra-subjective representation and the need to communicate the plan to multiple agents and knowledge bearers in order to mobilize productive forces.

Finally, regardless of how much skillful planning is prepared by renowned engineers, and despite the best intentions of government officials to anticipate issues and communicate the plan to diverse social stakeholders, the implementation of plans for resource utilization necessarily involves, for lack of a better word, a 'reaction' from the natural environment. This is the moment of natural objectivity – *the subject-independent environmental reactivity to the actions taken by*

45 For an attempt to develop a different perspective, see Karl A. Wittfogel, "Geopolitics, Geographical Materialism and Marxism", in: *Antipode* 17/1 (1985), pp. 21–71; John Bellamy Foster, "Marx's Theory of Metabolic Rift: Classical Foundations for Environmental Sociology", in: *American Journal of Sociology* 105/2 (1999), pp. 366–405.

46 Louis Althusser, *For Marx*, transl. by Ben Brewster, London 1977.

47 Erich Walter Zimmermann, *World Resources and Industries*, 2nd ed., New York 1951.

the forces of the material base. Such reactivity, which can be anticipated and predicted but not predetermined, brings a degree of potential fallacy to all objective considerations, thus rendering them *conditional*. Due to this contingency generated by the encounter between epistemic abstractions and their natural field of application, most activities that comprise the reproduction of society's material base require monitoring and adjustment. Such monitoring is often done by the popular strata through quotidian interactions with local environments, as well as by organized institutional efforts, such as scientific data gathering.

With the above discussion in mind, we pose the following research question regarding *conditional objectivity*:

> **RQ3.** How do different knowledge bearers and socio-epistemic groups within a knowledge economy contribute to the objectivity of the material base, and how is such objectivity tested over time?

4.3.1 Conditional Objectivity, Natural Reactivity, and Water Monitoring

The objectivation of the material base of early modern Venice was intimately connected with water. The latter can hardly be considered a resource in a reductively economic sense – that is, as a material good for value-making through production and circulation. Rather, water and its geography were the precondition for the existence of maritime Venice, both locally and geopolitically. Water provided the means of subsistence and health for local popular strata, it functioned as a means for transportation and commerce, and it served military purposes from defense to power projection. Therefore, it is not an exaggeration to say that the objectivity of Venice and its material forces was articulated through a multilayered relationship with water,[48] and that the pursuit of water knowledge was a priority in the reproduction of the Venetian material base. Nonetheless, as we argued earlier, the development of the water-knowledge economy was not a smooth, homogenous process but a contested, protracted endeavor whose path-dependencies were built up over centuries.

For the forces of production, which experienced the materiality of water and the lagoon on a daily basis, many labor activities were connected with water,[49] as water-based professions included artisanal work, textile and paper production, and transportation. Fishing was an essential activity for the city – so much, in fact, that it was strictly regulated. The techniques and times of the year for fishing were established along with the price of fish in the market.[50]

---

48 The analysis of the multiple layers of water use in Venice draws on Pietro Daniel Omodeo and Sebastiano Trevisani, "Historical Geoanthropology in Venice", in: *Journal of Interdisciplinary History of Ideas* 11/22 (2022), pp. 13:1–13:22.

49 On working practices in early modern Venice, see Anna Bellavitis, Martina Frank, Valentina Sapienza (eds.), *Garzoni: apprendistato e formazione tra Venezia e l'Europa in età moderna*, Mantova 2017.

50 Rivoal, "Agir en être collectif."

Moreover, rivers were liquid roads connecting the lagoon to mainland territories: Brenta to Padova, Sile to Treviso, and the Piave to locations where wood was cut and transported downstream from the Alps. In addition, water connected Venice to the Mediterranean world, especially to the Eastern shores. In was also connected to proto-industrial production – for example, the Arsenale was the shipyard in which the fleet of Venice and many technological inventions were developed in the Middle Ages and early modernity. In this case, the connection with military interests is ostensible.[51] Moreover, irrigation and agriculture are important aspects of water management. Together with land reclamation, they constituted a basic concern for water engineers. Agricultural interests weighted on hydrological interventions that transformed the territory. Furthermore, manufactures along rivers took advantage of hydromechanic power already in the late Middle Ages and the Renaissance. As Deborah Howards has shown,[52] the use of water-powered technologies in early-modern Veneto, particularly in the Alps, played an important economic function in the proto-industrial era. The interests of millers and manufacturers had to be considered by water engineers, too.

Regarding the relevance of water to the forces of reproduction and sustaining life, the scarcity of drinkable water in urban Venice was remarkable. Renaissance historian Sanudo expressed this scarcity in a concise and often quoted contrast: '*è in aqua et non ha aqua*' ('[Venice] is in water but has no water').[53] Before the nineteenth century, when the extraction of water from underground aquifers became technically possible, water was collected by means of cisterns spread all over the city. They were filled either by rain or by watermen, who transported the precious element by boat from the Brenta river. For this reason, the diversion of Brenta in the early seventeenth century meant diverting not only sediments but also drinkable freshwater. On this account, waterscape engineering proved to be a field that mattered at an existential level because decisions had to be made about biopolitical priorities. Interventions in rivers had to be carefully assessed for their many consequences on lagoon life in ecological and economic terms.

In terms of the knowledge economy, hydraulic knowledge established the interconnections of the different parts of the territory (of the hydrological basin) at a theoretical level, which were disconnected in practice. Indeed, knowledge about water interdependencies was key to managing, and sometimes cutting, the fluvial connections between the lagoon, Venice, and the Alps. For instance, beginning in the fifteenth century, it was recognized that deforestation caused the arrival of more abundant sediments in the lagoon due to major erosion. Such knowledge

---

51 Jürgen Renn and Matteo Valleriani, "Galileo and the Challenge of the Arsenal", in: *Preprints of the Max Planck Institute for the History of Science Berlin* 179 (2001), URL: https://www.mpiwg-berlin.mpg.de/sites/default/files/Preprints/P179.pdf (09.08.2024).

52 Deborah Howard (ed.), *Proto-industrial Architecture of the Veneto in the Age of Palladio*, Vicenza 2021.

53 David Gentilcore, "The Cistern-System of Early Modern Venice: Technology, Politics and Culture in a Hydraulic Society", in: *Water History* 13/3 (2021), pp. 1–31, pp. 3–4.

of material geographic interdependencies was the basis for regulations aimed at preserving forests not only for economic reasons (the value of wood for construction, heating, and the fleet) but also for the protection of the lagoon. In this respect, early modern Venice can be considered an instance of non-destructive uses of resources.[54] On the other hand, the comprehension of systemic interdependencies also enabled ambitious programs of territory reengineering – namely, the disconnection of the lagoon (by modifying river courses) from its hydrographic basin.

The reactivity of natural elements was often tested, and even experimented with, in the process of water management. For instance, in 1428, Doge Francesco Foscari decided that the Brenta river mouth should be redirected to the Fusina locality, despite the opposition of the fishermen from the San Nicolò community. However, the Doge argued that his decision would function as a kind of test to probe the consequences of Brenta's outflow in the area facing the city of Venice. 'We should try for one year,' Foscari supposedly said, 'and put the markers; if she [the Brenta, feminine in local parlance] silts up with earth, we will have it closed.'[55] After two and a half years, as Cornaro reports, the situation had become extremely serious and called for a revision of the earlier decision:

> That [river mouth] was opened at Lizafusina [Fusina]. Soon, the boat pilots said that there was much more water at the mouth than before. [The fishermen] of San Nicolò said that everything silted up. That [the river] ran in that manner for two and a half years and brought earth toward Zorzi Dalega [San Giorgio in Alga] up to a place called Croseta. Therefore, when the waters were low, people would walk to that place. So did the donkeys, as well. The reeds had reached as far as the boat shelter of the aforementioned friars. And the frogs sang there.[56]

The 'testing' of natural reactivity to the various geoengineering projects often fell on the forces of production and reproduction – that is, on those who lived and worked in relation to water, the objective foundation of the material base of early modern Venice. Just as importantly, water management projects were not implemented 'smoothly' in the sense that the upper epistemic echelons, including water engineers, could simply redraw and divide the terrain as they saw fit. More often than not, geoengineering would produce multiple unexpected consequenc-

54 Karl Appuhn, *A Forest on the Sea: Environmental Expertise in Renaissance Venice*, Baltimore 2009, ch. 2.

55 Cornaro, *Scritture sulla Laguna*, p. 78: "Provemo uno anno et femo meter i segnali et, se quella aterrerà, la faremo serar."

56 Ibid., p. 79: "La dicta [foce] fu aperta a Lizafusina [Fusina], et breviter i pedoti diceva che i trovava asa mazor aqua su la fusa [foce] che i non havea fato per avanti, et quelli [i pescatori] da San Nicolò diceva che per tuto se aterrava. In modo che quella corse per dicta via do anni et mezo et aterrò verso san Zorzi Dalega [San Giorgio in Alga] per fina uno luocho [che] se chiama la Croseta per modo che cum le aque basse se vegniva a pie' per fina a dicto luoco, et cusì i someri; et havea conducto el canedo per fina ala Cavana de dicti frati, sì che le rane cantava lì."

es, which would require further adjustments and even reiterations of entire projects. Therefore, an epistemic feedback loop was necessary between the various dimensions, strata, and communities of the material base by means of which the objectivity of the various abstractions could be evaluated. The establishment of the Water Office in the sixteenth century was an important step in the long-term development of the water-knowledge economy and a key component in testing the conditional objectivity of water knowledge abstractions.

In sum, the long-term success of the Venetian hydrological reproduction regime rested on two pillars: the transformation of the territory through water knowledge-driven actions, by which hydraulic interventions became inscribed in the local geomorphology, and the monitoring and adjustments carried out by the water officers and the popular strata, who would 'double-check' the effects of all engineering interventions. For instance, such monitoring was the rationale behind the water officers' interviews with fishermen to assess the consequences of the modifications to hydraulic settings,[57] as those who worked in the waters of the lagoon could best observe and report any changes. Therefore, on the one hand, hydrology acted as an epistemic force for material transformations and objectivity-making. On the other, labor and the living experience of the lagoon's inhabitants provided the *epistemological backing* for the validity of the water knowledge behind territory planning. The result was a water-knowledge economy that functioned as the conditioning structure for the objectivity of the material base, and by which natural reactivity could be observed and, if needed, responded to.

5 Conclusion

The hydrological knowledge of early modern Venice was marked by a profound sense of the anthropic capacity to shape and reshape Venetian waterscapes (e. g., coastal lines, lagoon channels, and rivers). Already in the sixteenth century, there was clear awareness, at least among politicians and water officers, that the configuration of the lagoon was the result of past decisions and that its future depended on processes of landscape engineering. However, the political and techno-scientific hubris of radical nature transformability (a social constructivism, or rather geoengineering, *avant la lettre*) was generally alien to the mentality of the late Middle Ages and early modernity. The Venetian transformations, although backed by the capital's oligarchy and its interest in maintaining the maritime configuration of Venice, resisted alienated forms of mathematical abstractions that considered water without relation to its environmental and social functions. New approaches to hydrological knowledge based on emergent Galilean science seem to have exhibited a bias toward reification and absolute positioning by invoking the power of mathematics at the expense of situated knowledge and ecological experience – with the latter being reduced to incipient experimentalism. Nonetheless, the Venetian Water Office adopted an involved approach to governance

57 See Omodeo, "The Invisible Fisherman."

and epistemic mediation, canvassing the popular strata regarding the effects of hydrological projects and participating in the daily maintenance of water-related resources. Thus, the overall attitude toward the anthropic transformability of the landscape indicates a knowledge economy located between the two extremes of complete subjugation of natural settings to human needs and a naturalist realism that sees the environment as something given independently of social relations.

Hydrology, the science of water and its flows, played a decisive function in waterscape reshaping. A large corpus of works connected to hydraulics, tidal flows, and mapping was created in early modern Venice in connection with local water management as well as with book printing and developments of academic culture, especially in Padua; these are additional aspects to be addressed in other studies on the water knowledge economy of Venice.[58] As externalist historian of science Boris Hessen once stressed, water in early modernity was a multilayered object of social intervention and scientific understanding.[59] Nonetheless, although water management required technical knowledge, water did not become an object of massive technological use connected with mechanistic visions. The latter were linked to emergent urban and manufacturing culture which was still limited in mercantile Venice. Indeed, early modern European society was still dominated by agricultural forms of experiencing nature, as Wolfgang Lefèvre has argued in his historical-materialist correction of the Hessen thesis (according to which the main driver of early modern science was technology while the chain of science 'production' could be summarized as follows: 'economics […] *present[s]* demands, which *pose* technical problems, which *generate* scientific problems').[60] In a mercantile and agricultural context, water was mainly connected with infrastructural interests (transportation, the harbor, defense), agriculture (irrigation, land reclamation), and, of course, fishing, as attested by the significance of the fishermen's experiences of the lagoon for the Venetian water knowledge economy.

Therefore, although one can legitimately consider the Venetian water knowledge economy to be an instrument of geomorphological transformation closely connected to the interests of a dominant class of capitalist oligarchy, interpretations of knowledge-making and change that adopt top-down, unidirectional explanatory models are insufficient. Such explanations may appear adequate at the macro level of geopolitics over long durations, but they present an im-

58 On hydraulic knowledge see, among others, Salvatore Ciriacono, "Cristoforo Sabbadino e l'idraulica europea del Cinquecento", in: Cristoforo Sabbadino, *Il sistema Laguna a metà Cinquecento: Opere scelte pubblicate nel 450° della morte*, ed. Pier Giorgio Tiozzo Gobetto, Mestrino 2011, pp. 13–28.

59 See Boris Hessen, *Manuscripts and Documents on the History of Physics: A Historical Materialist Textbook*, ed. by Pietro Daniel Omodeo and Sean Winkler, Venice 2022, pp. 191–202.

60 Wolfgang Lefèvre, *Naturtheorie und Produktionsweise, Probleme einer materialistischen Wissenschaftsgeschichtsschreibung: Eine Studie zur Genese der neuzeitlichen Naturwissenschaft*, Darmstadt 1978. See Gideon Freudenthal and Peter McLaughlin (eds), *The Social and Economic Roots of the Scientific Revolution: Texts by Boris Hessen and Henryk Grossmann*, ed. and transl. Philippa Schimrat, Dordrecht 2009, p. 4.

age of society and knowledge that minimizes the contributions of the forces of production and completely eliminates the reproductive dimension. There is no material base to consider along with its reproduction, no governance other than as domination, no knowledge economy except for top-down command, and certainly no natural reactivity. Even a cursory investigation of early modern Venice shows how inadequate such conceptualizations tend to be. The reproduction of the material base of Venice was centered on the understanding, use, and protection of water, which required the development of a robust knowledge economy. Multiple knowledge bearers – from fishermen to water officers to engineers and merchants – contributed to this water knowledge economy, whose existence was crucial for establishing, testing, and adjusting the conditional objectivity of water. Involved governance was a significant part of this process, and it is difficult to imagine that when the water officers solved issues related to rivers, canals, and public health concerns, they were merely applying knowledge instead of, in addition, expanding the Venetian knowledge base by drawing on the situated know-how of the forces of production and reproduction. None of this erases the merchant elite which ruled from the insular city and pursued its proto-capitalist imperial geopolitics. It does, however, demonstrate that there is more to societies and their histories than the actions, intentions, and plans of the ruling classes.

To sum up, water and its politics were at the core of the reproduction of the Venetian material base in early modernity. This hydrological reproduction regime depended on a water-knowledge economy with multiple knowledge bearers, an involved approach to governance, and persistent monitoring of the objective conditions of water by society. In fact, the knowledge economy that emerged as part of the hydraulic reproduction regime exhibited strong vertical and horizontal integration, despite tensions between competing visions for water usage and the direction of the future of the material base. It may not be an exaggeration to say that in early modern Venice, a kind of dispersed collective intelligence developed to leverage water for the survival, perseverance, and flourishing of Venetian society. Despite performing different, and even hierarchically segregated, functions, no social stratum could claim full ownership of the entire scope of water knowledge due to the complex natural reactivity of water bodies.

Acknowledgments

Pietro Daniel Omodeo would like to thank the following institutions and projects that have supported his current research: the UNESCO Chair *Water Heritage and Sustainable Development* at Ca' Foscari University of Venice; the FARE project *EarlyGeo-Praxis* (Grant of the Italian Ministry of University and Research, no. R184WNSTWH); the Max Planck Partner Group *The Water City* (Venice–Berlin–Jena); the project *Cosmography of Historical Waterscapes* (funded by Tsinghua University, Beijing); THE NEW INSTITUTE Centre for Environmental Humanities (NICHE) in Venice; and the Max Planck Institute of Geoanthropology, Jena.

The research of Justas Patkauskas was funded by the European Union (GA number: 101105880). Views and opinions expressed are however those of the author only and do not necessarily reflect those of the European Union or Research Executive Agency. Neither the European Union nor the granting authority can be held responsible for them.

Reference Lists

Archival Documents and Primary Sources

Archivio di Stato di Venezia, *Savi ed esecutori alle acque*, Atti.

Archivio di Stato di Venezia, *Compilazione leggi Pesca.*

Cornaro, Alvise, *Discorsi intorno alla vita sobria: edizione ricca di aggiunte*, Venezia 1826.

Cornaro, Marco, *Scritture sulla Laguna*, in: *Antichi scrittori d'idraulica veneta*, Vol. 1, ed. G. Pavanello, Venezia 1919.

Sanudo, Marin, *De origine, situ et magistratibus urbis Venetae ovvero La città di Venetia (1493–1530)*, Venice 2011.

Research Literature

Althusser, Louis, *For Marx*, transl. Ben Brewster, London 1977.

Appuhn, Karl, *A Forest on the Sea: Environmental Expertise in Renaissance Venice*, Baltimore 2009.

Arrighi, Giovanni, *The Long Twentieth Century: Money, Power, and the Origins of Our Times*, London 1994.

Bellavitis, Anna, Frank Martina and Sapienza Valentina (eds), *Garzoni: apprendistato e formazione tra Venezia e l'Europa in età moderna*, Mantova 2017.

Bentmann, Reinhard and Michael Müller, *Die Villa als Herrschaftsarchitektur: Versuch einer kunst- und sozialgeschichtlichen Analyse*, Frankfurt am Main 1971

Braudel, Fernand, *Capitalism and Material Life: 1400–1800*, New York 1975.

Braudel, Fernand, *The Mediterranean and the Mediterranean World in The Age of Philip II*, transl. Sian Reynolds, New York 1972.

Castellani, Erasmo, *Negotiating Sovereignty through Petitions in the Early Modern Mediterranean: Patterns of Political Expression in the Venetian Stato da Mar*, PhD dissertation, Duke University 2021.

Cazzola, Franco, *Uomini e fiumi: Per una storia idraulica ed agrarian della bassa pianura del Po (1450–1620)*, Roma 2021.

Ciccotti, Giovanni, Cini Marcello, De Maria Michelangelo and Jona-Lasinio Giovanni, *The Bee and the Architect: Scientific Paradigms and Historical Materialism*, Venice 2024.

Ciriacono, Salvatore, "Cristoforo Sabbadino e l'idraulica europea del Cinquecento", in: Cristoforo Sabbadino, *Il sistema Laguna a metà Cinquecento: Opere scelte pubblicate nel 450° della morte*, ed. P.G. Tiozzo Gobetto, Mestrino 2011.

Ciriacono, Salvatore, *Building on Water: Venice, Holland and the Construction of the European Landscape in Early Modern Times*, New York 2006.

Damerow, Peter, *Abstraction and Representation: Essays on the Cultural Evolution of Thinking*, Dordrecht 1995

Fiocco, Giuseppe, *Alvise Cornaro, il suo tempo e le sue opere*, Vicenza 1965.

Freudenthal, Gideon and Peter McLaughlin (eds.), *The Social and Economic Roots of the Scientific Revolution: Texts by Boris Hessen and Henryk Grossmann*, ed. and transl. Philippa Schimrat, Dordrecht 2009.

Foster, John Bellamy, "Marx's Theory of Metabolic Rift: Classical Foundations for Environmental Sociology", in: *American Journal of Sociology* 105/2 (1999), pp. 366–405.

Foster, John Bellamy, "Nature as a Mode of Accumulation: Capitalism and the Financialization of the Earth", in: *Monthly Review* 73/10 (2022), pp. 1–24.

Gentilcore, David, "The Cistern-System of Early Modern Venice: Technology, Politics and Culture in a Hydraulic Society", in: *Water History* 13/3 (2021), pp. 1–31.

Hessen, Boris, *Manuscripts and Documents on the History of Physics: A Historical Materialist Textbook*, ed. by Pietro Daniel Omodeo and Sean Winkler, Venice 2022.

Howard, Deborah (ed.), *Proto-industrial Architecture of the Veneto in the Age of Palladio*, Vicenza 2021.

Høyrup, Jens, "Practitioners – School Teachers – "Mathematicians": The Divisions of Pre-Modern Mathematics and Its Actors", in: *Writing and Rewriting the History of Science 1900–2000* (Les Treilles, 5–11 September 2003).

Ienna, Gerardo, Pietro Daniel Omodeo and Massimiliano Badino, *Epistemologia storica: Correnti, temi e problemi*, Roma 2022.

Lecourt, Dominique, *L'épistémologie historique de Gaston Bachelard*, Paris 1969.

Lefèvre, Wolfgang, *Naturtheorie und Produktionsweise, Probleme einer materialistischen Wissenschaftsgeschichtsschreibung: Eine Studie zur Genese der neuzeitlichen Naturwissenschaft*, Darmstadt 1978.

Luzzini, Francesco, "The Floating Price of Beauty: Water and Land Management in Venice through the Centuries", in: *Venice and the Anthropocene: An Ecocritical Guide*, eds. Cristina Baldacci, Shaul Bassi, Lucio De Capitani and Pietro Daniel Omodeo, Venice 2022, pp. 29–32.

Marchart, Oliver. *Post-foundational Political Thought: Political Difference in Nancy, Lefort, Badiou and Laclau*, Edinburgh University Press 2007.

Omodeo, Pietro Daniel, "History of Science and History of the Earth in the Anthropocene", in: *Physis* 57 (2022a), pp. 171–188.

Omodeo, Pietro Daniel, "Geopraxis: A Concept for the Anthropocene", in: *Journal of Interdisciplinary History of Ideas* 11/22 (2022b), pp. 10:1–10:52.

Omodeo, Pietro Daniel, "Hydrogeological Knowledge from Below: Water Expertise as a Republican Common in Early Modern Venice", in: *Berichte zur Wissenschaftsgeschichte: History of Science and Humanities* 45/4 (2022c), pp. 538–560.

Omodeo, Pietro Daniel, "The Invisible Fisherman: The Economy of Water Knowledge in Early-modern Venice", in: *Ichthyology in Context (1500–1880)*, eds. Paul J. Smith and Florike Egmond, Leiden 2023, pp. 362–391.

Omodeo, Pietro Daniel, *Political Epistemology: The Problem of Ideology in Science Studies*, Cham 2019.

Omodeo, Pietro Daniel and Sebastiano Trevisani, "Historical Geoanthropology in Venice", in: *Journal of Interdisciplinary History of Ideas* 11/22 (2022), pp. 13:1–13:22.

Omodeo, Pietro Daniel, Sebastiano Trevisani and Babu D. Senthil, "Benedetto Castelli's Considerations on the Lagoon of Venice: Mathematical Expertise and Hydro-Geomorphological Transformations in Seventeenth-Century Venice", in: *Earth Sciences History* 39/2 (2020), pp. 420–446.

Renn, Jürgen and Matteo Valleriani, "Galileo and the Challenge of the Arsenal", in: *Preprints of the Max Planck Institute for the History of Science Berlin* 179 (2001), URL: https://www.mpiwg-berlin.mpg.de/sites/default/files/Preprints/P179.pdf (09.08 2024).

Revest, Clémence, "Ciceronianismo e ideale repubblicano nell'età dell'espansione veneziana in Terraferma", in: *Storica* 82 (2022), pp. 17–63.

Rheinberger, Hans Jörg, *Historische Epistemologie zur Einführung*, Hamburg 2007.

Rivoal, Solène, "Agir en être collectif: L'État, la communauté des Nicolotti et l'approvisionnement de Venise à l'époque modern", in: *Tracés: Revue de Sciences humaines* 29 (2015), pp. 65–84.

Rivoal, Solène, *Les marchés de la mer : Une histoire sociale et environnementale de Venise au XVIIIe siècle*, Roma 2022.

Sabbadino, Cristoforo, *Discorsi sopra la laguna*, ed. Roberto Cessi, Venezia 1930.

Wittfogel, Karl A. and G. L. Ulmen, "Geopolitics, Geographical Materialism and Marxism", in: *Antipode* 17/1 (1985), pp. 21–71.

Zago, Roberto, *I Nicolotti: Storia di una comunità di pescatori a Venezia nell'età moderna*, Padova 1982.

Zilsel, Edgar, "The Sociological Roots of Science", in: *Social Studies of Science* 30/6 (2000), pp. 935–939.

Cristoforo Sabbadino's Manuscript Notes on Tides: A Document on Water Knowledge and Practice in Renaissance Venice from the Marciana Library of Venice

Ovanes Akopyan and Pietro Daniel Omodeo

1 Introduction: A Sabbadino Manuscript in the Marciana Library of Venice

The Biblioteca Nazionale Marciana of Venice preserves a rare manuscript by Cristoforo Sabbadino, the most reputed water expert of sixteenth-century Venice, which has thus far escaped the close scrutiny of historians of hydrology and early modern science. Its title page lists its contents: a series of interrelated topics gravitating around the *Flussi e reflussi de le acque*, that is, the "ebb and flow" (collocation Marc. It. IV 51. 5136). The aim of this paper is to make a transcription of the initial section of this manuscript available to the scientific community. Our selection, running from folio 2*r* to 7*v*, relates to the tides and their distant (cosmological, astrological) and proximate (meteorological) causes. We look at this manuscript as a document of early modern hydrological knowledge, connected with institutional and epistemic practices of resource management. In what follows, we first offer a brief prosopography of the author and his institutional context. At once, we consider the intellectual roots of Renaissance debates on tides. Then, we describe the manuscript and present the author's main argument in the section which is of concern here. In this manner, we point out the relevance of the author's cosmographic, astrological and natural discussion of the phenomenon for Venetian waterscape policies. The transcription of the manuscript follows as an appendix.

2 Cristoforo Sabbadino, a Venetian Water Officer

The author of the text under consideration, Cristoforo Sabbadino, served as *protomaestro* (or *proto*) and senior water engineer of the *Offitio delle Acque* of the Venetian Republic.[1] Born around 1487 (in a text composed around 1557 he confessed to be 70-years-old), he witnessed the peak of the Republic's early attempts to put its water resources under control. Sabbadino's family background and education

1 The most valuable contribution on Sabbadino's biography is still Roberto Cessi, "Prefazione," in Cristoforo Sabbadino, *Discorsi sopra la Laguna (parte 1)*, ed. by Roberto Cessi, Venice 1930, pp. VII–XXVI. Among the more recent publications on the *Offitio delle Acque* (or the *Magistrato alle Acque* in its later iteration) and Venice's water management, see above all Jane L. Stevens Crawshaw, *Cleaning Up Renaissance Italy: Environmental Ideals and Urban Practice in Genoa and Venice*, Oxford 2023, ch. 4.

DOI: 10.13173/9783447123693.047

helped him not only participate in such efforts but also lead them. His father, Paolo Sabbadino, worked in various capacities for the Magistrato alle Acque for 20 years, having risen eventually to the position of *protomaestro*.[2] Although his tenure does not seem to have been particularly successful and was marked by financial issues, Paolo must have provided his son with some basic introduction to the profession. The extent of such introduction is unclear, however. Evidence suggests that Paolo passed away around 1500, whilst Cristoforo's first hydrological interventions related to the adjustment of the Brenta dated back to the 1530s. This means that Sabbadino's formative years have remained untraceable to date. Among other things, we still do not have any information about whether Sabbadino ever entered the university or had professional contacts and collaboration with university circles. Be that as it may, it is evident that by the 1530s, he proved himself as a leading water expert in the Republic. For the subsequent 30 years, Sabbadino continued to be involved in virtually all hydrological discussions and projects carried out under the umbrella of the *Offitio* and largely determined the Republic's water policies.[3]

Sabbadino was a textbook practitioner, and his body of work demonstrates anew the centrality of the so-called artisanal tradition for the organization of early modern knowledge.[4] Based on an impressive amount of empirical data, his reflections on both the state of the lagoon and water streams in the Venetian mainland pursued highly practical goals. It appears at the same time that Sabbadino was not completely devoid of literary aspirations, as he summarized some of his findings about the alleged long-term rise of water levels in the lagoon in the form of a dialogue, the genre that experienced a renaissance in the sixteenth century.[5] But the choice of language (he wrote in Italian), the style and constant reference to practice and first-hand data suggest that the dialogue's intended audience was within Venetian political and institutional ranks rather than belonged to the *res publica literaria*.[6] The timing clearly favoured such experience-based undertakings: with the Republic dramatically increasing its presence in the *terraferma* and seeking to optimise the effective use of the new land resources, water management,

2 Sabbadino, "Opinion o modo di salvar la Laguna secondo lo aricordo del Sabbattino," in: *Discorsi sopra la Laguna (parte 1)*, p. 131.

3 Sabbadino's most important works on the Lagoon and water management, including his dispute with Aloise Cornaro, were published by Roberto Cessi in two volumes in 1930 and 1941, respectively. Some of those texts were later reprinted as Cristoforo Sabbadino, *Il sistema laguna a metà Cinquecento*, ed. by Pier Giorgio Tiozzo Gobetto, Chioggia 2011.

4 The importance of this tradition against the backdrop of early modern science has recently been brought to the fore in a variety of publications. For some examples, see Pamela H. Smith, *From Lived Experience to the Written Word: Reconstructing Practical Knowledge in the Early Modern World*, Chicago/London 2022; Thomas Morel, *Underground Mathematics: Craft Culture and Knowledge Production in Early Modern Europe*, Cambridge 2023.

5 Sabbadino, "Raggionamenti…," in: *Discorsi sopra la Laguna (parte 1)*, pp. 151–65.

6 It is also important to note that there is no evidence at our disposal concerning Sabbadino's knowledge of Latin.

especially in agriculture, became a pressing matter.[7] Concurrently, in the mid-sixteenth century Venice was as always battling its perpetual nemesis: the *acqua alta*. Although some environmental reconstructions demonstrate that during the early modern period, the rise of high waters in the north of the Adriatic was not as dramatic as in the Middle Ages and later beginning in the eighteenth century, it posed a lasting existential threat to the local community; moreover, coupled with the need to balance the water levels in the lagoon with the artificially altered streams of the *terraferma* flowing into the sea, it presented new challenges. Sabbadino was among several other Venetian scholars and engineers who tried to offer a reliable interpretation of the phenomenon of tides aimed at solving its most extreme and devastating consequences.[8]

3 Pre-modern Conceptions of Tides

Before introducing Sabbadino's manuscript on the causes of tides, it seems essential to provide a brief overview of pre-modern tidal theories in order to contextualize the Venetian's interpretation.[9] While an array of accounts recorded tides, just few authors before the early modern period suggested what could cause them. It is all the more significant considering that the tides, often called 'the most mysterious effect of nature',[10] were regarded as the most manifest example of the foundational interplay between the celestial and terrestrial realms. In antiquity, no theory seemed to achieve a consensus, with most authors devoting only brief passages to the phenomenon and not elaborating on the subject due to its obscurity.[11] Probably, the least unsystematic attempt was made by Pliny the Elder, who strongly influenced all subsequent authors concerned with natural history.[12] In the *Naturalis Historia*, largely building on previous observations, Pliny pointed to the fact that although tidal motions occur at regular intervals, their strength

7 On this aspect, see Salvatore Ciriacono, *Building on Water: Venice, Holland and the Construction of the Landscape in Early Modern Times*, New York 2006 [the first Italian edition – 1994].

8 Perhaps, the most intriguing example among such attempts was Veronese nobleman Lodovico Nogarola's dialogue *Timotheus, sive De Nilo* (1552), which touched upon the origin of water motion in the Veneto region in relation with the inundation of the Nile.

9 What follows with respect to ancient and medieval theories is a shortened version of Ovanes Akopyan, "Discussing Tides Before and After Newton: Roger Joseph Boscovich's De aestu maris", in: *Perspectives on Science* 30/6 (special issue *(De)Constructing Authority in Early Modern Cosmology*, ed. by Ovanes Akopyan and Pietro Daniel Omodeo) (2022), 1042–64.

10 This expression was first used among the ancients, in particular by Diogenes Laertius and Pliny the Elder. Already in the sixteenth century, In a letter to his fellow Venetian Giovanni Battista Ramusio, Girolamo Fracastoro claimed that among a whole variety of natural events, there were just three the causes of which were the most occult. One of them, he added, was the flow of water.

11 For a few surveys of ancient theories (which are unfortunately not devoid of some lacunae), see Lucio Russo, *Flussi e riflussi. Indagine sull'origine di una teoria scientifica*, Milan 2003, pp. 20–22, 51–62; Vincent Deparis, Hilaire Legros and Jean Souchay, "Investigations of Tides from the Antiquity to Laplace", in: *Tides in Astronomy and Astrophysics*, ed. by Jean Souchay, Stéphane Mathis and Tadashi Tokieda, Berlin/Heidelberg 2013, pp. 32–34.

12 Pliny, *Natural History* I.II.212–220.

might differ from day to day. To explain the paradox, Pliny distinguished daily and weekly cycles, and stated that interactions between the Sun and the Moon on the basis of fortnightly cycles could cause the tides. He did not further this argument, however, and exhibited no explicit understanding of the fortnightly cycle. Later, in his astrological *magnum opus Tetrabiblos*, Claudius Ptolemy assigned the consistency of tidal motions to the influence of the Moon. He argued that it governed diverse natural events as it was the source of humidity and the closest celestial body to the Earth.[13] However, Ptolemy did not go beyond this generic statement and limited himself to a short paragraph.

In the Middle Ages, particularly in the wake of the transmission of Islamic knowledge in the West in the twelfth and thirteenth centuries,[14] a variety of interpretations were put forth. Among these, three competing solutions were disseminated.[15] All of them, to a greater or lesser extent, were grounded in the notions initially, and usually in passing, formulated in ancient philosophy and advanced in the subsequent commentary tradition. The first, vitalistic theory claimed the existence of underwater chasms that periodically drew in and forced out water, similar to an animal's breathing, and caused the movement of the tide. This interpretation echoes Stoic philosopher Posidonius' conception of *pneuma* as the main driver of the phenomenon.[16]

The other two theories exploited Aristotle's *Meteorologica*, in which the Stagirite listed a number of potential principles behind the motion of water without clearly endorsing any of them.[17] Thus, the second medieval explanation, which was of a more physical nature, associated the flow and ebb with the water's qualities, the geographical specifications of bodies of water, and external influences, such as winds. In the third explanation, which took up Aristotle's and Ptolemy's assertion that 'the most general indication of the Moon is for water and earth', the Persian astrologer Abū Maʿšar al-Balḫī (known as Albumasar in Latin) developed the dominant astronomical/astrological theory based on the recognition of

---

13 Ptolemy, *Tetrabiblos* I.II.3.

14 The literature on the transmission of Islamic astrological and magical knowledge to the West is immense. See above all Charles H. Haskins, *The Renaissance of the Twelfth Century*, Cambridge, MA 1927; David Pingree, "The Diffusion of Arabic Magical Texts in Western Europe", in: *La diffusione delle scienze islamiche nel Medio evo europeo*, ed. Biancamaria Scarcia Amoretti, Roma 1987, pp. 57–98; Marie-Thérèse D'Alverny, *La connaissance de l'Islam dans l'occident medieval*, ed. Charles Burnett, Aldershot 1994; Charles Burnett, *Magic and Divination in the Middle Ages: Texts and Techniques in the Islamic and Christian Worlds*, Aldershot 1996; Wolfgang Hübner, "The Culture of Astrology from Ancient to Renaissance", in: *A Companion to Astrology in the Renaissance*, ed. Brendan Dooley, Leiden/Boston 2014, pp. 17–58; Liana Saif, *The Arabic Influences on Early Modern Philosophy*, Basingstoke/New York 2015.

15 Federico Bonelli and Lucio Russo, "The Origin of Modern Astronomical Theories of Tides: Chrisogono, De Dominis and Their Sources", in: *The British Journal for the History of Science* 29 (1996), pp. 386–88.

16 Russo, *Flussi e riflussi*, pp. 20–21.

17 Aristotle, *Meteorologica* II.1–2.

a correlation between tides, diurnal rotation, and the lunar cycle.[18] In his fundamental *Great Introduction to Astrology*, Abū Maʿšar suggested that water increases due to the Moon's ascension over a point in the sea and ebbs when the Moon retrogrades. As the Moon ascends over every part of the Earth during the length of a day, the flow and the ebb alternate. He argued that the position of the Moon in the heavens in relation to other celestial bodies, above all to the Sun, and in relation to particular constellations, was the strongest influence on the strength of tidal motions. This was not the only aspect that Abū Maʿšar considered important, however. Alongside a lengthy exposition of the astronomical/astrological hypothesis, he indicated that the wind and the geographical features of the place in which the event emerges were additional influences.

The *Great Introduction to Astrology* was translated twice into Latin in the twelfth century and quickly became the most influential astrological 'manual' in the European Middle Ages. Although Abū Maʿšar remained silent regarding the monthly and yearly cycles of tides, his interpretation gained wide readership among medieval Latin scholars.[19] It should also be noted that Abū Maʿšar conceived the *Great Introduction to Astrology* as a detailed commentary on Aristotle's natural philosophical teachings.[20] As Alain de Libera perfectly demonstrated, through a selection of magical writings that circulated in the West as though they had been composed by the Stagirite, astrologers effectively adapted a distorted Aristotelianism to legitimize their discipline.[21] The reputation of a science Aristotle had allegedly sanctioned with his authority paved the way for astrology to evolve into an integral part of the university curriculum.[22] The success of Abū Maʿšar astrological commentary on the Philosopher's natural philosophy significantly contributed to this turn of events.

As regards Abū Maʿšar's tidal theory, it became by extension seen as crafted within the Aristotelian tradition, even though Aristotle had never plainly favoured the lunar explanation, let alone complemented it with astrology. In similar fashion, some of the medieval scholastics adopted another supposition first articulated in the writings of Persian astrologer Māschā'allāh ibn Atharī and then

18 Abū Maʿšar al-Balḫī, *The Great Introduction to Astrology*, 2 vols., ed. Keiji Yamamoto and Charles Burnett, Leiden/Boston 2020, vol. 1, bk. 3, ch. 4–8, pp. 263–333.

19 Edgar Laird, "Robert Grosseteste, Albumasar and Medieval Tidal Theory", in: *Isis* 81, 4 (1990), 684–694; Charles Burnett, "Does the Sea Breathe, Boil or Bloat? A Textual Problem in Abū Ma'shar's Explanation of Tides", in: *Mélanges offerts à Hossam Elkhadem par ses amis et ses élèves*, ed. Frank Daelemans et al., Brussels 2007, pp. 73–79.

20 Richard Lemay, *Abu Ma'shar and Latin Aristotelianism in the Twelfth Century: The Recovery of Aristotle's Natural Philosophy through Arabic Astrology*, Beirut 1962.

21 Alain de Libera, *Penser au Moyen Âge*, Paris 1991, pp. 253–62.

22 Graziella Federici Vescovini, "I programmi degli insegnamenti del Collegio di medicina, filosofia e astrologia, dello statuto dell'Università di Bologna", in: *Roma, magistra mundi: itineraria culturae medievalis. Mélanges offerts au Père L. E. Boyle à l'occasion de son 75e anniversaire*, ed. Jacqueline Hamesse, Leuven 1998, pp. 193–223; Jean-Patrice Boudet, *Entre science et nigromance. Astrologie, divination et magie dans l'Occident médiéval (XII–XV siècle)*, Paris 2006, pp. 205–303.

amplified by Abū Maʿšar: that the effects on Earth of planetary bodies is analogous to magnetic attraction.[23] With respect to the issue of tides, it consequently implied the existence of a similarity between water motions and the attractive forces of a loadstone. With a few proponents in the first half of the thirteenth century, including William of Auvergne, this idea was later embraced by Pietro d'Abano.

The Renaissance discourse on tides inevitably drew upon medieval reflections, with the majority of Renaissance theories centred around two approaches that either sought to substantiate what the medieval predecessors had proposed (this was particularly relevant with regard to the lunar astronomico-astrological explanation) or dismissed the past notions as based on false premises.[24] The most significant example of the latter approach was offered by Giovanni Pico della Mirandola, who fiercely criticised Abū Maʿšar in his *Disputationes adversos astrologos* and labelled the Persian's interpretation a deliberately erroneous appropriation of Aristotle's natural philosophy.[25] However, despite Pico's famous attack against astrology, the former approach remained dominant until the mid-sixteenth century and the theory focused on the position of the Moon relative to other celestial bodies continued to be widely reproduced. A region under the permanent threat of flooding because of high tides, Venice was particularly invested in attempts to connect theorical reflections with practical solutions. Even a glance at the most influential sixteenth- and early seventeenth-century writings investigating with the origin of tides reveals that most of them were either composed in the Venetian Republic or published therein.[26] The few exceptions include texts that formed part of a larger cosmological worldview (such as Kepler's magnetic treatment of the tides or Galileo Galilei's heliocentric system) or scrutinized the case of Venice but were written elsewhere, for instance, in Florence and Rome. Perhaps, the most noteworthy among the texts concerned with the tides that were published in Venice prior to Sabbadino's manuscript and could have influenced it was Federico Crisogono's *Tractatus de occulta causa fluxus et refluxus maris*.[27]

This work, printed in 1528 alongside other writings by the Paduan professor, contained an effective explanation of the principal cycles of the tides based ex-

23 Nicolas Weill-Parot, "L'attraction magnétique entre influence astrale et astrologie au Moyen Âge (XIIIe – XVe siècle)", in: *Philosophical Readings* 7/1 (special issue *Medieval and Renaissance Astrology*, ed. by Donato Verardi) (2015), pp. 55–70.

24 For an overview of Italian Renaissance theories, see above all Pietro Daniel Omodeo, "Modelli esplicativi delle maree nel Rinascimento: una rassegna", in: *Galilaeana. Studies on Renaissance and Early Modern Science* 14 (2017), pp. 98–114.

25 Ovanes Akopyan, "Giovanni Pico della Mirandola on Tides," in: *Bruniana & Campanelliana* 1 (2018), pp. 135–145.

26 For an overview of Venetian astronomical accounts concerned with the origin of tides, Ventrice's *La discussione sulle maree tra astronomia, meccanica e filosofia nella cultura veneto-padovana del Cinquecento*, Venice 1989, remains indispensable.

27 Federico Crisogono, *De modo collegiandi, pronosticandi et curandi febres, necnon de humana felicitate ac denique de fluxu et refluxu maris*, Venice 1528. For an introduction to Crisogono's work, see Bonelli and Russo, "The Origin of Modern Astronomical Theories of Tides," 388–390.

clusively on the positions of the moon and the sun. The booklet was also accompanied by a set of concentric card disks, one fixed and two free to rotate about the center, which allowed the calculation of the relative positions of the earth, the Moon, and the Sun. It is presumed that this feature, as well as its concise character contributed to a great success of Crisogono's text, the argument of which was taken up by many subsequent scholars. Federico Delfino was one who explicitly drew on the booklet in his work on tides published in Venice in 1559, as did Ludovico Boccadiferro in 1570. Crisogono's tract was reproduced in its entirety by Paolo Galluccio in 1588, and his theory was later adopted in Venice by Annibale Raimondo and in France by Claude Duré. Despite some criticism of Crisogono's method expressed, for instance, in the writings of Simon Stevin, who came to the same mechanical explanation of the tides from a strictly mathematical perspective and rejected the astrological premises of the phenomenon, Crisogono heavily influenced every major author from within the university and academic context, including his fellow Dalmatian Marc' Antonio de Dominis.[28]

Taken as a whole, the details presented above reveal that in the 1550s, that is, around the time when Sabbadino penned his manuscript notes, the issue of the flow and ebb of water was extensively discussed within the Venetian context and among his personal acquaintances, such as Alvise Cornaro and Girolamo Fracastoro. Therefore, the text, which this article strives to bring to broader awareness, reflects a burgeoning intellectual environment at the intersection of practical knowledge and theoretical approaches, at a time when efforts to control and transform the natural landscape reached a new level.

4 The Marciana Manuscript and its Argument

Sabbadino's manuscript preserved in the Marciana can be aptly described as a medium-size practitioner's handbook. It comprises a collection of notes and information concerning the tides, water flows, astronomy, calendric computation and topography, which were useful for the work of an "Inzigner e Protho" "in the service of the water office of the Most Serene Venice" – as the author introduces himself at the beginning of the manuscript. The main topics of the handbook are listed in the titlepage as follows:

Ebb and flow of the waters
When waters grow and diminish
When the Sun rises
Perpetual wheel on fertile years and mobile festivities
Hand concerning mobile festivities
In what celestial sign is the Moon every day

28 Marc' Antonio de Dominis, *Euripus seu de fluxu et refluxu maris sententia*, Roma 1624.

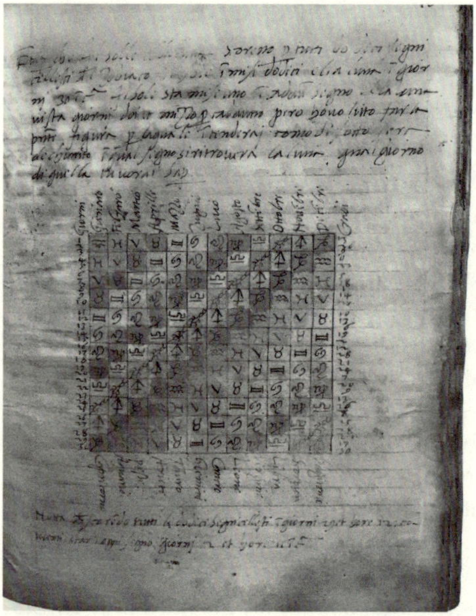

Fig. 1: A table of the cycles of the Sun and the Moon. In: Cristoforo Sabbadino, *Flussi e reflussi de le acque*, Marc. It. IV 51. 5136.

What planet dominates every hour of the day and the night
The determination of places in a drawing with winds and measure[29]

The first section, on the tides, sets the main topic of the handbook: water flows and the variation of their heights depending on cosmological factors that reach far beyond the local dimension of the lagoon of Venice or even the Adriatic Sea. Knowledge about the Moon, the Sun, their relative positions, the movement of the natural elements and meteorology is mobilized in the activity of a water officer. Sabbadino worked for an institution, which had the objective to protect the lagoon, as he clearly stated in the first lines of the manuscript. His work, as one reads, would be impossible without an adequate knowledge about water. This element was subject to the Moon's action. The text reads:

> I Cristoforo Sabbatino, in the service of the Water Office of the most Illustrious Serenity of Venice as an Engineer and Proto, in view of the fact that the task of this Office is to preserve the lagoon—in which the Lord God has situated the glorious City of Venice and placed here the waters in the manner of walls and fortresses—I took upon myself the heavy burden of demonstrating how salt waters increase and decrease with their ebbs and flows, both major and minor, to those who do not know. This is a subject that is necessary to know. For a clearer understanding by the readers, I draw an initial lunar depiction based on the knowledge that the Moon is the ruler of waters and seas, and the cause of major (and, in the opinion of many, minor) ebb and flow.[30]

For these reasons, the Moon occupies the central place in the manuscript's section on tides as well as in other parts. For Sabbadino, astronomy, comprising astrology, is particularly important for a correct understating of water flows. In his

29 Sabbadino, *Flussi e reflussi de le acque*, Marc. It. IV 51. 5136, titlepage.
30 Ibid., f. 1*r*.

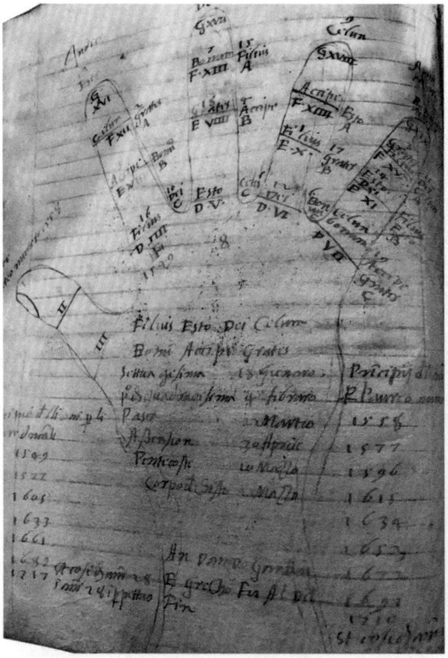

Fig. 2: A graph illustrating how to use one's hand for calendric computation. In: Cristoforo Sabbadino, *Flussi e reflussi de le acque*, Marc. It. IV 51. 5136.

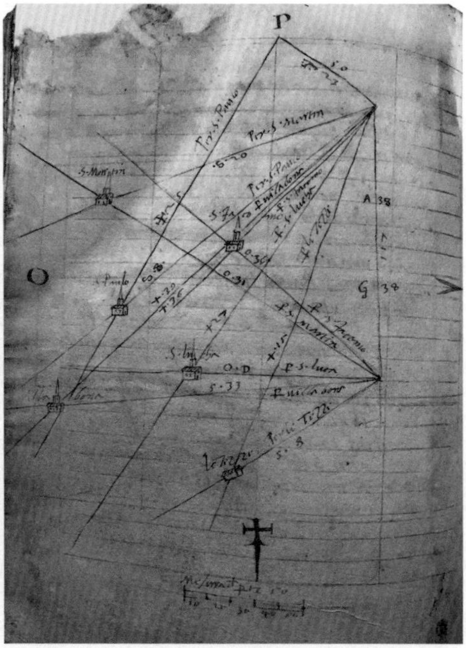

Fig. 3: A map of Venice featuring church towers as reference points. In: Cristoforo Sabbadino, *Flussi e reflussi de le acque*, Marc. It. IV 51. 5136.

opinion (in line with widespread astrological convictions of the time), the efficacy of heavenly influences on Earth is proved by the action of the Moon on the rhymical movements of waters. Sabbadino here connects this typical argument in favour of astrology with practical needs, as it constitutes background knowledge for the management and protection of Venice. Together with the Moon, the Sun and even the other planets are believed to act on Earth (actually, on water); hence, astrological knowledge looms large over the entire explanation of tides (figure 1).[31] Moreover, the cycles of the Moon and the Sun are also relevant for the computation of mobile festivities, in particular of Easter. Sabbadino writes on this topic, alongside tides, delving into practical methods of calendric computation, including how to use one's hand for the purpose (in the section 'Hand concerning mobile festivities') (figure 2).[32]

The drawing of maps and the measurements of angles and distances were crucial for the duties of a Venetian water officer. In the handbook, Sabbadino drew and explained the functioning of his measurement instruments. He explained

31 Ibid, f. 10*r*.
32 Ibid., f. 21*v*.

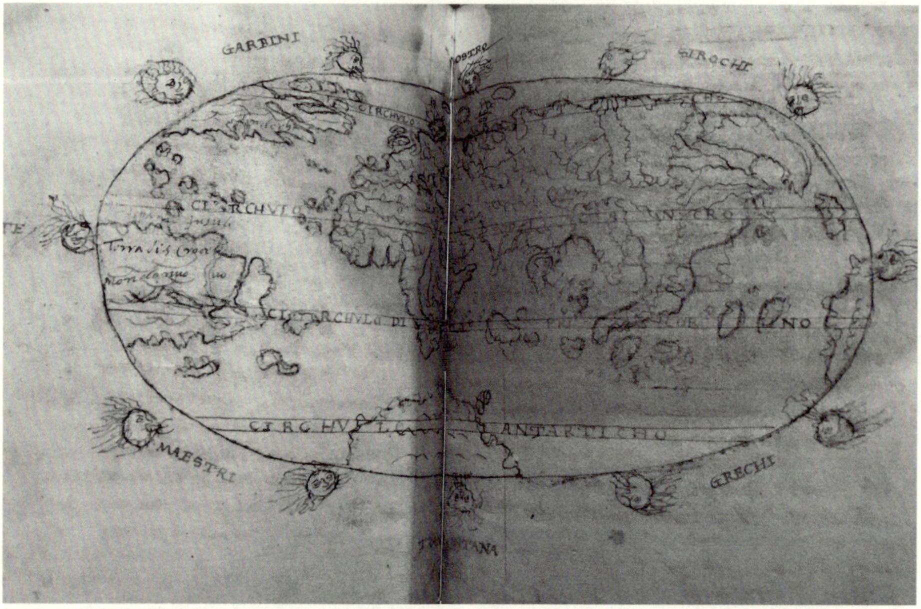

Fig. 4: A map of the world. In: Cristoforo Sabbadino, *Flussi e reflussi de le acque*, Marc. It. IV 51. 5136.

their application to triangulations devised to measure and draw Venice and its watery surroundings. A sketch, contained in the manuscript, documents his usage of church towers as reference points, and their targeting as the topographic basis for territorial maps (figure 3).[33] Moreover, a schematic depiction of the terrestrial globe aims to illustrate the orientation of winds and their names in the cartographic representation of the whole world offers a vision of Venice's planetary position. The water city is represented close to the center of the map, which is occupied by Jerusalem. The globe is composed of the *orbis terrarum* of the Ancients (Europe, Asia, Africa) plus the New World, which is labelled as *Mondo nuovo* echoing the title of Amerigo Vespucci's famous booklet on the newfound continent (figure 4).[34] As is apparent, the world of a Renaissance technician like Sabbadino is not confined to his local experience. Indeed, the local experience of a water practitioner of Venice in his time is situated within a framework marked by a deep awareness of cosmographic and cosmic relations.

The section on the tides thus has a clear cosmological and planetary dimension, although its relevance is explicitly linked to local practices (as the above quotation confirms). The explanation of the phenomenon of tides relates to a

33 Ibid., f. 17*v*.
34 Ibid., ff. 35*v*-36*r*.

drawing (figure 5), in the opening of the booklet, which shows the relation between the different phases of the lunar cycle, tidal motions and water heights. The Moon, as one reads, is the 'dominatrice delle acque', the dominator of waters and all humidity. Before he deals with the details of his tidal explanation, Sabbadino delves into relevant meteorological considerations connected with the circulation of humidity. During its monthly cycle, the Moon acts on the waters, attracting humidity in the form of vapors. These, in turn, cause wind, precipitations and even tempests (*fortune*):

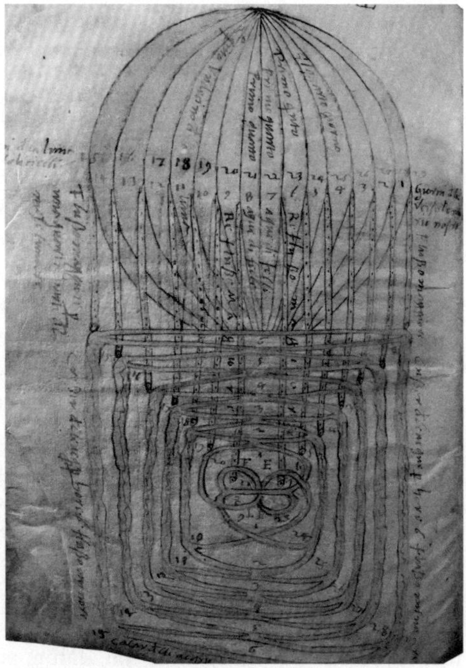

Fig. 5: A graph illustrating the correlation among different phases of the lunar cycle and the intensity of tidal motion. In: Cristoforo Sabbadino, *Flussi e reflussi de le acque*, Marc. It. IV 51. 5136.

> It is commonly believed that as the Moon progressively shows to us its light from day to day, the more it becomes charged with moisture, which it draws from both air and water. By its motion the vapors it feeds move; and winds, rain and snow are produced together with motions from which storms can be easily caused.[35]

Relative to the tides, Sabbadino explains that there are two periodicities. The 'minor cycle', which he calls 'flusso e riflusso minore' lasts one day; the 'major cycle', or 'flusso e riflusso maggiore' lasts one month. Moreover, the waters have two main motions. One is natural and is characterized by the flow of riverine waters to the sea and mostly moves westward. Sabbadino here repeats a trope that can be already found in ancient sources, based on the observation that the biggest rivers of the Mediterranean Sea discharge into the eastern part of the basin. Such natural motion is caused by the circulation of the heavens and, in fact, has the same direction of the daily rotation from east to west. In addition to it, one ought to take into account the motions that are caused by violence, that is, those that are produced by an external agent different from the circular action of the heavens. Sabbadino calls this category of motion 'motto sforciato'. He suggests that it is the consequence of the action of winds. In the Adriatic Sea, the winds known as *Tramontana, Maestro*

35 Ibid., f. 3*r*.

and *Greco* force the sea to move southwards, while *Sirocho*, *Ostro* and *Garbino* make it move towards the north. In one case, the Venetians used to say that 'the water moves from the Borino wind' (*l'acque vano da borino*), in another, that they 'move from Scirocco' (*da Sirocho*).[36] As for the flows to and from the lagoon, Sabbadino explains that the waters rise when the salty water enters through the harbours at the inlets and they diminish when it flows into the open sea. He remarks that there is an apparent misalignment between the lunar and the tidal flows, but this is only seemingly true and, indeed, depends on the observer's position in latitude.

The major motion of the waters is monthly. It can be observed by the fact that the waters grow more on certain days than on others. Sabbadino remarks that this phenomenon can be more easily perceived in closed waters, such as lagoons, than in the sea. In connection with the monthly cycles, certain days are characterized by a sort of stagnation, which local people call 'acque di felle', that is, 'rotten waters'. Sabbadino indicates that these days are the seventh and the eight of each month, as well as the twenty-second and the twenty-third. Apart from these transition days, experience teaches (*et questo si ha cavato dalla longa esperienzia che si ha havuto*) that the lunar month lasts 29 days and 12 hours. It can be subdivided into four periods. During two of them the waters grow. Sabbadino calls this phenomenon a 'multiplication': *le acque si moltiplicano.* During the two other periods, the waters diminish. Between the first and second period and between the third and fourth, it was observed that the waters stand for 36 hours.

After the description of the various phases of the monthly motion of water, Sabbadino offers an explanation of the phenomenon. According to him, they depend on an exchange of humidity between the body of the Moon and the sea (and what we would term the atmosphere). The main cause of the exchange is the necessity to cool the lunar disk, heated by the solar rays. Therefore, the relative positions of the Moon and the Sun are decisive and the appearance of the lunar disk in its various phases marks the varying intensity of thermic exchanges between this celestial body and terrestrial waters. When the Moon is closer and irradiated by the Sun in a more intense manner, it collects humidity for cooling; in turn, when it is less exposed to the solar action, it releases the humidity back. This has huge consequences not only for the sea levels and, indeed, for the tides, but also for meteorology more broadly, for instance, with regard to rain and precipitations.

Sabbadino mentions that some people believe that the tides are the effect of the direct action of the Sun on the waters, which the Sun hits (*percuote*) during its passage. However, he observes that such a theory has noticeable shortcomings, the most evident of which is that it cannot explain tidal effects during the night, that is, when the Sun is not directly above the moving waters. On this account, as one reads, it is more sensible to assume, in accordance with natural philosophy (*in base alla filosofia naturale*) that the sea has a cosmic motion that is proper to waters

36 Ibid., f. 4*r*.

as an element. This reference is an interesting witness that the theoretical background of the water officer of Venice includes not only mathematical astronomy but also natural philosophy, which at the time mainly amounted to Aristotelian physics and its Scholastic elaboration. Considering that the sixteenth century marked the pinnacle of the University of Padua, the mention of natural philosophy suggests that, as a practitioner and water expert, Sabbadino held Paduan literati in high esteem. The natural motion, as one reads, is well-ordered, akin to that of the heavens. Indeed, it directly follows the motion of the moon.

Relative to meteorology, winds account for variations of periodicity. Sabbadino offers some details about the varying durations. In winter, when the Scirocco wind blow from the South, the waters grow for seven or eight hours and decrease for four or five hours. By contrast, also in winter, when the Gregale wind (*vento Greco*) or the Tramontane (*Tramontana*) blow, the waters decrease for seven or eight hours and grow for a shorter amount of time, namely for four or five hours.

After the section on tides, Sabbadino addresses the motions of the Moon. As it is clear, astronomical knowledge about its period is fundamental for the comprehension of water motion and efficacious interventions in the lagoon. Sabbadino also includes tables relative to the standard growing and decreasing of waters during the month, that is, independently of the action of winds. As he explains, this is no abstract knowledge about the heavens but practice-oriented, that is, water related:

> As I have said, the rise and fall of the waters is caused by the lunar courses and movements and, according to another opinion of mine, by celestial motions and courses. But regardless of the causes, I wish to show all the hours when the waters begin to rise and fall, all the days of the lunation, which lasts 29 days and 12 hours, with the following table.[37]

5 Conclusion

Cristoforo Sabbadino's manuscript from the Biblioteca Marciana offers a unique insight into the entangled history of water management theory and practice in sixteenth-century Europe. It showcases the coexistence of a traditional theoretical framework alongside first-hand observations gathered "on the ground" in a political environment focused on the effective use of water resources and therefore devoting a good deal of attention to water phenomena. Set against the backdrop of Sabbadino's other projects for the Republic of Venice, his notebook exemplifies the state's growing environmental ambitions at a time when it developed means to implement any plans that it deemed necessary. At the same time, Sabbadino's

37 Ibid., f. 9*r*: "E perché detto per avanti, che il crescer e calar delle acque è causato dalli corsi et movimenti lunari, et per altra mia oppinione dagli moti e corsi cellesti, ma sia per qual causa si voglia, voglio con l'infrascritta tabula dimostrar tutte le hore che le acque cominciano a cresser et a calar tutti li giorni de la luna che sono 29 et hore 12."

work, while highly practical, emerged within distinct cultural settings where the origin of tides was widely debated as a crucial problem of natural philosophy undergoing significant changes. Although the extent to which Sabbadino's notebook was known outside the circles of Venetian practitioners and water experts remains unclear, it should nonetheless be viewed as both a consequence of and a solution to that philosophical and astronomical puzzle – a puzzle that would only be solved, according to the canon of a new 'classical' physics, in 1687 by none other than Isaac Newton.

Acknowledgments

Pietro Daniel Omodeo: I would like to thank the institutions and projects that support my current research: the UNESCO Chair *Water Heritage and Sustainable Development* at Ca' Foscari University Venice; the FARE project *EarlyGeoPraxis* (Grant of the Italian Ministry of University and Research, no. R184WNSTWH); the Max Planck Partner Group *The Water City* (Venice-Berlin-Jena); the project *Cosmography of Historical Waterscapes* (funded by Tsinghua University, Beijing), THE NEW INSTITUTE Centre for Environmental Humanities (NICHE) in Venice and the Max Planck Institute of Geoanthropology, Jena.
Ovanes Akopyan: This research has received funding from the European Union, through the HORIZON-MSCA-PF Project 101059723 "TIDES – A Long Way to a New Cosmology: Theories of Tides in Pre-Modern Thought." We would also like to thank Damiamo Acciarino without whose assistance the publication of Sabbadino's manuscript notes would not have been possible.

Appendix:
Transcription of the tidal part of the manuscript Marc. It. IV 51. 5136

FLVSSI E REFLVSSI DE LE ACQVE
QVANDO CRESCHONO E CALANO LE ACQVE
QVANDO SI LIEVA IL SOLE
RVOTA PERPETVA PER LI ANNI FERTILI E FESTE MOBILLI
MANO PER FESTE MOBILLI
IN QVAL SEGNO CELLESTE SI RITROVA LA LVNA OGNI GIORNO
QVAL PI[A]NETA DOMINI OGNI HORA DEL GIORNO E DELA NOTE
PER TVOR GLI LOCHI IN DIS[EGN]O PER LI VENTI E CON MISVRA

|Titlepage verso|

FIGVRA LVNARE

|1r|

Ritrovandomi, io Cristoforo Sabbatino, al servitio dell'offitio delle acque della Illustrissima Serenità di Vinetia, con il carico de Inzigner e Protho, e vedendo che in esso offitio non si tratta altro che di ritrovar modi di conservar la laguna nella qual il Signor Dio ha situato la gloriosa Città di Venetia e dato lì le acque per sue mura e fortezze, ho voluto tuor la prode fatica di dimostrar a quelli che no lo sanno como le aque salse crescono e discrescono con li loro flussi e reflussi e maggiori e minori, cosa molto necessaria a saperla. E per più chiara intelligentia degli lettori conoscendo la Luna esser dominatrice delle acque, degli mari e causarsi per quella il flusso e riflusso maggiore (et per opinion de' molti anco il minore), ho voluto formar la prima figura lunare. E dichiarando l'ordine di quella, le intenderano molte cose bisognose a saperle per conservar queste lagune, l'acqua delle quai sono quella istessa del mare.
Dirò adunque.
La figura rotonda et incarnata è tutto il corpo lunare, il qualle è sferico et oppaco, et ha la luce dal Sole, ma non la dimostra a noi, se non quando essa Luna si alontana da quello. Dirò il far della Luna. Quelli circuli, over linee, segnate per essa luna, se intendono gli giorni lunari, secondo che quella vada mostrando a noi la sua luce. Al primo circulo, il quale è il converso di quella là dove è segnato 1, se intende il suo primo giorno; e là dove è signato 2, il secondo. E così, di segno in segno e di giorno in giorno, si va fin al quartodecimo giorno de essa Luna, che è il principio della opposition sua con il Sole, detto 'l tondo, che alhora la mettà della Luna luce verso noi, l'altra mettà di essa Luna si rende per il ri|2v|verso, e tornerà dal segno 16, che è finito 'l tondo. Ai 17 poi è il secondo giorno, che quando comincia a lucer verso li cielli, per lo apressarsi al Sole. Il 18 poi è il terzo, e va seguitano fino al fine di essa Luna. Quelle trombe che si veggono distender dalla Luna gionger dove sono segnate le acque dimostrano il tra[sa]lire che fa essa Luna delle acque ogni giorno lunare, e lo ribassar le più corte, se intendono quando l'aigue del mare son più alte, lì in più loci, quando quelle son più bassi, nel motto maggiori di queste di duo dì, che, dalla prima alla settima tromba, sempre le acque vanno di giorno in giorno scemando e cadendo, como si dice di felle. Dalla ottava alla quintadecima tromba, le acque vano crescendo, fintanto che la Luna et quelle istesse scrivono dal tondo in o[rigine] fino al fine della Luna, è congiontion di quella con il Sole. La figura di sotto guarda, a modo de canali signata, significa [tanto] il cresser e calar dell'acque nel suo motto minore, il quale ogni sei hore como legendo, più chiaro le intenderesti.
E si dice la Luna esser madre de tutte le humiditati, perché quella le riceve e dal aere e da l'acqua, secondo che quella demostraremo in la sua luce e ne l'asconde, et dal qual viene, et che il cammino che fa la Luna lontanandosi dal Sole, e dimostraremo a noi la luce sua, ne fa conoscer alterni giorni e tempi negli quai spesse fiate nascono le fortune. E benché de tutti gli altri Pianete si conoschono li effetti loro, niente di meno, non si vegono così certi, como quelli che si causano negli tempi che la luna si va rivolgendo, per esser Pianeta più prossimo a noi degli altri, gli quali motti si conoscono, per il cresser et discresser delle |3r| acque degli

mari et con l'esser quelli in alcuni tempi più alti che ne gli altri, con il maggior e minor flusso e reflusso di quelli, la qual cosa è a noi certissima, né mai falla. E tra gli altri effetti che qui giuso si vegono causarli per essa Luna, uno è certissimo et ordinato, detto Acque di felle. Per il che, volendo raggionar di tali discorsi delle acque, ho voluto con l'arte fatta figura lunare, così imaginata, dimostrare (il meglio che ho potuto) gli effetti de essa Luna; come sono le acque di felle; et li giorni che esse acque crescono e calano; e quando e quanto si fermano; et alcuni giorni di essa Luna prodigiosi.

Dico prima che dalla congiontion, o veramente (come si dice) dal far della Luna, fino al suo fine, sono giorni 29 et hore 12, secondo che quella fa nel suo camino, contro e fuori del Zodiaco. Et perché egl'è comune oppinione che più che essa Luna si va dimostrando con la sua luce a noi di giorno in giorno, tanto più quella si va caricando d'humidità, trahendo quella e dal aere e da l'aigua, per il qual motto si moveno anco gli vapori de essi alimenti, e nascono dagli venti pioghie e nevi, motti dagli quai facilmente si causono le fortune.

Vari motti ordinari hano le aque degli mari per li movimenti di essa Luna. L'uno è 'l cresser et il calar che quello fano in hore 12, cioè sei crescendo et sei calando, et è detto flusso e reflusso minore; l'altro è il cresser che quelle, fino ogni quarto, parti de un corso lunare, et è detto flusso e reflusso maggiore. Il minore si causa da questi effetti: quando la Luna [esce] del Oriente, cioè del Levante nel Emisferio nostro, et |3v| ascendendo verso 'l mezzogiorno, le acque nel mezzo degli mari, con il suo globo l'arbasciano, et alle rive di quelli se inalciano, per ore sei **e** ½. Quando poi la Luna descende verso il Ponente nostro, le acque predette se alciano con il suo globo, et alle rive se arbasciano, per altre hore sei **e** ½. Per il che diviso un giorno lunare, che è de hore 23, minuti 12, in quattro parti, viene ad esser ogni quarta parte hore 5 e minuti 4-8 solare. Quando poi la Luna si parte dal Ponente nostro e va ascendendo verso il mezzogiorno degli antipodi, le acque parimente nel mezzo degli mari con il suo globo se arbasciano, et alle rive di quello crescono e se inalciano. E ritornando poi quell'al Oriente rivo, le acque sopradette nel mezzo s'inalciano e alle rive si arbasciano, et queste due fiate chelle acque crescono e calano intraviene in hore 24 de un giorno lunare: et è detto flusso e riflusso minore. Et è da saper che il cresser e calar delle acque de il mare, che è questo nostro Adriatico, como nelli altri seni et mari, non si conosce per quel corso che quelli tengono da loco a loco, come si vede nelle lagune serate tra gli litti; ma si conosce da il gonfiarsi e desgonfiarsi che quelli fano: alciando il globo nel mezzo verso 'l cielo et arbasciando quello verso motti over corsi: uno natural e l'altro sforciato. Il natural è il continuo corso che hanno gli mari per riva e da terra, descendendo principalmente da l'Oriente, et mandando con continuo corso verso Occidente; et così scoreno per riva e facendo questo corso, se l'acqua ritrova qualche seno, là entra in quello per una riva et esce per l'atra, in questo modo. |4r| Gionta l'acqua con il suo corso al stretto Gaditano, ditto di Gibilterra, la si caccia in quello per la riva del Africa, et circondando la riva del Mediterrano atorno atorno, la ritrova il sino Adriatico, et entra in quello per la riva della Velona et Albania, et scorendo la

Schiavonia, Istria, Friuli, Marca, Abrutio, Apulia, Calauria, Terra di Lavoro, Franza et Ispania, ritorna al stretto di Gibilterra, et per la riva de la Ispania esce nel Occeano Occidentale, et a questo modo circonda tutta la terra. Motto suo natural causato dal rotondo motto degli cieli; l'altro motto è sforciato, causato dagli venti, è questo che in questo mostro sino Adriatico regnano gli venti di Tramontana, Maestro, e Greco; l'acque scoreno verso mezzogiorno, e se per contrario, regnano gli venti Meridionali, come Sirocho, Ostro e Garbino, le acque tornano in drietto verso il Settentrione. Nel primo corso si dice l'acque vano da borino; e l'altro da Sirocho e così gli venti danno il corso alle acque nella superficie. Ma el più continuo è quello da borino, per regnar essi venti la maggior parte del anno, e per il discender questo sino Adriatico verso 'l Mediterano. Le acque veramente delli altri mari tengono il corso de li loro venti. In alcuni altri lochi tengono le acque altro corso: como nella Propontide, dita il Mar di Costantinopoli, al loco degli Dardanelli; là dove 'l regno di essa Propontide esce fuori nel mar Egeo, como si la fusse una fiumara, e pure s'alza. E la causa è questa: el loco degli Dardanelli è di strettezza di uno miglio **e** ½, la qual stretezza tiene l'acqua suspesa et alta; di modo che la cressente del Mar Egeo non puol farsi tanto alta che la superi quella della Propontide, et entri dentro et a filo la stretezza |4v| di esso loco, vi sono anco la grandissima quantità delle fiumare che sono nella Palude Meotide, detta Mar della Tana, et nel Ponto Eusino, detto il Mar Maggiore, et in essa Propontide, le quai continuatamente essendo in essi mari tengono multiplicata l'acqua, che la larghezza delli Dardanelli non è tale che ll'acqua si possi arbasciar, e ad egual livello di quella del Mar Egeo. Et è da saper che il cresser e calar delle acque de sei in sei hore si intende con boni tempi, e queti e non con fortune de essi mari, perché essi fortuni e venti abreviano e slongano hora il cressente et hora il descressente delle acque, ma non è però che il cresser et calar passi il tempo delle 12 hore, tra l'uno e l'altro. Nelle lagune veramente, in li quai entra et esce il mar salso, l'acqua tiene il corso venendo per li porti crescendo et calando uscendo per quelli nel mare. E per che detto che uscendo la Luna del Levante et ascendendo verso il Mezzogiorno, il globo del mare l'arbascia nel mezo et, arbasciandossi, l'acqua si alcia alle rive. Et ritrovati aperti li porti della laguna, e' entra per quelli, in essa escesse l'acque cresca ricrescendo meno, si vedrà molte volte l'acqua cresser la laguna, alla luna nostra ancora uscita dal Oriente, et alle fiate, essa luna sarà molto alta e l'acqua ancora discenderà fuori talmodo, non è però che questo ordine sia variato e fuori del suo termine: ma procede da questa causa: la luna cammina per el Zodiaco como fa 'l sole, il qual in uno anno lo circuisse tutto; e questa in mese uno lunare fa 'l medemo: la luna adunque serà negli segni invernali, como Sagitario, Capricorno et Aquario, in [...] li quali essendo essa Luna, quella non si vede nel emisperio nostro, se non hore otto [...] per il che lei tarda il mostrarsi a noi nel sito |5r| che siamo, dui hore in circa, et doi altre si asconde, avanti che le acque finiscano di calar. Alle fiate veramente quella serà negli segni estivi, como in Cancro, Gemini, e Leone, e starà nel emisperio nostro hore 16 **et** ½. E però il levar della luna se intende hore doi dopo uscita dal orizonte, et il tramontar suo, hore doi avanti che la si ascondi nel Ponente: perché partendo il circulo del ciello in quattro parte el bisogna che la luna stia in ogni quarta parte hore sei; e però in questi casi bisogna saper in qual segno si ritrova la luna nel zodiaco, et dar al giorno breve tante hore, et così alla notte, di modo che hore 12 resti per il giorno et altre 12 per la notte: facendo il giorno ella notte eguale, de ogni tempo de hore dodici.

L'altro motto delle acque è il flusso e riflusso maggiore, et è quello che si vede quando naturalmente le acque si alciano più uno giorno che un altro, il che si vede più facilmente nelle lagune che nel mare, e così quando si arbasciano et vedessi in questo muodo. Quando la luna è in la sua congiontion con il solle, cui è nel tempo che fa la luna, alhora le acque sono in la maggior altezza sua, e questo è il primo giorno di essa luna. Il secondo alquanto si arbasciano. Il terzo fa il medemo, e così vanno scemando fino al settimo et ottavo giorno di essa luna che è nel primo quarto de la sua revolutione nel qual tempo le acque per hore 36 fano poco alciamento over arbasciamento, e stano con poco corso, e dicessi le acque sono di felle. Il nono giorno di quella, le acque cominciano a gonfiarsi et como si dice a pontar. Il decimo giorno più, et così vanno crescendo di giorno in giorno fino alla opposition di essa luna con il solle, che è nel tondo di quella, nel qual tempo le acque sono nel esser |5v| che se ritrovano nel far della luna. Passato 'l tondo et cominciando ad alsarsi la luna al solle, le acque cominciano a calar, e scemarsi e così di giorno in giorno vano facendo, fino al 21 et 22 giorni di essa luna, che è il suo terzo quarto. Et a quel tempo le acque son nel istesso esser che erano nel suo primo quarto. Nelli qual tempi (e del primo e del terzo quarto di essa luna) si chiamano le acque di felle. Et da questo è nasciuto in proverbio tra marinari che si dice tra li 7 et 8 le acque non fano motto, tra li 22 et 23 le non vano né su né zo, e dicessi acque di felle, perché non avendo motto velloce li chiamano marce come il felle; et è falso il detto che alcuni dicono tra li 8 e li 9 l'acqua non si move, perché il nono giorno della luna le acque cominciano a pontar, et ad haver maggior motto, et il 23 di essa luna vano crescendo fino ala congiontion sua con il sole, di modo che così como partito un giorno lunare in quattro parte, nel qual giorno la luna circonda tutta la terra, dui giorni le acque crescono, e dui calano, e nel mezzo del calar e crescer si affermano. Così partito un mese lunare (che è di giorni 29 et hore 12, nel qual tempo la luna dimostra la sua luce a noi) in quattro parte: dui quarti le acque moltiplicano, e dui quarti si scemano, con il loro flusso e reflusso maggiore; et tra il primo e secondo quarto si fermano per hore 36, e l'istesso fano tra il terzo e quarto quarto, et questo si ha cavato dalla longa esperienzia che si ha havuto.

Le cause veramente da le quai poleno sortir li effetti sopra detti del flusso e riflusso maggiore con l'ordine della luna si poleno dir esser questi. Essendo la luna corpo denso et oppaco como la terra e posta nel cielo più propinquo ali ellementi percotendo in quella li raggi del sole contiene [in] parte il calore che patisse la terra, e rivolgendo essa |6r| parte calda verso l'aere e l'acqua per rifrigerarsi trae a sé e del aerre e de l'acqua de l'humor frigido per il che minuendo da l'aigua questa parte et frigidor over humor frigido quella si scema et si arbascia e così va facen-

do fino alla quarta parte di essa luna nel qual tempo essa dimostra ver la terra la quarta parte che la sua calidità per esser nella quarta parte del suo circulo over ciclo. Passata essa quarta parte di esso suo ciclo quella si va alontanando dal solle et il globo del aere, se intermedia tra essa luna et il solle per il che quella comincia a relassar la humidità tolta e da l'aere e da l'acqua, e così cominciano le acque ad augmentar e così vanno augmentando fino al tondo di essa luna, nel quarto tempo esse acque sono ne la istessa altezza che sono nel far di essa luna, passato il tondo et essa luna tornando ad alsarsi al sole comincia più a riscaldarsi et per rinfrigerarsi atraere asa' della humidità e de l'acqua e del aere e così esse acque vanno scemandossi e diminuendo fino al terzo quarto di essa luna nel qual tempo le acque sono in la istessa bassezza che erano nel primo quarto et entrando essa luna ne l'ultimo quarto per lo apressarsi al sole comincia a mostrar la sua luce verso li cieli e la parte che non luce et è frigida comincia a volgerla verso la terra e però comincia a relassar la humidità tolta come è detto, e le acque così vanno augmentando fino al fine di essa luna che è la congiontion con il sole.
Un'altra raggione vel dico, la qual è questa: alontanandossi la luna dal sole et essendo più propinqua alla terra delli altri cieli comincia a percuetere sopra il globbo degli mari alsandosi alla cima di quello et così esso globo per cosse reinizia a poco a poco ad arbasciarsi e le acque si vano inalciando verso le rive degli mari et così va facendo fino che essa luna è ascissa nela quarta parte del suo ciclo et alla metà di esso globo over [...] |6v| del mare passata essa quarta parte quella comincia a descender giuso dal globo et quello va respirando et alciandossi tirando l'acqua assé alciandossi nel mezzo et arbasciandossi alle rive et così opera nelli altri dui quarti di essa luna. La causa veramente da la qual procede il cresser e callar delle acque in le hore dodici, sei crescendo e sei calando procede che levandossi il solle et uscendo fuori nel Oriente comincia a percorrere nel globo de essi mari et ad arbasciarli per hore sei continue per il che arbasciandossi quelli nel mezzo l'acque loro si alciano alle rive e diciam noi l'acqua cresce passato e esso solle e il signo del meridie e discendendo verso il Ponente comincia a rilassar la percution di esso globo di mari et quelli ritornano ad alciarsi et così fanno per hore sei et così alciandossi nel mezzo le acque loro si arbasciano ale rive e diciam noi l'acqua calla alciando poi esso solle verso la mettà del ciclo delli antipodi, li globi di mari si arbasciano nel mezzo et le acque si alciano alli rivi ritornando dopo il solle verso Levante esse acque si alciano nel mezzo di essi mari e si arbasciano alle rive di quelli, et così in un giorno sollare ch'è di hore 24 le acque hore 12 s'arbasciano et 12 crescono così ogni 6 hore calando et ogni sei crescendo. Altri dicono questo causarsi dalla Luna la qual facendo parimente il suo corso atorno la terra et a qui in hore 24 et ½ fa il meddemo carico sopra il globo degli mari como farebbe il solle. Ma queste raggioni non si acordano del tutto inperoché la notte il sole non è sopra l'emisperio nostro e però non puol percuotere sopra i globi delli mari che sono in questa parte superior e massime nel Mediterraneo et in questo sino Adriatico. E parimente la luna. Io veramente dico che questo arbasciarssi e alciarsi li mari nel loro mezzo et globo è uno motto ordinato causato dalli motti delli cielli al

princi||7r||pio del motto di quelli, overo secundo l'oppinion filosofica, quando si cominciorno gli mari et così como essi cielli hano in motto continuo et ordinato, così hano gli mari che il 12mo in fiadar e refiadar ascendendo e discendendo. Et tengo che questo ordine serà continuo fino al fine del motto di essi cielli et questo basta quanto al moto delle acque al crescer e calar di quelli se nel flusso e reflusso maggiore como nel minore.

L'intraviene assai volte che nel flusso e riflusso minore il crescer delle acque sarà più longo che il calar di quelle, et alcune fiate el calar più longo che il cresser e massime in questo sino Adriatico dominato dalli venti Australi et Septentrionali. Se 'l venerà una fortuna di Siroco l'acqua crescerà 7 et 8 hore et andarà giuso calando 4 et 5 hore. Se nello inverno serà fortuna con vento Greco e Tramontana l'acqua andarà giuso 7 et 8 ore et crescerà 4 over 5; ma sia qual sorte di fortuna che si voglia abreviasi oppur lungassi il calor over il cresser tra l'uno e l'altro mare si passano le hore 12.

E perché fin qui ho raggionato degli motti delle acque e degli loro flussi e riflussi e maggiori e minori vorei anco raggionar d'alcuni accidenti che cadono per li corsi lunari et però ho formata la antista figura lunare nella quale vedrai tanti li giorni che essa luna dimostra la sua luce a noi dalla congiontion prima alla ultima et poi dirassi il resto.

Reference Lists

Sources

Abū Maʿšar al-Balḫī, *The Great Introduction to Astrology*, 2 vols., eds. Keiji Yamamoto and Charles Burnett, Leiden/Boston 2020

Sabbadino, Cristoforo, *Discorsi sopra la Laguna (parte 1)*, ed. Roberto Cessi, Venice 1930.

Sabbadino, Cristoforo, *Flussi e reflussi de le acque*, Marc. It. IV 51. 5136.

Sabbadino, Cristoforo, *Il sistema laguna a metà Cinquecento*, ed. Pier Giorgio Tiozzo Gobetto, Chioggia 2011.

Crisogono, Federico, *De modo collegiandi, pronosticandi et curandi febres, necnon de humana felicitate ac denique de fluxu et refluxu maris*, Venice 1528.

De Dominis, Marc' Antonio, *Euripus seu de fluxu et refluxu maris sententia*, Roma 1624.

Research Literature

Akopyan, Ovanes, "Discussing Tides Before and After Newton: Roger Joseph Boscovich's *De aestu maris*", in: *Perspectives on Science* 30/6 (special issue *(De)Constructing Authority in Early Modern Cosmology*, eds. Ovanes Akopyan and Pietro Daniel Omodeo) (2022), pp. 1042–1064.

Akopyan, Ovanes, "Giovanni Pico della Mirandola on Tides", in: *Bruniana & Campanelliana* 1 (2018), pp. 135–145.

Bonelli, Federico and Lucio Russo, "The Origin of Modern Astronomical Theories of Tides: Chrisogono, De Dominis and Their Sources", in: *The British Journal for the History of Science* 29 (1996), pp. 385–401.

Boudet, Jean-Patrice, *Entre science et nigromance. Astrologie, divination et magie dans l'Occident médiéval (XII–XV siècle)*, Paris 2006.

Burnett, Charles, "Does the Sea Breathe, Boil or Bloat? A Textual Problem in Abū Ma'shar's Explanation of Tides", in: *Mélanges offerts à Hossam Elkhadem par ses amis et ses élèves*, eds. Frank Daelemans, Robert Halleux, David Juste and Léopold Zimmer, Brussels 2007, pp. 73–79.

Burnett, Charles, *Magic and Divination in the Middle Ages: Texts and Techniques in the Islamic and Christian Worlds*, Aldershot 1996.

Ciriacono, Salvatore, *Building on Water: Venice, Holland and the Construction of the Landscape in Early Modern Times*, New York 2006.

D'Alverny, Marie-Thérèse, *La connaissance de l'Islam dans l'occident medieval*, ed. Charles Burnett, Aldershot 1994.

De Libera, Alain, *Penser au Moyen Âge*, Paris 1991.

Deparis, Vincent, Hilaire Legros and Jean Souchay, "Investigations of Tides from the Antiquity to Laplace", in: *Tides in Astronomy and Astrophysics*, eds. Jean Souchay, Stéphane Mathis and Tadashi Tokieda, Berlin 2013, pp. 31–82.

Federici Vescovini, Graziella, "I programmi degli insegnamenti del Collegio di medicina, filosofia e astrologia, dello statuto dell'Università di Bologna", in: *Roma, magistra mundi: itineraria culturae medievalis. Mélanges offerts au Père L. E. Boyle à l'occasion de son 75e anniversaire*, ed. Jacqueline Hamesse, Leuven 1998, pp. 193–223.

Haskins, Charles H., *The Renaissance of the Twelfth Century*, Cambridge, MA, 1927.

Hübner, Wolfgang, "The Culture of Astrology from Ancient to Renaissance", in: *A Companion to Astrology in the Renaissance*, ed. Brendan Dooley, Leiden/Boston 2014, pp. 17–58.

Laird, Edgar, "Robert Grosseteste, Albumasar and Medieval Tidal Theory", in: *Isis* 81/4 (1990), pp. 684–694.

Lemay, Richard, *Abu Ma'shar and Latin Aristotelianism in the Twelfth Century: The Recovery of Aristotle's Natural Philosophy through Arabic Astrology*, Beirut 1962.

Morel, Thomas, *Underground Mathematics: Craft Culture and Knowledge Production in Early Modern Europe*, Cambridge 2023.

Omodeo, Pietro Daniel, "Modelli esplicativi delle maree nel Rinascimento: una rassegna", in: *Galilaeana. Studies on Renaissance and Early Modern Science* 14 (2017), pp. 98–114.

Pingree, David, "The Diffusion of Arabic Magical Texts in Western Europe", in: *La diffusione delle scienze islamiche nel Medio evo europeo*, ed. Biancamaria Scarcia Amoretti, Roma 1987, pp. 57–98.

Russo, Lucio, *Flussi e riflussi. Indagine sull'origine di una teoria scientifica*, Milan 2003.

Saif, Liana, *The Arabic Influences on Early Modern Philosophy*, Basingstoke/New York 2015.

Smith, Pamela H., *From Lived Experience to the Written Word: Reconstructing Practical Knowledge in the Early Modern World*, Chicago/London 2022.

Stevens Crawshaw, Jane L., *Cleaning Up Renaissance Italy: Environmental Ideals and Urban Practice in Genoa and Venice*, Oxford 2023.

Ventrice, Pasquale, *La discussione sulle maree tra astronomia, meccanica e filosofia nella cultura veneto-padovana del Cinquecento*, Venice 1989.

Weill-Parot, Nicolas, "L'attraction magnétique entre influence astrale et astrologie au Moyen Âge (XIIIe – XVe siècle)", in: *Philosophical Readings* 7/1 (special issue *Medieval and Renaissance Astrology*, ed. Donato Verardi) (2015), pp. 55–70.

An Early Modern Controversy on Hydropolitics: The Dispute Over the Watershed of Mexico

Omar Rodríguez Camarena

1 Disputed Hydropolitical Projects and an Early Example from Below

The territory, especially in hydraulic matters, is not the background against which human history takes place, but the two are inextricably linked, as is their historical development. Different social groups coexisting in the same landscape and waterscape have diverse "hydrocultures" with different practices and ideas about the territory, and therefore they also promote different "hydropolitical projects".[1] This plurality of spaces and people means that the territory is always an object of struggle and negotiation, as are knowledge about it and projects for its future.[2] Territory 'embodies the contradictions, conflicts and struggles of that society',[3] and thus, like societies, territories are also always in constant production, reproduction and change.

These conflicts were of course more complex in a colonial environment, especially in the case of the watershed of Mexico, with its peculiarities due to its unique environment, within a series of lakes, and its political situation as the capital of multicultural New Spain. Thus, in the Basin of Mexico, not only have different cultures clashed, but also different lifestyles and practices related to water, which have changed throughout history, transforming the landscape itself. These are not only conceptual, but also practical and political struggles over the desired relationship between society and the environment.

Although the shores of its lakes had been inhabited by different peoples before, the transformation of the Basin of Mexico accelerated with the arrival of the Aztecs, who, after a pilgrimage in 1325, found their "promise land", located within the lakes of the Basin of Mexico. They had an extremely positive image of this waterscape, which they transformed in order to reclaim enough land to build

1 Rutgerd Boelens, Jaime Hoogesteger, Erik Swyngedouw, Jeroen Vos and Philippus Wester, "Hydrosocial Territories: A Political Ecology Perspective", in: *Water International* 41 (2016), p. 1.

2 Pietro Daniel Omodeo. "Hydrogeological Knowledge from Below: Water Expertise as a Republican Common in Early-Modern Venice", in: *Berichte zur Wissenschaftsgeschichte / History of Science and Humanities* 45/4 (2022), p. 539.

3 Brenda Baletti, "Ordenamento Territorial: Neo-Developmentalism and the Struggle for Territory in the Lower Brazilian Amazon", in: *Journal of Peasant Studies* 39/2 (2012) p. 578.

DOI: 10.13173/9783447123693.069

their city, Tenochtitlan, and even artificial plots for agriculture, called *chinampas*.[4] They built roads and canals to the city and a double aqueduct to bring fresh water from Chapultepec (Grasshopper Hill). The most impressive work was the construction of a large dike that separated the brackish water of Lake Texcoco[5] from the fresh water, creating the so-called *Laguna de México*.[6] They also built another smaller dike next to the city to protect it from flooding. However, this complex hydraulic management did not aim to create a sharp separation between water and land, or between the lakes and the city. Instead, they coexisted in a fluid and dynamic relationship.[7]

When the Spaniards and their indigenous allies, under the command of Cortés, conquered Tenochtitlan, not only were temples and palaces destroyed, but also much of the hydraulic infrastructure, such as the huge dike that separated fresh water from salt waters. Later, the reconstruction of the city and the imposition of European farming techniques, technologies and practices had a huge impact on the environment. The high indigenous mortality rate made way for the introduction of livestock and new agricultural products, which, together with the novelty of the plough and oxen and the intensification of logging, led to an increase in soil erosion and, consequently, the silting of the lakes.[8] As early as 1533, following worrying reports of increasing deforestation in the watershed, various measures were implemented to control it, but they failed.[9] Given that the rainfall in the first decades after the conquest of Tenochtitlan was moderate, all these changes did not pose a major problem, and the indigenous hydraulic infrastructure seemed unnecessary. As a result, the dike that protected the city from flooding was lost.

Things changed in 1555, when unusually heavy rains flooded the city for the first time under Spanish rule. This led viceroy Luis de Velasco to consult various sectors of this multicultural society in search of a solution. He listened not only to European engineers, but also to indigenous leaders and 'elders who understood these matters as people native to the land and raised in it'. This meant that their experience and historical knowledge of water management was valued.[10] However, two different ways of dealing with water can be seen from this period. Both aimed to protect the city from flooding, but were supported by different social

4 Marcos Mazari, Raúl Marsal and Jesús Alberro, "Los asentamientos del templo mayor analizados por la mecánica de suelos", in: *Estudios de cultura Náhuatl* 19 (1989), p. 179; Pedro Armillas, "Gardens on Swamps", in: *Science* 174/4010 (1971), p. 654.

5 Being a closed basin, the streams caused the accumulation of minerals in the lower part of the basin, which was Lake Texcoco.

6 Barbara Mundy, *The Death of Aztec Tenochtitlan, the Life of Mexico City*, Austin 2015, pp. 35–37.

7 Vera Candiani, *Dreaming of Dry Land: Environmental Transformation in Colonial Mexico City*, Stanford 2014, pp. 15–16 and 22.

8 Ibid., p. 29.

9 Alain Musset, *El agua en el Valle de México. Siglos XVI–XVIII*, Mexico 1992, pp. 64–65.

10 Emma Pérez-Rocha, *Ciudad en peligro: Probanza sobre el desagüe general de la ciudad de México, 1556*, Mexico 1996, p. 34.

groups.[11] On the one hand, the indigenous leaders affirmed that the best solution was to rebuild the old dike next to the city, which protected it from the waters of Lake Texcoco. On the other hand, Francisco Gudiel in the Spanish *cabildo*, or council, proposed controlling the level of the lakes by opening an outlet for their waters to the north.[12] The local representatives of the Crown were also divided over these alternative plans of action. The Spanish council agreed with Gudiel's proposal because it also offered the possibility of reclaiming more land for the settlers. On the other hand, the viceroy and the government supported the indigenous solution because it not only took into account the interests of the Spanish settlers, but also preserved the lakes and their resources for the common good. It was a more comprehensive water management based on local knowledge and experience that recovered the importance of the lakes to the natural and social life of the basin.[13] Altogether they opposed the more disruptive plan of the Spanish council and the settlers to open an outlet for the waters of the lakes. They sought to protect the native way of life associated with the lake of indigenous communities, which was also useful to the city, but without imposing only urban interests.[14]

Since viceroy Velasco supported the indigenous project of protecting the city with a dike as before, this was carried out. The work, which was directed by the indigenous leaders of the different towns, involved around six thousand natives and was completed in just three months.[15] But the conflicts over water management in the basin had only just begun. The viceroy had decided that he would supply the corn to feed the indigenous workers, while the city council or the

11 This is reminiscent of the case of Venice. Pietro Omodeo, Sebastiano Trevisani and Senthil Babu, "Benedetto Castelli's *Considerations on The Lagoon of Venice*: Mathematical Expertise and Hydro-Geomorphological Transformations in Seventeenth-Century Venice", in: *Earth Sciences History* 39/2 (2020).

12 Bejarano, *Libro del Cabildo e Ayuntamiento desta ynsine e muy leal ciudad de Tenuztitan Mexico*, vol. 6, Mexico [undated'], pp. 197–199; Luis González Obregón, *Memoria histórica, técnica y administrativa de las obras del desagüe del valle de México, 1449–1900*, vol.1, book II, Mexico 1902, pp. 62–67.

13 As Nancy Fraser has noted, in contrast to present-day environmentalism, which focuses only on the protection of nature, indigenous people under mercantile capitalism, but even now, 'did not separate protection of nature or habitat from defence of livelihoods, political autonomy, or social reproduction of their communities. They fought, rather, for all those elements together and for the forms of life in which they were integrated'. *Cannibal Capitalism*, London/New York 2022, p. 109.

14 This is similar to what happened in Venice, where there was an opposition between those in favour of land reclamation and those defending the preservation of the lagoon for the common good, the latter based on 'comprehensive knowledge which aimed to cope with systemic complexity'. Pietro Omodeo, Sebastiano Trevisani and Senthil Babu, "Benedetto Castelli's *Considerations on The Lagoon of Venice*: Mathematical Expertise and Hydro-Geomorphological Transformations in Seventeenth-Century Venice", in: *Earth Sciences History* 39/2 (2020), pp. 429 and 441. At the same time, water policies took into account the communities of the lagoon, mainly fishermen, and were thus implemented in a dialogical way through alliances between different sectors of the society. Pietro Daniel Omodeo, "Geopraxis: A Concept for the Anthropocene", in: *Journal of Interdisciplinary History of Ideas* 11/22 (2022), pp. 9:30–31.

15 Pérez-Rocha *Ciudad en peligro*, p. 117.

Spanish settlers would provide the meat and the necessary tools.[16] However, the Spanish council refused to pay its share for the work, although it was actually intended to protect the urban properties of the Spanish settlers. As a result, the Royal Court (*Real Audiencia*) launched an inquiry, which not only reclaimed these payments, but also highlighted the importance of the lakes.[17] Friars and local Hispanic governors were called as witnesses, as were indigenous leaders, including some of those who had proposed rebuilding the old dam to protect the city. They were questioned about the benefits of the lakes for their resources, their necessity for commerce and supplies by canoe, and even the unhealthy effects of their drying up.

It can be seen that the questions were formulated with a vision similar to that of the indigenous project, supporting the demand for payment for the natives' work, and the importance of the lakes as a common good for both Spaniards and indigenous people. For instance, the witnesses were asked if they knew that:

> [XVI] the drainage of the lagoon is quite difficult, and it could occupy a large number of Indians, who would be forced to abandon their farms and crops, and this city could not provide the necessary livelihood [...]
>
> [XVII] in this city, both the republic of the Spanish and that of the natives are supplied with the necessary means of subsistence, as well as building materials, by canoe, and if the said lagoon were to be drained, it would not be able to provide for all these people.
>
> [XVIII] that the Spaniards and the natives of this city have benefited from fishing in the lagoon, and from the grass, birds and other things from which they derive great benefit [...]
>
> [XIX] If you know that a lack of water in the lagoon would be very harmful to this city, since the bad smell generated in the said lagoon when parts of it dry up, could cause major diseases.[18]

---

16 Ibid; González, *Memoria histórica, técnica y administrativa*, pp. 59–61.

17 "Traslado de probanza hecha a petición del fiscal de la Audiencia de México, licenciado Maldonado, sobre el edificio de la Albarrada y desaguadero de la laguna de la ciudad. México, 14 de mayo de 1556". General Archive of the Indies. Patronato, 181, R. 30. Pérez-Rocha has transcribed this document in *Ciudad en peligro*.

18 '[XVI] si saben quel desaguadero de la dicha laguna es dificultosso, y en él se avían de ocupar gran cantidad de yndios, e avían de dexar forzosamente de entender en sus labranzas e sementeras, e esta ciudad no podría proveer de los mantenymientos necesarios, que se proveen, por estar ocupados en la dicha obra [XVII] si saben que en esta dicha ciudad se provee, así la república de los españoles, como la de los naturales, de los mantenimientos necesarios como [de] los materiales para los edificios con canoas, e si la dicha alaguna se desaguase no podría prover por ser mucha la gente. [XVIII] si saben que los españoles e naturales desta ciudad, es grande el provecho que reciben de la pesquería de dicha laguna, e de la yerba, e tule, aves e otras cossas, en que tienen grandes aprovechamientos; e si la dicha alaguna se desaguase, no avrían los provechos [XIX] si saben que si a la dicha alaguna, le faltase el agua sería muy dañosso a esta ciudad, por el mal olor que en la dicha laguna se engendra,

Once again, this inquiry shows that the Royal Court supported the indigenous project and a more comprehensive water management that took into account the richness and necessity of the lakes. Although, in the end, the Spanish council never paid for the dike, its construction represented the recognition by the New Spain authorities of the advantages of indigenous water management over the proposal of Hispanic settlers. Once again, indigenous competence in infrastructure construction was revalued when the city needed new fresh water sources. Spanish technicians attempted to build a new aqueduct from the northwest, but the arches were misaligned, and the slope was miscalculated, so the project was eventually abandoned. Then, in 1575, the city's indigenous rulers proposed to build another aqueduct from Chapultepec. Once again, the Spanish council, which was supposed to provide some materials for the work, did not receive the project very well. It finally began in 1576, but the work was constantly interrupted due to a very severe epidemic, so it was not completed until 1582.[19] The new aqueduct reached the indigenous market on the south side of the city, which was certainly useful to improve indigenous commerce and activities.

The water management of the Basin of Mexico in the second half of the 16th century, in particular the dike to prevent flooding, the subsequent inquiry and the new aqueduct can be seen as examples of "knowledge from below". It can be compared to the case of Venice, where the transversal collaboration between the Venetian senate, water officers and fishermen made it possible to preserve the lagoon for the common good.[20] Similarly, in the Basin of Mexico, a collaborative policy sought not only a more harmonious coexistence with water, as Barbara Mundy argues,[21] but also the achievement of a common good among the different social groups. Since this mediated knowledge economy involved not only local interests but also Crown representatives, it can be seen as an early instance of *glocal* policymaking. Although the integration of new regions in early globalization tended to have a negative impact on native societies and environments, the watershed of Mexico shows that in the early modern period some dialogical and bottom-up solutions that attempted to protect the common good could be implemented in the New World.

2 Geoanthropological Changes. The Transformation of a Basin Into a Valley

At the beginning of the 17th century, several changes occurred in the watershed. Mexico City suffered several floods that rekindled interest in the issue, and the problem was even discussed in printed texts. In 1606, the cosmographer Heinrich Martin, known in Mexico as Enrico Martínez, published his *Reportorio de*

guando partes de la dicha alaguna se seca, y ansí se a visto por espirencia otros años, que la dicha alaguna se seca, e por muy grande el mal olor que hay en esta ciudad e dello podría redundar grandes enfermedades.' Pérez-Rocha. *Ciudad en peligro*, pp. 35–36.

19 Mundy, *The Death of Aztec Tenochtitlan, the Life of Mexico City*, pp. 191 and 197–205.

20 Omodeo, "Hydrogeological Knowledge from Below".

21 Mundy, *The Death of Aztec Tenochtitlan, the Life of Mexico City*, p. 199.

los tiempos e historia de Nueva España (Mexico), and later, in 1615, Juan de Torquemada's *Monarquía Indiana* was printed in Seville. Among other things, these two books offered an explanation for the transformation of the basin after the Spanish colonization. According to these authors, the introduction of European farming, with the plough and cattle, caused an increase in soil erosion and, with the rains, the sediments gradually settled on the bottom of the lakes. This sedimentation process began to reduce the extension of the lakes, which in turn caused various problems. For instance, the reduction of the lakes, together with overexploitation, affected the fish population and fishing activities.[22]

The main problem that both Martinez and Torquemada pointed out was that, as a consequence of silting and the rise of the lakes' bottoms, their capacity to contain water diminished. This increased the risk of flooding for the city.[23] Since this process allowed the shallower parts of the lagoon of Mexico to be transformed into reclaimed land, it was not seen as something negative by the Spanish settlers. Therefore, unlike Venice, where the government protected the lagoon from land reclamation, the surrounding area from deforestation, and the aquatic life from overfishing,[24] in the Basin of Mexico no measures were taken to prevent the reclamation of these new dry lands or to try to control fishing. In general, the silting up of the lakes was not considered a problem as long as there were no heavy rains flooding the city, which was precisely the problem that arose at the dawn of the 17th century.

In 1604, Mexico City suffered a major flood, which worsened the following year. By that time, not only had the geohydrology of the basin changed, but the indigenous population had decreased, while the Spanish settlers were gaining influence. Thus, although the new viceroy, the Marquis of Montesclaros, once again asked for different opinions, this time the indigenous people were not consulted at all. The viceroy called for a 'general and perpetual drainage'. This decision shows the strength that the urban vision had acquired. After preliminary inquiries, a project to drain Lake Zumpango in the north was presented by 'architecture masters and cosmographers'.[25] The royal fiscal, Espinosa de la Plaza, opposed it, arguing that it was his duty to protect the indigenous people and that

22 Juan de Torquemada, *Monarquía indiana*, vol. 1, book III, c. XXVIII, Mexico 1964, pp. 423–424; Martínez, *Reportorio de los tiempos e historia de Nueva España*, Mexico 1606, 185–186; Candiani. *Dreaming of Dry Land*, p. 29. Unlike Venice, as far as we know, in the Mexican case no measures were taken to control fishing. Cfr. Pietro Omodeo, "Hydrogeological Knowledge from Below", pp. 543–545.

23 Torquemada, *Monarquía indiana*, vol. 1, book III, c. XXVIII, pp. 423–424; Martínez, *Reportorio de los tiempos e historia de Nueva España*, cap. XV. QUE TRATA, QUE SEA la causa de que algunas partes de esta Nueva España que solían ser lagunas y pantanales, se siembran y cultiven al presente, y de parecer que mengua la laguna de México, pp. 185–186.

24 Karl Appuhn, *Forest on the Sea: Environmental Expertise in Renaissance Venice*, Baltimore 2009. Pietro Omodeo and Sebastiano Trevisani, "Historical Geoanthropology in Venice", in: *Journal of Interdisciplinary History of Ideas* 11/22 (2022), pp. 12:11–12.

25 Cepeda and Carrillo, *Relación universal, legitima, verdadera, del sitio en que está fundada la muy noble, insigne, y muy leal Ciudad de Mexico*, Mexico 1637, ff. 6v–7r.

such a huge project would force the natives to abandon their farmlands. Thus, although the viceroy's position had changed, influential representatives of the Crown continued to support the indigenous population. The solution adopted was the traditional one of repairing dikes and causeways. This time, however, it was under the direction not of the indigenous rulers, but of the Franciscan friars. Torquemada was one of them.[26]

In 1607, along with another intense rainy season, a new viceroy arrived: Luis de Velasco II, whose father had been the viceroy who, half a century earlier, had supported the indigenous project of rebuilding the dike to protect the city. Meanwhile, the balance of power and alliances between social groups had changed, and with them, the ideas about the relationship between the city and the surrounding waters.[27] The decline of the indigenous peoples reduced their decision-making power in water management, and at the same time weakened the defense of lake life. The viceroy became more aligned with the settlers' interests. Unlike his father, he thought that dikes, river diversions and canals were not enough. Instead, he believed it was necessary to drain the lakes to provide a solution to the flooding of the city. Likewise, the common good was identified with that of the city's Spanish settlers and no longer with the life that revolved around the lakes. According to this shift in water policy, the Spanish government sought to protect urban interests, while the lakes and their resources were considered expendable. Therefore, since then the lake waters were depicted as an "enemy" of the city.[28] Although the Spanish people were aware that the risk of flooding had increased due to the intensification of soil erosion and the silting up of the lakes, they did not take any measures to reduce the anthropogenic causes of this process. Quite on the contrary, they gained confidence in their ability to change the local environment. Thus, the project of opening an outlet for the waters of the lakes, that is, transforming the closed basin into an open valley, was revived.[29]

Although several people were consulted once again, they all shared the urban vision, which was primarily interested in safeguarding the city and its properties. Thus, practically all of them agreed that a drainage of the lakes was the only solution to the flooding of the city.[30] In contrast to the more complex indigenous

26 Michael Mathes, "To Save a City. The Desagüe of Mexico-Huehuetoca, 1602", in: *The Americas* 26/4 (1970), p. 428.

27 Boelens, Hoogesteger, Swyngedouw, Vos & Wester have drawn attention to the opposite process: 'These projections of how these territories, their water and their people are and ought to be organized may commonly lead to the empowerment of certain groups of actors while disempowering other'. "Hydrosocial Territories: A Political Ecology Perspective", in: *Water International* 41/1 (2016), p. 5. In any case, we can say that projections and the relative power of social groups influence each other.

28 Cepeda and Carrillo, *Relación universal, legitima, verdadera*, pp. 10r–11v.

29 Omar Rodríguez Camarena, "Transformation and Persistence of the Basin-Valley of Mexico in the 16th and 17th Centuries", in: *Journal of Interdisciplinary History of Ideas* 11/22 (2022), pp. 14–21.

30 Cepeda and Carrillo, *Relación universal, legitima, verdadera*, pp. 13r.–13v. 'to governmentalize territories through 'new' discourses and ideologies creates specific forms of consciousness

solutions, the proposal of the engineers and the Spanish governor consisted in opening an outlet for the water of the lakes, which was a simpler solution despite its huge dimensions. In this way, the discussion became more limited, not only because the indigenous people were excluded, but also because there was no longer any real discussion of other water management alternatives.[31] Since all the participants in the discussion agreed on the need to build a drainage for the lakes, the only question was how to do it, thus, it became a technical or engineering problem. Billy Vaughn Koen has defined the engineering method as 'the strategy for causing the best change in a poorly understood situation within the available resources'.[32] In our case, the new, more technical approach was linked to an understanding of the environment that was indeed impoverished by the loss of the ability to deal with complexity. At the same time, what was considered to be a resource changed.[33] The image of the lakes changed from being a valuable resource to representing a negative element for the city,[34] while urban life and properties became the most important resources to protect.

To solve this engineering problem, several projects were presented, all of them planned by Europeans, of which that by the cosmographer Enrico Martínez was selected. He proposed to open an outlet for the water of the lakes in the north of the valley;[35] the drainage works had a length of more than thirteen kilometers, with a huge tunnel of more than six kilometers. Despite its enormous dimensions, ten months later the first outlet for the waters of the lakes was created thanks to the labor of 60,000 indigenous people from different communities of the watershed. These communities were thus affected by the temporary abandonment of their livelihood for the benefit of the properties and well-being of the city's inhabitants.[36]

Although a first outlet for the water lakes was opened, it was not enough, so the flooding problems continued and the traditional water management systems,

---

that are called upon (presumably in a self-evident manner) in order to defend particular water policies, authorities, hierarchies, and management practices.' Boelens et al., "Hydrosocial Territories: A Political Ecology Perspective", p. 7.

31 'Discourses about "hydrosocial territory" join power and knowledge to ensure a specific political order as if it were a naturalized system, by making fixed linkages and logical relations amongst a specified set of actors, objects, categories and concepts that define the nature of problems as well as the solutions to overcome them.' Ibid.

32 Billy Vaughn Koen, *Discussion of the Method. Conducting the Engineer's Approach to Problem Solving*, Oxford 2003, p. 7.

33 Fernando Broncano has delved into these issues. "La ingeniería como una disciplina humanística. El ingeniero como intérprete de los artefactos", in: ACOFI (ed.), *Acciones y cambios en las facultades de ingeniería*, Colombia 2011, p. 251.

34 Even more than before, the cyclical changes in water levels and, at the same time, between water and land, were seen as a serious problem for the city, in stark contrast to the perspective of the lake communities, who saw them as a vital rhythm for the generation of a wide variety of resources.

35 Cepeda and Carrillo, *Relación universal, legitima, verdadera, del sitio en que está fundada la muy noble, insigne, y muy leal Ciudad de Mexico*, ff. 13v–14v.

36 Candiani, *Dreaming of Dry Land*, pp. 48–50, 54–57 and 64.

including dikes, continued to be necessary. However, since then the main plan was to drain the water from the watershed in order to protect the city, and later, to make room for urban expansion.[37] Although some more comprehensive alternatives for the water management in the Basin-Valley of Mexico had been proposed from time to time,[38] the disagreements among engineers usually concerned only the best drainage project, not the idea of drainage itself. This has concealed a deeper conflict between the urban vision and that of its surroundings, and between the urban settlers and the indigenous communities on the shores of the lakes; at the same time, an epistemological turn took place that sidelined the complex experience of water management from below in order to value only the quantitative and simplistic knowledge of European technicians who would implement an action plan, the draining of the lakes, that had already been decided. In this way, this new social and natural arrangement, which privileged the city over the lakes and European technology over indigenous experience, become a 'dominant governance system' based on 'modernist water-scientific conventions'.[39] This shift in the management of Mexico's waters was not an open discussion based on arguments; on the contrary, it narrowed the debate, the options and the number of participants.[40] Much as the modern experiments of the time were a kind of 'public space with restricted access',[41] water management and decision-making in the Basin-Valley of Mexico was public and open, but only to those who were trained in European techniques and were aligned with urban interests.

Therefore, the historical process of the transformation of the Mexican waterscape can be seen as an example of the imposition of an epistemocratic vision

37 For an analysis of this process of environmental transformation, see Candiani, *Dreaming of Dry Land* and Matthew Vitz, *A City on a Lake. Urban Political Ecology and the Growth of Mexico City*, Durham/London 2018.

38 In the mid-19th century, Francisco de Garay developed a comprehensive plan for water management. For some unsuccessful 20th-century alternatives see Sergio Miranda Pacheco, "El Frankenstein urbano. Ecólogos, urbanistas e ingenieros frente a la crisis hidrológica de la Ciudad de México a mitad del siglo XX", in: *HALAC. Historia Ambiental Latinoamericana y Caribeña* 10/2 (2020), pp. 162–202.

39 Boelens *et al* have made this point in general terms: 'powerful hydrosocial territories envision to position and align humans, nature and thought within a network that aims to transform the diverse socionatural water worlds into a dominant governance system [...] with 'dominance' often characterized by divisions along ethnic, gender, class or caste lines, frequently sustained by modernist water-scientific conventions'. "Hydrosocial Territories: A Political Ecology Perspective", p. 6.

40 We think of this process in a similar way as Stephen Toulmin's alternative interpretation of the implications of 17th-century science: 'In addition to reconsidering the historical assumptions underlying the received view, which depicted the 17th century as a time when the conditions of work in the sciences strikingly improved, we also need to look again at the deeper belief that 17th-century science and philosophy developed an original concern for rationality and the claims of Reason [...] Rather than expanding the scope for rational or reasonable debate, 17th-century scientists narrowed it.' *Cosmopolis. The Hidden Agenda of Modernity*, Chicago 1992, p. 20.

41 Steven Shapin and Simon Schaffer, *Leviathan and the Air-Pump. Hobbes, Boyle, and the Experimental Life*, Princeton 1985, p. 336.

that was assumed and imposed by excluding alternative options for water management.[42] The urban perspective of the settlers was then presented as a matter of public welfare in general, and the drainage project as the only and objective solution to the flooding.[43] These transformations can be seen as part of the modern process of opposition of culture to the "other", nature,[44] in this case, the lakes, but also the rich life of indigenous communities and different species whose livelihoods were closely linked to the lakes, but who were considered expendable by the urban and modernizing views. In this case, the "other" was suppressed: not only the waters, but also the indigenous communities on the shores of the lakes, whose experience and knowledge were no longer taken into account, since they were only coopted as labor for drainage.

3 Conclusions: Alternative Hydropolitics Across History

Territories, especially those related to water resources, are always contested by different groups with conflicting interests, visions and projects. The case of the Mexico watershed helps us understand the complexity of the confrontations over water management and landscapes that developed over time, involving different cultures, materialities and levels of governance that connected the local and the global. Hence, although different ideas, practices and interests have coexisted in the Valley of Mexico, their relationships have tended to be unequal. This process of social and geographical transformation has important epistemological and political implications, since a particular vision and project of society and nature was ultimately imposed on the environment and surrounding communities. Although the Basin of Mexico, even within the lakes, had been altered by the Aztecs and other groups, the changes took a different course after the European colonization, transforming waterscapes, biota and culture. This was already evident in the 16th century, when the introduction of livestock, European agriculture and logging increased the erosion and led to the progressive siltation of the lakes, which eventually resulted in the loss of the smaller Lagoon of Mexico. The Spanish government even encouraged the introduction of European goods such as cattle and new production processes such as ploughing, but it proved unsuccessful in controlling the increasing deforestation, and in the case of fishing and silting, no measures were taken. However, in an attempt to preserve both the

42 Ambrosio Velasco calls "epistemocracy" the 'justification of political dominance based on a supposed superior rationality and true knowledge'. The epistemocratic view ascribes to itself the capacity to discern what is fair and true, which 'is placed above any other justification of political dominance, such as the will of the community itself'. Ambrosio Velasco, "Republicanismo indiano y crítica a la epistemocracia colonial", in: *Cuyo. Anuario de Filosofía Argentina y Americana* 42 (2023), pp. 30–31.

43 Candiani, *Dreaming of Dry Land*, pp. 4–5.

44 Lorraine Daston, "How Nature Became the Other: Anthropomorphism and Anthropocentrism in Early Modern Natural Philosophy", in: *Biology as Society, Society as Biology: Metaphors*, ed. Sabine Maasen, Everett Mendelsohn and Peter Weingart, special issue of *Sociology of the Sciences* 18 (1995), pp. 37–56.

city and the lake's resources, the government at least initially sought to recover indigenous experience and knowledge. At a time when the New Laws issued by the Crown sought to protect the indigenous peoples from overexploitation,[45] the Spanish government of the Basin of Mexico, in the second half of the 16th century, consulted the natives and supported their proposals against the more disruptive plans of the Spanish settlers. As in Venice, two different positions on water management were developed and supported by different social groups: one aimed at preserving the lakes, the other at progressive land reclamation. In Mexico, the viceroy and representatives of the Crown initially supported the more complex indigenous approach, which took into account not only the security of the city but also the resources that the lakes provided for the common good. For this reason, they opposed the plan of the Spanish council and settlers to open an outlet to drain the lakes and prevent flooding in the city. A year later, in the inquiry launched to try to get the Spanish council to pay what it owed for the works, the royal court clearly acknowledged the importance of the lakes, the diversity of natural products they offered and their function for transportation and commerce. The court opposed the negative effects that the drainage works could have on the indigenous communities and even on the general health. This water management can be seen as a successful example of "knowledge from below", which guarantees a better coexistence of the city and the waters, taking into account local knowledge and expertise.[46] It is also an early example of a *glocal* negotiation that took into account local solutions, supported even by the viceroy and representatives of the Crown, in order to protect the common good. As in the contemporary case of Venice, the management of the waters of Mexico can be seen as a valuable example of a more pluralistic and 'more democratic approach' that shows 'how limits could be placed on the alienation of the commons'[47] and the possibility of a more horizontal management of communal resources,[48] even in the early Ibero-American world.

But in contrast to Venice, where bottom-up policies for the preservation of the lagoon prevailed throughout its history, in the watershed of Mexico, the hydropolitics changed in the 17th century, which in the long term would drastically

45 The so-called New Laws were aimed at the 'good treatment and conservation of the Indians', thus they banned slavery and extinguished the system of *encomienda* or permanent assignment of indigenous people to colonizers, replacing it with the *repartimiento* system, which was only for temporary work. *Leyes y ordenanças nueuamente hechas por su Magestad para la gobernación de las Indias y buen tratamiento y conseruacion de los Indios*, Alcalá de Henares 1542. In any case, opposition from the colonizers and overwhelming economic interests never allowed New Laws to be really implemented.

46 The indigenous solution was also more successful than the Spanish in introducing fresh water.

47 Pietro Daniel Omodeo, "Geopraxis: A Concept for the Anthropocene", in: *Journal of Interdisciplinary History of Ideas* 11/22 (2022) 9, pp. 9, 30–31.

48 Pietro Daniel Omodeo and Sebastiano Trevisani, "Historical Geoanthropology in Venice", p. 15.

altering the landscape. The power of the indigenous people declined, while the urban interests of the settlers gained strength. This imbalance of power eventually changed the perception of the lakes, which were no longer regarded as a valuable resource but as a threat to the city. This influenced decisions: the viceroy and the Crown representatives favored European engineers over indigenous experts, and the drainage project was seen as the only solution to protect the city. Such a vision neglected the importance of the lakes for the benefit of the community as a whole. As a matter of fact, the common good was associated mainly with urban interests. A huge geo-anthropological project was launched to transform the closed basin into an open valley.

Despite the previous advantages of indigenous water management, their local expertise was no longer taken into account. Even on a more general level, there was no real discussion about what the best water management option was. Rather, it was assumed that opening an outlet for the waters was the only way to prevent flooding. The complexity of water management was thus reduced to the engineering problem of opening an outlet to control the water of the lakes; the task became the exclusive competence of European engineers and politicians, while indigenous people were only used as labor. This geo-anthropological model became the "dominant governance system", and its legacy has prevailed until today. As such, it can be understood as an instance of the establishment of an epistemocracy which pretends to determine what is not only the best hydropolicy, but also the common good. In this way, the urban perspective was presented as general and equated with the public good: its own particular interests were hidden, while alternative options were erased, with negative impacts on indigenous communities and the environment. Thus, not only did "nature", in this case the lakes, become the "other", the opposite of human civilization, but so did the indigenous way of life. Both became expendable in the name of preserving urban privilege and lifestyle.

Recovering the diversity of alternative hydropolitics developed throughout history in a landscape that has undergone such extensive anthropogenic transformations as the Basin-Valley of Mexico can help clarify the conceptual and practical options that were possible even within the Ibero-American empire. From this case we can learn about more communitarian alternatives that were developed at the inception of modernity in the watershed of Mexico. Later, the adoption of water solutions based on European engineering and science implied the imposition of a narrower approach, linked to an urban vision with their particular interests, and not necessarily better for the community as a whole. Although this model succeeded in transforming the basin into an urban valley, it had a major impact on the surrounding communities and water environment. In this way, through historical studies, we can learn about alternative developments that were still an option in the early modern world and were later set aside to develop a more centralized and vertical hydropolitics. Recovering the diversity of visions and interests of the communities involved in a more sustainable way for the general common good in the past can offer us alternatives to the challenges we currently face in water management.

Acknowledgments

This work was developed as part of my postdoctoral research in the FARE Project *"EarlyGeoPraxis". Positioned Cosmology in Early Modernity: The Geo-Praxis of Water and Land Management in Venice* at Ca' Foscari University of Venice. I would also like to acknowledge the support of THE NEW INSTITUTE Centre for Environmental Humanities (NICHE) at Ca' Foscari, especially its director, Francesca Tarocco. I would like to thank Pietro Daniel Omodeo and Helge Wendt for inviting me to contribute to this volume. This paper was also developed in collaboration with the research project "Critique of Epistemocracy, Pluralism, Epistemic Equity and Democracy" at the National Autonomous University of Mexico (UNAM).

Reference Lists

Sources

Bejarano, *Libro del Cabildo e Ayuntamiento desta ynsine e muy leal ciudad de Tenuztitan Mexico*, vol. 6, Mexico [undated].

Cepeda and Carrillo, *Relación universal, legitima, verdadera, del sitio en que está fundada la muy noble, insigne, y muy leal Ciudad de Mexico*. Mexico 1637.

Leyes y ordenanças nueuamente hechas por su Magestad para la gobernación de las Indias y buen tratamiento y conseruacion de los Indios, Alcalá de Henares 1542.

Martínez, Enrico, *Reportorio de los tiempos e historia de Nueva España*, Mexico 1606.

Pérez-Rocha, Emma, *Ciudad en peligro: Probanza sobre el desagüe general de la ciudad de México, 1556*, Mexico 1996.

Torquemada, Juan de, *Monarquía indiana*, vol. 1, Mexico 1964.

"Traslado de probanza hecha a petición del fiscal de la Audiencia de México, licenciado Maldonado, sobre el edificio de la Albarrada y desaguadero de la laguna de la ciudad. México, 14 de mayo de 1556". General Archive of the Indies. Patronato, 181, R. 30.

Research Literature

Appuhn, Karl, *Forest on the Sea: Environmental Expertise in Renaissance Venice*, Baltimore 2009.

Armillas, Pedro, "Gardens on Swamps", in: *Science* 174/4010 (1971), pp. 653–661.

Asmussen, Tina and Pietro Omodeo, "Foreword to Early Modern Geological Agency", in: *Earth Sciences History* 39/2 (2020), pp. 363–370.

Baletti, Brenda, "Ordenamento Territorial: Neo-developmentalism and the Struggle for Territory in the Lower Brazilian Amazon", in: *Journal of Peasant Studies* 39/2 (2012), pp. 573–598.

Baldacci, Cristina, Shaul Bassi, Lucio de Capitani and Pietro Daniel Omodeo (eds.), *Venice and the Anthropocene: An Ecocritical Guide*, Venice 2022.

Boelens, Rutgerd, Jaime Hoogesteger, Erik Swyngedouw, Jeroen Vos and Philippus Wester, "Hydrosocial Territories: A Political Ecology Perspective", in: *Water International* 41/1 (2016), pp. 1–14.

Broncano, Fernando, "La ingeniería como una disciplina humanística. El ingeniero como intérprete de los artefactos", in: ACOFI (ed.), *Acciones y cambios en las facultades de ingeniería*, Colombia 2011, pp. 249–265.

Candiani, Vera, *Dreaming of Dry Land: Environmental Transformation in Colonial Mexico City*, Stanford 2014.

Daston, Lorraine, "How Nature Became the Other: Anthropomorphism and Anthropocentrism in Early Modern Natural Philosophy", in: *Biology as Society, Society as Biology: Metaphors*, eds. Sabine Maasen, Everett Mendelsohn and Peter Weingart, special issue of *Sociology of the Sciences* 18 (1995), pp. 37–56.

Fraser, Nancy, *Cannibal Capitalism*, London/New York 2022.

González Obregón, Luis, *Memoria histórica, técnica y administrativa de las obras del desagüe del valle de México, 1449–1900*, vol.1, book II, Mexico 1902.

Koen, Billy Vaughn, *Discussion of the Method. Conducting the Engineer's Approach to Problem Solving*, Oxford 2003.

Mathes, Michael, "To Save a City. The Desagüe of Mexico-Huehuetoca, 1602", in: *The Americas* 2674 (1970), pp. 419–438.

Mazari, Marcos, Raúl Marsal and Jesús Alberro, "Los asentamientos del templo mayor analizados por la mecánica de suelos", in: *Estudios de cultura Náhuatl* 19 (1989), pp. 145–182.

Miranda Pacheco, Sergio, "El Frankenstein urbano. Ecólogos, urbanistas e ingenieros frente a la crisis hidrológica de la Ciudad de México a mitad del siglo XX", in: *HALAC. Historia Ambiental Latinoamericana y Caribeña* 10/2 (2020), pp. 162–202.

Mundy, Barbara, *The Death of Aztec Tenochtitlan, the Life of Mexico City*, Austin 2015.

Musset, Alain, *El agua en el Valle de México. Siglos XVI–XVIII*, Mexico 1992.

Omodeo, Pietro Daniel, "Hydrogeological Knowledge from Below: Water Expertise as a Republican Common in Early-Modern Venice", in: *Berichte zur Wissenschaftsgeschichte / History of Science and Humanities* 45/4, Special Issue: Knowledge from Below (December 2022), pp. 538–560.

Omodeo, Pietro Daniel, "Geopraxis: A Concept for the Anthropocene", in: *Journal of Interdisciplinary History of Ideas* 11 (2022) 9, pp. 1–52.

Omodeo, Pietro Daniel and Sebastiano Trevisani, "Historical Geoanthropology in Venice", in: *Journal of Interdisciplinary History of Ideas* 11/22 (2022), pp. 1–21.

Omodeo, Pietro Daniel, Rodolfo Garau and Giulia Rispoli, "Historical Geoanthropology", in: *Journal of Interdisciplinary History of Ideas* 11/22 (2022), pp. 1–12.

Omodeo, Pietro Daniel, "Venice. City of the Anthropocene", *Anthropocene Curriculum* (2022), URL: https://www.anthropocene-curriculum.org/contribution/venice-city-of-the-anthropocene (24.08.2024).

Omodeo, Pietro Daniel, Sebastiano Trevisani and Senthil Babu, "Benedetto Castelli's *Considerations on The Lagoon of Venice*: Mathematical Expertise and Hydro-Geomorphological Transformations in Seventeenth-Century Venice", in: *Earth Sciences History* 39/2 (2020), pp. 420–446.

Regier, Jonathan, "Scenes with the Earth as Actor: Agency and the Early-modern Earth", in: *Earth Sciences History* 39/2 (2020), pp. 409–419.

Rodríguez Camarena, Omar, "Transformation and Persistence of the Basin-Valley of Mexico in the 16th and 17th Centuries", in: *Journal of Interdisciplinary History of Ideas* 11/22 (2022), pp. 14:1–35.

Seitzinger and others, "International Geosphere–Biosphere Programme and Earth system science: Three decades of co-evolution", in: *Anthropocene* 12 (December 2015), pp. 3–16.
Shapin, Steven and Simon Schaffer, *Leviathan and the Air-Pump. Hobbes, Boyle, and the Experimental Life*, Princeton 1985.
Toulmin, Stephen, *Cosmopolis. The Hidden Agenda of Modernity*, Chicago 1992.
Velasco Gómez Ambrosio, 'Las ideas republicanas para una nación multicultural de Alonso de la Veracruz', in: *Innovación y tradición en Fray Alonso de la Veracruz*, ed. Carolina Ponce Hernández, Mexico 2007, pp. 67–77.
Velasco Gómez, Ambrosio, "Republicanismo indiano y crítica a la epistemocracia colonial", in: *Cuyo. Anuario de Filosofía Argentina y Americana* 42 (2023), pp. 19–42.
Vitz, Matthew, *A City on a Lake, Urban Political Ecology and the Growth of Mexico City*, Durham/London 2018.
Wendt, Helge, "Epilogue: The Iberian Way into the Anthropocene", in: *The Globalization of Knowledge in the Iberian Colonial World*, ed. Helge Wendt, Berlin 2016, pp. 297–314.

Saving Water: Scarcity and Resource Management in Landlocked Territories of Early Modern Central Europe

Alexander Schunka

1 Water and Scarcity

In his famous book *The City of the Sun* (*La città del Sole*) of 1602/1623, the Italian Dominican philosopher Tommaso Campanella mentions that the inhabitants of this utopian community collected and recycled rainwater in a quite professional manner in order to always have a sufficient amount of it available.[1] Campanella did not merely invent an "utopian" practice here: people in some European regions, especially in the Mediterranean, practiced rainwater collecting in cisterns and large reservoirs during the early modern era.[2] Cisterns attracted the attention of travelers such as the Englishman John Evelyn, who visited Venice in the mid-seventeenth century, or the German pastor Salomon Schweigger, who recorded the sophisticated Ottoman water supplies of Constantinople but also mentioned the remaining large Byzantine cistern.[3] At roughly the same time, European travelers to Asia wrote with some admiration about the large water tanks they encountered on the Indian subcontinent.[4] There was certainly a broad awareness of the importance of water and its potential scarcity in the premodern world, just as it was common knowledge among philosophers, physicians and agricultural practitioners since antiquity that water collected from rain provided the best quality of drinking water.[5]

1 Tommaso Campanella, "The City of the Sun" (1602), in: *Ideal Commonwealths*, ed. Henry Morley, London 1885, pp. 217–263, here pp. 233–234. – I am grateful to Sophie Adelaide Reboldi (Berlin) for valuable discussions and assistance in finalizing the text.

2 Johann Heinrich Zedler, "Cisterna", in: *Grosses vollständiges Universal-Lexicon Aller Wissenschaften und Künste* 16 (1734), cols. 161–162; idem, "Aqua Pluvia, das Regen-Wasser", *ibid.*, 2 (1732), cols. 988–989. See David Gentilcore, "The Cistern-System of Early Modern Venice: Technology, Politics and Culture in a Hydraulic Society", in: *Water History* 13 (2021), pp. 375–406.

3 Salomon Schweigger, *Ein newe Reyßbeschreibung auß Teutschland Nach Constantinopel und Jerusalem* […], Nürnberg 1608, pp. 127–128. On the centralized water supply system of Ottoman Constantinople see Deniz Karakaş, "Water for the City: Builders, Technology, and Private Initiative", in: *A Companion to Early Modern Istanbul*, eds. Shirine Hamadeh and Çiğdem Kafescioğlu, Leiden 2021 (Brill's Companions to European History 26), pp. 308–339.

4 Alexander Schunka, "South Asian Ports and Water Scarcity in the Eyes of Seventeenth- and Eighteenth-Century European Visitors", in: *Crossroads* 19/1 (2020), pp. 52–73, here pp. 62–63.

5 See, for instance, Johann Coler, *Oeconomia Ruralis et Domestica*, vol. 1, Mainz 1645, p. 57; see also Gentilcore, "Cistern-System", p. 386.

DOI: 10.13173/9783447123693.085

In central Europe, north of the Alps, rainwater collection was not practiced on a large scale, with certain exceptions in coastal areas such as Amsterdam or the North Sea islands, where freshwater wells were lacking and groundwater was brackish.[6] In an important advice book of 1682, the Austrian nobleman Wolf Helmhard von Hohberg conceded that while many people considered rain water to be of the best quality, its storage in cisterns for long time periods diminished its original value compared to flowing water from springs and wells.[7] According to Hohberg's contemporary, the author Johannes Colerus, rain was a very unpredictable phenomenon that was in God's hands.[8] Regions blessed with sufficient wells and streams did not have to rely on rain water collection.

As in the world of today, early modern European societies depended on a sufficient availability of water. The concerns about its collection in cisterns and reservoirs illustrate the links between practical issues of water provision on the one hand, and uncontrollable outside influences such as weather, climate, and topography on the other. Certainly, topographical conditions influenced not only the local availability of freshwater, but also the perceptions of water users, including scholars. It seems that even manuals of political theory and state building addressed water (as a means of infrastructure and supply of a community) to the extent that their learned authors had experienced it as a scarce resource.[9]

While a supply of freshwater was generally difficult to obtain in arid regions as well as in coastal areas, the present chapter focuses on water scarcity beyond deserts and ports, namely in the landlocked territories of early modern central Europe. It is connected to recent debates on the concept of scarcity in the histo-

6 Michael August Friedrich Prestel, *Der Boden, das Klima und die Witterung von Ostfriesland: sowie der gesammten norddeutschen Tiefebene in Beziehung zu den land- und volkswirthschaftlichen Interessen, dem Seefahrts-Betriebe und den Gesundheits-Verhältnissen*, Emden 1872, pp. 339–348; Filip van Roosbroeck, "The Water Supply of Early Modern Amsterdam: A Drop in the Bucket?", in: *The Low Countries Journal of Social and Economic History* 16/2 (2019), pp. 71–91. On the general problem of freshwater scarcity in coastal regions see Schunka, "South Asian Ports".

7 Wolf Helmhard von Hohberg, *Georgica Curiosa. Das ist: Umständlicher Bericht und klarer Unterricht von dem adelichen Land- und Feld-Leben*, vol. 1, Nürnberg 1682, p. 40: "Viel wollen zwar/ das Regenwasser sey das subtileste und beste/ weil es aber nicht allzeit frisch zu bekommen/ allein in Cisternen aufbehalten wird/ daselbst von der Lufft nicht kann gereiniget werden/ also ohne Bewegung offt lang stehen muß; duncket mich das Quellbronnen-Wasser/ sonderlich was aus Bergen und erhabenen Hügeln entspringet/ sey das gesündeste und bequemlichste."

8 "Vom Regen kan nichts gewisses prognosticiret werden." Coler, *Oeconomia Ruralis*, vol. 1, p. 118.

9 See, for instance, the scant treatment of this resource by the famous cameralist scholar from Saxe-Gotha, Veit Ludwig von Seckendorff (*Teutscher Fürsten Stat* […], Frankfurt am Main 1656), versus the book of his contemporary Johann Joachim Becher (*Politische Discurs von den eigentlichen Ursachen dess Auff- und Abnehmens der Städt, Länder, und Republicken*, 2nd ed., Frankfurt am Main 1673, pp. 777–780). See the modern analysis of the topic regarding the Italian Renaissance by Roger D. Masters, *Fortune is a River: Leonardo Da Vinci and Niccolo Machiavelli's Magnificent Dream to Change the Course of Florentine History*, New York et al. 1998.

riography of the environment and natural resources.[10] Based on the assumption that early modern Europeans lived in a state of constant scarcity, researchers have concluded that people either had to orient their lives towards the limited availability of resources (which implied, for instance, saving or sharing), or they tried to remedy this perceived scarcity by increasing the exploitation of nature. These problems seem particularly relevant for landlocked societies where a potential water scarcity had an impact on social relations, economic actions and the political stability of a community.

Thus, the availability and potential scarcity of water is more than a material issue. Drawing on the work of anthropologist Marcel Mauss, scholars have seen water as a 'total social fact.'[11] What mattered (and still does) are questions of its fair access and distribution, including strategies to ensure its sustainability and availability in the future. In this respect, almost all early modern societies can be termed 'waterworlds,' in which, according to Danish scholars Kirsten and Frida Hastrup, water combines its qualities as a material and social resource and stands for a totality of connections among different social groups that organize their lives largely as a relationship between people and water.[12] Water regimes are everyday phenomena: they apply not only in exceptional cases such as natural disasters, and they are not necessarily a phenomenon of coastal regions. In the landlocked societies of early modern central Europe, water regimes seldom managed an abundance of water (in the sense of floods and dike building), but rather dealt with a lack of or insufficient access to this resource. Here, scarcity can be related to geography and infrastructure, but also to one's particular place in society. Different groups therefore had varying needs and means of accessing this resource. This makes water scarcity not an objectifiable and measurable criterion, but rather connects the problem to individual and collective actors and their perceptions within particular circumstances.

How, then, can societies maintain their necessary cohesion and not break apart over issues of the just and equitable distribution of goods such as water? In the wake of Elinor Ostrom's work on *Governing the Commons*, historians have concluded that 'collective action among stakeholders is possible only when the resources are perceived to be scarce.'[13] Thus, a fair distribution of water – according to contemporaneous perceptions – guaranteed an orderly and stable society.

10 Fredrik Albritton Jonsson and Carl Wennerlind, *Scarcity: A History from the Origins of Capitalism to the Climate Crisis*, Cambridge 2023. See also Annette Kehnel, *Wir konnten auch anders: Eine kurze Geschichte der Nachhaltigkeit*, München 2021.

11 I refer to Ben Orlove and Stephen C. Caton, "Water Sustainability: Anthropological Approaches and Prospects", in: *Annual Review of Anthropology* 39 (2010), pp. 401–415, here p. 401.

12 Kirsten Blinkenberg Hastrup, "Waterworlds: Framing the Question of Social Resilience", in: *The Question of Resilience: Social Responses to Climate Change*, ed. idem, Copenhagen 2009, pp. 11–30, here pp. 15–16. See also Kirsten and Frida Hastrup, "Introduction: Waterworlds at Large", in: *Waterworlds: Anthropology in Fluid Environments*, eds. idem, New York/Oxford 2022, pp. 1–22; Orlove and Caton, "Water Sustainability", pp. 403–404.

13 Eduardo Araral et al., "Water Commons: A Critical Appreciation and Revisionist View",

This would imply that access to and management of water could not develop as a top-down process (as Karl August Wittfogel, for instance, had imagined earlier),[14] but involved collaboration across social boundaries to resolve potential conflicts.

Addressing early modern strategies and interactions to save water, this chapter relies on a selection of documents from two landlocked territories of central Europe in the seventeenth and eighteenth centuries, namely the Duchy of Saxe-Gotha (in today's Thuringia) and the Electorate of Brandenburg (-Prussia). Both territories differed to some extent in their topographical preconditions: Saxe-Gotha simply lacked rivers and waterways, while in Brandenburg rivers, canals, and swamps were manifold. Nevertheless, water users in both German states felt that their access to this resource was insufficient to meet their needs. While the perceptions of water scarcity differed, both societies required specific strategies to make water available and to guarantee its fair distribution.

The following part of the present chapter focuses on water supply in urban communities. The next section then turns to infrastructural uses of rivers and canals, with a special focus on the role and needs of millers. The final part addresses in a more general perspective the rhetorics of cooperation and their relation to practical action.

2 Scarcity and Distribution: Water Arrangements in Urban Communities

Central European cities in the seventeenth and eighteenth centuries faced particular problems of water distribution, especially if they were the sites of princely courts. The households of Baroque monarchs, with their numerous servants, required ever-increasing amounts of water for their daily supplies as well as for representational purposes (notably gardens, greenhouses, grottoes and fountains).[15] At the same time, the courts depended in various respects on local artisans, merchants, workers, and business entrepreneurs who belonged to the city's population and who needed water for production as well as for everyday uses such as drinking, cooking, washing, and sanitation.[16]

The city of Gotha (the capital of the most important early modern territory among the fragmented states of Thuringia, and home to a gigantic ducal castle built in the 1640s that still overlooks the town) was one of the more unusual princely residences in the Holy Roman Empire, as it was *not* located near a river. This topographical fact contributed to the constant water scarcity faced by the inhabitants of Gotha, including the ducal family and courtiers. Water from the hills

---

in: *Routledge Handbook of the Study of the Commons*, ed. Blake Hudson et al., London 2019, pp. 144–156, here p. 149.

14 Karl August Wittfogel, *Oriental Despotism: A Comparative Study of Total Power*, New Haven 1957.

15 See, for instance, the contributions in *Wasser im Barock*, ed. Albert Baur, Mainz 2004 (Geschichte der Wasserversorgung 6).

16 See Ansgar Schanbacher, "Umwelt und Ressourcen in der frühneuzeitlichen Stadt Mitteleuropas", in: *Nachhaltigkeit in der Geschichte: Argumente – Ressourcen – Zwänge*, eds. idem, Arnd Reitemeier and Tanja Susanne Scheer, Göttingen 2019, pp. 111–134.

of the nearby Thuringian Forest was provided to the town by two canals, which served for the transport of timber and the provision of freshwater. These canals also played an important role for municipal businesses and the population. The significance of the *Leinakanal* and the additional *Flößgraben* for the community as a means of infrastructure and water supply can be seen in how precisely their cleaning was organized.[17] The so-called *Leinafege*, the compulsory and unpaid cleaning of the canals by peasants and city dwellers, who stood in shallow water and cut the tall river weed with sickles twice a year around Ascension Day and St John's Day, was a recurring, community-building experience for many. It remained a regular event into the twentieth century.[18]

In Gotha, the use of the available water required a fine equilibrium among different individuals and groups. If users such as peasants or craftsmen drew too much water from the upper reaches of the canal for their own purposes, causing a short supply in the lower reaches, conflicts were inevitable. Gotha's court officials notoriously laid their own water pipes in their townhouses for private sanitation, thereby generating water shortage and complaints. While these overexploiters interfered with a presumed local harmony of water distribution, little could be done because they were protected by their close relationship with the court.[19] Although the duke's court officials did not seem to have the best of reputations, especially when it came to issues of water management, they still had to use the public water resources for themselves and their families just like everyone else. However, when at one point too much water was diverted directly by the ducal court, where it was used, among other things, to irrigate the citrus fruits of the prestigious gardens, the municipal millers soon took the joint initiative to stop grinding grain for the ducal militia.[20]

Negotiations between the duke and the town eventually led to quite sophisticated efforts by engineers to measure and limit the amount of canal water now running through pipes by calculating their diameters, incline and flow rate.[21] Nevertheless, when water was lacking in town, the Duke had to reduce the running of his representational fountains to the time when he was actually present (a similar scheme had been practiced at Versailles under Louis XIV).[22] Conflicts

17 For instance: Landesarchiv Thüringen – Staatsarchiv Gotha [hereafter: StAG], Kammer Stadt Gotha, 329, Acta den bey hiesiger Residenz sich veroffenbahreten Waßer-Mangel und deßen Remedur betr., f. 87r, Mandat Herzog Friedrichs II. zur Leinafege (Gotha 16.09.1718).

18 Helga Raschke, *Kultur und Natur am Leinakanal*, Gotha 2024, pp. 161–164.

19 StAG, Kammer Stadt Gotha, 329, Acta den bey hiesiger Residenz sich veroffenbahreten Waßer-Mangel und deßen Remedur betr., 1719, ff. 139–149.

20 Ibid., Kammer Stadt Gotha, 329, Acta den bey hiesiger Residenz sich veroffenbahreten Waßer-Mangel und deßen Remedur betr., ff. 2r–3r (Gotha 17.02.1705). See also ibid., Kammer Stadt Gotha, 671, passim.

21 Ibid., Kammer Stadt Gotha, 660, Acta die neue Wasserkunst hinterm Schloße betreffend, passim.

22 Ibid., Kammer Stadt Gotha, 671, Acta cameralia die alhiesige Wasserleitungen und Remedur des vorfallenden Wassermangels betr., f. 43r (14.07.1740): "zu Vermehrung des Waßers, damit das Publicum in der Stadt nicht Noth leide." In Versailles, a signaling system was practiced

over the use of water ultimately required an amicable settlement that even a ruler had to accept.

These examples illustrate that all parts of society depended on Saxe-Gotha's canals and on more or less consensual agreements regarding the use of their water. Still the canals were not the only sources of freshwater for the city of Gotha and its inhabitants, where in 1650 altogether 29 public wells existed. Other than the *Leinafege*, Gotha's communal wells were maintained by organized *Brunnennachbarschaften* (resident associations for the upkeep of wells), which were presided over by a *Brunnenmeister* and participated in the public life of the city.[23] The cleaning of the wells took place regularly in late June around St John's Day (the dryest period of the year), at about the same time as the cleaning of the canals, and according to municipal authorities was likely to end in a local drinking bout.[24] This was also the moment when a new *Brunnenmeister* was elected. Unlike the Christian calendar, St John's Day (June 21) marked the turn of the year from the perspective of local water management.[25] Water in Gotha, its scarcity as well as its forms of distribution and maintenance, structured space and time.

As far as its wells were concerned, Gotha was far from unique. In many other early modern cities, public wells and fountains were multi-functional objects. They served as a water supply for the community, provided a means of fighting the frequent city fires, and had important social functions as daily meeting places for people from different social backgrounds – not to mention their representational aspects, as in the case of Augsburg's well-known fountains.[26] Wells were usually maintained on a communal and regular basis, following special laws and regulations. It was in the interest of the rulers and local authorities that these wells were constantly operating well, not so much because they provided drinking water for the population, but because they served to fight city fires.[27] Thus, in the electorate of Brandenburg, according to a Berlin "Brunnenordnung" (*Well Regulation*) of 1660, there were almost 50 public wells and fountains and slight-

among servants to turn on the fountains only when the king was going to appear. On Versailles see Ian Thompson, *The Sun King's Garden. Louis XIV, André Le Nôtre and the Creation of the Gardens of Versailles*, London 2006, pp. 237–238.

23 Hans Kayser, "Brunnennachbarschaften in Gotha", in: *Mitteilungen des Vereins für Gothaische Geschichte und Altertumsforschung* 31 (1939–1940), pp. 88–120, here p. 89.

24 Ibid., pp. 92, 98.

25 *Instruction der Brunnennachbarschaften in Gotha* (1673), printed ibid., p. 92. See also ibid., p. 94: "Wenn das Jahr ümb und der Tag St. Johannis Baptistae herbeykommen […]."

26 On the famous fountains of Augsburg see Martin Kluger, *Augsburgs historische Wasserwirtschaft: der Weg zum UNESCO-Welterbe. Wasserbau und Wasserkraft, Trinkwasser und Brunnenkunst in Augsburg (um 1400–1921)*, Augsburg 2015.

27 *Corpus Constitutionum Marchicarum, Oder Königl. Preußis. und Churfürstl. Brandenburgische in der Chur- und Marck Brandenburg, auch incorporirten Landen publicirte und ergangene Ordnungen, Edicta, Mandata, Rescripta [et]c.* […], ed. Christian Otto Mylius, vol. 5, 1, Berlin 1740, cols. 149, 161, 284. On the problem of frequent city fires in the early modern era see Cornel Zwierlein, *Prometheus Tamed: Fire, Security, and Modernities, 1400 to 1900*, Leiden 2021 (Library of Economic History 13).

ly less than 400 private ones in the twin cities of Berlin and Cölln. These wells usually provided groundwater. This number of wells was quite high in relation to the approximately 8,000 inhabitants of both cities in the second half of the seventeenth century. While in the slightly smaller city of Gotha[28] the excessive use of water for private purposes was a matter of debate and conflict, in Berlin any owner of a private well was subject to a heavy penalty if he or she failed to keep it in order. Anyone found to be soiling or destroying a public fountain faced an even heavier fine, ranging from prison to public shaming and expulsion. Moreover, every member of the community had to pay a regular fee for the maintenance of public fountains.[29]

One difference between the examples of Gotha and Berlin-Cölln was that other than Gotha, Berlin-Cölln was located near a river, namely the Spree. Whereas Gotha lacked water, the capital of Brandenburg was a "hydraulic" or "amphibious" city in an increasingly "hydraulic" or "amphibious" territory – given the canal-building plans of the late seventeenth century and the enormous enterprises to drain swamps in the eighteenth.[30] Friedrich Nicolai, in his famous topographical work *Beschreibung der königlichen Residenzstädte Berlin und Potsdam* (1769), presents much evidence of how the geographical layout of Berlin and Cölln was structured in close connection with their waterways. Overall, water plays a surprisingly prominent role in his book.[31]

The supply of Berlin's municipal wells with groundwater was part of a water system that included the river Spree and the local canals such as the *Cöllnische Stadtgraben* or *Kupfergraben*, where several mills were located. Nicolai himself hints at the fact that Berlin's water resources were interconnected: The water for the royal castle originated from a mill (*Werdersche Mühle*) owned by the prince elector that was located on a nearby branch of the river. Water was pumped from there through copper pipes up to a large basin on the castle roof. It then flowed several floors down in pipes to supply the inhabitants and staff of the royal castle, including its annexes such as the court apothecary.[32]

---

28 On estimates of Gotha's population see Helga Raschke, "Gotha als Residenzstadt von Sachsen-Gotha-Altenburg und Sachsen-Coburg und Gotha", in: *Residenzstädte und ihre Bedeutung im Territorialstaat des 17. und 18. Jahrhunderts*, Gotha 1991 (Veröffentlichungen der Forschungs- und Landesbibliothek Gotha 29), pp. 9–26, here p. 26.

29 "Brunnen- und Gassenordnung Berlin-Cölln" (14.08.1660), in: *Corpus Constitutionum Marchicarum*, vol. 5, 1, cols. 313–334.

30 Karl-Heinz Manegold, "Technik, Handelspolitik und Gesamtstaat: Brandenburgische Kanalbauten im 17. Jahrhundert", in: *Technikgeschichte* 37 (1970), pp. 101–129; Hans-Joachim Uhlemann, *Berlin und die Märkischen Wasserstraßen*, Berlin 1987; David Blackbourn, *The Conquest of Nature: Water, Landscape, and the Making of Modern Germany*, New York/London 2006, pp. 21–75.

31 A search in Friedrich Nicolai, *Beschreibung der königlichen Residenzstädte Berlin und Potsdam und aller daselbst befindlichen Merkwürdigkeiten*, Berlin 1769, provides more than 100 references to water.

32 Ibid., pp. 54–55, 85, 328.

These linkages within Berlin's early modern water supply system may offer an implicit explanation for the numerous laws and regulations toward its inhabitants against soiling the town's waters. Thus, access to the Spree and the use of its water were highly regulated. Laws issued by the authorities (usually originating from specific grievances) reveal that people regularly dumped their waste into the river, where even a 'mountain' of waste could be seen.[33] Moreover, there were irregular platforms in several parts of the Spree where women did their laundry. While the problem of drinking water is not explicitly discussed in monarchical edicts, both waste and laundry practices contributed to a narrowing of the river and an interference with its course, which affected trade and the water level of the local sluice, as well as reducing the much-needed water for the local millers.[34]

The amount to which water management related to infrastructural issues will be discussed in the next section of this chapter, but it has been illustrated so far that the strategies to save water for the benefit of the population differed in the two urban communities presented here. In the case of Saxe-Gotha, and particularly in its capital city and surroundings, the available amounts of this resource had to be negotiated and shared among different groups of stakeholders, such as the duke, his courtiers and officials, the city population including its several businesses, and finally the peasants upstream. In Brandenburg, on the other hand, where water was abundantly available, it was important for the authorities to guarantee – in a top-down fashion – the access to water and to ensure sufficient water quality for their subjects. While communal strategies prevailed in the Duchy of Saxe-Gotha, water management in the Electorate of Brandenburg corresponded much more closely with state building initiatives from "above," linking the issue to the improvement of water infrastructures.

3 Rivers, Canals, and Millers: The Infrastructural Dimension

As has already been illustrated, diverging needs and attitudes towards the use of water involved all groups within early modern societies. However, water was of special importance to those who had to make their living from it: namely millers (who needed flowing water to power their mills), fishermen (who had to care for breeding their fish in ponds or dammed-up river sections), and peasants in need of irrigation for their fields (who often drove their cattle through rivers and canals, destroying the banks and thus changing the course of waterways).[35]

Watermills were a significant feature in the landlocked territories of early modern central Europe. In the German lands (just as, for instance, among settlers in colonial North America[36]), mills usually had wide catchment areas. Only

33 *Corpus Constitutionum Marchicarum*, vol. 5, 1, col. 303: "ein grosser Berg in der Spree".

34 Several laws and regulations address this problem, for instance ibid., col. 355 (1707).

35 See, for instance, *Corpus Constitutionum Marchicarum [...] Continuatio prima [...]*, ed. Christian Otto Mylius, Berlin/Halle 1744, col. 369 (1740). Similar complaints existed in Saxe-Gotha.

36 I am planning a publication on water management and milling among German Protestant settlers in colonial Pennsylvania.

during extraordinary events, such as the plague of 1709, did the electoral government of Brandenburg temporarily reduce the milling districts in the country by erecting pop-up mills (as we would perhaps call them today) on a provisional basis to prevent people from traveling long distances and spreading the disease.[37]

As already shown in the case of Saxe-Gotha, millers could claim a certain authority within early modern society. They produced the flour that nourished the people. In an economic regard and as information brokers, the owners or tenants of a mill were part of a local elite. They were also important intermediaries between the authorities and the village. It was not uncommon that millers had received a good school education and formed professional dynasties over several generations.[38] Most importantly from a water management perspective, millers were the key local experts in hydraulic engineering.[39] It was thus difficult for political authorities to overrule millers due to their knowledge and their needs. Within a history of natural resources, even the well-known story of the Prussian miller Arnold and King Frederick the Great in the late eighteenth century – traditionally interpreted as a jurisdictional case, but in fact a quarrel about a local miller's authority over water management – may deserve a new interpretation.[40]

Conflicts of interest between millers and ruling elites were to some extent the local effects of larger processes of the time. They often emerged in the context of monarchical attempts to improve the waterways of a territory in order to participate in a wider European and even global economy of production and trade.[41] This included the building of canals, something which became increasingly common among numerous "Absolutist" European states from the seventeenth

---

37 See the "Pest-Ordnung" (1709) in: *Corpus Constitutionum Marchicarum*, vol. 5, 4, col. 302.

38 Dietmar Bleidick, "Mühle", in: *Enzyklopädie der Neuzeit Online*, 2019, https://doi.org/10.1163/2352-0248_edn_COM_313996. Gerd-Christian Treutler, "Mühlenwesen (Kurmark, plattes Land)", in: *Historisches Lexikon Brandenburg*, URL: https://www.brandenburgikon.net/index.php/de/sachlexikon/muehlenwesen (04.12.2024).

39 On the worlds of a Franconian miller and his diary in the seventeenth century see Alexander Schunka, "Water's Dangers: Swimming and Drowning in the Early Modern Era", in: *Healing and Harm: Essays in Honor of Mary Lindemann*, ed. Erica Heinsen-Roach et al., New York 2024, pp. 70–80.

40 David M. Luebke, "Frederick the Great and the Celebrated Case of the Millers Arnold (1770–1779): A Reappraisal", in: *Central European History* 32/4 (1999), pp. 379–408; Monika Wienfort, "Gesetzbücher, Justizreformen und der Müller-Arnold-Fall: Recht und Justiz in Friedrichs Staat in europäischer Perspektive", in: *Friedrich der Große in Europa: Geschichte einer wechselvollen Beziehung*, eds. Bernd Sösemann and Gregor Vogt-Spira, Stuttgart 2012, vol. 2, pp. 33–46.

41 On the bigger picture see Marcus Popplow and Detlev Ellmers, "Verkehr und Transport", in: *Enzyklopädie der Neuzeit Online* (2019), https://doi.org/10.1163/2352-0248_edn_COM_372640; Eckhard Schinkel, "Kanal", ibid. (2019), https://doi.org/10.1163/2352-0248_edn_COM_289329; Marcella Lorenzini, "Infrastructure Financing in the Early Modern Age: The Beginning of a 'Little Divergence'", in: *Infrastructure Finance in Europe. Insights into the History of Water, Transport, and Telecommunications*, eds. Youssef Cassis et al., Oxford 2016, pp. 61–80. See also the contributions in *Public Goods Provision in the Early Modern Economy: Comparative Perspectives from Japan, China, and Europe*, eds. Masayuki Tanimoto and Roy Bin Wong, Berkeley 2019.

century onwards.[42] The canal-building efforts of Brandenburg-Prussia since the later seventeenth century are particularly well-known. Brandenburg's canals soon connected the river systems of the Baltic and North Seas, contributing to the electorate's rise to kingdom (from 1701) and European power. This went along with an enormous increase in population and economic significance of its capital Berlin (-Cölln) around 1700. On a more limited scale, other territories such as the Duchy of Saxe-Gotha followed similar plans to develop their own, albeit much fewer and smaller, waterways in order to also participate in an evolving Atlantic economy.[43]

In many of these cases, however, the authorities and their local representatives soon realized that the needs of local water users, such as millers in particular, had to be considered. Perhaps the most important among several reasons why Saxe-Gotha's plans to improve its waterways failed, was the number of mills along them: A ducal official traveling along the rivers Unstrut and Saale realized that more than thirty mills spread over a distance of about one hundred miles. Most of these mills would have had to be relocated or rebuilt, which soon appeared as an impossible task.[44]

Some decades later, in the more "aquatic" Electorate of Brandenburg, millers had to cope with a number of detailed regulations from above (whose contents usually hint at local problems in need of a solution). For example, millers were ordered not to dam up the water in the rivers Spree and Havel – which they apparently did in order to compensate for seasonal variations in water levels and to produce an even flow throughout the year. But while such dams were beneficial to the work of millers, they caused problems for nearby farmers, as the water flowed uncontrollably across fields, not only irrigating but also destroying local agriculture. It was evident that the diverging needs of two important fractions of water users had to be satisfied, namely millers and peasants, since 'these [mills] abundantly supply the cities and the countryside with the required flour and cater to their customers, and that the harmful flooding of the meadows can be avoided.'[45] However, besides the millers' damming practices (which were deemed illegal by the government), the laws hint at another group of potential culprits: 'By experience,' local fishermen were also blamed for causing irregularities, such as not keeping the rivers clean and clear. According to the authorities,

42 On France and the *Canal du Midi*, see Chandra Mukherjee, *Impossible Engineering: Technology and Territoriality on the Canal Du Midi*, Princeton 2015.

43 See Uwe Jens Wandel, "Herzog Ernsts Schiffahrts- und Kanalpläne", in: *Ernst der Fromme: Staatsmann und Reformer (1601–1675)*, eds. Roswitha Jacobsen and Hans-Jörg Ruge, Bucha bei Jena 2002, pp. 227–248; Alexander Schunka, "Hiob Ludolf und die globalen Ambitionen im Herzogtum Sachsen-Gotha des 17. Jahrhunderts", in: *Hiob Ludolf and Johann Michael Wansleben: Oriental Studies, Politics, and History between Gotha and Africa, 1650–1700*, eds. Asaph Ben-Tov, Jan Loop, and Martin Mulsow, Leiden 2024, pp. 81–100.

44 See the reports in StAG, Kammer immediate, 1204 (1658).

45 *Corpus Constitutionum Marchicarum*, vol. 4, 4, cols. 173–175 ("Edikt zum Mühlenwesen", 1716).

the fishermen's negligence contributed to the rivers changing their course and flooding nearby farmlands.[46]

Again, the interactions and conflicting needs of local stakeholders called for cooperative action and dialogue, which in the Brandenburg case was imposed from above. A particularly sophisticated form of collaboration was applied to the water users along the *Finow-Kanal,* completed under Frederick II (the Great) in 1747. This was one of the most important waterways of the territory, connecting the Oder and Havel river systems to the northeast of Berlin.[47] Here, the shipping of goods had to be accommodated with the needs of millers, so that transport did not interfere with milling. Therefore, the water level of the canal was regulated in a particularly detailed manner: the lockmaster was responsible for damming the canal overnight and letting the water flow only in 'economical' (*sparsam*) portions during the day. Moreover, the water level in the *Finow-Kanal* was checked and adjusted several times a day, for instance two hours before work started in the morning and then again at noon. This daily rhythm was supplemented by a weekly rhythm to take account of the fact that less water was needed over the weekend. Occasional floods and seasonal variations also had to be taken into consideration, such as an increase of water in spring and its decrease in autumn, i.e. during harvest time, when it was particularly important to keep the mills running well. The miller of the adjacent city of Neustadt (today part of Eberswalde) was provided with additional instructions on how to operate his mill according to the expected water level. Since the amount of water in the canal depended on daily, weekly and seasonal rhythms and could be very low at times, fishermen had to give up their traditional eel farming but could expect a compensation.[48]

It would certainly be worthwhile to undertake an in-depth research on what all these regulations meant in practice, something the present chapter cannot provide.[49] But just as in the case of Saxe-Gotha, evidence suggests that water arrangements had both spatial and temporal dimensions – when accommodating different needs of this resource along a newly built canal required a new time management for their users. All in all, saving water in Brandenburg-Prussia (where the resource was generally abundant) meant that the local needs of different stakeholders had to be addressed and their access to water was restricted to some extent in order to ensure the necessary cooperation within a fragmented society.

46 Ibid., col. 175: "Und da aus der Erfahrung bekandt, daß der Abfluß des Wassers im Früh-Jahre sonderlich durch das lange Graß, so in gedachten Ströhmen wächset, wie nicht weniger durch die zum Theil übel, theils auch über die Gebühr angelegte Fisch-Wehre gehemmet, und solchergestalt in die Wiesen durch der Unterthanen selbst-eigene Schuld gestauet werde."

47 On the Finow-Kanal see, with the relevant literature, Felix Koschmieder, "Finowkanal (18./19. Jahrhundert)", in: *Historisches Lexikon Brandenburgs,* URL: https://brandenburgikon.net/index.php/de/sachlexikon/finowkanal2 (07.12.2024); Uhlemann, *Wasserstraßen,* pp. 35–46.

48 On the mills and other uses of the Finow-Kanal see *Corpus Constitutionum Marchicarum […]: Continuatio tertia […],* Berlin/Halle 1748, cols. 165–169 (1747).

49 I am planning a more thorough investigation of the everyday implications in the near future.

4 Cooperation and Conflict: The Rhetorics and Practices of Saving Water

The degree to which different individuals and groups of water users along the *Finow-Kanal* were forced to cooperate with each other may appear quite striking. This involved lockmasters, millers and fishermen, but regulations also included local authorities, water-related industries, ship's captains, and, finally, the royal administration on several levels. What is also important here is the degree of intervention into individual liberties in order to preserve water as a common good. The examples presented so far do not hint at an overarching and clear hierarchy of importance among the participants. Rather, it seems that certain preferences (if any) were given on an ad-hoc basis, depending on local circumstances. While more research is needed on the practical consequences and potential conflicts arising from these negotiations, it is still fascinating to see how seventeenth- and eighteenth-century forms of (or perhaps rather attempts at) cooperation resemble Elinor Ostrom's ideas of 'governing the commons.'[50] What needs to be considered from an early modern perspective is the general importance of face-to-face communication, including relationships of mutual trust within small social units. Underlying this is the idea of a well-ordered society, including the God-given and sufficient, albeit limited, availability of goods that all parts of society must protect and keep in order.[51]

A final and brief look at the governmental rhetorics of water saving and distribution may illustrate this point. Admittedly, most of the following examples are taken from statements by governmental authorities, i.e. from "above." But, as already mentioned, many of these laws and regulations were the results of initiatives from "below", originating in supplications and petition letters by individuals and communities, or in proposals from city magistrates. It was therefore quite common for these texts to retain even incorporated parts of the original wording.

50 Especially those regarding communal pastures in a Swiss village, but also irrigation in Spain: Elinor Ostrom, *Governing the Commons. The Evolution of Institutions for Collective Action*, Cambridge 1990, here pp. 61–65, 71–76. For early modern Europe, see the contributions in *Ländliche Gemeingüter/Rural Commons: Kollektive Ressourcennutzung in der europäischen Agrarwirtschaft/Collective Use of Resources in the European Agrarian Economy*, eds. Niels Grüne et al., Innsbruck 2016 (Jahrbuch für Geschichte des ländlichen Raumes 12). Cf. the contributions in *The Commons in a Glocal World: Global Connections and Local Responses*, eds. Tobias Haller et al., London 2019, as well as Tine De Moor, "From Historical Institution to Pars Pro Toto: The Commons and their Revival in Historical Perspective", in: *Routledge Handbook of the Study of the Commons*, eds. Blake Hudson et al., London 2019, pp. 319–333.

51 As a general overview see Marc Raeff, *The Well-Ordered Police State. Social and Institutional Change through Law in the Germanies and Russia (1600–1800)*, New Haven 1983. See, as a more recent overview in German, Reiner Prass, *Grundzüge der Agrargeschichte*, vol. 2: *Vom Dreißigjährigen Krieg bis zum Beginn der Moderne (1650–1880)*, Köln 2016, pp. 24–37, 58–70, who also hints at some of these aspects. The specialist literature on these topics is vast, but overviews are scarce. Cf. Tine De Moor's call for more historical research: De Moor, "The Commons", p. 320. With a focus on water, see Susan Richter, "Wasser als göttliche Gabe und menschliches Naturrecht: Brunnen- und Wasserordnungen der Frühen Neuzeit", in: *Gute Ordnung: Ordnungsmodelle und Ordnungsvorstellungen in der Reformationszeit*, eds. Irene Dingel and Armin Kohnle, Leipzig 2014, pp. 124–140.

Since the sixteenth century, the rulers of Brandenburg attempted to maintain or restore a God-given order by banning certain groups from transgressing it. A common accusation made by the authorities against fishermen, for example, was that they did not pay enough attention to the spawning season. As a result, stocks of pike and other fish were 'greatly devastated' (*sehr verwüstet*).[52] If only the disorder among the fishermen came to a halt and Godly order was restored, 'then our country and people will enjoy fish and fishing in a more fruitful way.'[53] But the fishermen were not the only ones to blame for possible disruptions of this God-given equilibrium. Other groups of potential transgressors were accused for an 'untimely water-greed' (*unzeitigen Wasser-Geitz*).[54] And Gotha's *Brunnennachbarschaften* were required to ensure *Fried und Einigkeit* ('peace and unity') over water.[55] It was the responsibility of collectives and individuals when the sensitive balance of water distribution got out of control and had to be restored by interventions from above.[56]

However, administrators of a monarch and his government were not the only ones who felt the need to restore a God-given order. In Saxe-Gotha, the city magistrate of its capital city called for a 'moderate use' of water by all groups involved: 'Personal interest must give way to the public interest.'[57] The arguments and rhetorics in the landlocked Protestant territories of Brandenburg and Saxe-Gotha resemble each other, just as the joint strategies for maintaining this equilibrium by regularly renovating wells and fountains, cleaning rivers, millraces and canals. While water structured the spaces of a city and a territory (as, for instance, in the topographical accounts of visitors), the temporal dimensions of water management (as in strategies for coping with seasonal differences, canal cleaning times, the rituals of *Brunnennachbarschaften*, daily and weekly routines of lockmasters and millers, and probably much more) illustrate the place of water in people's lives. Collective ideas and practices certainly contributed to how water and its management were inscribed into the minds of the people involved.[58]

It is nevertheless important to note that the image of peaceful cooperation among water users within a well-ordered early modern society and across social hierarchies was to some extent no more than an illusory ideal. Conflict and

52 *Corpus Constitutionum Marchicarum*, vol. 4, 2, col. 246 (1682). On the problem of fishing in Brandenburg from the perspective of an early modern history of natural resources see Julian Pfau, "Fischfang und Ressourcenkonflikte im frühneuzeitlichen Kurbrandenburg", unpublished MA Thesis, FU Berlin 2021.

53 *Corpus Constitutionum Marchicarum*, vol. 4, 2, col. 183 (1551): "und unser landt und leutte derselben diste fruchtbarlicher geniessen und gebrauchen mögen."

54 Ibid., *Continuatio tertia*, col. 166 (1747).

55 Kayser, "Brunnennachbarschaften", p. 92.

56 *Corpus Constitutionum Marchicarum*, vol. 4, 4, col. 175 ("Edikt zum Mühlenwesen", 1716).

57 StAG, Kammer Stadt Gotha, 329, f. 147v: "das Privat-Interesse [...] dem publico weichen."

58 See *Corpus Constitutionum Marchicarum: Continuatio tertia*, f. 165; ibid., vol. 5, 3, f. 245. Cf. also, from a different world region, Sylvia Rodríguez, "Acequias: Trust and Hydrosocial Territory", in: *Journal of the Southwest* 64 (2022), pp. 582–615.

competition over water involved political quarrels with neighboring states, both for Brandenburg-Prussia and Saxe-Gotha,[59] as well as collective action from within. Under certain circumstances, a minor local government official (*Wasserknecht*) trying to enforce fishing rights on behalf of his ruler could be threatened to be thrown into the water by disobedient villagers.[60] Rather than propagating peaceful cooperation in a harmonious early modern society, water management reveals an ad hoc system of multiple checks and balances following possibly divergent traditional logics. Water users from different social groups eventually had no choice but to reconcile their interests with those of others: they were all dependent on a scarce resource.

This system of checks and balances also applies to water management within larger state building initiatives. Whenever the ruling authorities of the Baroque era launched projects to build dams and canals, it appeared difficult to gain support on a local level and even to recruit reliable workers. Local communities tended to see the building of canals and the draining of swamps (as in eighteenth-century Prussia) as an unacceptable intrusion on their land use, which could lead to conflict and renegotiations of water regimes. Governmental water management thus had to include the needs of their subjects and harmonize them as much as possible with the aspirations of state-building and population growth.[61]

By investigating the water regimes in early modern landlocked territories, this chapter has illustrated the degree to which traditional societies had to rely upon cooperative forms of resource management. Early modern water management also shows that sustainable uses of this resource mattered, not least because of the perceived scarcity of water.[62] However, this does not mean that early modern "waterworlds" were any static, or that responsible action to the environment in the early modern era should be romanticized.[63] Canal-building, demographic changes, proto-industry and transregional trade all point to important processes that necessitated constant renegotiations of water regimes while they may have raised an increasing general awareness of its sustainable uses.

Analyzing water regimes in early modern landlocked societies does perhaps not yield as dramatic results as research on coastal areas, and the ordinary cases of daily negotiations may not be as spectacular as early modern coping strategies with natural disasters. Whereas the empirical examples from the Thuringian

59 On Gotha see Schunka, "Hiob Ludolf", pp. 86–88. On Brandenburg see the instructive collection of documents by Konrad Wutke, *Die schlesische Oderschiffahrt in vorpreussischer Zeit: Urkunden und Aktenstücke*, Breslau 1896 (Codex Diplomaticus Silesiae 17).

60 StAG, Kammer Stadt Gotha, 329, ff. 46–47 (1718).

61 See, for instance, Heinrich Kaak, "Rulers and Ruled in Flood Protection during the Eighteenth Century: The Prussian Example", in: *Public Goods Provision*, pp. 172–201; Alexander Schunka, "Migranten und kulturelle Transfers", in: *Friedrich der Große in Europa*, vol. 2, pp. 80–96, here pp. 90–94.

62 Alexander Schunka, "Nachhaltigkeit in der Ressourcengeschichte der Frühen Neuzeit", in: *Jahrbuch der Stiftung Thüringer Schlösser und Gärten* 27 (2024), pp. 10–18.

63 This tendency can perhaps be found in Kehnel, *Wir konnten auch anders.*

Duchy of Saxe-Gotha and the Electorate of Brandenburg-Prussia may, strictly speaking, offer only limited points of comparability, this chapter has revealed the extent to which water management and water saving strategies could be organized from above as well as from below. It has highlighted the importance of sharing and saving water in the early modern era, regardless of whether this resource appears as plentiful or scarce – because what mattered was not just a measurable quantity, but quality, demand and access. Moreover, the cooperative distribution of water structured the mindsets of the people involved, in a spatial as well as temporal perspective.

Finally, a contemporaneous and general awareness of water scarcity explains why early modern German travelers and learned authors shared an interest in water saving strategies in other parts of the world. Even seemingly "utopian" forms of water management were linked to local practice. Thus, when the city of Freudenstadt in the Black Forest of Württemberg was founded in 1599, its architect Heinrich Schickhardt was familiar with the water systems of Italy as well as those of Johann Andreae's utopian community of *Christianopolis*. Both were reflected in the town's layout, including a sophisticated and symmetrical arrangement of fountains to remind the population every day of water as a gift from God.[64]

Reference Lists

Manuscript Sources

Landesarchiv Thüringen – Staatsarchiv Gotha,
- Kammer Stadt Gotha, 329, 660, 671.
- Kammer immediate, 1204.

Printed Sources

Becher, Johann Joachim, *Politische Discurs von den eigentlichen Ursachen dess Auff- und Abnehmens der Städt, Länder, und Republicken*, 2nd ed., Frankfurt am Main 1673.

Campanella, Tommaso, "The City of the Sun" [1602], in: *Ideal Commonwealths*, ed. Henry Morley, London 1885, pp. 217–263.

Coler, Johann, *Oeconomia Ruralis et Domestica*, vol. 1, Mainz 1645.

Corpus Constitutionum Marchicarum, Oder Königl. Preußis. und Churfürstl. Brandenburgische in der Chur- und Marck Brandenburg, auch incorporirten Landen publicirte und ergangene Ordnungen, Edicta, Mandata, Rescripta [et]c. [...], ed. Christian Otto Mylius, 6 vols., 4 Continuationes, Berlin(/Halle) 1737–1755.

Hohberg, Wolf Helmhard von, *Georgica Curiosa. Das ist: Umständlicher Bericht und klarer Unterricht von dem adelichen Land- und Feld-Leben*, vol. 1, Nürnberg 1682.

Nicolai, Friedrich, *Beschreibung der königlichen Residenzstädte Berlin und Potsdam und aller daselbst befindlichen Merkwürdigkeiten*, Berlin 1769.

64 On the context see Claus Bernet, "Die Gründung von Freudenstadt: Neue Ansätze zur wichtigsten deutschen Idealstadt", in: *Blätter für Deutsche Landesgeschichte* 143 (2007), pp. 107–131. Further research is in preparation.

Prestel, Michael August Friedrich, *Der Boden, das Klima und die Witterung von Ostfriesland: sowie der gesammten norddeutschen Tiefebene in Beziehung zu den land- und volkswirthschaftlichen Interessen, dem Seefahrts-Betriebe und den Gesundheits-Verhältnissen*, Emden 1872.

Schweigger, Salomon, *Ein newe Reyßbeschreibung auß Teutschland Nach Constantinopel und Jerusalem* […], Nürnberg 1608.

Seckendorff, Veit Ludwig von, *Teutscher Fürsten Stat* […], Frankfurt am Main 1656.

Wutke, Konrad, ed., *Die schlesische Oderschiffahrt in vorpreussischer Zeit. Urkunden und Aktenstücke*, Breslau 1896 (Codex Diplomaticus Silesiae 17).

Zedler, Johann Heinrich, ed., *Grosses vollständiges Universal-Lexicon Aller Wissenschaften und Künste*, 64 vols., Halle/Leipzig 1731–1754.

Research Literature

Araral, Eduardo, et al., "Water Commons: A Critical Appreciation and Revisionist View", in: *Routledge Handbook of the Study of the Commons*, eds. Blake Hudson et al., London 2019, pp. 144–156.

Baur, Albert (ed.), *Wasser im Barock*, Mainz 2004 (Geschichte der Wasserversorgung 6).

Bernet, Claus, "Die Gründung von Freudenstadt: Neue Ansätze zur wichtigsten deutschen Idealstadt", in: *Blätter für Deutsche Landesgeschichte* 143 (2007), pp. 107–131.

Blackbourn, David, *The Conquest of Nature: Water, Landscape, and the Making of Modern Germany*, New York/London 2006.

Bleidick, Dietmar, "Mühle", in: *Enzyklopädie der Neuzeit Online* (2019), https://doi.org/10.1163/2352-0248_edn_COM_313996.

De Moor, Tine, "From Historical Institution to Pars Pro Toto: The Commons and their Revival in Historical Perspective", in: *Routledge Handbook of the Study of the Commons*, eds. Blake Hudson et al., London 2019, pp. 319–333.

Gentilcore, David, "The Cistern-System of Early Modern Venice: Technology, Politics and Culture in a Hydraulic Society", in: *Water History* 13 (2021), pp. 375–406.

Grüne, Niels, et al. (eds.), *Ländliche Gemeingüter/Rural Commons: Kollektive Ressourcennutzung in der europäischen Agrarwirtschaft/Collective Use of Resources in the European Agrarian Economy*, Innsbruck 2016 (Jahrbuch für Geschichte des ländlichen Raumes 12).

Haller, Tobias, et al. (eds.), *The Commons in a Glocal World: Global Connections and Local Responses*, London 2019.

Hastrup, Kirsten, "Waterworlds: Framing the Question of Social Resilience", in: idem, *The Question of Resilience: Social Responses to Climate Change*, Copenhagen 2009 (Historisk-Filosofiske Meddelelser 16), pp. 11–30.

Hastrup, Kirsten and Frida Hastrup, "Introduction: Waterworlds at Large", in: eaedem, *Waterworlds: Anthropology in Fluid Environments*, New York/Oxford 2022, pp. 1–22.

Jonsson, Fredrik Albritton and Carl Wennerlind, *Scarcity: A History from the Origins of Capitalism to the Climate Crisis*, Cambridge 2023.

Kaak, Heinrich, "Rulers and Ruled in Flood Protection during the Eighteenth Century: The Prussian Example", in: *Public Goods Provision in the Early Modern Economy. Comparative Perspectives from Japan, China, and Europe*, eds. Masayuki Tanimoto and Roy Bin Wong, Berkeley 2019, pp. 172–201.

Karakaş, Deniz, "Water for the City: Builders, Technology, and Private Initiative", in: *A Companion to Early Modern Istanbul*, eds. Shirine Hamadeh and Çiğdem Kafescioğlu, Leiden 2021 (Brill's Companions to European History 26), pp. 308–339.

Kayser, Hans, "Brunnennachbarschaften in Gotha", in: *Mitteilungen des Vereins für Gothaische Geschichte und Altertumsforschung* 31 (1939–1940), pp. 88–120.

Kehnel, Annette, *Wir konnten auch anders: Eine kurze Geschichte der Nachhaltigkeit*, München 2021.

Kluger, Martin, *Augsburgs historische Wasserwirtschaft: der Weg zum UNESCO-Welterbe. Wasserbau und Wasserkraft, Trinkwasser und Brunnenkunst in Augsburg (um 1400–1921)*, Augsburg 2015.

Koschmieder, Felix, "Finowkanal (18./19. Jahrhundert)", in: *Historisches Lexikon Brandenburgs*, URL: http://www.brandenburgikon.de (07.12.2024).

Lorenzini, Marcella, "Infrastructure Financing in the Early Modern Age: The Beginning of a 'Little Divergence'", in: *Infrastructure Finance in Europe. Insights into the History of Water, Transport, and Telecommunications*, eds. Youssef Cassis et al., Oxford 2016, pp. 61–80.

Luebke, David M., "Frederick the Great and the Celebrated Case of the Millers Arnold (1770–1779): A Reappraisal", in: *Central European History* 32/4 (1999), pp. 379–408.

Manegold, Karl-Heinz, "Technik, Handelspolitik und Gesamtstaat: Brandenburgische Kanalbauten im 17. Jahrhundert", in: *Technikgeschichte* 37 (1970), pp. 101–129.

Masters, Roger D., *Fortune is a River: Leonardo Da Vinci and Niccolo Machiavelli's Magnificent Dream to Change the Course of Florentine History*, New York et al. 1998.

Mukherjee, Chandra, *Impossible Engineering: Technology and Territoriality on the Canal Du Midi*, Princeton 2015.

Orlove, Ben and Stephen C. Caton, "Water Sustainability: Anthropological Approaches and Prospects", in: *Annual Review of Anthropology* 39 (2010), pp. 401–415.

Ostrom, Elinor, *Governing the Commons: The Evolution of Institutions for Collective Action*, Cambridge 1990.

Pfau, Julian, "Fischfang und Ressourcenkonflikte im frühneuzeitlichen Kurbrandenburg", unpublished MA Thesis, FU Berlin 2021.

Popplow, Marcus and Detlev Ellmers, "Verkehr und Transport", in: *Enzyklopädie der Neuzeit Online* (2019), https://doi.org/10.1163/2352-0248_edn_COM_372640.

Prass, Reiner, *Grundzüge der Agrargeschichte*, vol. 2: *Vom Dreißigjährigen Krieg bis zum Beginn der Moderne (1650–1880)*, Köln 2016.

Raeff, Marc, *The Well-Ordered Police State: Social and Institutional Change through Law in the Germanies and Russia (1600–1800)*, New Haven 1983.

Raschke, Helga, *Kultur und Natur am Leinakanal*, Gotha 2024.

Raschke, Helga, "Gotha als Residenzstadt von Sachsen-Gotha-Altenburg und Sachsen-Coburg und Gotha", in: *Residenzstädte und ihre Bedeutung im Territorialstaat des 17. und 18. Jahrhunderts*, Gotha 1991 (Veröffentlichungen der Forschungs- und Landesbibliothek Gotha 29), pp. 9–26.

Richter, Susan, "Wasser als göttliche Gabe und menschliches Naturrecht: Brunnen- und Wasserordnungen der Frühen Neuzeit", in: *Gute Ordnung: Ordnungsmodelle und Ordnungsvorstellungen in der Reformationszeit*, eds. Irene Dingel and Armin Kohnle, Leipzig 2014, pp. 124–140.

Rodríguez, Sylvia, "Acequias: Trust and Hydrosocial Territory", in: *Journal of the Southwest* 64 (2022), pp. 582–615.

Roosbroeck, Filip van, "The Water Supply of Early Modern Amsterdam: A Drop in the Bucket?", in: *The Low Countries Journal of Social and Economic History* 16/2 (2019), pp. 71–91.

Schanbacher, Ansgar, "Umwelt und Ressourcen in der frühneuzeitlichen Stadt Mitteleuropas", in: *Nachhaltigkeit in der Geschichte: Argumente – Ressourcen – Zwänge*, eds. idem, Arnd Reitemeier and Tanja Susanne Scheer, Göttingen 2019, pp. 111–134.

Schunka, Alexander, "Migranten und kulturelle Transfers", in: *Friedrich der Große in Europa. Geschichte einer wechselvollen Beziehung*, eds. Bernd Sösemann and Gregor Vogt-Spira, Stuttgart 2012, vol. 2, pp. 80–96.

Schunka, Alexander, "South Asian Ports and Water Scarcity in the Eyes of Seventeenth- and Eighteenth-Century European Visitors", in: *Crossroads* 19/1 (2020), pp. 52–73.

Schunka, Alexander, "Water's Dangers: Swimming and Drowning in the Early Modern Era", in: *Healing and Harm: Essays in Honor of Mary Lindemann*, ed. Erica Heinsen-Roach et al., New York 2024, pp. 70–80.

Schunka, Alexander, "Hiob Ludolf und die globalen Ambitionen im Herzogtum Sachsen-Gotha des 17. Jahrhunderts", in: *Hiob Ludolf and Johann Michael Wansleben: Oriental Studies, Politics, and History between Gotha and Africa, 1650–1700*, eds. Asaph Ben-Tov, Jan Loop and Martin Mulsow, Leiden 2024, pp. 81–100.

Schunka, Alexander, "Nachhaltigkeit in der Ressourcengeschichte der Frühen Neuzeit", in: *Jahrbuch der Stiftung Thüringer Schlösser und Gärten* 27 (2024), pp. 10–18.

Tanimoto, Masayuki and Roy Bin Wong (eds.), *Public Goods Provision in the Early Modern Economy. Comparative Perspectives from Japan, China, and Europe*, Berkeley 2019.

Thompson, Ian, *The Sun King's Garden: Louis XIV, André Le Nôtre and the Creation of the Gardens of Versailles*, London 2006.

Treutler, Gerd-Christian, "Mühlenwesen (Kurmark, plattes Land) ", in: *Historisches Lexikon Brandenburg*, URL: https://www.brandenburgikon.net/index.php/de/sachlexikon/muehlenwesen (04.12.2024).

Uhlemann, Hans-Joachim, *Berlin und die Märkischen Wasserstraßen*, Berlin 1987.

Wandel, Uwe Jens, "Herzog Ernsts Schiffahrts- und Kanalpläne", in: *Ernst der Fromme. Staatsmann und Reformer (1601–1675)*, eds. Roswitha Jacobsen and Hans-Jörg Ruge, Bucha bei Jena 2002, pp. 227–248.

Wienfort, Monika, "Gesetzbücher, Justizreformen und der Müller-Arnold-Fall: Recht und Justiz in Friedrichs Staat in europäischer Perspektive", in: *Friedrich der Große in Europa. Geschichte einer wechselvollen Beziehung*, eds. Bernd Sösemann and Gregor Vogt-Spira, Stuttgart 2012, vol. 2, pp. 33–46.

Wittfogel, Karl August, *Oriental Despotism: A Comparative Study of Total Power*, New Haven 1957.

Zwierlein, Cornel, *Prometheus Tamed: Fire, Security, and Modernities, 1400 to 1900* (Library of Economic History 13), Leiden 2021.

Gratia Dei: Marine Resources of the Northern Seas in the Albums of Adriaen Coenen, a Sixteenth-Century Dutch Practical Expert

Florike Egmond

About our noble herring
The king above all other fishes
Our great golden mountain in Holland
By the grace of God almighty
Also [of] Zealand and Flanders.[1]

These words are part of a longer eulogy of the herring written by Adriaen Coenen (1514–1587) from Scheveningen, a Dutch fish auctioneer and long distance fish merchant who was himself the son of a fisherman and a fisherman's daughter. Coenen had no Latin and no further formal education than the local school. However, like the most innovative naturalists of his time who investigated and described marine life, Coenen created surveys of the aquatic world, which were not published however. He personally painted and wrote several large and highly visual albums during the 1560s–80s. His *Visboeck* (*Fish Book*, 1577–81) and *Walvisboeck* (*Whale Book*, c. 1584–85) depict and describe *aquatilia* of the North Sea and North Atlantic, but he also goes into fishing techniques, fishing grounds and seasons, monsters and other strange marine creatures, fishes of rivers and lakes, beached whales, and much more.[2]

Coenen's manuscript albums do not consist of pages with handwritten text accompanied by images. The oblong *Walvisboeck* comes closest to our notion of a picture book: the painted images fill nearly the whole page and there is only a small amount of text. In contrast, the circa 400 folios of the *Visboeck* all have a coloured background. Most of its folios contain groups of coloured images with painted frames as well as framed handwritten text blocks (Fig. 1). The latter are written in a lively sixteenth-century Dutch, but also include quoted passages in German and French. Coenen's Dutch texts are always written in the first person

1 Adriaen Coenen, *Visboeck*, manuscript album, The Hague, Koninklijke Bibliotheek, Ms 78 E 54; here f. 26; here further abbreviated as CoenenKB. In all folio references I follow the numbering by the KB, not Coenen's original one.

2 See note 1 above; and Adriaen Coenen, *Walvisboeck*, Antwerp, Erfgoedbibliotheek Hendrik Conscience, EHC 707256; here further indicated as *Whale Book*; and his unfinished *Haringkoningboek* (c. 1586–87), Cologne, Historisches Archiv, Ms 296.

DOI: 10.13173/9783447123693.103

and contain a wealth of detail based on his own experience and observations. He clearly separates these from the quoted passages and summaries, both visually and textually. As he put it: when I have not seen something myself, 'I write my authors', meaning I mention my sources.[3] His works are much more, therefore, than a *loci* collection with some short comments. Coenen's albums are to my knowledge the richest and most personal extant sources regarding marine life, fishing and the expertise regarding the sea of the coastal population of the North Sea in the sixteenth century.[4]

1 Marine Resources and Practical Expertise

This essay is a case study that focuses on what Coenen as an eminently practical expert tells us about the *aquatilia* of the northern seas as resources. It thus concentrates on a central theme in his albums, which was moreover closest to his personal experience. As fish auctioneer of Scheveningen, wholesale fish merchant, collector and salesman of curious things of the sea, and local notable of a fishing village, it was literally Coenen's business to be extremely well-informed about the value of fishes and all aspects of the trade in fish. He knew everything about fish processing (cleaning, salting, smoking or drying fish by hanging them out on lines in the drying gardens); transportation modes (salted in barrels or dried and packaged); pricing and profits; seasonal fluctuations of supply and demand; and the preferences of the market. Regarding the latter, he describes mussels and codfish, for instance, as food for both poor and rich. Squid was eaten in France, but regarded as inedible in Holland. The rich in Holland very much appreciated small young rays, called 'maidens', especially boiled and then braised in butter. These undersized rays could not be dried and sold for exportation according to fish trade regulations and thus were only available for the local market.[5] Refined tastes are also evident from the fact that the wealthy inhabitants of The Hague preferred to eat haddock and cod caught on hooks baited with shrimps rather

---

3 CoenenKB f. 112v.

4 My joint investigation with Peter Mason into Coenen's life and works began in the early 1990s and has resulted in various publications in Dutch and English on topics that range from his biography and worldview to, for instance, fishing, fish descriptions and classification, Coenen's empirical attitude to evidence, etc. See in particular Florike Egmond and Peter Mason (eds.), *The Whale Book. Whales and Other Marine Animals as Described by Adriaen Coenen in 1585*, London 2003; Florike Egmond, *Het Visboek. De Wereld volgens Adriaen Coenen*, Zutphen 2005; Florike Egmond, *Eye for Detail. Images of Plants and Animals in Art and Science, 1500–1630*, London 2017, esp. pp. 156–160, 194–208; and Florike Egmond, "On Northern Shores: Sixteenth-Century Observations of Fish and Seabirds (North Sea and North Atlantic)", in: *Naturalists in the Field. Collecting, Recording and Preserving the Natural World From the Fifteenth to the Twenty-First Century*, ed. Arthur MacGregor, Leiden/Boston 2018, pp. 129–148. On Coenen's work as a source for fish and fisheries information, see Floris P. Bennema and Adriaan D. Rijnsdorp, "Fish Abundance, Fisheries, Fish Trade and Consumption in Sixteenth-Century Netherlands as described by Adriaen Coenen", in: *Fisheries Research* 161 (2015), pp. 384–399.

5 CoenenKB f. 225 (mussels), f. 124r (ray).

Fig. 1: A typical decorated page, showing various kinds of ray. Coenen, Visboeck, f. 123v. Adriaen Coenen, Visboeck [Fish Book], 1577–81, Holland. C. 400 folios. The Hague, Koninklijke Bibliotheek, Ms 78 E 54, URL: https://www.kb.nl/themas/middeleeuwen/visboek-van-adriaen-coenen (18.03.2025).

than haddock and cod fished in differed ways further out in the ocean.[6] It would be a misrepresentation of Coenen's work and expertise, however, to reduce them to merely economy-related aspects. Fish prices, tonnages of catches, market aspects and so on actually play a minor role in his albums.

Those albums are organized around fishes and other *aquatilia*, not around fishing or selling. First and foremost, Coenen was passionately curious about living nature. Until his death, in his seventies, he continued to investigate and collect information regarding the seas and whatever was living in and on them. He collected strange fishes and had their portraits painted; he stuffed and dried water animals and even showed some for money. He kept a sea tortoise for a while alive in a tub at his house. This fascination with living nature went back to his youth – perhaps even to the late 1520s–early 1530s: 'since I was inquiring and loved seeing curious things from an early age'.[7] Since his young years he used to carry a small notebook in which he wrote down his observations and made sketches of interesting fish, meteorological phenomena and whatever else struck him: 'and I also included this in my memory booklet in which I had also drawn other rare fishes that had arrived in my times'; he also had a 'small writing room' in his house where he must have painted and written his albums.[8]

Coenen consistently presents himself as a modest self-taught naturalist-*curiosus* with high quality expertise based on a lifelong professional practice of working with fish. But Coenen's writings and images reflect not only his individual experience. They also encapsulate the collective knowledge of multiple generations of his fellow villagers, fishermen, mariners, fish merchants and other connected professionals as embodied in practice and transmitted via oral traditions that include (folk) tales and proverbs, sometimes in local dialect.

The increasing attention of historians to artisanal expertise, bodily knowledge, the importance of 'making and doing' in the creation and transmission or circulation of knowledge is currently extending itself to other kinds of practical experts.[9] Farmers, gardeners, miners, seafarers, foresters, and fishermen – to name

6 CoenenKB f. 40v.

7 CoenenKB f. 407r. On the early origin of Coenen's interest and its implications, see Florike Egmond, "Looking Beyond the Margins of Print: Depicting Water Creatures in Europe, c. 1500–1620", in: *Ichthyology in Context (1500–1880)*, eds. Paul Smith and Florike Egmond, Leiden/Boston 2024, pp. 147–243, here pp. 218–225.

8 CoenenKB f. 407r (memory book) and f. 314v (writing room).

9 To name but a few examples that concern knowledge of either the seas or the inner earth: Henrique Leitão, "Instruments and artisanal practices in long distance oceanic voyages", in: *Centaurus* 60 (2018), pp. 189–202; Wim de Winter, "Southern-Netherlandish Observations and Knowledge Production of *Naturalia* on the Seas: The Writings of Michael de Febure (1721)", in: *Early Modern Low Countries* 3/2 (2019), pp. 265–282; Philippa Hellawell, "'The best and most practical philosophers': Seamen and the Authority of Experience in Early Modern Science", in: *History of Science* 58/1 (2020), pp. 28–50; Francesco Luzzini, "Sounding the Depths of Providence: Mineral (Re)generation and Human-Environment Interaction in the Early Modern Period", in: *Earth Sciences History* 39/2 (2020) pp. 389–408; Tina Asmussen and Pamela O. Long, "Introduction: The Cultural and Material Worlds of Mining in Early

but a few categories – are usually regarded as neither artisans nor professionals. Their great expertise nonetheless built upon sensory experience. It was embodied, transmitted via oral traditions and practices as well as texts, and most of all it was deeply connected with nature, the earth, and the seas. Their practices were directly relevant to early modern knowledge making regarding nature, therefore. Those practices also reflect, though usually indirectly, how early modern humans imagined their relationship with nature and its resources.

While Adriaen Coenen was definitely a practical expert, his knowledge was by no means based on practice alone. He can certainly not be regarded as a representative of 'folk' knowledge unspoilt by erudition. Nor is it likely, in fact, that such a straightforward dichotomy ever existed in European history. Coenen did not have much formal education but he was a literate person and probably a member of the Scheveningen chamber of rhetoric. He fused his practical experience of *aquatilia* with learned natural knowledge as written down by the most famous contemporary naturalists, such as Pierre Belon, Conrad Gessner, and Guillaume Rondelet, and the great naturalists of antiquity, in particular Pliny. Coenen had access to various vernacular editions of their publications thanks to local patrons near The Hague and Scheveningen who belonged to the landed aristocracy and the *noblesse de robe* connected with the Habsburg government.[10]

That access itself and Coenen's relations with these patrons were predicated upon and triggered by his great interest in and expertise about marine life. Some precisely dated examples of that interest go back to the early 1540s and 1550s. This was not a case, therefore, of a man with limited education whose interest in nature derived from published learned works. The inspiration and fascination were there from his youth, *before* the great works on *aquatilia* of the 1550s had even been published.[11] In terms of social mobility and self-presentation, his albums even provided him with an entry into far more elevated circles than the local nobility. Coenen presented an early fish album (now lost) personally to Prince William of Orange, then leader of the Dutch Revolt, hoping for a court position as page for his young son. And in the last years of Coenen's life he personally exchanged fish drawings and information with the renowned naturalist Rembert Dodoens (1517–1585), former physician of the Habsburg Emperor Maximilian II. Like Coenen, Dodoens spent his final years in Leiden.[12]

Modern Europe", in: *Renaissance Studies* 34/1 (2020), pp. 8–30; and Marianne Klemun, "Classification and Experience. Rocks and Taste. 'Vulgar' Reasoning in the Earth Sciences", in: *De Achttiende Eeuw* 48/1–2 (2016), pp. 113–126.

10 Although Coenen did not have Latin, he could read German, French and perhaps some English. A full survey of Coenen's published sources has not yet been made, and it is often unclear which specific editions he was able to consult.

11 See for a survey of the printed works and of the chronology of the sixteenth-century interest in aquatilia, Egmond, "Looking Beyond the Margins of Print".

12 See CoenenKB ff. 37v–38, 49v (gift of the album to Prince William of Orange). On the Dodoens (also: Dodonaeus) connection, see further Egmond, *Het Visboek*, pp. 56–58.

While Coenen's fascination with marine nature thus appears to have originated spontaneously, the published works by the great naturalists of his own time undoubtedly influenced the encyclopaedic format of his albums and his self-presentation as a describer of fishes. Coenen's approach to evidence shows a combination of common sense combined with respect for sources, a critical attitude towards evidence, and an overwhelming respect for eye-witnessing that were probably partly innate but also enhanced by his reading of works by the sixteenth-century naturalists. For Coenen practice-based experience and personal observations always overruled other kinds of information in terms of credibility, even if that meant humbly disagreeing with authorities of the calibre of Pliny, Belon, Rondelet, or Gessner.[13]

Coenen was no natural philosopher. He does not generalize and rarely uses abstract concepts. He never uses the term *resources*, but speaks rather more concretely of the wealth, abundance, riches, or in the contrary case of scarcity or dearth of fishes. His terminology thus resonates with that used for harvests, suggesting a mental link between the resources of land and water. Such links are familiar from the mirroring of animal names between land and water animals that is still evident in names like sea wolf, sea louse, sea horse, and so on. Such links also re-echo in a literary genre known in the Italian (especially Neapolitan) context as *egloghe pescatorie:* highly erudite, book-length poems in Latin that focus almost completely on fish and fishermen, while transposing the format of Virgil's bucolic eclogues to the domain of the sea.[14] Interestingly, a transfer from land and agriculture to the marine world of fishermen – though lacking an arcadian idealization – also occurs in several literary texts and songs that originated in Bruges during the 1540s–60s.[15]

Yet, it is simplistic to regard this land-water mirroring and a possible parallel between their resources as typical of an *early modern* approach or mentality. After all, not only names like sea wolf or sea horse but also harvest-related notions of riches, dearth, and ripeness of fishes are still in use at present.[16] Nor do Coenen's writings suggest that local fishermen imagined themselves as *cultivating* the seas, and he is quite explicit about the differences between obtaining knowledge of land and of water creatures: 'We are amazed by the strange and significant rar-

13 See Egmond, *Eye for Detail*, pp. 156–160, 194–208, and Egmond, "On Northern Shores".

14 See esp. Daniela Caracciolo, "L'enciclopedia ittiologica di Giulio Cesare Capaccio ed i suoi rapporti con il collezionismo Napoletano", in: *Napoli Nobilissima* serie 5/X (2009), pp. 3–20; and Daniela Caracciolo, "Per una Wunderkammer letteraria, Mergellina, la 'fatica marittima' di Giulio Cesare Capaccio", in: *Annali di critica d'arte* 5 (2009), pp. 33–80.

15 See Noel Geirnaert, "Piscatorial Elements in Sixteenth-Century Literature in Bruges: Fantasy Scenes and Compassionate Eulogies", in: *Ichthyology in Context*, eds. Smith and Egmond, pp. 325–339.

16 Modern terms like herring grounds and spawning grounds also refer to land and territory rather than water. Cf. the terminology used in Louis Sicking and Darlene Abreu-Ferreira (eds.), *Beyond the Catch. Fisheries of the North Atlantic, the North Sea and the Baltic, 900–1850*, Leiden/Boston 2009.

ities of the world that can be found on land; how many more strange and wondrous creatures must exist in the seas, as has been known for a long time, because one cannot investigate the sea in the same manner as is possible on land'.[17]

Perhaps a comparison with *mining* is more apposite, although it is not reflected in Coenen's vocabulary and would probably have been far removed from his personal experience. Fishing exploits the resources of the waters, mining those of the earth. In both cases human beings reach for something of value that is largely invisible, hidden below the surface, sometimes at great depths. In both cases, refined expertise is needed to read or interpret those surfaces (steam, smells, colour changes, turbulence, whirls, opacity or clarity, et cetera) in order to find and access what is below them. In both cases these hidden spheres are full of dangers, while promising potential treasures.[18] Knowledge and experience can protect those who enter these spheres. And precisely the fact that so much may happen just below the surface, invisibly, makes it easy to understand why in both spheres arcane knowledge, lore, and beliefs in dangerous creatures abound.

2 Fishing Zones: Locating Marine Resources

The expertise required to access nature's marine resources concerned two main domains of knowledge. Like all seafarers, Dutch fishermen needed to know how to survive on the northern seas and orientate themselves – a theme on which Coenen has almost nothing to say. More specifically, Dutch fishermen needed to have a clear idea of *which* kind of *aquatilia* they wanted to obtain from the seas and *how* to do so. This required expertise regarding the variety of *aquatilia* that lived in these seas, *where* they could be located and at what times. Naturally, not all *aquatilia* were seen as useful to human beings, as resources, and the concept of 'useful' was not limited to the category of the edible. Coenen's also mentions marine resources such as precious ambergris, kelp and various kinds of seagrasses and seaweeds, chalky shells that were used for paths, feathers of gulls and shelducks; rough sharkskin to cover shafts of knives, and of course numerous small fishes that served as bait. Yet other *aquatilia* had curiosity value or were used as decoration; some were collector's items. Best known among the latter are the Jenny Hanivers, the shells of marine turtles, saws of saw fish, whale bones, narwhal teeth known as horns of unicorns, and special shells. Nearly all of these figure in Coenen's albums.

Some marina naturalia are actually called useless (*onnut*) by Coenen. These include various kinds of seaworms and shells, jellyfish, sea mice, sea nettles, starfish, sea urchins, and other often nameless growths. Coenen included them in his albums even though they were regarded as inedible and usually thrown away.[19]

17 CoenenKB f. 20v.
18 See the literature on mining in note 9 above. Although hunting would seem to be a closer comparison for fishing, it is almost absent from Coenen's terminology.
19 On 'useless' as a general category, see e.g. CoenenKB ff. 12r, 40.

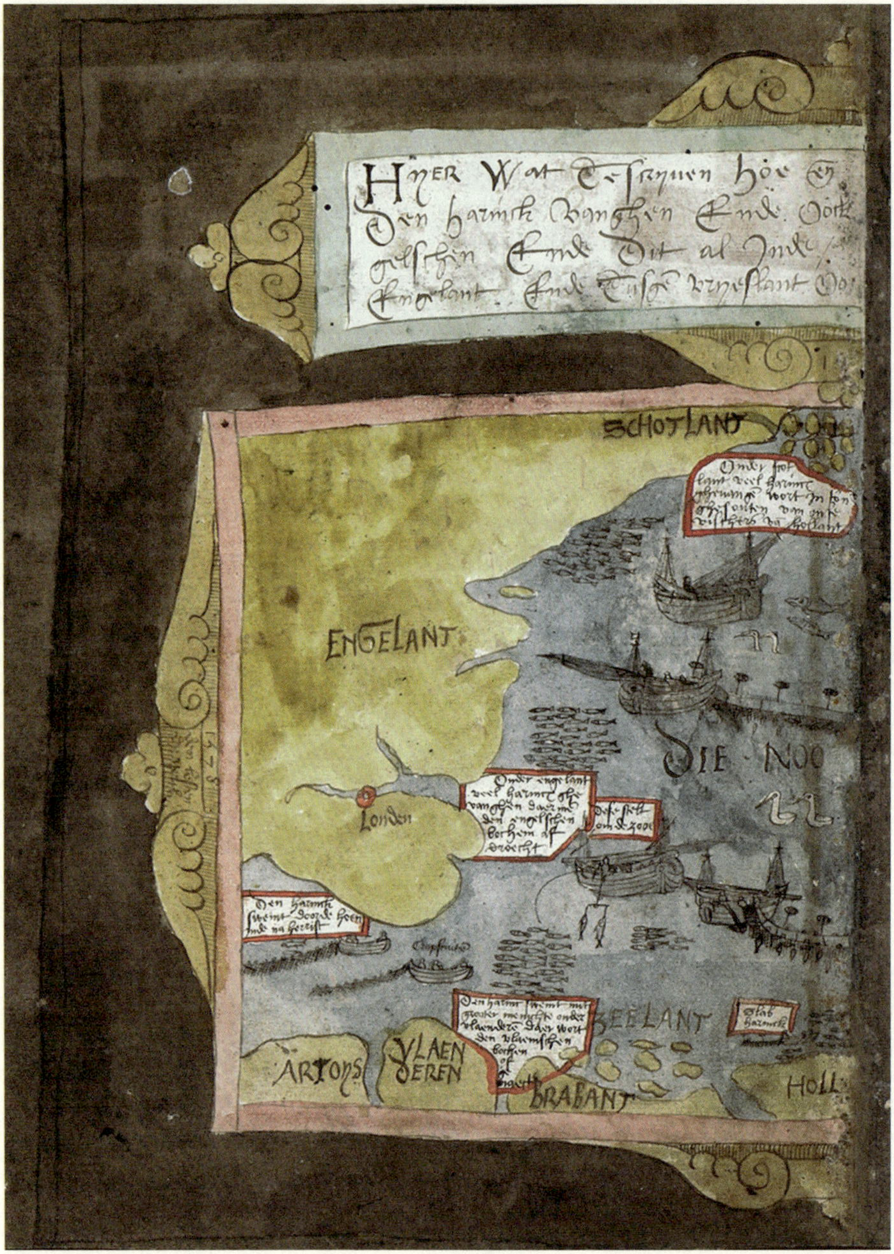

Fig. 2: Double-page map showing the North Sea as a space of activity. Coenen, Visboeck, ff. 28v–29r. Adriaen Coenen, Visboeck [Fish Book], 1577–81, Holland. C. 400 folios. The Hague, Koninklijke Bibliotheek, Ms 78 E 54, URL: https://www.kb.nl/themas/middeleeuwen/visboek-van-adriaen-coenen (19.03.2025).

-19-
FRIESLANT
RT ZEE
DENEMARKEN
HOLST

Fig. 3: Whales migrating along the Dutch coast. Coenen, Visboeck, detail of ff. 167v–168r. Adriaen Coenen, Visboeck [Fish Book], 1577–81, Holland. C. 400 folios. The Hague, Koninklijke Bibliotheek, Ms 78 E 54, URL: https://www.kb.nl/themas/middeleeuwen/visboek-van-adriaen-coenen (19.03.2025).

Though the objects themselves might be useless, knowledge of them was clearly not.

The maps that Coenen personally drew are particularly suggestive. A double-page map in the section about the herring (Fig. 2) puts the North-Sea and Channel at the center of the image. Here, land is not framed by seas, but the sea is the focus and framed by coastlines. In fact, the map is a perfect representation of the North Sea as a connecting space of activity – a mini-version of Braudel's Mediterranean – that links Britain, extending all the way up to Scotland and the northern islands Fair Isle and Shetland, to Norway, Denmark, Northern Germany, the Low Countries and Western France. Strikingly, on Coenen's maps the seas are visually packed with activities and indications, whereas the land is relatively bare. He depicts various types of fishing boats, fishing techniques with different types of nets, marine creatures such as sharks and seals, and numerous seabirds. This map also depicts shoals of herring, while text balloons indicate which types of herring were caught in which 'regions' of the sea, and whether they were eventually sold dried, smoked or otherwise processed. Here we see a horizontal, region-

al distribution, therefore, which combines geographical expertise concerning the locations of fishing grounds with temporal notions of the seasons in which those areas were usually fished.

Coenen thus understood the sea as what we would call a richly varied *habitat* in which some *aquatilia* seemed simply present in certain zones, while others, such as herring, salmon, whales, plaice, and cod, followed recurring routes and migrations. The fishermen, whose work and lives were themselves structured by these migrations, had come to know them by experience transmitted via the generations. They knew that such migration patterns were connected with the seasons and were conscious that some were linked with the life and reproductive cycles of these *aquatilia*. Pilchard (*pelser*), weever (*pieterman*) and many other fishes seasonally came closer to the Dutch coast, and Coenen compares some of their migrations with those of finches, who migrate in a south-westerly direction in the autumn: 'as we see fishes do every day, big and small, coming from the north and moving towards the southwest, which can be better seen close to the coast rather than in the deeper waters'.[20]

20 CoenenKB f. 41–41v.

Geographical knowledge of the sea and its fishes was not limited to economically relevant species such as cod, plaice, herring, haddock, or mackerel. It also regarded large sea mammals such as whales (Fig. 3), which at this time were not yet commercially hunted by the Dutch.[21] Coenen writes for instance, that a herd of large whales passed once or twice every year close by the Dutch coast and could be easily observed from his village. They always came from the north and moved in a west-south-westerly direction; they were never observed returning northwards. They 'leap out of the water, some half out of it, others completely, and it seems as if they follow each other swimming and breaching (…)'. This could last for two or three hours and the local fishermen said 'they migrate to find a bride'. This happened generally during calm and beautiful weather, but some three days after such a passage usually a heavy storm occurred.[22]

In naming the herring *Gratia Dei* Coenen referred to the crucial double contribution of the herring to the prosperity of Holland. Herring was, on the one hand, a fundamental food especially for the poorer inhabitants of the towns in Holland. Herring fishing and the connected industries and trade provided a major source of employment, moreover. In the fifteenth and sixteenth centuries it was one of the most important sources of wealth in Holland next to the textile industry and beer brewing.[23]

The well-known technique of gibbing was already some 200 years old by Coenen's time. If done out at sea, the herring catch could be kept much longer on board, which allowed for far longer fishing trips. The large herring busses developed in the fifteenth century were big enough to process considerable quantities of herring, salt them, and pack them into barrels. They could stay on the open seas for many weeks and allowed Dutch fishermen to access fishing grounds as far as the Orkneys and Shetland.[24] Coenen describes three types of ships used by the Dutch herring fishers: the large herring busses (*haringbuizen*); smaller *boeten* and the yet smaller and narrower *pinken*. The two larger types mostly had their home ports within the Dutch river delta. Like most other fishing villages located along the coast of Holland with its dunes and sandy beaches, Scheveningen had no port: here the smaller flatbottomed fishing boats were pulled up on the beach. Scheveningen entrepreneurs who owned large busses usually docked them in the safer river ports of Holland such as Maassluis, Schiedam, Rotterdam.

21 Dutch commercial whaling started in the seventeenth century and mainly concerned Arctic fishing grounds, not the North Sea.

22 CoenenKB ff. 167v–168r.

23 For the long section on the herring see CoenenKB ff. 24–33, here esp. f. 30v. For an economic analysis of early modern Dutch herring fisheries with references to Coenen, see Christiaan van Bochove, "The 'golden mountain': an Economic Analysis of Holland's Early Modern Herring Fisheries", (eds.) Sicking and Abreu-Ferreira, *Beyond the Catch*, pp. 209–243.

24 See Sicking and Abreu-Ferreira eds., *Beyond the Catch*, as well as Bennema and Rijnsdorp,"Fish Abundance", for further references to the literature (often in Dutch) about early modern fisheries on the North Sea.

The herring fishermen undertook two to four long trips per season, using very long nets, and remaining out at sea for five to eight weeks on end. During their first trip they went to the seas north of Scotland where they caught two types of herring: the fatty *maatjesharing* – as yet without roe – that was perfectly suitable for salting and use as brined herring; and the full herring – with roe – that was more suited to be fried or boiled. During the second trip, they fished for full herring as well as empty herring (that had spawned) and herring that was on the point of spawning. In each Dutch port inspectors checked that these different types of herring were not mixed and sold together; only full herring was regarded as top quality. The fishermen also caught *slab*-herring in the autumn during trips close to the Dutch coast that generally lasted no longer than a single night.

Coenen also provides descriptions and occasionally maps for other fishes that were important to the Dutch economy, such as plaice, flounder, sprat, turbot, and various other flat fish as well as round fish like cod, herring, and mackerel. He always begins with a description of the fish itself and its flavour, and then comments on the fishing seasons, the relevant ports in Holland, processing techniques, and the main market places or staples. These descriptions point to two further parameters of Coenen's marine expertise besides regional knowledge of the seas and seasonality: verticality and long-term changes.

His account about the plaice is a good example. The Scheveningen fishermen usually started to fish for plaice by early February once the haddock catches started to diminish. By March plaice began to move from deeper waters in the North Sea and to gather in shallower zones closer to the sandy coast of Holland. Fishermen naturally hoped that such a gathering (*leck*) would occur in front of their own coastal village, so that they could fish close to home for months: 'they take up their position there, as is marvellous to see. And there they are piled up together so thickly that I have heard fishermen say that after the whole *leck* has been caught (in the course of two or three months) the sea is two or three fathoms deeper than when the *leck* began.'[25]

A detail of one of Coenen's maps shows how mackerel were caught using either special nets or a very long line with a lead weight at the end and marked with a red piece of cloth (*draap*) which the fishing boats dragged behind them; vertically attached to this long line were shorter sticks or stiff lines with baited hooks that attracted fish like mackerel that swam not deep down near the sea bottom but closer to the surface.[26] The depth at which these hooks would float, and where the fishermen expected to encounter mackerel, would depend on a combination of the weight of the line plus hooks, bait and lead, and the speed of the fishing boat.

As also suggested by their tales about the movements of plaice from deeper to more shallow zones, Coenen and the fishermen must have had a fair knowl-

25 CoenenKB ff. 140–140v; cf. ff. 135v–136.
26 CoenenKB, ff. 31–32v on mackerel fishing.

edge of the depth levels of the North Sea and the presence of certain types of fish in certain depth zones. Coenen's occasional references to fathoms suggest that the fishermen also measured depths. Perhaps we could therefore speak of a multi-dimensional notion of the largely invisible underwater domain: horizontal regionality and vertical depth combined with temporal notions of seasonality and long-term changes.

Local oral history certainly remembered the years in which huge gatherings of plaice occurred close to the coast, and a local saying suggested that a year with excellent catches of common dab was a bad one for plaice fishing. Local traditions thus recorded and transmitted long-term temporal patterns in catches.[27] Coenen infrequently but explicitly addresses long-term changes that he personally witnessed in the course of his long life. He saw some very drastic changes in the stocks of gurnard and salmon, for instance. Tub gurnards were abundant, he writes, both in his very young years (c. 1520s–1530s) and in the 1580s, but they were scarce in the middle of the sixteenth century.[28] The changes in salmon stocks were even more dramatic. Salmon were caught in the Dutch river delta as well as in the North Sea not far from the coast of Holland. In Coenen's father's days (turn of the 15th century) salmon were caught so rarely in the North Sea by fishermen from Scheveningen that a single salmon sold for the price of a sturgeon or a whole fat pig. During Coenen's youth, in contrast, salmon was abundant and extremely cheap; by about 1580 salmon had become scarcer again and more expensive.[29]

Coenen's descriptions of species composition and abundance are accurate enough to be used by the modern experts Floris Bennema and Adriaan Rijnsdorp as a source for the study of historical changes in marine ecology.[30] Coenen never suggests causal explanations for the long-term changes, however, whether in the form of changing weather patterns, climate, or human overfishing. In fact, there is no indication that he regarded fishes as a *limited* resource, and this may well have something to do with his view of nature, about which more will be said below.

3 Reading the Signs of the Sea

Knowledge of the sea as an element and as a habitat of fishes, the ability to read the signs of the sea, the weather, and the sea creatures was of crucial importance to fishermen in order to survive, physically and economically. Coenen shows great respect for this type of expertise that was mainly transmitted via practice and oral tradition, and gives many brief examples. Some of these refer to characteristics of the sea water, such as its thickness, limpidity, or colour. Successful salmon fishing in the North Sea, for instance, required very specific conditions. Winter salmon was caught from early January, mainly when there was a strong

27 CoenenKB f. 137.
28 CoenenKB ff. 148v–149 on tub gurnard.
29 On salmon, see CoenenKB ff. 25, 42, 43–45, cf. 202, 205v–206v.
30 Bennema and Rijnsdorp, "Fish Abundance", compared Coenen's information with trawl survey data from around 1900 and 1990.

west-south-westerly wind and a light drizzle, which made the water thick.[31] Fishermen who changed the bait on the hooks for haddock-fishing from shrimps or allis shad to small herring noted that haddock far preferred the former two types of bait and disdained the herring: 'the haddock blows that bait off the hook as if it was saying 'it doesn't please me'; the fishermen can see this because of the clarity of the water'.[32]

Coenen explicitly speaks of signs (*tekenen*) in his examples of how the fishermen interpreted the behaviour of sea birds: 'such signs have the fishermen'.[33] The gatherings and sudden movements or migrations of sea birds announced a significant weather change or indicated the presence of shoals of fish. If many guillemots (*zeekoeten*) were seen, for instance, this predicted a good year for plaice, since guillemots knew how to follow the plaice, which moved to shallower waters in years when they were particularly numerous.[34] And if the Scheveningen fishermen observed many gannets and other fish-eating birds in the waters off the Scottish isles, they stayed in the area and expected a good catch. But storm petrels (*malefijters*), 'small birds like large swallows, black, with flat feet like duck', forecast storms and thunder when they gather in large numbers and float on the waves not far from the fishing boats.[35] And when flocks of black and white oyster catchers arrived on the Dutch beaches, storm and rain usually followed, as the saying went: 'a proverb among our fishermen says: if three [oystercatchers] are seen together, it means 3 *reef* wind; when 4 are together, it means 4 *reef* wind, and the more there are together the stronger the wind will be. And this usually does indeed happen'.[36]

The fact that fishermen in Holland regarded certain animals as rivals may also tell us something about their notion of fishes as a resource. Sharks and specifically dogfish (*hondekens*) ate the whiting that was caught on the fishermen's lines, cutting the fish clean in half with their razor-sharp teeth and often leaving half of them on the hooks. Sharks also ate herring that was stuck with its gills in the stiff and fine-meshed nets.[37] The marine mammal that Coenen names as *hil* (probably a type of dolphin) stole herring from the nets without damaging them. And Coenen calls seals downright thieves that operate close to the herring busses[38], while in the waters off Scotland gannets and other seabirds dived and stole herring from lines and nets that were being hauled in: 'And they cause grave damages to the fishermen. These birds are very greedy. They gobble so many herring that

31 CoenenKB f. 43.
32 CoenenKB ff. 141v–142.
33 CoenenKB f. 114.
34 CoenenKB f. 114.
35 CoenenKB ff. 113v–115 (various seabirds); ff. 113–113v (malefijters).
36 CoenenKB, f. 114v.
37 CoenenKB ff. 108, 126.
38 CoenenKB ff. 28v–29 (hil and seals).

they discharge entire herrings from behind. For that reason, our fishermen use an expression about a man who can eat enormously and say "what a gannet is he"'.[39]

Scheveningen fishermen may have been as annoyed with human as with animal rivals and competitors. Coenen's descriptions of fishing from various villages along the sandy Dutch coast and from ports in Holland and Zealand indicate not merely a level of specialization (fishing at long distances or closer to the coast; fishing for cod, herring, salmon et cetera), but also the presence of (inter)local regulations. While these especially addressed the selling of fish and guarantees of quality and size, Coenen gives one example that points to the existence of certain prohibitions and catch limitations.[40] Harbour porpoise (*bruinvis*; also known at the time as sea-pig) were regularly caught with special nets along the coast of Holland to the north of Scheveningen. The fishermen of Scheveningen were not allowed to use such nets. Apparently, this was connected with the proximity of Scheveningen to one of the mouths of the river Maas, whose fresh water created a zone with exceptionally limpid water right in front of Scheveningen.[41]

Perceiving certain animals as fish thieves implies that the fishermen thought of the fishes as rightfully belonging to themselves. And the regulations regarding the use of certain nets suggest that notions of fair or unfair competition existed with regard to fishes as a resource. It is hard to make out, however, whether this points to a notion of fishes as a *limited* resource.

4 The Sea as a Domain of Dangers, Monsters and Portents

While promising rich catches and potential treasure, the sea was also a hidden domain full of lurking dangers and strange phenomena, expressed in sayings and tales about sea monsters that circulated in fishing communities (Fig. 4). These entered into Coenen's albums via two main channels: first, via local oral traditions; and secondly, via published works, old and new. Coenen's printed sources on sea monsters included especially Olaus Magnus, *Historia de gentibus septentrionalibus* (1555); the anonymous *Dierenpalleijs* [Palace of Animals] (1520), a compilation in Dutch, illuminated with many woodcuts, of stories and images that went back to medieval sources and derived from the late fifteenth-century *Hortus Sanitatis*; and Cornelius Aurelius's, *Divisie-kronijk* (1517) also known as the *Cronyck van Holland* [Dutch Chronicle].[42]

39 CoenenKB ff. 113–113v.

40 See on regulations and the role of the Dutch *College van de Grote Visserij* (Council of the Great Fisheries; created during the 1580s), Sicking and Abreu-Ferreira (eds.), *Beyond the Catch.*

41 CoenenKB ff. f.132v–133.

42 Coenen probably consulted the German version of Olaus's work: *Olai Magni Historien der mittnachtigen Länder,* Basel 1567; *Der dierenpalleijs ende die vergaderinge van den beesten d'aerden, van den vogelen d'lucht, van den visschen ende monsteren d'wateren,* Antwerp 1520, with many woodcut illustrations. Cornelius Aurelius, *Divisie-kronijk. Die chronijcke van Hollant, Zeelant ende van Vrieslandt. Beginnende van Adams tijden,* Leiden 1517; it went through 53 editions between 1538 and 1802.

Fig. 4: One of Olaus Magnus' sea monsters, copied by Coenen. Visboeck, detail of f. 64v. Adriaen Coenen, Visboeck [Fish Book], 1577–81, Holland. C. 400 folios. The Hague, Koninklijke Bibliotheek, Ms 78 E 54, URL: https://www.kb.nl/themas/middeleeuwen/visboek-van-adriaen-coenen (19.03.2025).

Coenen's interest in such phenomena is undoubted. Curiosities of the seas were a personal resource for him: a source of income as well as a fund of pleasure, enjoyment and knowledge that in its turn helped to establish his status and self-image as a fish and marine expert. In 1576, for instance, Coenen managed to buy the sword and head of a ten-foot long swordfish from a local fisherman who had caught the animal and hung the head with sword from the facade of his house. Coenen had never come across one before in almost half a century of observations: 'therefore there must be very few of these [sword]fish in our seas, or they make themselves hard to catch'.[43] While copying or summarizing Olaus Magnus's stories about sea monsters, Coenen nearly always adds personal comments or examples, and claims that the North Sea had as many rarities to offer as the seas near Olaus's Norway.[44]

What Coenen actually *believed* about strange marine creatures is harder to establish. He certainly did not regard the well-known Jenny Hanivers as real sea dragons, and neither did his customers. In fact, Coenen personally created them. In the course of decades he sold thousands of small rays and a few monkfish that he had dried in the shape of sea-dragons. They were used as decoration in Dutch

43 CoenenKB f. 96r.

44 See e.g. CoenenKB ff. 37v–38. On seamonsters as perceived in early-modern Norwegian works, see Ronny Spaans, "'My Eyes Have Never Yet Beheld Him.' Demythologising Arctic Sea Monsters in the Poetry of the Norwegian Priest and Fish Merchant Petter Dass (1647–1707)", *Ichthyology in Context*, eds. Smith and Egmond, pp. 420–453.

Fig. 5: Sea devil from local folklore. Coenen, Visboeck, detail of f. 86v. Adriaen Coenen, Visboeck [Fish Book], 1577–81, Holland. C. 400 folios. The Hague, Koninklijke Bibliotheek, Ms 78 E 54, URL: https://www.kb.nl/themas/middeleeuwen/visboek-van-adriaen-coenen (19.03.2025).

households, often displayed dangling below chandeliers.[45] Coenen also repeatedly relegates local tales about strange marine creatures to bygone days, old women, a 'heathen' past, and the uneducated lower classes. According to local lore, for instance, the arrival from the east of large numbers of dragonflies predicted the arrival of plundering soldiers. Coenen dismisses this as old wives' tales (*oude wijven verhalen*). He links the mass appearance of these insects with a dry wind from the east and compares their east-west movements with the migration of birds.[46]

Scheveningen lore as reported by Coenen spoke of various ghostly appearances and in particular of sea devils (*kuijker* or *hoesgen nicker*) with flashing eyes as big as sapphires who showed themselves by night close to the seashore but did not harm human beings and even helped them to sort shrimps (Fig. 5). Belief in these creatures was widespread in Coenen's young years, but he calls it phantasy (*fantasien*) or delusion (*wangeloof*) and relegates it to a past 'when we were still heathens'. Coenen had never been able to find anyone who had actually seen these sea devils; his informants always referred him to yet another person.

45 CoenenKB f. 96 (monkfish) and f. 122v (dragons from rays).
46 CoenenKB f. 311–311v.

In various further cases when fishermen spoke of strange sea creatures Coenen repeats the conclusion that he has never been able to find an eye witness: 'it is always hearsay'.[47] He was no less critical of book-knowledge. While he could try and check sources of local tales, this was impossible for the printed works since, as he writes, those monsters lived too far away: 'I find many kinds of mermaids and mermen in writing and many books speak of them. But I have never found as yet, to this year 1579, anyone who has seen them with their own eyes'.[48]

While discussing many of these strange marine creatures, Coenen therefore usually left the question of their existence open. He was caught between his critical sense and the desire for reliable evidence in the shape of eye-witness accounts, on the one hand, and his respect for older authorities, on the other hand. Even more important was his firm belief in God's omnipotence, which made it impossible for him to discard the *potential* existence of such creatures.[49] Interestingly, in the case of the local sea devils with the flashing eyes, Coenen splits his argument in two: sea devils and similar phenomena were probably created by the Devil and should not be given credibility, but the presence of strange, wonderful and amazing creatures in the sea, as observed every day by the inhabitants of the coast, was a sign of God's omnipotence.[50]

In a rather similar way Coenen keeps the interpretational options open when dealing with the issue of whether the arrival of strange creatures from the sea should be regarded as portents. On the one hand, a large segment of Coenen's *Visboeck* is devoted to such

> … rare, big fish and strange monsters of the sea, that have arrived at certain times here in Holland and also in other faraway countries or have manifested themselves in the seas or have sometimes been caught at sea. And when such strange monsters and rare fish showed themselves or were thrown upon the shores, something exceptional always happened afterwards, such as great mortality or warfare or in these times the deaths of important lords, kings and rulers.[51]

These words suggest that Coenen shared the fairly widespread conviction that the appearance of abnormal natural phenomena foretold extraordinary events: 'Since rare and miraculous figures, forms and shapes outside the regular path of nature, among both humans and animals, usually mean something special as monsters'.[52] The hand of God manifested itself via deviations in the normal patterns of nature.

47 CoenenKB ff. 178 and 290 (sea devils, phantasy, delusion), and f. 189v (hear say).
48 CoenenKB f. 193.
49 CoenenKB, e.g. ff. 23, 73, 113–113v, 151v.
50 CoenenKB f. 290.
51 CoenenKB f. 12r, dated 1578.
52 CoenenKB ff. 323. It is uncertain whether these are Coenen's own words or a quotation.

Coenen's actual practice contradicts these statements. The most spectacular arrivals that occurred close to home, on his own coast, show him from his most matter of fact and critical side. Discussing the appearance of two giant squids in 1546 and 1566, Coenen records that the common people linked the squid of 1566 with the Sea Beggars and the dramatic events of that year in the Dutch Revolt. But he immediately points out that no strange events had actually followed the arrival of the 1546 squid.[53] In his lengthy reports on the arrival of several other remarkable water creatures – a huge and a small sunfish (*Mola mola*); a spectacularly coloured and huge *lampris guttatus* – he was far more interested in investigating, measuring and preserving them than in looking for their significance. This is particularly manifest in his reportage on the spectacular beaching in 1577 of three very large whales near Scheveningen – the traditional omen of impending doom. Coenen measured the creatures and assisted in auctioning them off. In his pages-long description he devotes not a single word to their possible significance.[54]

Whether fishermen's tales about sea devils and marine monsters can be regarded as a way of coming to terms with the dangerous deep and its secrets remains an open question here. Interestingly, Coenen distances himself to some extent from those beliefs and from the common people, even though he highly praises the expertise of the fishermen in reading the signs of the sea. He did not go regularly out to sea himself. He was no uneducated fisherman. Yet, he was no learned author either, and he tends to leave the final interpretation of curious natural events to those with more education. Coenen thus moves back and forth between traditional beliefs and what we might call an empiricist attitude towards evidence. Overriding all is his belief in an omnipotent God.[55]

5 God and the Resources of Nature

There is hardly a page of his albums on which Coenen does not explicitly state that he sees God as the moving force behind the bounties of nature, including those of the seas. To Coenen God was first and foremost a wise, good, and omnipotent ruler of Nature and creator of wondrous things. An introductory passage in the *Fish Boock* sums this up very well:

> Thus when we hear or see his wondrous works, we can do no better than praise, acclaim, and honour him. And fear him with a childlike friend-

53 See CoenenKB ff. 62v–63 (giant squid of 1566), and ff. 46v–48 (giant squid of 1546).

54 See CoenenKB f. 151v and Coenen, *Whale Book* f. 14; CoenenKB f. 264 (lampris guttatus); and esp. CoenenKB ff. 53v–58 (beached whales 1577).

55 Coenen's religious stance is not so easily defined: born before the Reformation, he was for many years close friends with influential patrons who remained staunch Catholics, while he himself switched position (almost certainly after 1566) and became a Protestant together with nearly all Scheveningen inhabitants including their priest. Yet, Coenen was very much a man of the moderate center groups and hated any type of religious persecution. An analysis of Coenen's religious attitudes in the complex context of Reformation, Iconoclasm and the Dutch Revolt has not yet been undertaken.

> ly trepidation, because he is omnipotent and good. Because (…) all the spheres of heaven, all that grows on the earth, all beasts in the fields, wild and tame, all birds in the air, all fishes in the waters He has given us humans for our needs. Therefore I have brought together in this book much about fishes, so that we may now and for ever honour and praise God Almighty for his amiable gifts every time we see his wonders and eat his tasty fishes, this is my desire, Amen.[56]

It was God's hand that made natural resources available to human beings, or on the contrary withheld them.

The very presence or absence of fishes and other marine naturalia, the small or large size of catches, fish migrations, abundance or scarcity, long-term changes in their presence, the appearance of strange marine creatures all ultimately reflected the will of God as expressed through Nature. Though certainly influenced by natural processes, they were a result of God's actions. Aged 63, Coenen wrote for instance, that for much of his life he had seen how fishes migrated every year from the deeper zones of the North Sea to closer to the coast of Holland and Zealand, on God's orders, one species after another, 'as if God commanded them'.[57]

Coenen's perspective certainly did not exclude looking for *natural* explanations for changes in migratory patterns, for long-term scarcity of certain fishes, or for other phenomena. And Coenen made lifelong efforts to understand such patterns in nature. Nor did he disregard human agency, as we have seen. Without expert fishing techniques, excellent knowledge of fishes, and the ability to read the signs of the seas, no fish would be caught and marine resources would remain inaccessible to human beings. But that access to nature's bounty was never unmediated. He thought that the Scheveningen fishermen were presumptuous when they believed that an abundant catch was the consequence of their expertise as fishermen alone: 'Thus our fishermen usually believe that good catches can be attributed to their practice and diligence' and 'those fishermen commonly think that they catch fish depending on how well they position their nets, but I consider that they depend on trust in God and that he provides.[58] According to Coenen not even the most expert fishermen would catch anything if God did not grant them the fruits of Nature: 'It is said that He gives a catch to whom He wants and when He wants. As He said to Peter cast that net, and in the name of the Lord many fishes were caught'.[59]

In Coenen's perspective human agency and nature's works thus came far below God's will in terms of relevance. In spite of their huge economic relevance, marine resources were in a fundamental sense not a matter of economics for Coenen.

56 CoenenKB f. 21, cf. f. 84v. Although Coenen briefly mentions the Flood, he is neither a philosopher nor a theologian and hardly engages with the concept of sin.

57 CoenenKB ff. 171v–172.

58 CoenenKB f. 227v; and CoenenKB f. 272.

59 CoenenKB f. 227v (cf. f. 272).

Reference Lists

Manuscript Sources

Coenen, Adriaen. *Visboeck* [*Fish Book*], 1577–81, Holland. C. 400 folios. The Hague, Koninklijke Bibliotheek, Ms 78 E 54, URL: https://www.kb.nl/themas/middeleeuwen/visboek-van-adriaen-coenen (19.03.2025)..

Coenen, Adriaen. *Walvisboeck* [*Whale Book*], c. 1584–85, Holland. C. 125 folios. Antwerp, Erfgoedbibliotheek Hendrik Conscience, EHC 707256, URL: https://dams.antwerpen.be/asset/jUZJkHhUZFeQeePAieiY0tyw (19.03.2025)..

Coenen, Adriaen. *Haringkoningboek*, c. 1586–87. C. 25 folios, unfinished, Cologne, Historisches Archiv, Ms 296.

Printed Sources

Anonymous, *Der dierenpalleijs ende die vergaderinge van den beesten d'aerden, van den vogelen d'lucht, van den visschen ende monsteren d'wateren,* Antwerp 1520.

Aurelius, Cornelius, *Divisie-kronijk. Die chronijcke van Hollant, Zeelant ende van Vrieslandt. Beginnende van Adams tijden,* Leiden 1517.

Olaus Magnus, *Historia de gentibus septentrionalibus,* Roma 1555.

Olaus Magnus, *Olai Magni Historien der mittnachtigen Länder,* Basel 1567.

Research Literature

Asmussen, Tina and Pamela O. Long, "Introduction: The Cultural and Material Worlds of Mining in Early Modern Europe", in: *Renaissance Studies* 34/1 (2020), pp. 8–30.

Bennema, Floris P. and Adriaan D. Rijnsdorp, "Fish Abundance, Fisheries, Fish Trade and Consumption in Sixteenth-Century Netherlands as Described by Adriaen Coenen", in: *Fisheries Research* 161 (2015), pp. 384–399.

Bochove, Christiaan van, "The 'golden mountain': an Economic Analysis of Holland's Early Modern Herring Fisheries", in: *Beyond the Catch. Fisheries of the North Atlantic, the North Sea and the Baltic, 900–1850,* eds. Louis Sicking and Darlene Abreu-Ferreira, Leiden/Boston 2009, pp. 209–243.

Caracciolo, Daniela, "L'enciclopedia ittiologica di Giulio Cesare Capaccio ed i suoi rapporti con il collezionismo Napoletano", in: *Napoli Nobilissima* series 5/X (2009), pp. 3–20.

Caracciolo, Daniela, "Per una Wunderkammer letteraria, Mergellina, la 'fatica marittima' di Giulio Cesare Capaccio", in: *Annali di critica d'arte* 5 (2009), pp. 33–80.

Egmond, Florike, "Looking Beyond the Margins of Print: Depicting Water Creatures in Europe, c. 1500–1620", in: *Ichthyology in Context (1500–1880),* eds. Paul Smith and Florike Egmond, Leiden/Boston 2024, pp. 147–243.

Egmond, Florike, "On Northern Ahores: Sixteenth-century Observations of Fish and Aeabirds (North Sea and North Atlantic)", in: *Naturalists in the Field. Collecting, recording and preserving the natural world from the fifteenth to the twenty-first century,* ed. Arthur MacGregor, Leiden/Boston 2018, pp. 129–148.

Egmond, Florike and Peter Mason (eds.), *The Whale Book. Whales and other marine animals as described by Adriaen Coenen in 1585,* London 2003.

Egmond, Florike, *Eye for Detail. Images of Plants and Animals in Art and Science, 1500–1630,* London 2017.

Egmond, Florike, *Het Visboek. De Wereld volgens Adriaen Coenen*, Zutphen 2005.
Geirnaert, Noel, "Piscatorial Elements in 16th-Century Literature in Bruges: Fantasy Scenes and Compassionate Eulogies", in: *Ichthyology in Context (1500–1880)*, eds. Paul Smith and Florike Egmond, Leiden/Boston 2024, pp. 325–339.
Hellawell, Philippa, "'The best and most practical philosophers': Seamen and the Authority of Experience in Early Modern Science", in: *History of Science* 58/1 (2020), pp. 28–50.
Klemun, Marianne, "Classification and Experience. Rocks and Taste. 'Vulgar' Reasoning in the Earth Sciences", in: *De Achttiende Eeuw* 48/1–2 (2016), pp. 113–126.
Leitão, Henrique, "Instruments and Artisanal Practices in Long Distance Oceanic Voyages", in: *Centaurus* 60 (2018), pp. 189–202.
Luzzini, Francesco, "Sounding the Depths of Providence: Mineral (Re)generation and Human-Environment Interaction in the Early Modern Period", in: *Earth Sciences History* 39/2 (2020) pp. 389–408.
Spaans, Ronny, "'My Eyes Have Never Yet Beheld Him.' Demythologising Arctic Sea Monsters in the Poetry of the Norwegian Priest and Fish Merchant Petter Dass (1647–1707)", in: *Ichthyology in Context (1500–1880)*, eds. Paul Smith and Florike Egmond, Leiden/Boston 2024, pp. 420–453.
Winter, Wim de, "Southern-Netherlandish Observations and Knowledge Production of *Naturalia* on the Seas: The Writings of Michael de Febure (1721)", in: *Early Modern Low Countries* 3/2 (2019), pp. 265–228.

Who Knows? Fishery Knowledge, Ichthyological Studies, and the Migratory Life of the Rhine Salmon

Barbara Orland

1 Introduction

Since fisheries science and industrial fishery management face a crisis, because they are unable to stop the international declines in fish populations, they react with a growing recognition of the local ecological expertise held by artisanal fisheries. Fishermen become scientifically relevant informants about fish behavior and abundance trends, about individual fish species, their feeding habits, reproductive cycles, and about environmental conditions at spawning sites. Fishery biologists reflect what they call ethnoichthyology and argue that the engagement between local fishermen and scientists may help to improve fishery management.[1] While collaboration is tackled locally, scientific discourse goes even beyond. Scientists started to analyze traditional ecological knowledge and compare it with scientific ways of knowing. 'It should not automatically be assumed that it is the fishers that are wrong, and the scientists are right', one author argues. Discrepancies may simply arise from the complementary character of the two fields of knowledge: 'the former [fishermen] may be based on a long temporal series of observations sometimes transmitted over several generations as traditional knowledge grounded in a local realm, while the second assembles shorter temporal but more systematic observations rarely covering more than 2 or 3 years but seeks generalizations on a broader spatial scale.'[2] The tenor of these publications is that cooperation between ichthyologists and fishermen has only recently been discovered. From a historical point of view, however, it makes you wonder if there has ever been a phase in the systematic study of fish, in which scholars did not depend on fishery. Is it not rather the case that the acquisition and documentation of local knowledge was a fundamental precondition of the growth of

1 Hind divides several waves of fisher's knowledge research: the first and mainly amateurs' approach should have taken place during the early twentieth century; a second wave, the 'ethnographic turn' started around the mid-1970s, 'a movement rebelling against hard quantitative science', the third wave he describes as 'applied social science', while the ongoing fourth wave reinvented quantitative biology depending on fishery data. Edward J. Hind, "A review of the past, the present, and the future of fishers' knowledge research: a challenge to established fisheries science", in: *ICES Journal of Marine Science October* 72 (2014), pp. 341–358.

2 Renato A.M. Silvano, John Valbo-Jorgensen, "Beyond fishermen's tales: contributions of fisher's local ecological knowledge to fish ecology and fisheries management", in: *Environment, Development, Sustainability* 10 (2008), pp. 657–675.

DOI: 10.13173/9783447123693.127

ichthyology? Recent scholarship gives an idea into the centuries-old collaborative relationships between fishery and knowledge production.[3]

My work builds on this recent research. First, I want to know more about the alleged complementarity of both knowledge fields. How do they differ? Because it is reasonable to assume that most fisher families (including those who made their living from deep-sea fishing) lived in local communities, where skills were passed on mainly by observation, manual imitation, and oral tradition, often in a local dialect, I am further interested in the tension between the local and the universal. While reading ichthyological writings about salmonids I confronted them with records from the Upper Rhine valley, between Schaffhausen, Basel, and Strasbourg, a region, where salmon fishing was practiced since earliest times and until the early 20th century, and where people reflected about salmon migration cycles, even if they did not know much about the North Sea and the Dutch Rhine Delta as a habitat for fish.[4] They simply observed that the salmon swam up the Rhine and that it began to spawn at certain places in the main river and its tributaries. Yet how did they explain fish migration? And how far did fishery experiences enter ichthyology?

I will argue that most ichthyologist's publications represent some kind of fishery expertise. Many vernacular expressions were transferred to a scientific nomenclature. This, however, raises the question of authorship. Fishermen and -women (fishery in the Rhine valley was a family business), usually did not belong to the literate high culture. Their knowledge became mainly accessible through texts written by non-fishermen. Where did these authors come from and what motivated them to explore the practices of fishing? None of the authors quoted below were fishermen, yet there is one exception – the book of the Strasbourg fisherman Eduard Baldner from 1666[5], to whom I dedicate an excursus. It should also be mentioned that during the noticeable decline of fishing on the Rhine since the early 20th century, several local historians conducted and documented conversations and interviews with the last fishermen in various villages.

3 See in particular: Pietro Daniel Omodeo, "Hydrogeological Knowledge from below: Water expertise as a Republican common in early-modern Venice", in: *Berichte zur Wissenschaftsgeschichte* 45 (2022), pp. 538–560; Pietro Daniel Omodeo, "The invisible fishermen: The economy of water knowledge in early-modern Venice", in: *Ichthyology in Context (1500–1880)*, eds. Paul J. Smith and Florike Egmond, Leiden/Boston 2023, pp. 364–391; Richard C. Hoffmann, *Fisher's craft and lettered art: tracts on fishing from the end of the Middle Ages*, Toronto 1997.

4 This is mentioned in several historical works on the region's fishing traditions. See e.g.: Daniel Bruckner, *Versuch einer Beschreibung historischer und natürlicher Merkwürdigkeiten der Landschaft Basel*, VI. Stück, Klein Hüningen, Basel 1751, p. 605; Johann Vetter, *Die Schiffart, Flötzerei und Fischerei auf dem Oberrhein (Schaffhausen-Basel) sowie: Geschichte der alten Schiffergesellschaften genannt 'Rhein-Genossenschaft' und, "Laufenknechte"*, Karlsruhe 1864, p. 1; Götz Kuhn, *Die Fischerei am Oberrhein: geschichtliche Entwicklung und gegenwärtiger Stand*, Stuttgart 1976, p. 20.; Max Baumann, *Fischer am Hochrhein: zur Geschichte der Fischerei zwischen Säckingen und Basel*, Aarau 1994, p. 6.

5 Leonhard Baldner, *Vogel-, Fisch- und Thierbuch*, Strassburg 1666, URL: https://orka.bibliothek.uni-kassel.de/viewer/image/1343227732549/1/ (15.08.2024).

Particularly noteworthy is Paul Hugger's ethnographic study of the fishing village of Klein-Hüningen, today a district of the town of Basel.[6] But there is also archive material that has received little attention. I mention a family of fishermen from Basel whose history is inextricably linked with the study of the Rhine salmon. Aside from the fact that this family dominated and modernized the region's salmon fishing industry from 1834 onwards, some of its members stood out for their concrete collaboration with academic scientists.

2 Multiple Terminologies

The vernacular names of the species reflect the peculiarities of the various locations, Albertus Magnus noted in 1260.[7] Consequentially, he did not only report that Pliny the Elder mentioned the salmon in the Rhine or that Hildegard von Bingen knew about the salmon in the Danube. He also introduced the different names he knew, the *Lachs* (*lahsen, asox*) and the *Salm,* with the justification that this fish could be found in different regions and rivers. The salmon is 'better in the Rhine River' than in Aquitania (as Pliny has taught) and 'especially at Cologne' one catches the finest salmon.[8] Whether the salmon undergoes physiological changes or whether the different names refer to distinctive species, played a minor role. Albertus assumed rather the opposite: different rivers offer different living conditions and thus must change the character of the fish

What appears to be linguistic ambiguity from a modern point of view, a confusion that should puzzle observers for centuries, as Peter Coates put it in his history of the salmon[9], in premodern times was no problem but a natural fact. It was generally accepted that no creature on earth has a fixed constitution which does not vary. While some scholars used distinct terms to describe variations of one fish that transforms physically over time, others thought that separate terms designate different fish.[10] Not until the middle of the 16th century, when the famous physician and naturalist Conrad Gessner wrote his almost encyclopedic fish book and tried to bring order to ichthyology the diversity of terms and concepts began to become tiresome. Gessner only accepted the three words *Lachs, Salmen,* and *Sälmling,* which were common in German-speaking Switzerland. Trouts (*Forellen* in German) he described as like salmon, but as a distinct fish. And the *Huch* or *Huchen,* the Danubius salmon, he counted to the trouts. But despite his need for

6 Hugger, Paul, *Kleinhüningen: von der 'Dorfidylle' zum Alltag eines Basler Industriequartiers,* Basel 1984. See also the different works of the local teacher from Lörrach Karl Herbster, e.g. "Salmenwöge am Hochrhein", in: *Mein Heimatland* 18 (1931), pp. 17–19.

7 Albertus Magnus, *De Animalibus libri vigintisex,* Venice 14, p. 243, URL: https://d-nb.info/gnd/118637649 (17.08.2024).

8 Albertus Magnus, *On Animals. A Medieval Summa Zoologica,* eds. Kenneth F. Kitchell and Irven Michael Resnick (2 vols.) Baltimore 1999, vol. 2, book 24, p. 1697.

9 Peter Coates, *Salmon,* London 2006, p. 8.

10 See Marie-Agnès Lucas-Avenel, "Des poissons, des mots et des signes: les signes monastiques des noms de poissons au XIe siècle", in: *Annales de Normandie* 62 (2012), pp. 139–174, here pp. 20, 21.

order, even Gessner could not entirely do without local idiosyncrasies. He created composites that referred to local terminologies. In Gaul, he wrote, the name of the female salmon is *Beccard*. From the German physician Johannes Kentmann he took *Kupferlachs* and *Kupfersalm* for the fish living in the Elbe or spoke of *Salmon Rondeletius* referencing the first anatomical descriptions of the salmon by Guillaume Rondelet.[11]

Gessner's successors in the seventeenth and especially in the eighteenth century achieved only limited success in their collective desire to order. Organizing and classifying remained an activity shaped by personal preferences. Researchers such as John Ray and Francis Willughby, who emphasized the need for a thorough reform of ichthyology and tried to give a clear understanding of the concept of species, did not completely dispense with the previous descriptions. Guided by Gessner and especially by the two ichthyological standard works of the late 16th century, written by Guillaume Rondelet and Pierre Belon, they only added observations made while dissecting fishes during their travels in France, Germany, and Italy (1663–1666).[12] Even the influential taxonomy of the Swedish naturalists Peter Artedi and Carl Linné of the early 18th century brought little new to the salmon terminology.[13] They created the family of salmonids but divided it into ten subspecies. A reduction of the names in circulation was not achieved, as they added categories developed from anatomical or morphological differences, e.g. *salmo albula*, the white salmon, or latinized popular terms. The fish known as *Huchen* in Vienna became *salmo hucho*, and the fish known as *Aesche* in the Upper Rhine became *salmo thymalius*.[14]

In negotiating terminology, the academic authority of the respective authors was decisive. But because standardization takes time, scientific authority can be challenged for long. At the end of the 18th century, it was still not certain that Linné's taxonomy would prevail in ichthyology. Accordingly, local vernacular names were increasingly identified as the real problem of science. In 1780, the German teacher Heinrich Sander complaint that fishermen, sailors, boatmen and market women, with their 'distorted' language, thwarted the laborious work of natural scientists in distinguishing species and determining names. If it is by nature dif-

11 Conrad Gessner, *Historiæ animalivm liber IV.: Qui est de piscium & aquatilium animantium* natura, Francofurti 1604, pp. 824–828.

12 See Sachiko Kusukawa, "Historia piscium (1686) and Its Sources", in: *Virtuoso by Nature: The Scientific Worlds of Francis Willughby FRS (1635–1672)*, ed. Tim Birkhead, Leiden/Boston 2016, pp. 305–334.

13 See Peter Artedi, *Ichthyologia, sive, opera omnia de piscibus*, ed. Carl Linnaeus, Leiden 1738.

14 See as an example of a popularized version of the Artedi/Linné classifications: Georg Heinrich Borowski, *Gemeinnützige Naturgeschichte des Thierreichs: darinn die merkwürdigsten und nützlichsten Thiere in systematischer Ordnung beschrieben und alle Geschlechter in Abbildungen nach der Natur vorgestellet werden*, vol. 5, Berlin 1784, pp. 135–138.

ficult to clearify the differences in external limbs, age, or gender, but the hardest thing of all is to understand the life cycle of fish.[15]

Over the course of two centuries, fish science had undergone some epistemological transformation. No longer regional habitats explained the characteristics of fish, their regular appearance, or their behavior in different locations. Rather the opposite, researchers took physiological, anatomical, and morphological parameters as primary tools for identifying and distinguishing one species from another. Yet because the salmon was, as I said, a fish with many faces, one now had to pay more attention to its migration behavior in relation to its physical constitution. This correlation, however, is a 'complete mystery and a terrible puzzle', as one author put it in the middle of the 19th century. Because of the 'natural difficulties of investigation, or at least of ascertainment', the salmon, more than any other under water creature, has been the subject of 'visionary theories, narrow empiricism, stiff assertions, easy credulity, and obstinate unbelief.'[16] Salmons can be observed by man only vaguely and occasionally during one half of the year, and during the other half it is not only invisible as to its habits, but quite unknown as to its residence. After the fish has left the rivers, 'we are ignorant not only of what he is doing, but of where he has gone.' Sciolism is on the side of science, while 'few half-facts gathered from a merely local experience' is on the side of the 'practical men'.[17]

3 Narrating the Migratory Life of the Salmon

This harsh criticism of ichthyology, combined with the call for more systematically prepared experiments, touched on a subject that was by no means unknown to earlier generations of researchers. By nature, river fishes move quickly from place to place, more so than their counterparts in lakes or the ocean. It took no special scientific training to come up with the idea that the fish's migrations might have something to do with their search for food or reproduction. However, only with the taxonomic enterprises since Gessner they gained greater attention. If taxonomies were to explain more than just classifying and organizing fishes into groups, if they were to serve as a tool for understanding the life cycle of salmon, then they needed to include the description, identification, and nomenclature of the various stages of fish development. Again, in the words of Russell: 'Without some knowledge of how, when, and where the fish breeds, dwells, and feeds, it is unless to speak and unsafe to act.' Did the names that were bandied about for the young fish really correspond to the developmental stages of the salmon, he asked. 'Is the Parr the young of the Salmon in earliest infancy? (…) At what age does the

15 Heinrich Sander, "Beiträge zur Naturgeschichte der Fische im Rhein. Erstes Stük 1780", in: *Kleine Schriften nach dessen Tod herausgegeben*, ed. Georg Friedrich Götz, vol. 1, Dessau/Leipzig 1784, p. 233.

16 Axel Russel, *The Salmon*, Edinburgh 1864, pp. 31–32.

17 Ibid., p. 32.

Smolt emigrate to Salt water? (…) After what length of absence does the emigrant return to fresh water? (…) In what shape does he return, Grilse or Salmon?'[18]

Gessner and his contemporaries had posed the question differently and much more fundamentally. In the middle of the sixteenth century, it was still impossible to say for sure whether the salmon caught between Basel and Schaffhausen was a migratory sea fish, a pure river fish, or a mixture of the two: 'Some people think that the salmon belongs to the fishes that are born in the sea, but when they grow up, they move to the rivers because of the sweet water'.[19] Gessner doubted that the fish were attracted by the fresh water and decided to believe the old fishermen. The fishermen have learned from their own experience that the fish came up from the sea to spawn in the rivers in winter, he declared. Only when the young salmon is strong enough it swims downstream into the sea, like the larger animals. Gessner knew that Rhine fishermen had their own insights about the life and reproduction cycle of the salmon. They reflected it in names and proverbs, some of which have been handed down since the Middle Ages. The names *Salm* and *Lachs* did not refer to different species. They referred to the seasons. Leonhard Baldner noted in 1666 that the salmon began to swim up in the 'Hornung' (February) and came back down in the 'Pfingstmonat' (May/June) and only then were called *Lachs*.[20] Despite their very different appearance, *Lachs* and *Salmen* were not considered to be two different species. In Basel there was a saying: 'They call him *Salmen*, as long as the day increases, *Lachs*, as soon as the day decreases.'[21] When the largest migrating flocks arrived the Upper Rhine from May to July, fishermen started the salmon fishing; fishing for the young they called the catch of *Sälmling*, and *Lachs* fishing took place during and after the spawning season. Here, as elsewhere, different names had been given to the various stages of the fish's development – *St. Jakobssalmen*, *Wintersalmen* or *Laichlachs*.

4 Fishermen as Transmitter of Knowledge

Authors of ichthyological writings needed first-hand knowledge to shed light on the complex behavior of fish. Understanding their life and reproductive cycle could only be done by observing them from the shore. But that was the domain of craftsmen. A good example of the resulting mixture of theory and practice is the 18th century *Natural History of the Fishes of Germany* from Marcus Elieser Bloch, a Berlin physician and correspondent member of several scientific societies.[22] Still at the end of the nineteenth century one of his successors, the zoologist Albert

18 Ibid.

19 Quoted from the German edition: Conrad Gessner, *Fischbuch: Das ist ein kurtze, doch vollkommne beschreybung aller Fischen so in dem Meer und süssen Wasseren, Seen, Flüssen, oder anderen Bächen jr wonung habend, sampt jrer waren conterfactur,* Zürych 1563, p. 375.

20 Baldner, *Vogel-, Fisch- und Thierbuch*, p. 146.

21 Bruckner, *Versuch einer Beschreibung*, p. 634.

22 Marcus Elieser Bloch, *Ökonomische Naturgeschichte der Fische Deutschlands,* 3 Theile, Berlin 1783–1785.

Günther from the British Museum, valued his descriptions 'made from nature' serviceable or even the best existing in literature.[23] Günther alluded to the fact that Bloch›s book was partly based on direct observations taken from the waters around Berlin. Yet in this region salmon was rare. Talking to local fishermen or examining freshly caught fish, as Bloch often did, was not possible.[24] Therefore, Bloch's main insights about salmon derived from the literature available to him. Wherever he mentioned practical knowledge (including phrases and sayings from disparate regions), it had been collected and written down by other authors.

Bloch took disparate sources from northern Europe, America, and Kamchatka, as well as from the countries bordering the Rhine. Summarizing the fishermen's knowledge about migration, he reflected that the salmon is at the transition from a river fish to a sea fish. For since he is born in 'sweet waters' but receives his growth in the sea, both waters have a claim on him. The salmon's strong urge to reproduce is the primary motivator behind its migration from the safety of the sea, where it finds abundant food, to the rivers, where fishermen employ a range of techniques to catch it. Empirical evidence, he told his readers, showed that this migration route extended from the North Sea to Basel. When the ice begins to melt along the coasts in the spring, it drives the salmon upstream. 'He usually comes in the spring with the wind that the fishermen call the Lachs wind.'[25] From February to March, however, the fishermen not only listen to the wind, Bloch goes on to explain. They also pay attention to the sounds of the water: 'The salmon, when swimming, keeps itself in the middle of the river and close to the surface of the water, and since it makes a lot of noise when it swims, one hears it from afar, like a storm; but when the weather is stormy or hot, it goes into the depth, and then one does not notice its passage.'[26] Hence, wind and water, as well as seasonal changes, determine the direction and speed of the migrations.

Bloch often reported observations from the riverbanks of specific regions. For example, he mentioned a group behavior of salmon observed in the Upper Rhine valley. About thirty animals usually swim up the Rhine in pairs and at an appropriate distance from each other. The group is led by the biggest *Rogner* (the popular term for females was *Rogner*, the males were called *Milchner*). Then the larger males follow in pairs, and at the end arrive the smaller males. The fishermen know that once the latter are in the net, the fish run is over. Only if the fish swarm is stopped by an obstruction, such as a waterfall, a log, or the sound of

23 Albert C. L. G. Günther, *An introduction to the Study of Fishes*, Edinburgh 1880, pp. 14, 15.

24 More on Bloch and his methods can be found in: Johannes Müller, "Distance, Geography, and Anecdote in M. E. Bloch's Natural History of Fishes", in: *Ichthyology in Context (1500–1880)*, ed. Paul J. Smith and Florike Egmond, Leiden/Boston 2023, pp. 612–631.

25 ‚Er geht gewöhnlich im Frühjahr mit dem Wind, den die Fischer den Lachswind nennen.' Bloch, *Ökonomische Naturgeschichte*, Theil 1, p. 130.

26 ‚Der Lachs hält sich beim Schwimmen mitten im Strohme und nahe an der Oberfläche des Wassers und da er bei seinem Zuge viel Geräusch macht, so hört man sie, gleich einem Sturme von weitem rauschen; wenn hingegen die Witterung stürmisch oder heiss ist, so geht er in die Tiefe und alsdann wird man nichts von seinem Zuge gewahr.' Ibid., p. 133.

fishing nets, the group briefly lefts the order to seek safety. After overcoming the obstacle, order will be quickly restored. Since the salmon swims just below the surface of the water, they make loud noises that the fishermen pay attention to. Yet in bad weather and stormy winds, they disappear into the depths, much to the chagrin of the fishermen. Because then it happens that a swarm passes by before the fishermen can react.

Another topic in which Bloch drew on the intimate knowledge of fishermen was the resting and spawning grounds of fish. Even though the entire Rhine was fished from its sources in the Alps to its estuary in the Netherlands, there existed areas that offered particularly favorable fishing grounds. These were often the mouths of tributaries into the Rhine. Near Basel, these good conditions were found at the delta of the Wiese, a small river that entered the Rhine nearby some hills formed after the last ice age by debris and gravel deposits of the Feldberg glacier. Because of this obstacle, the Rhine between Basel and Strasbourg had a much stronger fall and a furcation (a strongly branched course).[27] Only near the shore, in the shallow side arms and in the floodplain, the current decreased significantly. While wandering fish have no problem with large currents and fast flowing water, their long migrations are strenuous so that they occasionally need a spot to rest. The salmon 'likes to seek out such waters whose banks are densely overgrown with trees, for it loves the shade and the cold water', Bloch explained.[28] The delta of the Wiese was such a place. Here, all migratory fish (not just salmon but e.g. eel) were able to remain in the shelter of the river's margins without disturbance. As a spawning ground this delta also offered the best food conditions: 'small fish, aquatic insects, and worms.'[29] Bloch reported that between Basel and Strasbourg, not only the one-year-old fish were sold as a delicious delicacy.[30] In springtime, the fish could become particularly fat, a clear difference to the Elbe salmon, which was significantly lower in quality than Rhine salmon. On their way to their spawning grounds, however, the salmon stopped eating leading to a state of emaciation on arrival. Notwithstanding these exertions, every salmon returned to the spawning places on the Rhine, where it was born. The salmon finds the water 'in which it once spawned' as easily as the swallow finds the building in which it had built its nest.[31] Once arrived the large females would use their tail fins to dig burrows in which to lay their eggs. The males then sprayed the eggs

27 Centralbureau für Meteorologie und Hydrographie im Grossherzogtum Baden, *Der Rheinstrom und seine wichtigsten Nebenflüsse von den Quellen bis zum Austritt des Stromes aus dem Deutschen Reich*, Berlin 1889, pp. 60–61.

28 Dagegen vermeidet er ,solche Flüsse, deren Mündungen mit Gebäuden besetzt sind, wie solches die Schweden durch Anlegung neuer Fischerwohnungen zum grössten Schaden der alten Fischerdörfer erfahren haben.' Bloch, *Ökonomische Naturgeschichte*, Erster Theil, p. 134.

29 Ibid.

30 Ibid., p. 139. See also Wilhelm, Gottlieb Tobias, *Unterhaltungen aus der Naturgeschichte*, vol. 10, Augsburg 1800, p. 217.

31 Bloch, *Ökonomische Naturgeschichte*, Erster Theil, p. 131.

with milk.[32] Courted by rival males, it could take weeks for the females to lay all their eggs. The fish larvae hatched, depending on the water temperature, after a few weeks, and then spent up to two years in their home waters. During this time, they didn't just get bigger but also changed their color scheme. The year-old *Sälmling* (parr) got a silvery skin (smolt) before he dropped down the river to the sea.

Most of Bloch's stories and descriptions were taken over from others. Even when he did refer to fishery, it was not first-hand knowledge from local fishermen Bloch had visited. At his time, observations originally made by fishermen had already been written down in some way and circulated among the community of interested naturalists. As historian Johannes Müller put it, Bloch depended on so-called second-order observation, drawn from various sources, and often enriched with anecdotes and stories, 'that circulated in- and outside the world of learning.'[33]

5 Excursus: The Strasburg Fisher Eduard Baldner

As a rule, fishermen did not write about their work and experiences. Authors who collected and disseminated their knowledge about fish behavior thus created visibilities and made available fishing information that would otherwise have remained hidden. It was the absolute exception that a fisherman would put his experience on paper himself. Eduard Baldner, a fisherman from Strasbourg, became famous for writing down his knowledge of fish (birds and other animals) in the Low German-Elsässic language and illustrating it with pictures by well-known Strasbourg painters. Until 1974 this work existed only as a manuscript, of which Baldner had made several copies during his lifetime. Today, a digitized copy can be viewed online at the University Library of Kassel.[34]

Baldner explained in the preface, that the idea to write came to him one day in 1646, when, as a particularly lucky hunt, he brought home some strange birds and took them to a painter. From then on, he spent twenty years of collecting, classifying, describing, and drawing every bird, fish, insect, and worm he could find. The date and place of capture of particularly rare animals are recorded. Only Gessner's writings were familiar to him, all other observations came from his own hunts. This makes the work a unique and reliable inventory of the fauna of the Upper Rhine region, Armin Geus rightly points out.[35]

In the second part of the three-part manuscript, dedicated to fish, Baldner described 45 species of fish and crustaceans. The species are arranged according to their size and economic importance. The salmon is the third most important species after the sturgeon and the Wels. Baldner also mentioned salmon-like fishes and stated that these can be identified by the presence of a small feather located

32 Ibid., p. 633.
33 Müller, "Distance, Geography, and Anecdote", p. 628.
34 See Baldner, *Vogel-, Fisch- und Thierbuch*, s. p.
35 Armin Geus, "Das Vogel-, Fisch- und Tierbuch des Leonhard Baldner, Strasbourg 1666", in: *Deutsches Schiffahrtsarchiv*, 1 (1975), pp. 201–209, here p. 202, URL: https://nbn-resolving.org/urn:nbn:de:0168-ssoar-49593-8 (14.08.2024).

behind the dorsal feather. But he distinguished the species not just according to their external appearance, he also conducted detailed dissections and provided comprehensive measurements and weights. And he permitted himself some criticism of Gessner. The carp evolves from 'Rogen' and 'Laich' and not 'as Mr. Doct. Gessner writes' from feces.[36]

The manuscript was not printed until the early twentieth century.[37] However, some copies were already circulating during Baldner's lifetime. When John Ray and Francis Willughby traveled through Holland, France, Germany, and Italy in the 1660s, they came to Strasbourg to meet Baldner and buy a copy of the manuscript.[38] Later, mainly regional ichthyologists such as the zoologist and physician Carl Theodor Ernst Siebold from Freiburg/Munich used Baldner's work extensively. He had found the manuscript 'to his greatest delight' in the Natural History Cabinet in Strasbourg and had already learned that another copy was in the State Library in Kassel.[39] According to Siebold, in the eighteenth century another Strasbourg naturalist named Reiseisen added the Latin names from Linné to the manuscript.[40] In any case, ichthyological research referred to Baldner's work, and until the nineteenth century he was the only fisherman to be honored as an educated natural scientist.

6 The Entrepreneurial Fisher Family Friedrich Glaser & Sons

While the story of Eduard Baldner epitomizes the classic image of the early modern naturalist, in this final section I mention a family of fishermen who established a completely new form of collaboration between ichthyology and fisheries. There exists no consistent history of the Basel-based Glaser family. However, from 1834 onwards they appear again and again in the files of the State Archives of Basel – files relating to different areas of activity. The Glasers' primary source of income has been derived from fishing, for which they needed an appropriate fishing license. These were contracts, which the fishermen had to sign with the towns and communities for one year at a time. The leaseholders of the banks of the Upper Rhine, the so-called 'fish meadows' (Fischweiden), generally used them by themselves, and in most cases, the entire family was involved in the catch. But the Glaser's over time began to collect and lease out 'fish meadows' contracts. Fellow fishermen became employees and tenants of them. An exemplary contract from 1899 between the Glaser company and a locomotive engineer shows that any kind of short- or long-term contract with laymen was practiced

36 Baldner, *Vogel-, Fisch- und Thierbuch*, s.p.

37 1903 published Robert Lauterborn the text without illustrations. See Robert Lauterborn, *Das Vogel, Fisch- und Thierbuch des Strassburger Fischers Leonhard Baldner aus dem Jahre 1666*, Ludwigshafen 1903.

38 Geus, "Das Vogel-, Fisch- und Tierbuch", p. 203.

39 Carl Theodor Ernst von Siebold, *Die Süsswasserfische von Mitteleuropa*, Leipzig 1863, pp. 33–35.

40 Ibid, p. 33.

and not aligned with the annual cycle of public licenses.[41] By 1912, the Glaser's dominance in the Upper Rhine fisheries had grown to such an extent that their attempt to become the sole leaseholder of the entire Rhine in the city of Basel met with resistance from the police. The police department feared that the company would abuse his monopoly position and lead to overfishing.[42]

The leasing of additional fishing licenses resulted in significant additional revenue, so that other businesses besides commercial fishing provided new sources of income for the family. The Glasers ran a profitable store in the city of Basel that sold fish, deer meat, and other delicacies. Friedrich Glaser Jr. in 1892 explained that trading fish was a beneficiary of modern transportation technology. First, the railroads had made it possible to bring even frozen fish from Siberia and America to Basel. Then, the ocean steamships led to an impressive increase in the consumption of fresh sea fish. What was once only available to the wealthy class at the turn of the 20th century had become a staple food.[43] The Glasers benefited in all cases, and with prosperity the family was able to enhance its reputation. Friedrich Glaser Sr. was a member of the Fisherman's Guild, he earned the title of Fish Master and held honorary positions within the Guild. His son, Friedrich Glaser Jr., increasingly engaged with the wider public. One clever marketing strategy was the publication of a fish cookery book, given away or sold to customers. This brochure that advertised the Glaser fishmonger's shop, and, at the end of the booklet, published all the certificates and prizes that the company had received on various occasions since 1858, had its fifth edition in 1892.

But the Glaser family not only produced fishermen, fishmongers, delicatessen merchants, cookery book authors and guild masters. In 1852 Friedrich Glaser Sr. became a scientific assistant of the first French egg hatching institute. Named *Imperial piscifactoire* (Imperial fish factory) this institute 1852 was situated in the floodplain of the Rhine River North of Basel and near the small town Huningue in the Alsace region of France.[44] Altogether, this was a highly sophisticated hydrological system with several buildings and much technical equipment, among others fifteen distinct fishpond types, fifteen water channel types, and six water basin types. The founding director was Victor Coste, a professor of embryology at the College de France in Paris. He used this building for his scientific studies and experiments.[45] The French Ministry of Agriculture and Napoleon III., who

41 StABS, Fischerei-Acten B1, Rheinfischerei, Allgemeines und Einzelnes.

42 Ibid.

43 Friedr. Glaser Sohn, *Kochbuch*, Selbstverlag o.J. (1892), p. 3.

44 See Victor Coste, *Die neuesten und wichtigen Verbesserungen in der Fischzucht, oder: Praktische Anleitung, durch künstliche Befruchtung des Fischrogens alle fliessenden und stehenden Gewässer auf leichte und wohlfeile Weise mit Fischen jeder Gattung sehr zahlreich zu besetzen*, Quedlinburg/ Leipzig 1853, pp. 65–72.

45 A few years later Coste also founded the *Station marine et biologique de Concarneau* in Bretagne, and, in 1860, he was elected the French General inspector for ocean and river fishing in France.

approved a start capital of 30000 francs, supported Coste's idea that science and technology are ripe to improve the nature of fish breeding.

The institute became Europe's first and for a long-time greatest breeding facility and artificial fish farming industry. Figures were circulated that promised breathtakingly high success rates. Huningue was said to have produced millions of fish for European waters in a very short time. The reality was somewhat different. Records do not show high yields. In fact, absolute figures were rarely given. The most revealing tables are those showing the losses in relation to the different stages of development of the fish.[46] If there was any success at all, it was in the production of fertilized eggs and the first stages of fish development, a success that would not have been possible without direct cooperation with the local fishermen. Although Huningue insisted that the method used had been invented by two fishermen from the Vosges, it depended first and foremost on the support of Friedrich Glaser Sr., who organized the delivery of large quantities of already fertilized eggs and taught the institute's technical staff how to extract eggs and sperm from the spawning animals. Together with his fellow fishermen he collected the sensitive goods in the surrounding areas of Basel and transported them in less than 24 hours safely to Huningue. In 1858, he was awarded a medal by France for this special support.

7 The Glaser-Miescher Collaboration

The year-long collaboration between his son, Friedrich Glaser Jr., and Friedrich Miescher, a renowned natural scientist and professor of physiology proved to be of even greater relevance to science. For the first time, the migrations of the Rhine salmon were systematically investigated. Today, Miescher is mainly known for his isolation of nucleic acid in 1869, which paved the way for the later identification of DNA. Yet shortly after this work, after he got his habilitation at the University of Basle and became professor of physiological chemistry in 1871/72, he started yearlong research about the salmon, mainly because the male's sperm of the salmon contained a particularly high amount of nucleic acid. His uncle, the well-known Basel anatomist and embryologist Wilhelm His, who himself studied fish eggs and the development of fish embryos, and – thanks to the support of Friedrich Glaser – was able to analyze the eggs within the ovarium of the salmon, brought Miescher in contact with Glaser.[47] According to His, without Glaser the researchers would not have been able to get the resources they needed.

46 *Notice historique sur l'établissment de pisciculture de Huningue…*, ed. Ministère des travaux publics. Direction générale des ponts et chaussées et des chemins de fer, Strasbourg 1862, pp. 71–79.

47 Wilhelm His, 'F. Miescher', in: *Die histochemischen und physiologischen Arbeiten von Friedrich Miescher, gesammelt und herausgegeben von seinen Freunden*, vol. 1, Leipzig 1897, p. 13.

Miescher's collaboration with the fisherman began in 1871, when Glaser supplied him with salmon sperm fluid in large quantities.[48] After he had undertaken several chemical analyses of the sperm, Miescher came out with a first version of his fertilization theory in 1874, arguing that from a chemical point of view there does not exist a particular fertilization material. Fertilization could only be the result of a higher influence. From a physiological perspective, however, his primary interest was in metabolism. In particular, he sought to examine the already mentioned characteristic of the salmon, according to which the fish lacked any dietary intake throughout its journeys. A comparison of fish from the Lower and Upper Rhine suggested that the salmon started its journey as a well-fed animal with underdeveloped sex glands. During its monthlong migration from the sea into the Rhine, the fish developed its sex glands, testes, and ovaries. At the outset of the spawning season, the female's ovaries reached approximately a quarter of her total body weight. However, by the conclusion of the season, the fish had once again become emaciated.

To study this phenomenon, Miescher and Glaser collected thousands of salmons over the years. From 1874/75 onwards they measured and weighed their musculature and organs, further examined the mammary glands histologically and chemically at various stages of development. In the notes to these salmon studies, which are preserved in Miescher's papers in the University library of Basel, there are numerous references to Glaser's participation. Comments such as '… according to Mrs. Glaser' show that even Glaser's wife occasionally was involved.[49] In 1880 an eighty pages paper was published that beside Friedrich Miescher as the main author mentions Friedrich Glaser as supporting author. Moreover, the content very clearly considered not just scientific results of Miescher's laboratory studies but drew upon the commercial records of the Glaser company and statistical data provided by Dutch fishers and merchants. As Miescher notes in his writings, Glaser supported him with a wealth of valuable insights and observations pertaining to the living conditions of the Rhine salmon and several unusual occurrences that he had observed.[50] He further acknowledged that although he was the primary author of the text, Glaser verified every section that reflected his observations as the major owner of the salmon fishery between Laufenburg and Basel. This enabled the two authors to present a comprehensive report on the salmon caught in the Rhine, including average weights and catch rates for each month, or annual figures that gave an impression of the large seasonal fluctuations. Miescher and Glaser were thus able to statistically prove

48 See "Das Leben des Rheinlachses Manuskripte, Notizen, Tabellen und Materialien", in: Nachlass Friedrich Miescher II (1844–1895), UB Basel, UBH NL 47.

49 See "Manuskript 20. Oktober 1881", UB Basel, UBH NL 47:9:1.

50 See Friedrich Miescher (unter Mitarbeit von Friedrich Glaser), "Statistische und biologische Beiträge zur Kenntnis vom Leben des Rheinlachses im Süsswasser", in: *Die histochemischen und physiologischen Arbeiten von Friedrich Miescher, gesammelt und herausgegeben von seinen Freunden*, vol. 2, Leipzig 1897, pp. 116–191, here p. 117.

what had been a complaint of Upper Rhine fishermen for centuries. By comparing catch rates on the Dutch and Swiss parts of the Rhine, the authors explicitly attributed the extinction of the salmon to the actions of Dutch fishermen. Most of the total catch at the Upper Rhine was obtained during the spawning months of November and December, representing approximately 20% of the total catch. Yet among 100 juvenile salmon captured in the Netherlands, 5 to 6 individuals from the Upper Rhine population were unable to reproduce. In absolute terms, the catch quotas achieved in the Dutch section of the Rhine were markedly disparate from those observed in Switzerland. In 1878, the ratio was 10 to 1.[51]

By combining statistics, measurements, occasional observations, microscopic and chemical analyses, the two authors attempted to write a life history of the Rhine salmon. They presented an impressive synthesis of empirical observations, biological insights, and statistical analyses, offering new hypotheses to unanswered questions about phenomena that have been previously described as 'mysterious.' One such phenomenon was the observation that animals with enlarged bodies and underdeveloped reproductive organs are consistently captured during the winter breeding season. It is evident, they concluded, that multiple migrations are occurring concurrently. Additionally, it is plausible that the salmon does not consistently migrate, but rather remains in a single location for an extended period and beyond the spawning season.

> I am therefore of the opinion, for which I will provide further evidence, that our winter salmon, which arrive in Basel from November to March, also remain in our area throughout the summer and autumn, and that they gradually reach sexual maturity together with the larger flocks of later immigrants arriving from May onwards, and then spawn with them from mid-November to mid-December.[52]

Miescher and Glaser proceeded to address the other long-standing question at what age salmon first begin to migrate and spawn. It is noteworthy that both sexes exhibit a striking absence of certain sizes in the vicinity of Basel, Miescher explained, a clear proof of the fact 'that not a single salmon actually grows up in the Rhine.' Once the juvenile fish have reached a sufficient size, they undertake their first migration, swimming down the Rhine into the North Sea. This occurs approximately one year after they are born. They remain in the North Sea for two to three years, attaining a weight of 3 kg, until they migrate for the first time to spawn. Another migration takes place after 4–5 years when they weigh

51 Ibid., pp. 120–122.

52 'Ich bin somit der Ansicht, für welche ich noch weitere Beweise beibringen werde, dass unsere vom November bis März in Basel anlangenden Wintersalmen auch durch den ganzen Sommer und Herbst in unserer Gegend bleiben und dass sie gemeinsam mit den vom Mai an heraufkommenden grösseren Schaaren späterer Einwanderer allmählich die Geschlechtsreife erreichen, um dann mit ihnen von Mitte November bis Mitte December zu laichen.' Ibid., pp. 129–130.

about 6–13 kg.[53] Yet it must be a matter for investigation by Dutch researchers as to whether this migration is occurring because of the food situation in the North Sea.

8 Conclusion

Longstanding vernacular names and practices regarding the existence of certain animals, their physical characteristics and behavior, and their utility for human nutrition or medicine have been an important source of information for ichthyological writers. The older ichthyology also adopted the ancient view that the differences and parallels between animal species were a manifestation of their respective habitats, and that the environment was also responsible for their migratory behavior. Some authors postulated that the quality of the waters was a primary driver of these movements, while others proposed that the spawning grounds were the most crucial factor. As long as there was no intention to define unique markups, all theories could coexist. However, when naturalists of the early modern period changed their empirical orientation and began to seek clear anatomical and physiological characteristics to collect, organize, and classify animal species, they quickly reached the limits of the available knowledge. Although it was possible to describe the animals objectively, it proved to be difficult to explain their migratory behavior. Dissections, which could easily be carried out on fish bought at the market, were not enough to understand migration processes. One either had to go to the banks of the rivers or rely on the observations told by fishermen. To my opinion, the writers of the early modern period took every piece of information they could get. Their main goal was to organize the existing expertise in the best and most efficient way possible. Ichthyological writings thus were a mixture of textbook-knowledge with deep historical roots, second-order observation, drawn from various sources, and anecdotes and stories told by local fisher. Despite these efforts, studying the migratory behavior of salmon remained a complicated subject.

Until the time of the Miescher-Glaser collaboration in the 1870s, there had been no similarly sophisticated study of salmon migration. No one before or since has combined the artisanal and practical knowledge of fishermen with the laboratory work of a biologist in such a detailed and thoughtful way. Zoologists and ichthyologists in the decades that followed have repeatedly emphasized that these results were unique and would shape the knowledge about salmon for a long time to come.[54] But while Miescher's publications were considered fundamental works on salmon, the Glaser name slowly faded from the scene and sooner or later was forgotten. This cannot necessarily be interpreted as ignorance towards the fisherman. In my opinion, it expresses a further change in ichthyological research and writing methods. Miescher worked in a transition phase. At the turn

53 Ibid., p. 156.

54 See e.g. Friedrich Zschokke, *Der Lachs und seine Wanderungen*, Stuttgart 1905. Most of it is a summary of the work of Miescher and Glaser.

of the 20th century, academic ichthyology underwent a period of expansion and professionalization, marked by the establishment of more professorships and research institutes. The advancement of scientific standards and the introduction of novel research techniques and measurement technologies prompted a shift in the field of fishery science away from the shore. Seen in this light, the rediscovery of fisheries expertise and the renewed interest in collaboration between scientists and fishermen is simply another stage in the evolution of a relationship that has been a dynamic process throughout its history.

Reference Lists

Archival Sources

Library of the University of Basel

"Das Leben des Rheinlachses Manuskripte, Notizen, Tabellen und Materialien", in: Nachlass Friedrich Miescher II (1844–1895), UBH NL 47.

"Manuskript 20. Oktober 1881", UBH NL 47:9:1.

Staatsarchiv Basel-Stadt

StABS, Fischerei-Acten B1, Rheinfischerei, Allgemeines und Einzelnes

Printed sources

Baldner, Leonhard, *Vogel-, Fisch- und Thierbuch*, Strassburg 1666, URL: https://orka.bibliothek.uni-kassel.de/viewer/image/1343227732549/1/ (15.08.2024).

Bloch, Marcus Elieser, *Ökonomische Naturgeschichte der Fische Deutschlands*, 3 vols. Berlin 1783–1785.

Borowski, Georg Heinrich, *Gemeinnützige Naturgeschichte des Thierreichs: Darinn die merkwürdigsten und nützlichsten Thiere in systematischer Ordnung beschrieben und alle Geschlechter in Abbildungen nach der Natur vorgestellet werden*, vol. 5, Berlin 1784.

Bruckner, Daniel, *Versuch einer Beschreibung historischer und natürlicher Merkwürdigkeiten der Landschaft Basel, VI. Stück, Klein Hüningen*, Basel 1751.

Centralbureau für Meteorologie und Hydrographie im Grossherzogtum Baden, *Der Rheinstrom und seine wichtigsten Nebenflüsse von den Quellen bis zum Austritt des Stromes aus dem Deutschen Reich*, Berlin 1889.

Coste, Victor, *Die neuesten und wichtigen Verbesserungen in der Fischzucht, oder: Praktische Anleitung, durch künstliche Befruchtung des Fischrogens alle fliessenden und stehenden Gewässer auf leichte und wohlfeile Weise mit Fischen jeder Gattung sehr zahlreich zu besetzen*, Quedlinburg/Leipzig 1853.

Gessner, Conrad, *Historiæ animalium liber IV: Qui est de piscium & aquatilium animantium natura*, Francofurti 1604.

Gessner, Conrad, *Fischbuch: Das ist ein kurtze, doch vollkommne beschreybung aller Fischen so in dem Meer und süssen Wasseren, Seen, Flüssen, oder anderen Bächen jr wonung habend, sampt jrer waren conterfactur*, Zürych 1563.

Glaser Sohn, Friedrich, *Kochbuch*, Selbstverlag 1892.

Günther, Albert C.L.G., *An Introduction to the Study of Fishes*, Edinburgh 1880.

Herbster, Karl, "Salmenwöge am Hochrhein", in: *Mein Heimatland* 18 (1931), pp. 17–19.

His, Wilhelm, 'F. Miescher', in: *Die histochemischen und physiologischen Arbeiten von Friedrich Miescher, gesammelt und herausgegeben von seinen Freunden*, vol. 1, Leipzig 1897
Lauterborn, Robert, *Das Vogel, Fisch- und Thierbuch des Strassburger Fischers Leonhard Baldner aus dem Jahre 1666*, Ludwigshafen 1903.
Magnus, Albertus, *De Animalibus libri vigintisex*, Venice 1495.
Magnus, Albertus, *On Animals: A Medieval Summa Zoologica*, eds. Kenneth F. Kitchell and Irven Michael Resnick, vol. 2, Baltimore 1999.
Miescher, Friedrich (unter Mitarbeit von Friedrich Glaser), „Statistische und biologische Beiträge zur Kenntnis vom Leben des Rheinlachses im Süsswasser", in: *Die histochemischen und physiologischen Arbeiten von Friedrich Miescher, gesammelt und herausgegeben von seinen Freunden*, vol. 2, Leipzig 1897.
Ministère des travaux publics, Direction générale des ponts et chaussées et des chemins de fer (eds.), *Notice historique sur l´établissment de pisciculture de Huningue …*, Strasbourg 1862.
Russel, Axel, *The Salmon*, Edinburgh 1864.
Sander, Heinrich, "Beiträge zur Naturgeschichte der Fische im Rhein, Erstes Stück 1780", in: *Kleine Schriften nach dessen Tod herausgegeben*, ed. Georg Friedrich Götz, vol. 1, Dessau/Leipzig 1784.
Siebold, Carl Theodor Ernst von, *Die Süsswasserfische von Mitteleuropa*, Leipzig 1863.
Vetter, Johann, *Die Schiffart, Flötzerei und Fischerei auf dem Oberrhein (Schaffhausen-Basel) sowie: Geschichte der alten Schiffergesellschaften genannt 'Rhein-Genossenschaft' und, "Laufenknechte"*, Karlsruhe 1864.
Wilhelm, Gottlieb Tobias, *Unterhaltungen aus der Naturgeschichte*, vol. 10, Augsburg 1800.
Zschokke, Friedrich, *Der Lachs und seine Wanderungen*, Stuttgart 1905.

Research Literature

Baumann, Max, *Fischer am Hochrhein: Zur Geschichte der Fischerei zwischen Säckingen und Basel*, Aarau 1994.
Coates, Peter, *Salmon*, London 2006.
Geus, Armin, "Das Vogel-, Fisch- und Tierbuch des Leonhard Baldner, Strasbourg 1666", in: *Deutsches Schiffahrtsarchiv* 1 (1975), pp. 201–209, URL: https://nbn-resolving.org/urn:nbn:de:0168-ssoar-49593-8 (14.08.2024).
Hind, Edward J, "A Review of the Past, the Present, and the Future of Fishers' Knowledge Research: A Challenge to Established Fisheries Science", in: *ICES Journal of Marine Science* 72 (2014), pp. 341–358.
Hoffmann, Richard C, *Fisher's Craft and Lettered Art: Tracts on Fishing from the End of the Middle Ages*, Toronto 1997.
Hugger, Paul, *Kleinhüningen: Von der 'Dorfidylle' zum Alltag eines Basler Industriequartiers*, Basel 1984.
Kuhn, Götz, *Die Fischerei am Oberrhein: Geschichtliche Entwicklung und gegenwärtiger Stand*, Stuttgart 1976.
Lucas-Avenel, Marie-Agnès, "Des poissons, des mots et des signes: Les signes monastiques des noms de poissons au XIe siècle", in: *Annales de Normandie* 62 (2012), pp. 139–174.

Müller, Johannes, "Distance, Geography, and Anecdote in M.E. Bloch's Natural History of Fishes", in: *Ichthyology in Context (1500–1880)*, eds. Paul J. Smith and Florike Egmond, Leiden/Boston 2023, pp. 612–631.

Omodeo, Pietro Daniel, "Hydrogeological Knowledge from Below: Water Expertise as a Republican Common in Early-Modern Venice", in: *Berichte zur Wissenschaftsgeschichte* 45 (2022), pp. 538–560.

Omodeo, Pietro Daniel, "The Invisible Fishermen: The Economy of Water Knowledge in Early-Modern Venice", in: *Ichthyology in Context (1500–1880)*, eds. Paul J. Smith and Florike Egmond, Leiden/Boston, 2023, pp. 364–391.

Silvano, Renato A. M. and John Valbo-Jorgensen, "Beyond Fishermen's Tales: Contributions of Fisher's Local Ecological Knowledge to Fish Ecology and Fisheries Management", in: *Environment, Development, Sustainability* 10 (2008), pp. 657–675.

Weaving Nets and Networks: Le Masson du Parc's Strategies for a Project on Fisheries

Aina Trias Verbeeck

1 Introduction

The research leading to this topic began with the reconstruction of the production context of a manuscript on fisheries written in Barcelona in 1722 by the naturalist Joan Salvador i Riera (Barcelona, 1683–1726). During the archival consultations on this subject, lesser-known documentation related to the manuscript and its French counterpart was identified. The present study arose from analysing those documents and aims to provide a clearer understanding of the actors responsible for collecting and transmitting practical knowledge about the sea and its resources and how this knowledge was organized within academic institutions and state administrations in early 18th-century France.

This research traces the relationships between bureaucratic and naturalist agents involved in the construction of knowledge about the sea and its resources. This approach aligns with Foucault's concept of *gouvernementalité*, as echoed by researchers like Laboulais.[1] It reflects the tension between overlapping and coexisting information collection processes within both administrative and scholarly environments, which were responding to changes in governmental logistics. Also, Darnton's thorough study of publication practices in the Enlightenment supports this reference framework.[2] Further, researchers such as Perrot and Bourguet have worked extensively on the formal dynamics of information gathering, widely studying questionnaires, notebooks and their methodologies.[3] It is remarkable how they established the principle of an omnipresent desire for knowledge, which drove and increased the collection of objects and data. I will explore how, in France, this was rooted in the personality and vision of Jean-Baptiste Colbert, who was determined to promote the Sciences in order to assess

1 This and similar ideas are explored in the volume edited by Lothar Schilling and Jakob Vogel (eds.), *Transnational Cultures of Expertise: Circulating State-Related Knowledge in the 18th and 19th centuries*, Berlin/Boston 2019.

2 Robert Darnton, *The Business of Enlightenment: A Publishing History of the Encyclopédie, 1775–1800*, Cambridge, MA 1979.

3 Marie-Noëlle Bourget, *Déchiffrer la France. La statistique départementale à l'époque napoléonienne*, Paris 1988 and 2001. Jean-Claude Perrot, *L'âge d'or de la statistique régionale française (an IV–1804)*, Paris 1977.

DOI: 10.13173/9783447123693.145

the nation's resources and legislate accordingly.[4] These investigations serve as a framework for the current case study and reflect upon the origins, continuities and discontinuities of such practices, even questioning their linearity. The time frame of my case study may be the main difference from these previous works, being centred on the second half of the 18th century and later. I will follow the actors involved and their connections. Information gathering is a necessity for survival and one logical, recurrent means of collecting information has been to ask for it from an array of interlocutors, followed by different ways of organizing the resulting data, from *Dioscorides* to 21th-century citizen science.[5]

Trends in early modern thought and practices in the 16th and 17th century contributed to the genesis of the modern state configuration and of theories for its ideological support, based on various authors from Machiavelli to Hobbes, including Bodin, Mariana and Botero. The need to find ways to increase power and wealth implied ways of generating knowledge and policies and of assessing resources. Those objectives would develop hand in hand with the deployment of scientific interests, pushing disciplinary boundaries and laying the groundwork for a more accurate and organized science in the Illustrated era. While content and methods changed over time, this did not necessarily happen in a linear, progressive or cumulative advance. The present study draws on the early 18th-century materials described here to open up questions about continuities and discontinuities in the methodologies. Organizational trials based on them were reused and reformulated according to specific needs, interests and circumstances.

In this chapter, François Le Masson du Parc (Douai, 1671–Paris, 1741) is presented along with the multiple layers that shaped his life, activity and output between 1717 and 1722.

From a historiographical point of view, part of this research has been based on the interstices of the archives: the documents found and their connections make visible the greater part of the knowledge production ecosystem – what it took to launch a publication project. Although the project of Le Masson du Parc on which I am working was never published, yet it contributed to broadening knowledge, combining and applying developments that brought together scientific and administrative interests in managing the marine environment in the first decades of the 18th century. Further, a description is provided of the sources consulted, of various natures, offering a better understanding of the methodologies used to collect and transfer data. This has been possible after analysing a wide range of related bibliographies and different sources located in the Paris and Barcelona

4 On Colbert and his administration: Jacob Soll, *The information master: Jean-Baptiste Colbert's secret state intelligence system*, Ann Arbor 2010; and: Lewis Wade, *Privilege, economy and state in Old Regime France: Marine insurance, war and the Atlantic Empire under Louis XIV*, Woodbridge 2023.

5 Aina Trias-Verbeeck, "Bajo el mar: fauna y flora marinas en los Dioscórides renacentistas", in: *Dioscórides ante el mundo: Usos plurales de un ‚libro-laboratorio' en la Edad moderna*, eds. Elisa Andretta and José Pardo-Tomás, Madrid 2024.

archives. It constitutes a very concrete case study that allows a probably partial but nonetheless accurate reconstruction of circumstances, connections and events to give a glimpse into the complex network of *oikonomiai* of knowledge in which the sea had a unifying role.[6]

2 François Le Masson du Parc, a Naval Career

Le Masson du Parc is known for his reports on fisheries along the French coasts following his appointment as Navy Inspector in 1726. However, comparatively little has been explained about his fisheries project in other geographical areas. His envisioned history of fisheries, *Histoire des pêches*,[7] was never published, but, from the documentation examined, it seems the six volumes were at an advanced or final stage, with some even in printing-proof form. The original manuscripts may still exist, scattered across various locations or private collections.[8]

Based on data gathered from the records of the Archives Nationales, the *Histoire des pêches* between 1714 and 1722 consisted of six volumes, each dedicated to a different aspect of fisheries: *Pêches hors d'Europe*; Pêches d'Europe hors du Canal; *Grandes pêches du Canal; Les petites pêches des grèves et des roches, et embouchures des rivières; Coquillages, varech, vers infestant les vaisseaux*; and *Oiseaux de mer*.

The significant amount of documentation generated by Le Masson du Parc and his collaborators, although left incomplete, has been recognized as providing the foundation for Duhamel du Monceau's celebrated *Traité général des pêches et histoire des poissons* (1769–1782). Political, economic or personal interests may have played a role in preventing the original texts from being published, and the

6 This article develops some of the results of my doctoral thesis *The sea in a cabinet. The fishing manuscript of Joan Salvador, 1722: contexts of production and reception*, supervised by José Pardo-Tomás, which was defended at CSIC-IMF/Universitat Autònoma de Barcelona in September 2024. The research has been done as part of the project IberMatMed, *Saberes de las dos Indias. La materia medica en el mundo colonial ibérico, ss. XVI–XVII* (PID2019-106449GB-100), and with the support of the Marie Sklodowska-Curie, Grant Agreement 101007579 SciCoMove: *Scientific Collections on the Move*.

7 The original title would have been "Histoire des pesches" according to archival notes and correspondence.

8 The archive of Le Masson du Parc was acquired by Duhamel du Monceau. These documents were deposited at the *Château de Denainvillers*, where they remained until the end of the First World War. The documentation began to be sold in 1932. A considerable part of this called *Fonds Denainvillers* was recovered and is preserved in the French national archives (AN), series *Archives Personals* (AP) of the Du Monceau brothers: AN 127AP. The rest of the *Fonds* documents, not necessarily including further material from Le Masson du Parc, are to be found in libraries and archives in Bordeaux and Lyon, in France, and the Houghton Library, Harvard University, in the United States. These locations are confirmed in Martine Jaoul and Madeleine Pinault, "The Collection 'Description of Arts and Métiers': Study of Unpublished Sources at the Houghton Library Université Harvard", in: *Ethnologie Française* 12/4 (1982), pp. 335–360. Some of Le Masson du Parc's works ended up in private hands, or remained with the entities with which he worked. To date, three originals have been located, which need further investigation: one on marine birds (private collection), one on algae and sea grasses (*MNHN*) and one on echinodermata (*Académie des Sciences*).

materials became dispersed due to discontinuities in transmission and conservation. This fragmentation of the legacy is likely what led to it being regarded as almost anecdotal.

Today, his contributions are recognized primarily for his role as a fisheries inspector in France, without much attention being given to his extensive career and contributions to maritime knowledge in the early 18th century. Although data on his life are limited, studies by André Zysberg and Dennis Lieppe, particularly regarding several of his *procès-verbaux*, provide insight into his biography. Furthermore, research by Romain Grancher hints at Le Masson du Parc's early environmental concerns or, at least, questionings, in the early 18th century.[9]

Born in Douai, northern France, on 3 September 1671, François Le Masson du Parc was the first-born son of Louis Le Masson, captain of the Royal Regiment of Ships, and Anne-Elisabeth Ruffin. François had two sisters, Pétronille and Marie-Catherine. He lost his mother at the age of seven and a half and was orphaned just before his twelfth birthday when his father died in June 1683.[10] Clearly, he was born into a well-off provincial bourgeois family, and his solid intellectual formation may partially explain his ambitions and the quality of his career development.

To date, there is no information about him until the age of 25, when a marriage certificate dated 27 December 1696 places him in Rouen. He had a daughter and was widowed before 1708, the year when a second marriage record appears in Le Havre. His second wife was Marie Dassier, daughter of Jules-César Dassier d'Adinville, originally from Paris. This marriage likely played a role in shaping his professional circles, as Dassier's connections and those of other Navy figures likely influenced Le Masson du Parc's naval career.

Le Masson du Parc entered the naval service as an écrivain extraordinaire at Le Havre in August 1703 and was appointed écrivain ordinaire in June 1716. This aligns with correspondence from the Navy archives dated 27 August 1716, which explains that he had been working at the admiralty in Dieppe under the orders of M. Le Brun since at least 1707. Claude Jacques Le Brun, who had recruited Le Masson, was a Navy official who eventually appointed him as his private employee, paid from his own funds.

By 1714, Le Masson held a position as a coast guard, but these positions were abolished in 1716, adding to his professional instability. Through his own initiatives and the support of several officers, he officially obtained a position in

9 André Zysberg, "Le Masson du Parc Inspecte la Côte du Bessin en Juillet 1724", in: *Cahier des Annales de Normandie* 35 (2009), pp. 211–225. Dennis Lieppe. "Étude d'introduction", in: *Pêches & pêcheurs du domaine maritime aquitain au XVIIIe siècle: Amirautés de Bayonne & de Bordeaux: Procès-Verbaux des visites faites par ordre du Roy concernant la pesche en mer (1727)*, eds. Dennis Lieppe et al., Camiac-et-Saint-Denis 2004. And Romain Grancher, "Gouverner les ressources de la mer. Une histoire environnementale de l'inspection des pêches françaises au XVIIIe siècle", in: *Cahiers d'histoire* 36/1 (2018), pp. 45–68.

10 According to the documentary reconstruction by Lieppe and the several archives he consulted, in Lieppe, "Étude", pp. 5–6.

Dieppe in 1717.[11] During this period, his administrative duties brought him into close contact with local fishermen and their concerns. His interest in fisheries expanded beyond administration, aligning with practices in natural history and integrating a wide range of knowledge and experiences. Records suggest he maintained regular communication with the *Conseil de Marine*,[12] reporting on various fisheries-related issues, including a perceived scarcity in Normandy. For instance, in 1715, while serving as Le Brun's replacement, he addressed the problems in the herring fishery and delivered a report.[13] In 1717, he submitted a mémoire to the Council detailing fisheries in Dieppe and the surrounding regions, as well as one on oyster fishing and conservation.[14] These reports, supported by Le Brun's recommendations, likely contributed to his appointment in June 1717.

The reports demonstrate his growing expertise on fisheries. Whether he undertook these efforts on his own initiative or in response to external requests remains unclear, but he prepared and signed them in his own name. His ambitious project was clearly influenced by the broader national agenda: to write a comprehensive history of fisheries in France and abroad, addressing the practical needs of those involved in these activities.

Le Masson sought to reconcile two positions: the Colbertian technocratic vision that aimed to regulate the sea's resources, and the practical needs he observed in the field. His goal was to socialize and transmit maritime knowledge through coherent regulations and to effectively manage conflicts and resources.

In March 1722, he wrote proactively to the *Conseil de Marine*, setting out how, after several years of work, the sections of his history concerning the French coasts along the English Channel were ready for publication. He included proofs from the printing press and sought approval and funding from the Navy, stating that the work was prepared to be presented to the public under the patronage of HSH *Monseigneur l'Amiral*.[15] The letter, thus, reveals that at the beginning of 1722 several volumes were ready and in the phase of launching the first printing proofs and awaiting their approval and financing from the Navy or another government body.

---

11 The record is kept in the municipal archives of Le Havre, Lieppe, "Étude", p. 13.

12 The *Conseil de Marine* was part of the *polysynodie*, a governance system introduced by the Regent, Philippe d'Orléans, in 1715. It took over the duties of the *Secrétaire d'État de la Marine*, keeping the organization and staff of the former office while sharing some responsibilities with other councils. The *Conseil de Marine* was dissolved in 1723 when King Louis XV reached his majority and the traditional system was restored. The position of *Secrétaire d'État de la Marine* was reinstated, briefly held by Joseph Fleuriau de Morville, and occupied by Jean-Frédéric Phélypeaux, comte de Maurepas, until 1749.

13 AN MAR/B3 234, f. 444.

14 AN MAR/B3 242, f. 35.

15 'qu'après avoir travaillé pendant plusieurs années à l'histoire des pêches, celles qui concernent les côtes de France dans la Manche sont actuellement sous presse pour être données au public sous la protection de S.A.S Monseigneur l'Amiral et qu'on se propose d'exécuter suivant les épreuves cijointes.' AN 127 AP1.

This meticulous project, combined with Le Masson du Parc's connections to high-ranking officials and the strong reputation he built, led to a royal commission in 1723 to investigate fisheries along the coasts of Flanders and Picardy.

In 1725, Le Masson du Parc was recruited by the office of Antoine-Denis Raudot (1679–1737),[16] at the Secretariat of State for the Navy, under Jean-Frédéric Phélypeaux, Comte de Maurepas (1701–1781), one of the pillars of the restored ministerial configuration of Louis XV (on which, see note 9). A year later, in April 1726, Raudot successfully petitioned Maurepas to recommend Le Masson du Parc to the king, securing his appointment as *Commissaire de la Marine* and *Inspecteur des Pêches*, a title practically created for him.[17]

As the culmination of his career, Le Masson was appointed First Secretary of the Fishing Detachment of the Secretariat of State for the Navy in 1737. He remained in this position until his death in 1741, at the age of seventy, leaving behind his third wife but no confirmed offspring.

3 The Naturalist Dimension of Le Masson du Parc

These professional accounts outline the journey of a provincial bourgeois, Le Masson du Parc, toward a naval career. An essential factor was the broader context of the period, marked by evolving perceptions of scientific practices and the formation of academic elites. This era also witnessed changing views of nature, particularly the marine world, and significant developments in natural history.

In early 18th-century Europe, early modern natural history – i.e. all matters concerning nature – was transforming into new forms of practice, corresponding to the political, economic activities of each territory. The relation between knowledge production and state administration became tighter and more complex.[18] In this context, a growing interest in naturalist practices emerged within urban scholarly circles, where scientific knowledge, techniques and methodologies were increasingly valued as markers of social class and status. The pursuit of nature transitioned from purely utilitarian knowledge to a quest for understanding and order, consolidating the foundation of naturalistic knowledge and practices.[19] The

16 Antoine-Denis Raudot (1679–1737), intendant of New France, where he worked alongside his father from 1705 to 1711. He then took up a post at the Secretariat of State for the Navy, in charge of royal regulations on fishing. According to Dennis Lieppe's analysis, Le Masson du Parc must have known him from his time as a coastguard a decade earlier, when Raudot also served in Normandy. For more on this relation and their natural history outputs, see the fourth chapter of Fred Blanchard, "Étude d'un recueil d'histoire naturelle coloniale et de plusieurs anecdotes illustrées de Nouvelle-France, ayant appartenu au Duc de Richelieu et issu des activités du Secrétariat de la Marine et des colonies entre 1715 et 1736", in: *Société d'Histoire de la Guadeloupe* 197 (2024), pp. 3–201.

17 Lieppe, "Étude", p. 19–20.

18 Isabelle Laboulais, "Territorialisation and logistics of knowledge and learning: The case of mineral resource surveys in France in the Eighteenth Century", in: eds. Lothar Schilling and Jakob Vogel, *Transnational Cultures of Expertise*, pp. 149–165.

19 On natural history, its configuration and practices: Nicholas Jardine, James A. Secord and E. C. Spary (eds.), *Cultures of Natural History*, Cambridge 1996; Gianna Pomata and Nancy

collection and exchange of curiosities and rarities became widespread, and rooms, galleries and cabinets were dedicated to accumulating, organizing and displaying specimens, which served as symbols of power and became objects of curiosity and business, as an attempt to dominate nature through material and visual culture. Naturalistic practices were closely intertwined with commercial ventures, political and economic exploration and the quest for new territories and resources. These environments also prompted new inquiries into the mysteries of the sea.

In France, the need to control maritime activities amidst the creation and expansion of empires and nation-states – whose successes and failures often played out at sea – led to various initiatives and organizational innovations. Under the leadership of Prime Minister Jean-Baptiste Colbert (Reims, 1619–Paris, 1683), France sought to establish itself as a European economic power. Colbert, a key proponent of the *Ordonnance maritime* of 1681, initiated studies for this project in the mid-17th century, drawing upon legal codes from previous centuries as references. The impact of the 1681 *Ordonnance* endured until the late 18th century, laying the groundwork for national regulations not only in France but also in other nations from the 19th century onwards.[20] During the early decades of the 18th century, the *Ordonnance* was in full implementation, resulting in disputes, controversies and revisions. These developments shaped not only the legal framework but also the complex processes of acquiring maritime information and constructing interpretations of the sea. In 1666, Colbert founded the *Académie des Sciences*, tasking its members with developing a project to provide scientific and technical support to French arts and crafts. This initiative, known as *Descriptions des Arts et Métiers, faites ou approuvées par messieurs de l'Académie Royale des Sciences*, aimed to systematize, manage and optimize economic resources, reflecting the growing recognition of science as a vital national asset. The project sought to systematize existing knowledge and enhance the prestige of both theoretical and applied science.

Most texts produced during this period emerged from a specific context characterized by Colbert's administrative and legislative endeavours and his scientific initiatives. These were intertwined with commercial interests, many linked to colonial expansion and the contested nature of the sea and its resources, which contrasted with the private ownership of land. By the late 17th and early 18th centuries, the regulation, control and management of maritime activities had become a growing concern for European states. Simultaneously, discourses

G. Siraisi (eds.), *Historia: Empiricism and erudition in early modern Europe*, Cambridge, MA 2005; Philippe Glardon, "The relation between text and illustrations in natural history treatises of the mid-sixteenth century", in: *A Cultural History of Animals: Volume 3: The Renaissance (1400–1600)*, ed. Bruce Boehrer, Oxford/New York 2017, pp. 119–146.

20 Ellen Krefting, "Ordering the Ocean in Old Regime France: Freedom, Risks and Riches in *L'ordonnance de la marine* 1681–1760" [work in progress, personal communication]. Margarita Serna Vallejo, "La Ordenanza francesa de la marina de 1681: Unificación, Refundición y Fraccionamiento del Derecho Marítimo en Europa", in: *Anuario de historia del derecho español* 78/79 (2009), pp. 233–260.

surrounding the concept of the ocean, as distinct from terrestrial territories, were taking shape. This issue sparked an intense conceptual debate throughout the 17th century, continuing well into the 18th century. Central to this debate was the contested perception of the sea: whether it should be seen as a naturally free entity, not subject to possession or sovereignty, or as a domain that could be dominated by a lord or state. Over the decades, the notion of the ocean's intrinsic freedom seemed to prevail over the concept of *mare clausum* – the idea that the sea could be subject to appropriation – as reflected in Colbert's *Ordonnance maritime* and further emphasized in Valin's widely circulated annotated edition.[21]

Nevertheless, even proponents of *mare liberum* – the principle of the open sea – tended to apply this concept primarily to the high seas. Coastal areas and their resources, as addressed in Colbert's ordinance, were subject to specific uses and prerogatives. Although the ordinance ostensibly supported free access, it introduced bureaucratic controls over fishing activities, resulting in what amounted to conditional freedom. This debate, far from being resolved, remains crucial in understanding the relationship between human practices and the environments in which they occur, as well as the resources involved – an essential theme in environmental history.[22]

The idea of *mare liberum* was also intertwined with the perception of the sea as an inexhaustible resource, a belief that persisted alongside concerns about scarcity and finitude. In the late 18th century, a Spanish *Diccionario* on fisheries was published.[23] In its introduction, the author, Sáñez-Reguart (ca. 1740–1797), encapsulated this view by asserting that, unlike mines, 'the sea gives and will always give.'[24] Thus, the notion of an infinite sea has coexisted for centuries with apprehensions about depletion, perhaps legitimizing exploitative extractive practices. Leading the Navy and the implementation of the scientific reference entity were the pillars of Colbert's strategy, which triggered administrative and management changes, but also redefined the value of information and knowledge – theoretical and practical – as a tool in the nation's politics and economy.[25] The encyclopaedic publishing projects that would mark the historiographical beginning of the

21 René Josué Valin, *Nouveau commentaire sur l'ordonnance de la Marine, du mois d'août 1681*, La Rochelle 1766.

22 On the commons: Garrett Hardin, "The Tragedy of the Commons", in: *Science* 162 (1968), pp. 1243–1248. The works of Joan Martínez-Alier are relevant to understanding the links between ecology, economy and social justice throughout history, i.e., Joan Martínez-Alier, *Land, Water, Air and Freedom: The Making of World Movements for Environmental Justice*, Cheltenham 2023. Also on these issues: Partha Dasgupta, "The Economics of the Environment", in: *Environment and Development Economics* 1/4 (1996), pp. 387–428.

23 It is considered the first published historical dictionary on fisheries in Spanish.

24 Antonio, Sáñez-Reguart, "Introducción", in: *Diccionario histórico de los artes de pesca nacional*, Madrid 1791–1795, p. VI.

25 About Colbert and his role in shaping the French nation-state of the *Ancien Régime*: Jacob Soll, *The Information Master: Jean-Baptiste Colbert's Secret State Intelligence System*, Ann Arbor 2010. See also: Lewis Wade, *Privilege, Economy and State in Old Regime France: Marine Insurance, War and the Atlantic Empire under Louis XIV*, Woodbridge 2023.

Age of Enlightenment were derived from the scientific elites. Darnton's extensive study[26] of the complexity and profitability of the encyclopaedic enterprise serves to situate and understand the previous decades in which the ideas that would give rise to these works were conceived. The *Déscriptions* – although still unpublished at the time – had an initial period of data collection, memoirs and illustrations between the end of the 17th century and the first decades of the 18th century. The first known materials produced for the purpose of generating the compendia commissioned by Colbert have been dated to 1693.[27] For decades, memoirs and information accumulated, providing structure and form for the processes of information gathering about knowledge and techniques in the French territory. These works did not begin to be published until decades later, in 1761, perhaps spurred on by the appearance of another ambitious project such as *L'Encyclopédie* in 1751. In any case, even then the *Déscriptions* project was a precursor to *L'Encyclopédie*, as well as a rival, or, rather, two contemporary ways of handling and publishing the information gathered by experts, craftsmen and scientists.

In these decades, the *Académie* was being consolidated as an official, prestigious entity that enjoyed widespread social recognition beyond its members and circle of associates. By being promoted and protected by the monarchy, knowledge and scientific advances became activities with a new relevance or status, perceived as interesting, important and necessary for the progress of the nation.[28] Or, at the very least, its activity was a point of reference and influence for a young, studious and diligent scholar, such as François Le Masson du Parc at that time. The circumstances surrounding the projects of legislation, the creation of the *Académie des Sciences* and the writing of the *Déscriptions* are intertwined, making evident the influence that these ideas had on the practices and relationships of the politicians and academics of the time. Both the drafting of laws and naturalist practices facilitated circulation. Research on correspondence within the Republic of Letters has highlighted how naturalists functioned as conduits for the exchange, reception and dissemination of knowledge and materials. These dynamics were often driven by personal interests, spanning from personal obsession to social and professional aspirations, or broader strategic and policy-related considerations.

At the beginning of the 18th century, Europe and most consolidated colonies – French, Spanish, Portuguese, British … – witnessed a growing enthusiasm for acquiring, systematizing and disseminating knowledge. Particularly in France,

26 Robert Darnton, *The Business of Enlightenment: A Publishing History of the Encyclopédie, 1775–1800*, Cambridge, MA 1979.

27 Georges Huard, "Les Planches de l'Encyclopédie et Celles de la *Description des Arts et Métiers* de l'Académie des Sciences", in: *Revue d'histoire des sciences* 4/3–4 (1951), pp. 238–249.

28 Alice Stroup, *A Company of Scientists: Botany, Patronage, and Community at the Seventeenth-Century Parisian Royal Academy of Sciences*, Berkeley 1990. A reference, albeit botanical, to illustrate this idea of the social recognition and the role of the *Académie* in those first decades of its existence. These tensions are also perceived and described in Marco Storni, "Cartography, Geodesy and the Heliocentric Theory: Yves Simonin's Unpublished Papers", in: *Centaurus* 63/1 (2021), pp. 102–124.

the effort to accumulate information was reinforced as the end of Louis XIV's reign raised the challenge of maintaining the whole monarchic structure and the strong impulse given to transoceanic projects. This interest extended beyond national borders, reflecting a desire to understand not only local domains but also neighbouring or distant regions. Due to the spatial overlap, there was a strong interest in the fishing practices of adjacent areas. Guidelines for gathering information on craft practices had become widespread, mobilizing relevant societal sectors, particularly within government institutions, which recognized the value of such data. The knowledge of the 'artisans of the sea' took on a relevant role in the growing structures of power, organization and regulation, as 'men of the land' lost control over the reality beyond the shores.

The precise motivations behind Le Masson du Parc's creation of the *Histoire des pesches* remain uncertain. The most plausible hypothesis suggests that a combination of personal, professional, political and economic factors influenced him through his professional and social networks. The early 18th-century surge in scientific, technical and applied sciences, alongside the activities of the *Académie des Sciences*, provides essential context for understanding Le Masson du Parc's efforts between 1714 and 1726.

4 Salvador – Jussieu – Le Masson du Parc: Triangulation of an Unpublished Work

Le Masson du Parc aimed to expand his network and gather information on fishing practices beyond the Channel and Europe. He designed questionnaires[29] and trialled ways of getting them answered. The first evidence of these efforts is encountered in a letter from a French merchant in Amsterdam in May 1720, in response to a request for Dutch fishing data.[30] Such information was highly appreciated, reflecting the broader trend of valuing applied knowledge. This period saw an emerging mentality focused on systematizing technical and practical knowledge, influenced by the Colbertian ordinance of 1681, which had been met with resistance and dissatisfaction by fishermen. There was also a strong commitment to various forms of fishing, with internal organizations and hierarchies linked to local resources. Additionally, concerns arose about a perceived decline in fisheries, attributed to competition and detrimental new techniques like trawling, particularly noted in Normandy according to Le Masson du Parc's treaty and related documents.

The Dutch letter exemplifies the value of this information, which motivated a refusal to answer his questions on the part of shipowners, fishermen and whalers contacted. This unproductive trial could have made Le Masson du Parc devise other ways of achieving his objectives. There are hints that he used contacts in the *Compagnie des Indes* to circulate questionnaires and obtain specimens, although

29 The AN127AP archives contain multiple examples from drafts and copies of these questionnaires.

30 AN 127AP3.

so far little evidence has been gathered to illustrate this option. Instead, the following sections will explain the deployment of Le Masson du Parc's work and questionnaires through scholarly and consular networks in order to ensure both international relevance and institutional validation for his project.

While working in Dieppe, he was in contact with scholars in France, some also active in the naval administration, to ensure his project would have the supervision and compliance of the contemporary scientific authorities. The earliest connection traced between Le Masson du Parc and naturalist circles relates to a manuscript about fishing on the Catalan coast. This manuscript, written in French by Joan Salvador, was a reply to the questions (*mémoire*) previously sent by Le Masson du Parc through Antoine de Jussieu (Lyon, 1686–Paris, 1758). The document is kept in the library of the *Muséum National d'Histoire Naturelle* in Paris, hereafter referred to as the *Muséum*, under the reference Ms 432, which is how I shall cite it. Correspondence between Salvador and Jussieu concerning Ms 432 is kept in the *Fons Salvador* at the Institut Botànic de Barcelona.[31] The letters regarding the proposal of collaboration date from early 1722, and contacts between Jussieu and Le Masson du Parc in this regard may have taken place in December 1721, according to a marginal note in one of the manuscripts kept in AN 127AP. In turn, the documents located in the archive of the botany section of the *Muséum*, under the shelfmark Ms CRY 307, are essential to understanding Le Masson du Parc's multidimensionality. The preserved letters date from February and March 1722. In them, Le Masson du Parc writes to Jussieu about personal and family issues along with the progress, doubts and difficulties related to his work, revealing information about the network of activities, collaborators and contacts that he drew on to advance his project, as detailed below.

Joan Salvador's friendship with Antoine de Jussieu began in 1705–1706, when both met at the *Jardin du Roi* in Paris during their training period under the tutelage of Tournefort. They travelled around the Iberian Peninsula (1716–1717) and correspondence and exchanges between them were abundant until Joan's death in 1726. The influence of this relationship is evident, even symbiotic, as both made use of each other's knowledge, standing and contacts when establishing strategies to obtain new seeds, species or even access to institutions, as shown by the appointment of Joan Salvador as a corresponding member of the *Académie des Sciences* through the mediation of his French friend.[32]

31 About the Salvador collection: José Pardo-Tomás, *Salvadoriana. El Gabinet de Curiositats de Barcelona*, Barcelona 2014.

32 In a letter Jussieu wrote to Réaumur, the latter being responsible for the *Déscriptions*, in November 1716, during the trip through the Iberian Peninsula that he made with Joan Salvador, Jussieu commented on esparto grass, of which inflorescence and seeds were found, and mentioned that, if this were not the case, he would have had it drawn for his [Réaumur's] *histoire des arts*. Emma Sallent Del Colombo and José Pardo-Tomás, "En Busca de la Iconografía Perdida. Philippe Simonneau y los Dibujos del 'Viaje de España y Portugal', 1716–1717", in: *Cuerpos Representados: Objetos de Ciencia Artísticos en España, Siglos XVIII–XX*, eds. Alfonso Zarzoso and Maribel I. Morente, Vitoria 2020, p. 35.

Jussieu's intermediary role likely arose from a recognition of the mutual benefits of collaboration between his two correspondents, Joan Salvador and François Le Masson du Parc. This collaboration offered Salvador the chance to produce a report on fishing, enhancing his reputation in French naturalist circles and providing a foundation for future work. For Le Masson du Parc, it provided a trial and validation for his methodology of gathering information through questionnaires via diplomatic channels. Jussieu's involvement could have been rooted in his connections with the *Académie des Sciences* and the preparation of the *Déscriptions des arts et métiers*, showing his legitimate interest in the project's success beyond personal friendships.

The documentation in the botanical library of the *Muséum*, under shelfmark Ms CRY 307, comprises manuscripts, illustrations and letters, revealing a previously unknown relationship with Parisian scientific circles, repositioning Le Masson du Parc's project within the practices of early 18th-century natural history. These practices aligned with the technical, commercial and political interests of the government. Le Masson du Parc's initiative was influenced by the prevailing intellectual currents and the demands of contemporary scholars. His aim was to create a comprehensive work that would advance his career while addressing the governance needs of fishing activities, maintaining rigour and precision. To achieve this, he sought the support and advice of esteemed scientists for the publication of his work.

Le Masson du Parc was not part of the *Académie des Sciences* circle, nor did he intend to join, possibly deterred by the institution's restrictive habits, which often rejected practical knowledge – the methodology he employed.[33] However, through Jussieu and other contacts, Le Masson du Parc was well-informed and provided with documents, corroborating his practical objective while understanding the academic practices and needs, and he maintained a fluid relationship in order to secure necessary approvals and financial support.

The two letters reveal Le Masson du Parc's active exchange of information and materials with his scholarly contacts, including discussions with Jussieu. This correspondence highlights an extensive network of collaborators, encompassing booksellers, editors, illustrators and engravers, all involved in the preparation of his *Histoire des pesches*. Le Masson du Parc mentioned M. Giffard, a bookseller and editor, from whom he was awaiting printer's proofs and notes concerning the forthcoming seascapes. It is suggested that Le Masson du Parc brought manuscripts or sample volumes on a visit to Paris. In the next letter, he refers to thirteen or fourteen completed proofs by M. Giffard, which he wanted by Easter in order to present them to interested parties in Rouen, where he intended to spend holidays.

33 These issues have been addressed by Storni, "Cartography, geodesy, …", and the research by J. van Besouw (work in progress, personal communication).

Another frequent contact was the engraver M. Audran.[34] In the first letter, he asked whether Jussieu had presented the first three proofs by Audran to the Admiral and Mr. De Valincourt, as previously agreed. Le Masson du Parc remarked that this could be advantageous for his career advancement, though he had limited expectations despite his efforts and financial contributions to the project.

In the second letter, Le Masson du Parc reiterated the necessity of reminding the Regent of his intentions. He requested Jussieu to inquire of M. Audran or M. Gistan if they had retrieved the plates, which had been completed to a higher standard than anticipated, and to obtain one of the three proofs for him to present to the Council and His Holiness. Furthermore, he mentioned Mr. Bertrand and Mr. Hardion as additional reviewers of his work, with the latter described as a reviewer and someone with connections to the Council of the Navy or its affiliates. Le Masson du Parc also conveyed that several contacts had reassured him that the Council would likely not obstruct the distribution of his *Mémoires* to the necessary consuls abroad.

'M. Chevalier' appears in the letters to Jussieu, always in relation to the visual components accompanying the compendium. I have identified these name references with Pierre Le Chevalier. A little information can be gained from the introduction to two of his manuscripts,[35] and from a recent study of his works with Le Masson du Parc under Maurepas and Raudot's direction.[36] A manuscript in the French National Library, authored by Pierre Le Chevalier himself, further elucidates this relationship and adds data to the constellation surrounding Le Masson du Parc's enterprise. According to the preface, Le Chevalier had been working for Le Masson du Parc since 1716, the year he was in Dieppe replacing Le Brun, and likely already involved in the fishing treatise project. He also mentioned being hired by Raudot, indicating the participation of multiple people and interests throughout the project's development.

From the letters and other documentation, several strategies that Le Masson du Parc employed to collect information and specimens, both from the coasts he frequented and from foreign countries, can be reconstructed. These strategies were not always premeditated or elaborate but were often methodical and efficient, leveraging his contacts. Notably, he had the support of several officials, including Raudot. He also maintained relationships with other high-ranking naval officials, such as Ambroise Daubenton, who managed French naval and trade

34 Most likely Jean Audran (1667–1756) or another member of the Audran family, renowned painters, engravers and muralists in Paris.

35 Jean-François Détrée, "Grande et petite marée", in: *Actes des congrès nationaux des sociétés historiques et scientifiques* 124/8 (2002), pp. 115–124; Eric Rieth (ed.), *Galerie de portraits de navires du milieu du XVIIIe siècle: L'album de dessins de Pierre Le Chevalier, Dieppe, 1752*.

36 Fred Blanchard, "Étude d'un recueil d'histoire naturelle coloniale et de plusieurs anecdotes illustrées de Nouvelle-France, ayant appartenu au Duc de Richelieu et issu des activités du Secrétariat de la Marine et des colonies entre 1715 et 1736", in: *Société d'Histoire de la Guadeloupe* 197 (2024), pp. 3–201.

affairs in Spain in the early 18th century and directed the Bureau of the Consulate from 1711. Daubenton's connections and consular position made him an ideal intermediary for Le Masson du Parc's objectives. Annotations in Le Masson du Parc's documents indicate that Daubenton facilitated information gathering, as seen in preserved notes, including a list of required illustrations of Barcelona, also delivered to Salvador by Jussieu. Other documents are addressed to Italy, Portugal and Spain, detailing requests for drawings and models.

Le Masson du Parc also sought the assistance of other officials, such as Mgr. Le C. de Monville and Mr. Bertrand from Raudot's office, to distribute his *Mémoires* and manage related costs, further suggesting support and financing from his superiors. A listing dated 1725 aligns with illustrator Le Chevalier's details that Raudot financed his work with Le Masson du Parc during that time.

This network of mentions and contacts with Jussieu illustrates the scope and dynamics of Le Masson du Parc's strategy when his *Histoire des pesches* was well advanced but lacked the international reach he envisioned in early 1722. He sought to disseminate his work through consular channels, as reflected in his correspondence with Jussieu and a formal letter to the *Conseil de la Marine* from March 1722. Indeed, through consular routes, Le Masson du Parc established an efficient global flow of his *Mémoires*. By converting his requests into royal orders, many consuls sought to comply. Registers of the circulars sent to consulates are recorded in the books of foreign affairs dispatches, such as the order sent to Italian consuls on 6 August 1722 and the order to consuls in Spain and Portugal on 17 September 1722 addressed to all consuls in both countries, urging them to send the *Conseil* information enlightening them about the fisheries in the harbours and coasts of their departments.[37]

Through this deployment of the consular network, Le Masson du Parc aimed to provide practical, applied and potentially social solutions to the problems around him. He must have been familiar with a wide range of situations due to his life experience and professional dedication in different coastal administrations, including environmental problems and social concerns such as labour and structural issues of the coastal communities and their relationship with the resources and natural environment that surrounded them. While the project served his personal and professional ambitions, his primary concern was the management of fishing activities and their products. He sought to create an accessible *Histoire des pesches*, combining natural history practices, such as detailed visual documentation from observation, with an emphasis on the practical aspects, particularly the materiality of fishing nets and their importance for effective fishing practices.

The lack of a final published work allows a focus on the intermediate documents and the information they contain. These scattered documents provide insight into Le Masson du Parc's activities, strategies and methodologies over several years. His naturalistic practices went beyond observation and writing,

37 AN MAR/B/7 113.

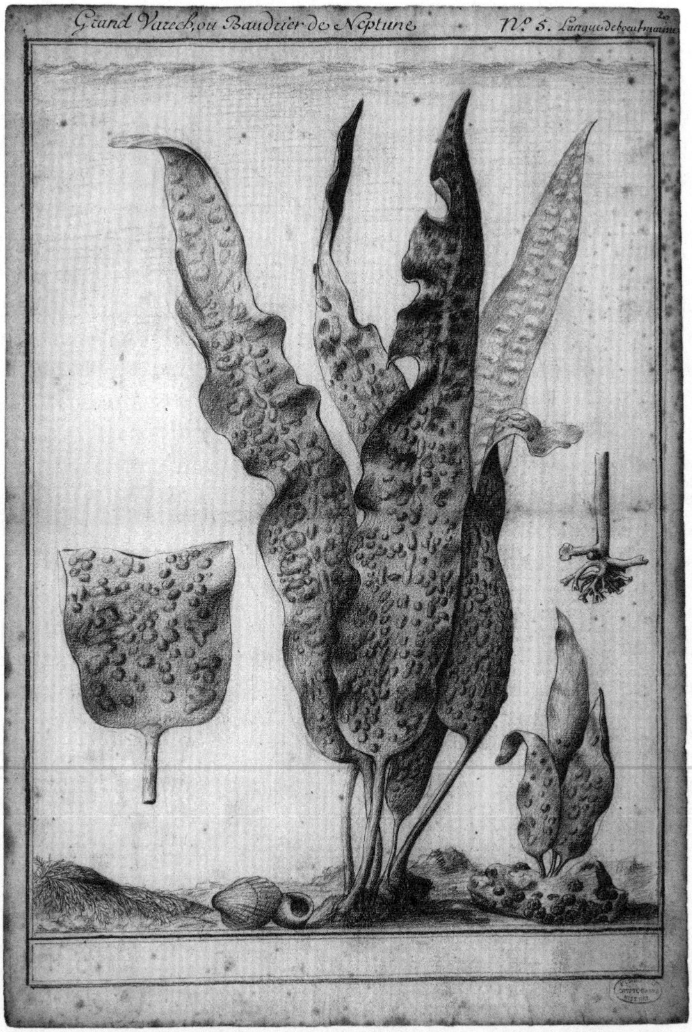

Fig. 1: Illustration presumably by Pierre Le Chevalier of Grand Varech ou Baudrier de Neptune, now Saccharina latissima. One of the eight designs, six of them representing detailed algae in their ecosystem. The drawings are preserved in the correspondence between Le Masson du Parc and Antoine Jussieu, 1722, were the botanist was asked to add the correct scientific names. MNHN, Ms CRY 307.

recognizing the importance of visual support in natural history treatises since the 15th century. Materials such as drawings of algae sent to Jussieu illustrate intermediate steps in creating the final image. The plates preserved in Ms CRY 307 have blank bottom space for annotating the correct scientific names, which Le Masson du Parc expected Jussieu's help with.

In his correspondence with Jussieu, he emphasized documenting and describing things clearly for non-experts, acknowledging his lack of scholarly aptitude and aiming to inform those unfamiliar with the sea. Developed visual support was essential for this purpose, hence Le Chevalier's collaboration was crucial.

In addition, Le Masson du Parc engaged in specimen collection, a common practice in naturalist activity of the time. He collected specimens to serve as models for drawings or to form a collection. In his second letter to Jussieu, he expressed satisfaction with the results of fishing during Lent, having obtained over fifty specimens of fish, insects, zoophytes and plants not mentioned by Rondelet, Belon or Johnston. In a letter to the Council of the Navy in March 1722, he noted that he acquired originals from other places when local specimens were unavailable.[38] According to Blanchard, Le Masson du Parc established a cabinet of marine specimens in Paris,[39] confirming the material dimension of his practices and the existence of his collection.

Le Masson du Parc combined the rigour of naturalist work with practical objectives. To accurately inform and be informed about fishing practices, he incorporated two key actions: visits to fishermen and the exchange of materials. Hunting and fishing treatises from the 17th to 19th centuries detailed the craftsmanship of threads and nets but often overlooked practical usage and differences between different locales. Le Masson du Parc knew it was challenging for many to verify compliance and correctly interpret diagrams and rules on-site. Therefore, he added a material dimension to his research, gathering information directly from the fishermen. His aim was to establish empirically-based standards for techniques and practices in order to achieve realistic control. His interest in who fished what and with which equipment led him to request net samples along with the questionnaire responses. Some samples, like Joan Salvador's, have been preserved.

Several types of questionnaires have been reviewed in combined archival work. The already mentioned Salvador manuscript, Ms 432, written in response to Le Masson du Parc's questions, included differing wording and versions when compared to other questionnaires, arguably due to the development in how he executed the information gathering process. For instance, later questionnaires were prepared with more precision and variables depending on their destination. The compendium sent to Barcelona via Jussieu and worked on by Joan Salvador is the only one identified to date that was sent through naturalist networks. It

38 'je me suis fait apporter de dessus les lieux les originaux que je n'ai pu avoir en France,' in Lieppe, "Étude", p. 17.

39 In Blanchard, "Étude d'un recueil", p. 145, there is a reference to Charles-César Baudelot de Dairval, *De L'Utilité Des Voyages Et De L'Avantage que la recherche des Antiquitez procure aux sçavans*, 1727. In its section on Parisian cabinets, p. 437, we find this brief description: 'Monsieur le Masson du Parc, en travaillant à l'histoire des Pêches des Poissons de mer (…) a fait un amas de Poissons singuliers, de Litophitons, de Coquillages et de Concretions marines, qui peuvent très-bien contribuer à augmenter de beaucoup l'Histoire de ce que la mer renferme de plus curieux dans son sein.'

Fig. 2: Sample of sardinal net in the cover envelope. Salvador to Jussieu. Ms 432, MNHN.

can be understood as a pilot test for the deployment that occurred months later through consular means.

The special value of the Salvador copy delivered to Jussieu, Ms 432, lies in its unique characteristics and components. To begin with, it is one of the few preserved documents produced by the Salvador family. More interestingly, this copy is the only one containing visual and material support. The manuscript contains a paper envelope on its cover with a sample of small mesh *sardinal* net. In Salvador's letter to Jussieu of November 1722, he mentioned the lack of time to include several illustrations, translations of names and a piece of large mesh *sardinal*, all of which Le Masson du Parc had requested. Further analysis of subsequent questionnaires is necessary to determine whether such requests were systematically included and fulfilled. So far, the responses from Barcelona are the only ones that preserve a material sample.

Besides collecting documents from different naturalists abroad, it is understood that Le Masson himself or colleagues investigated fishery practices in other French regions, as part of the underlying interests promoted in the different spheres: political, economic and scientific. An example of this environment is found in AN MAR/C/8 27–29, a *mémoir* on fisheries from the Bay of Arcachon, possibly created through Le Masson du Parc's visits and inspections, or following the same procedures. This document, a kind of "sample book" of nets, evidences the need for materiality in applying knowledge about fishing and the sea. Material samples ensured unequivocal communication and interpretation of measurements, techniques, knots, thicknesses or colours. Text and drawings

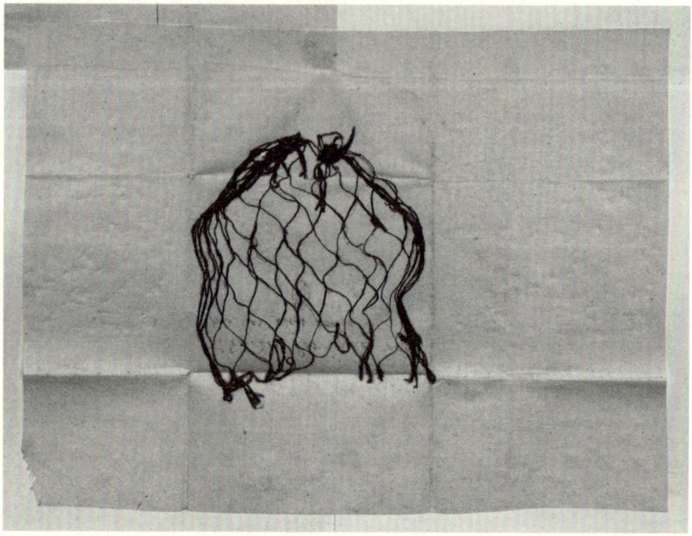

Fig. 3: Net sample in mémoire 1726. AN MAR/C/8 27–29.

were insufficient; technological exchange, like the exchange of seeds or shells for identification and study, was crucial in economic activities where scientific knowledge was developed and applied for profit or resource management. This necessity for materiality in applying knowledge about fishing and the sea is crucial for understanding and systematizing practices. Archival rarities like these allow us to glimpse lost links in the transfer between scholarly practices and applied sciences, highlighting the historiographical prioritization of preserving texts over objects and other materials often discarded during conservation processes.

The peculiar nature and scarcity of these documents suggest they resulted from a specific conjunction: concerns about declining fish stocks met the determination of figures like Le Masson du Parc, who sought to unravel the causes and provide solutions. Once a common reference system was established, the knowledge of who fished with which type of net and mesh no longer required material samples in communications. With a generalized understanding of working net and mesh types, production probably specialized in models that were permitted and that had proven effective, becoming standardized.

5 Conclusions: The Multiple Faces of Le Masson du Parc and Knowledge *oikonomiai* in Circulation

It has been possible to largely reconstruct the trajectory and facets of Le Masson du Parc in the years preceding his appointment as fisheries inspector in 1726. Le Masson du Parc combined two positions that he seemed to attempt to reconcile, or perhaps they were not as separate as current fragmentation and archival dispersion might suggest. On one hand, there was the Colbertian political vision

– what might be termed technocratic – of organizing both the sea and the crafts, trades and resources associated with it. On the other hand, there was the necessity perceived by Le Masson du Parc from his own experience, which led him to want to produce a useful work with the aim of socializing and transmitting maritime knowledge through coherent regulations to achieve effective control of both conflicts and resources.

His infrastructure and network of contacts were based on personal connections with agents from various social, commercial and economic domains. High-ranking officials were crucial for gaining favour and advancing his proposals, but his collaborators were also indispensable. The rigour and precision of his work earned him the support of recognized scholars, and maintaining a good reputation among members of the naval elite provided the diplomatic legitimacy needed in order to be granted the opportunity to use the French consular structure to send and receive the necessary questionnaires to complete his work. His intention was to provide solutions for the correct daily development of fishing practices in communities and the regulation of that activity.

It is worth noting that most influential figures in his career were themselves interested members of various initiatives within these entities. The members of this erudite elite held positions in various bourgeois domains – scientific, political, diplomatic – thus maintaining control within the upper class over all matters considered beneficial to the nation. Le Masson du Parc, a provincial bourgeois well-connected with Parisian circles, conceived an intelligible and useful work with a seemingly socializing intent, reminiscent of what would be seen decades later in Diderot.

The relational framework of Le Masson du Parc facilitated the circulation of materials across various domains, revealing a complex network of infrastructures, relationships and informal practices. During this period, the copying, appropriation and multiplication of knowledge were commonplace, extending far beyond official academic circles. During the early modern period and onwards, knowledge was exchanged in private spaces, offices, markets, ports, ships and official institutions, highlighting the diverse settings in which scientific processes unfolded.[40] These exchanges were not limited to formal channels: family ties, friendships, commercial relationships and diplomatic structures also determined the movement of people, objects and knowledge, shaping the flow of information. It is equally essential to consider the influence of what did not circulate: the concealed, lost, manipulated or obstructed knowledge, often responding to geo-

40 On heterogeneous places of science: Irina Podgorny, Nathalie Richard and Laura Cházaro (eds.), *Lugares de encuentro, científicos vocacionales, redes y prácticas científicas en el mundo iberoamericano y más allá. Estudios Interdisciplinarios de América Latina y el Caribe* 35/1 (June 2024). Neus Ibáñez Cortina and Aina Trias Verbeeck (eds.), "Lugares de encuentro y culturas de la curiosidad", in: *Dynamis* 44/2 (2024). Florike Egmond, "Visual immersion: Daniele Barbaro's fish album and the wave of interest in aquatic creatures in mid sixteenth-century Europe", in: *Notes and Records: The Royal Society Journal of the History of Science* 76/1 (2022), p. 1–18.

political interests. The network traced underscores the collective construction of knowledge, involving a wide array of agents, spaces and actions that influenced the evolution of practices and disciplines. The final, recognized author or works were those able to leave traces, typically men with the means and power to publish. The cases of Le Masson du Parc and Joan Salvador expose the limitations of traditional historical constructions, which have mostly relied on printed and published materials.

In the context of fisheries, mainstream historiography might identify Duhamel du Monceau's *Traité* as the first significant work in France and Sáñez-Reguart's *Diccionario* in Spain. However, archival materials reveal lesser-known figures such as Le Masson du Parc, Joan Salvador, Le Chevalier, Raudot and various consuls, as well as anonymous contributors such as fishermen, informants, captains, traders, intermediaries and family members. These individuals were crucial in compiling the information that underpinned projects like Le Masson du Parc's and surely other forgotten initiatives. Although these works were not always published – as in the case of the *Histoire des pêches* – they laid the groundwork for later, more widely recognized works, surpassing earlier treatises and preparing the foundation for subsequent publications.

Books and treatises, while marking significant milestones, are the culmination of complex, long-term processes driven by motivations and interests that largely precede the publications. The risk of constructing historical narratives solely around published works is that it overlooks the preceding efforts that made those publications possible.

Mixed documentation, including textual, visual and material elements, provides a rich resource for research, offering insights into scientific practices beyond the examination of published documents, contributing to our understanding of the organization, dedication and skills involved in producing scientific knowledge. Archival research reveals the intricate connections between knowledge generation, personal, economic, political and commercial interests, and the policies of a place, as well as the roles and relationships of the agents involved in the transmission and circulation of that knowledge.

Reference Lists

Archival Sources

Fons Salvador — archive, letters and library at Institut Botànic de Barcelona.

Ms 432 — Manuscript on fisheries by Joan Salvador i Riera, 1722. *Archives et collections anciennes, Bibliothèque de recherche. Muséum national d'histoire naturelle*, Paris.

Ms CRY 307 — Letters, manuscript and drawings by François Le Masson du Parc and Pierre Le Chevalier, *Bibliothèque de botanique. Muséum national d'histoire naturelle*, Paris.

French national archives (AN), series *Archives Personals* (AP) — 127AP corresponds to the Du Moceau brothers' documentation. In AN 127AP 1–4 we find Le Masson du Parc's preserved documents and related papers.
French national archives (AN), Archives de la Marine (MAR) — Referenced materials: AN MAR/B/3 234 f. 444; AN MAR/B/3 242 f. 35; AN MAR/B/7 113; AN MAR/C/8 pp. 27–29.

Printed Sources

Baudelot de Dairval, Charles-César, *De L'Utilité Des Voyages Et De L'Avantage que la recherche des Antiquitez procure aux sçavans*, 1727. Accessed through Heidelberg University Library.
Sáñez-Reguart, Antonio, *Diccionario histórico de los artes de pesca nacional.* Madrid, 1791–1795. Accessed through Biblioteca digital hispánica, ID: bdh0000023088.
Valin, René Josué, *Nouveau commentaire sur l'ordonnance de la Marine, du mois d'août 1681.* La Rochelle 1766. Accessed through Archive.org ID urn: oclc: record: 848672780

Research Literature

Blanchard, Fred, "Étude d'un recueil d'histoire naturelle coloniale et de plusieurs anecdotes illustrées de Nouvelle-France, ayant appartenu au Duc de Richelieu et issu des activités du Secrétariat de la Marine et des colonies entre 1715 et 1736", in: *Société d'Histoire de la Guadeloupe* 197 (2024), pp. 3–201.
Bourget, Marie-Noëlle, *Déchiffrer la France. La statistique départementale à l'époque napoléonienne*, Paris 1988.
Camarasa, Josep Maria, "Salvadorianae II. Les Jussieu et les Salvador: Deux Familles de Naturalistes au Début du XVIIIe Siècle", in: *Les naturalistes français en Amérique du Sud, XVIe–XVIIIe siècles. Actes du 118e Congrès national des sociétés historiques et scientifiques, Comité des Travaux Historiques et Scientifiques*, ed. Yves Laissus, Paris 1995, pp. 69–102.
Darnton, Robert, *The Business of Enlightenment: A Publishing History of the Encyclopédie, 1775–1800*, Cambridge, MA, 1979.
Dasgupta, Partha, "The Economics of the Environment", in: *Environment and Development Economics* 1/4 (1996), pp. 387–428.
Détrée, Jean-François, "Grande et petite marée", in: *Actes des congrès nationaux des sociétés historiques et scientifiques* 124/8 (2002), pp. 115–124.
Egmond, Florike, "Visual immersion: Daniele Barbaro's fish album and the wave of interest in aquatic creatures in mid sixteenth-century Europe", in: *Notes and Records: The Royal Society Journal of the History of Science* 76/1 (2022), pp. 1–18. https://doi.org/10.1098/rsnr.2021.0084
Grancher, Romain, "Gouverner les Ressources de la Mer. Une Histoire Environnementale de l'Inspection des Pêches Françaises au XVIIIe Siècle", in: *Cahiers d'histoire* 36/1 (2018), pp. 45–68.
Hardin, Garrett, "The Tragedy of the Commons", in: *Science* 162 (1968), pp. 1243–1248.
Huard, Georges, "Les Planches de l'Encyclopédie et Celles de la *Description des Arts et Métiers* de l'Académie des Sciences", in: *Revue d'histoire des sciences* 4/3–4 (1951), pp. 238–249.
Ibáñez Cortina, Neus, Aina Trias Verbeeck and Neus Nualart (eds.), "Lugares de encuentro y culturas de la curiosidad", in: *Dynamis* 44/2 (2024).

Jaoul, Martine and Madeleine Pinault, "The Collection 'Description of Arts and Métiers': Study of Unpublished Sources at the Houghton Library Université Harvard", in: *Ethnologie Française* 12/4 (1982), pp. 335–360.

Krefting, Ellen, "Ordering the Ocean in Old Regime France: Freedom, Risks and Riches in *L'ordonnance de la marine* 1681–1760" [2024, work in revision, personal communication].

Lieppe, Dennis, "Étude d'introduction", in: *Pêches & pêcheurs du domaine maritime aquitain au XVIII*[e] *siècle: Amirautés de Bayonne & de Bordeaux: Procès-Verbaux des visites faites par ordre du Roy concernant la pesche en mer (1727)*, eds. Dennis Lieppe et al., Camiac-et-Saint-Denis 2004.

Lieppe, Dennis, Anne-Marie-Cocula, François Parc, Bernard Larrieu, Jean Bernard, Christian Daney and Yves Laborie (eds.), *Pêches & pêcheurs du domaine maritime aquitain au XVIII*[e] *siècle: Amirautés de Bayonne & de Bordeaux: Procès-Verbaux des visites faites par ordre du Roy concernant la pesche en mer (1727)*, Camiac-et-Saint-Denis 2004.

Martínez-Alier, Joan, *Land, Water, Air and Freedom: The Making of World Movements for Environmental Justice*, Cheltenham, 2023.

Pardo-Tomás, José, *Salvadoriana. El Gabinet de Curiositats de Barcelona*, Barcelona 2014.

Perrot, Jean Claude, *L'âge d'or de la statistique régionale française (an IV–1804)*, Paris 1977.

PPodgorny, Irina, Nathalie Richard and Laura Cházaro (eds.), *Lugares de encuentro, científicos vocacionales, redes y prácticas científicas en el mundo iberoamericano y más allá. Estudios Interdisciplinarios de América Latina y el Caribe* 35/1 (2024).

Rieth, Eric (ed.), *Galerie de portraits de navires du milieu du XVIII*[e] *siècle: L'album de dessins de Pierre Le Chevalier*, Dieppe, 1752.

Sallent Del Colombo, Emma and José Pardo-Tomás, "En Busca de la Iconografía Perdida. Philippe Simonneau y los Dibujos del 'Viaje de España y Portugal', 1716–1717", in: *Cuerpos Representados: Objetos de Ciencia Artísticos en España, Siglos XVIII–XX*, eds. Alfonso Zarzoso and Maribel I. Morente, Vitoria 2020, pp. 21–40.

Serna Vallejo, Margarita, "La Ordenanza francesa de la marina de 1681: Unificación, Refundición y Fraccionamiento del Derecho Marítimo en Europa", in: *Anuario de historia del derecho español* 78–79 (2009), pp. 233–260.

Soll, Jacob, *The Information Master: Jean-Baptiste Colbert's Secret State Intelligence System*, Ann Arbor 2010.

Storni, Marco, "Cartography, Geodesy and the Heliocentric Theory: Yves Simonin's Unpublished Papers", in: *Centaurus* 63/1 (2021), pp. 102–124.

Stroup, Alice, *A Company of Scientists: Botany, Patronage, and Community at the Seventeenth-Century Parisian Royal Academy of Sciences*, Berkeley 1990.

Trias Verbeeck, Aina, "Bajo el mar: fauna y flora marinas en los Dioscórides renacentistas", in: *Dioscórides ante el mundo: Usos plurales de un 'libro-laboratorio' en la Edad moderna*, eds. Elisa Andretta and José Pardo-Tomás, Madrid 2025.

Wade, Lewis, *Privilege, Economy and State in Old Regime France: Marine Insurance, War and the Atlantic Empire under Louis XIV*, Woodbridge 2023.

Zysberg, André, "Le Masson du Parc Inspecte la Côte du Bessin en Juillet 1724", in: *Cahier des Annales de Normandie* 35 (2009), pp. 211–225.

Mineral Extraction from Water in Georgius Agricola's Knowledge Economy of Mining

Helge Wendt

1 Introduction

In this contribution, the significance of water as a carrier of minerals in the mining work of Georgius Agricola is presented as an aspect in which knowledge of mining, hydraulic engineering, mineralogy and metallurgy intersects with legal requirements and economic possibilities of mineral extraction. Although this historical account centers on a single author, an *economy of knowledge* is revealed, in which different areas of knowledge and different groups of actors with their respective epistemic traditions come together. The extraction of substances from water is treated here under the heading of mining and mineralogy, whereas Paracelsus, for example, addressed this topic from the perspective of "alchemy" concurrently with Georgius Agricola.[1] However, in his works Agricola does not address this field of knowledge as a completely integrated area of knowledge and practice, and so the main aim of this article is to reconstruct the epistemological traditions used by Agricola himself and to define the field.

The article aims to examine water in Agricola's writings as a resource that was involved in multiple contexts of meaning. An economy of knowledge emerges, in which, alongside a competing approach to water as a material, the particular concern was in concretizing different forms of knowledge for the purposeful use of water.

2 Water in the Early Modern Anthroposphere

In the 16th century, water was perceived less as a diverse and difficult-to-understand material than as a substance with which a multitude of sometimes competing practices were associated.[2] As part of this anthroposphere, water was also present in mining in many ways, as will be explained below. The particular focus on the topic of mineral extraction from water opens a thematic field that points

1 Simon Brandl, *Mystik und Magie im Frühparacelsismus: Erkundungen um Alexander von Suchtens Traktat ‚De tribus facultatibus'*, Berlin/Boston 2021, pp. 114, 157.

2 Hasok Chang's great work on the role of water in the chemical revolution of the 18th century (*Is Water H2O? Evidence, Realism and Pluralism*, Dordrecht et al. 2012.) should serve as a form of demarcation here. Unlike two hundred years later, in the 16th century there is no classification of types of water; instead, the approaches discussed mainly focus on the possibilities of the liquid substance with its mechanical, energetic and chemical potential.

DOI: 10.13173/9783447123693.167

from the early modern period to the modern era. In the formation of a proto-anthropocene, human forms of resource use were expanding. The use of water had already diversified in many ways by the Middle Ages: Water was the basis to produce beverages or was drunk directly. Water was a driving force for mills. Water was an important chemical and mechanical agent in various manufacturing processes, such as cloth and leather production or in agriculture, the fishing industry and food production.[3] Over the centuries, as in the use of other natural resources, the use of water also developed in a regionally specific way. The variety of its anthropological uses was much greater than, for example, in some of the technical uses of coal.

The abovementioned basic forms of water use were, like those of wood, the same in most human cultures, and water always acquired a religiously connoted status and played an important role in the development of social and political hierarchies. Just like the use of wood, the use of water was also subject to standardizing regulations, which, among other things, were intended to prevent the use of water by one legal subject from harming other subjects in their intentions to use it. Michael Fessner and Christoph Bartels see an expansion of the legal position of the sovereigns in the area of mining. This development was due particularly to the economic crises that arose in the first half of the 16th century, especially as a result of confessional disputes.[4] However, technical innovations and reoriented production processes also created opportunities for a sovereign to redefine his legal position in the mining sector with the help of mining regulations. The general and special jurisdiction of the mining industry, which led to legal proceedings and claims, was also the result of a nascent statehood.[5]

Disputes about the right and mode of use can be found in the archives, for example in the Saxon State Archives. Individuals are accused of diverting water for private use by circumventing the levies and thus harming others who needed the water for their mining activities.[6] In the mining regulations of Schemnitz from 1466, a group of individuals were granted the right to use the water flowing through a gallery that they had built themselves. This individual right of use was to be reviewed annually by a magistrate's court, in which a mining official was consulted alongside the owner of the tunnel and the plaintiff.[7]

---

3 Bernd Herrmann, *Umweltgeschichte. Eine Einführung in Grundbegriffe*, Berlin/Heidelberg 2016, p. 136.

4 Michael Fessner and Christoph Bartels, "Von der Krise am Ende des 16. Jahrhunderts zum deutschen Bergbau im Zeitalter des Merkantilismus", in: *Geschichte des Deutschen Bergbaus*, vol. 1: *Der alteuropäische Bergbau. Von den Anfängen bis zur Mitte des 18. Jahrhunderts*, ed. Wolfhard Weber, Münster 2012, pp. 453–455.

5 Ibid.

6 Sächsisches Staatsarchiv, 40001 Oberbergamt Freiberg, Nr. 601, ff. 28r.–28v.

7 Eva Jaschik (ed.), "Bergordnung für Schemnitz/Banská Štiavnica von 1466", in: *Das Stadt- und Bergrecht von Banská Štiavnica/Schemnitz. Untersuchungen zum Frühneuhochdeutschen in der Slowakei* (Veröffentlichungen des Germanistischen Instituts), Oulu 1986, pp. 5–6, URL: https://

These sources show that fundamental questions of social relations were connected with the use of water. The relationship between subjects and the prince and the relationships between different subjects were regulated by law. In addition to these social effects, the sources also reveal the massive interventions in natural conditions caused by water management in the mining industry. Discharging and damming up water changed the natural courses of the waters and interfered with the seasonal fluctuations in water volumes. The construction of tunnels changed the natural conditions of rock formations and influenced hydraulic conditions. The use of water and the emission of flue gases in mining and metallurgy in the early modern period therefore represented significant, regional anthropogenic environmental influences – both in the European colonies in South America and in Europe itself.[8]

3 Natural Water in Human Mining Activities

The focus of this article is on water as a carrier material for metallurgically usable substances, and not on the technical solutions for water use. In his work on mining and metallurgy, Georgius Agricola of course had a multifaceted view of the potential uses and dangers of water for the human activity of mining and the associated metallurgical practices. He regarded water as a resource, as a raw material that could be put to productive use. Despite this "humanization" of water, Agricola also highlights aspects that lay outside the realm of human use and did not concern human activities. These aspects were not external to the spheres perceptible or observable by humans and may have had indirect effects on humans. For Agricola, however, they are described as largely autonomous – such as hydraulic properties, the accumulation of water in a mine or hydropower.

The important aspect of Agricola's knowledge about the generation of water and its underground course has been investigated by Isabel F. Barton. She not only examined Agricola's writings on the different ways in which underground water works, but also presented a history of ideas about geological water since Greek antiquity, since Agricola was influenced by different authors from European Antiquity. This contextualization of knowledge regarding water in the 16th century can be followed up more broadly by outlining the significance of water in other contemporaneous writings. The 16th-century French scholar Bernard Palissy, for example, in his work *Discours admirables de la nature des eaux et fonteines*, written as a dialog between Theory and Practice, makes Theory say the following:

---

e-docs.geo-leo.de/server/api/core/bitstreams/9f78e155-32a9-44dd-b1ba-02ac94b16d50/content (09.04.2025).

8 Herrmann, *Umweltgeschichte. Eine Einführung in Grundbegriffe*, pp. 144–145; Thomas Wickman, "Narrating Indigenous Histories of Climate Change in the Americas and Pacific", in: *The Palgrave Handbook of Climate History*, eds. Sam White, Christian Pfister and Franz Mauelshagen, London 2018, p. 397.

> don't you know that water is one of these elements, indeed even the first of them all, without which nothing could be initiated? I do not say anything about the animal, nor the vegetal, nor the mineral, nor even about the stones, as I will make you understand when I talk about them.[9]

In their essay "The cultural and material worlds of mining in early modern Europe", Tina Asmussen and Pamela O. Long emphasize how authors such as Georgius Agricola and Andreas Ryff stylized mining as a civilization-preserving achievement of European culture in the 16th century. These two mining experts of the Renaissance period believed that the prosperity of princes and citizens could not be preserved without a positive turn towards mining.[10] In this respect, it is hardly surprising that Agricola portrays the use of water in a very positive light from a technical perspective. If the right experts make the right decisions, then the negative effects of water consumption in mining and the surrounding areas would be unnoticeable. Moreover, the advantages of using water correctly and profitably outweigh the disadvantages that could arise through competition over watercourses or pollution.

The topic of water was frequently researched as both a supporting and a jeopardizing part of the technical development of mines in the early modern period. Franziska Neumann emphasizes this double-sided significance of water for career paths in the mining administration in Saxony in the 16th and 17th centuries.[11] For Fessner and Bartels, the use of water power was among the technological innovations that Central European mining had undergone since the 16th century.[12] How the power of water could be used to drive water wheels, for example, is fascinating thanks to the diverse structural and mechanical solutions that emerged in the Middle Ages and early modern period. Waterwheels were used to drive pumps or hoisting machines, or could set mills, weather machines, hammer

9 Bernard Palissy, *Discours admirables, de la nature des eaux et fonteines, tant naturelles qu'artificielles, des metaux, des sels & salines, des pierres, des terres, du feu & des emaux. Avec plusieurs autres excellens secrets des choses naturelles. Plus un traité de la marne, fort utile & necessaire, pour ceux qui se mellent de l'agriculture. Le tout dressé par dialogues, esquels sont introduits la theorique & la practique. Par M. Bernard Palissy, inventeur des rustiques figulines du Roy, & de la Royne sa mere. A treshaut, et trespuissant sieur le sire Anthoine de Ponts, chevalier des ordres du Roy, capitaine des cents gentils-hommes, & conseiller tresfidele de Sa Majesté.*, eds. Antoine de Ponts and Martin Le Jeune, Paris 1580, pp. 72–73. Original: 'ne sçais tu pas que l'eau est l'un des elements, voire le premier entre tous, sans lequel nulle chose ne pouroit prendre cõmencement ? ie dy nulle chose animee, n'y vegetatine, n'y minerale, ne mesme les pierres, comme ie te feray entendre en parlant d'icelles.'

10 Tina Asmussen and Pamela O. Long, "Introduction: The Cultural and Material Worlds of Mining in Early Modern Europe", in: *Renaissance Studies* 34/1 (2020), pp. 8–30, https://doi.org/10.1111/rest.12581.

11 Franziska Neumann, *Die Ordnung des Berges: Formalisierung und Systemvertrauen in der sächsischen Bergverwaltung (1470–1600)*, Göttingen 2021, pp. 120–125; 263–265.

12 Fessner and Bartels, "Von der Krise am Ende des 16. Jahrhunderts zum deutschen Bergbau im Zeitalter des Merktantilismus", pp. 463–466.

mills and bellows in motion.[13] Water was thus part of the mechanics of mining. In some cases, above-ground water was used to drive the machines, by collecting it into a usable quantity by detour and damming, and it could be brought into a desired flow form. After all, the force and speed of flow were of great importance for the proper functioning of the technical equipment. In some cases, however, water flowing underground was also used, which was directed and channeled through galleries. This underground water was first tapped by mining and by digging pits, galleries and shafts. It consisted of seeping water or groundwater that accumulated in the soil layers. As a result of the digging, this water, flowing out of the rock, collected in the technical infrastructure created by the miners and became not only a disruptive element, but one that endangered this infrastructure. Directed drainage in a gallery enabled the disruption and risks to be reduced and at the same time made available a resource whose power potential could be utilized.

Legal documents increasingly recorded the regulation of natural water through technical intervention since the end of the 15th century. Among other things, contracts were concluded in which entrepreneurs made a commitment to the sovereign to find technical means to free a mine from flooding and help drain it. One example of such a contract is the agreement concluded between Dukes Ernst and Albrecht of Saxony on the one hand and Hans von Stauffenberg on the other to make the mine on the Geisingberg, near the town of Altenberg in Saxony, usable again by means of a drainage system: 'Contract to erect a Device on Mount Geysing, to drain the mountain …'[14]

In the anthroposphere, water was considered a usable resource on account of its mechanical power. Its importance consisted in the fact that it could set technical structures in motion. This form of water utilization thus relates to a theme of energy history. The power of running water was converted into a mechanical force and became a resource. In the course of the construction of waterworks, legal disputes arose about the effect of the technical solutions installed at great expense, as shown, for example, by a document on problems in the Freiberg mine, in which the sovereigns complain about the ineffectiveness of a drainage gallery and at the same time make suggestions for solving ongoing problems.[15] Knowledge about the construction of so-called "arts" held such a special position in

13 Heinz Krümmer, "Bergbauurkunden der Markgrafen von Meißen aus der zweiten Hälfte des 14. Jahrhunderts und ihre Bedeutung bis zur Agricola-Zeit", in: *Georgius Agricola, 500 Jahre: Wissenschaftliche Konferenz vom 25.–27. März 1994 in Chemnitz, Freistaat Sachsen*, ed. Friedrich Naumann, Basel 1994, pp. 299–306, https://doi.org/10.1007/978-3-0348-7159-4_32; Klaus Mauersberger, "Maschinenwesen und Maschinenkunde im 16. und 17. Jahrhundert", in: *Georgius Agricola, 500 Jahre*, ed. Friedrich Naumann, Basel 1994, pp. 380–391, https://doi.org/10.1007/978-3-0348-7159-4_40.

14 Friedrich August Schmid, *Diplomatische Beiträge zur Sächsischen Geschichte*, Vol. 1, Dresden/Leipzig 1839, p. 18.

15 Sächsisches Staatsarchiv, 40001 Oberbergamt Freiberg, Nr. 3352, f. 34.

mining that it was decisive for the careers of officials in Saxony's mining administration of the 16th century.[16]

There is another form of using the mechanical power of water associated with medieval and early modern mining. Water was used in various stages of ore processing to flush away ore components for which there was initially no further use. The water was passed at a regulated speed through a trough, or a whole series of troughs and water basins, so that the heavier, ore-containing components could settle, while the lighter and, in the view of the period, useless substances were washed away. This changed the chemical composition of the water, which now carried the substances extracted during the washing process and mixed with cleaner water and created sediments in its course.

These forms of use and the special infrastructures that were built for them show that water was an integral part of the early modern Technosphere: Collecting basins, canals, galleries, wooden channels and pipes, dams and barrages, overflows, drains and sluices led to technical systems that extended into larger landscape areas. These technical infrastructures not only had effects directly in the mining area, but changed the water in its course, chemical composition and seasonal variance also in the lower-lying watercourses.

The energetic use of water in the mining sector is therefore more similar to arable soil on which various crops grow. Although the soil loses nutrients through cultivation, it is ploughed up and worked in other ways, and after the harvest the soil remains arable land that can be reused in the same way after a few months of fallow. After its mechanical use for washing out ores or for conversion into mechanical power, the water continued on its way as a stream, with only a small part lost due to human intervention.[17] Unlike this energetic use, however, in the chemical use of the water the liquid part of the water was largely consumed. Water had to be evaporated in order to extract the material of interest, and in most applications there was no further reason to collect it and return it to the natural cycle. Even if any water was nevertheless returned after chemical use, the chemical composition of the initial material had been changed by the removal or addition of some substances. Although it can be assumed that the entire volume of water, for example from a spring, was not used up for the chemical yield, but only a small proportion of its volume, this extractive use nevertheless represented a strong alteration of the chemical composition of the watercourse.

16 Neumann, *Die Ordnung des Berges*, pp. 123–124.

17 Gerhard Mathé, "Agricola und die Geologie", in: *NTM International Journal of History & Ethics of Natural Sciences, Technology & Medicine* 2/1 (1994), pp. 13–26, https://doi.org/10.1007/BF02914993.

4 Agricola's View of the Chemical Use of Water

In Georgius Agricola's writings, the two energetic uses of running water were complemented by a third form in the realm of chemical practice. In addition to the mechanical, technical or energetic uses of water in mining in the early modern period, water has this other side that affects the anthroposphere. Some waters contain high proportions of substances in which humans have an interest. For example, salt was extracted from seawater by either letting it evaporate in the sun or boiling it in pans until the liquid components had evaporated and only the mineral substances remained. In addition, Agricola, who was not only a mining expert but also a physician and mayor, described other substances that could be extracted from water. In this form of use, water became a resource in its own right, even if only a small proportion of the ingredients it contained could be extracted.

The components of solid or other liquid substances could be dissolved with the aid of cold or warm water. Either the dissolved substances were of no further interest to the metallurgist and the mixture was discharged, or it was the substances dissolved from their natural solution in water that the metallurgist now wanted to recover in as pure a form as possible by further processing the solution or brine. Here again, the chemical composition of water changed through human activity. Water was withdrawn from the natural cycle and in some cases returned chemically altered. In some cases, it was evaporated and the gaseous, chemically heterogeneous particles were released into the air, thus influencing the atmosphere and the water cycle.[18]

The use of water in mining brings different areas of knowledge into direct exchange with each other. The exploitation of water in mining for the purpose of extracting certain substances required knowledge about the basic resource of water. In addition, knowledge of how to identify a particular substance in a particular water had to be activated. Finally, an enormous amount of detailed knowledge was required to extract the specific substance from the water mixture using chemical processes and then to process the dissolved parts in such a way that the desired material was obtained.

The exchange of different areas of knowledge arose from a mining interest, namely, to extract a certain substance in as pure a form as possible. Certain pre-mining and pre-chemical experience with a particular water source must have existed, however, before a metallurgy expert like Georgius Agricola could formulate the claim that a sufficiently large quantity of the substance could be extracted from a particular spring by means of chemical processes.

Agricola's claim was not merely a description of common mining practices. Rather, his aim was to raise awareness among miners and decision-makers in this field. He presented his knowledge as reliable knowledge that had been developed and tested in close association with practice. For him, there was no doubt about

18 William Ruddiman et al., "Does Pre-Industrial Warming Double the Anthropogenic Total?", in: *The Anthropocene Review* 1/2 (2014), p. 152, https://doi.org/10.1177/2053019614529263.

the advantages of the forms of water use he described and, as mentioned above, the metallurgical exploitation of spring water represented a greater benefit than the environmental and social problems that could arise from the extraction, detour and addition of other substances.

5 Discussing Geological Water

Agricola discussed water types that had a high mineral content as a secondary topic of the second book of the *De Re Metallica*, how the "good miner" could gain knowledge of deposits and the "right" way to exploit them. Most of these deposits could only be exploited by the miner digging a pit and creating a mine. This was different for the extraction of substances from water, although here, too, intervention in nature and changes to the landscape were necessary. Agricola placed the section on the extraction of minerals from water between the sections on the construction of a mine and the extraction of mineral sands:

> Nunc dicam de his ad quæ assequenda metallico non opus est fossionibus, quod ea uis aquarum secum ex uenis efferat : quorum duo genera sunt, fossilia, eorumue ramenta, & succi. Cum autem fontes sint ora uenarum, è quibus iam dicta emittuntur, eos primum metallicus considerat, utrum habeant arenam cum metallis aut gemmis permistam, an aquam alicuius succi plenam effundant : si quid metallorum uel gemmarum in fontium lacunis subsederit, non ipsorum modo arenæ sunt lauandæ, se etiam riuorum qui ab eis deducuntur, & fluminum in quæ rursus illi exonerant: sin fontes ex sese aquam aliquo succo infectam emiserint, ea itidem colligenda est: quanto enim ab ortus sui loco longius defluxerit, pluresque combiberit aquas simplices, tanto fit dilutior, tantoque magis eam uires deficiunt : …[19]

19 Agricola, *De re metallica*, pp. 23–24; Georg Agricola, *Zwölf Bücher vom Berg- und Hüttenwesen. In denen die Ämter, Instrumente, Maschinen und alle Dinge, die zum Berg- und Hüttenwesen gehören, nicht nur aufs deutlichste beschrieben, sondern auch durch Abbildungen … aufs klarste vor Augen gestellt werden (1556).* transl. and ed. Carl Schiffner, Berlin 1928, pp. 27–28.
'Nun will ich von den Erzeugnissen reden, zu deren Gewinnung der Bergmann nicht zu graben braucht, weil die Kraft des Wassers sie aus den Lagerstätten freimacht. Es gibt hiervon zwei Arten, nämlich Mineralien oder ihre Bruchstücke und Lösungen oder ihre Erstarrungsprodukte. Wenn im Ausbiß der Lagerstätten, aus denen die erwähnten Produkte stammen, Quellen auftreten, so untersucht der Bergmann diese, ob sie Sande mit Erzkörnern oder Edelsteinen durchmischt oder gelöste Mineralien führen. … Enthält das Wasser der Quellen gelöste Mine-//28//ralien, so muß es aufgestaut werden; je weiter es nämlich vom Entstehungsort wegfließt und je mehr es somit reines Wasser aufnimmt, desto verdünnter wird es und desto mehr verliert es an Gehalt.'
Hoover and Hoover (1950, p. 33) translate as following: 'Now I will discuss that kind of minerals for which it is not necessary to dig, because the force of water carries them out of the veins. Of these there are two kinds, minerals – and their fragments – and juices. When there are springs at the outcrop of the veins from which, as I have already said, the above-mentioned products are emitted, the miner should consider these first, to see whether there are metals or gems mixed with the sand, or whether the waters discharged are filled with juices. In case metals or gems have settled in the pool of the spring, not only should the sand from it

Agricola does not propose a typology of different types of water but distinguishes only between those that contain a certain amount of minerals and those that do not. If the issue of typology applies at all to this chapter, it is to the different types of stretches of water, which Agricola enumerates, such as brooks, rivers, ponds and lakes. These types offer different conditions to which the miner has to adapt if he intends to win minerals from water. Furthermore, a high mineral content in water may hint at mineral deposits in adjacent rocks through which the water had run. That this kind of water was central to the miner's interests is evidenced by the fact that it is also an issue in the following part of the book, on sands, which were themselves a product of water activities.[20] These types of deposits were also mentioned by Palissy, who stated that it was possible to find mineral deposits in neighboring rocks. In his view, the water that ran through clay soils mines would absorb minerals. Therefore, this water hinted with a high degree of certainty at the presence of deposits.[21] The miner, as Agricola also explained, should follow the water back upstream to reach and exploit those deposits.

Agricola highlighted a second possibility, as the miner might envisage using the mineral-rich water as a raw material. In that case, Agricola advised damming up the water and preventing the mineral content from draining away.

To detect the type and degree of mineral saturation, any mining expert should employ a bodily method. Agricola recommended tasting the water to distinguish possibly "six different mineral solutions" from one another, namely salt, soda, alum, vitriol, sulphur and the so-called *Erdwachs* (mineral wax). *Erdwachs* was a bituminous material that was easily recognizable, as it changed spring water to a dark, blackish color.[22]

The utility of these types of water is defined by Agricola in the twelfth book of his *De Re Metallica,* as follows:

> However, *succi* are naturally or artificially made out of solids and of waters, that moistens *succi,* either to make liquid *succi* or mixed stones.[23]

6 Succi: Water-Providing Substances

Agricola discusses the issue of 'condensed products won from solutions' in the twelfth and last book of *De Re Metallica.* He challenges the opinion that this theme does not belong here among those normally linked to the knowledge of mining

be washed, but also that from the streams which flow from these springs, and even from the river itself into which they again discharge. If the springs discharge water containing some juice, this also should be collected; the further such a stream has flowed from the source, the more it receives plain water and the more diluted does it become, and so much the more deficient in strength.'

20 Agricola, *De re metallica,* p. 24.

21 Palissy, *Discours admirables,* pp. 21–22.

22 Agricola, Schiffner, *Zwölf Bücher vom Berg- und Hüttenwesen,* p. 29.

23 Agricola, *De re metallica,* p. 439. Original: 'Succi autem concreti conficiuntur uel ex aquis, quas natura, aut ars, succis infecit, uel ex ipsis succis liquidis, uel ex lapidibus mistis.'

and ore treatment. In his attempt to depict the wide spectrum of knowledge and to picture the whole economy of knowledge of mining, he explains that condensed products originate from waters 'which were enriched either through natural processes or through artificial measures with those substances, with liquid substances or with mixed minerals.'[24]

Three phenomena observed by Agricola led in a natural manner (i.e. without any human intervention) to so-called 'condensed products' – which in modern terminology would be named solutions:

1 Saturated water
2 Substances dissolved in water
3 Water that contains a mixture of an undistinguished number of different dissolved minerals

This aspect of water, as a carrier of minerals, has hardly been treated in historiography. Agricola's own knowledge about those dissolved substances was gained mainly from two sources: First, he could rely on his own experience and observation. Second, he could make use of his reading of ancient and contemporary writings, which helped him to find examples that backed up his thesis. He argued that minerals dissolved in water could play a certain role in mining and metallurgy. In addition to this thesis, he presented other technologies for extracting substances, for example by evaporation in the sun or by any artificial heat source.

The early 20th-century team led by Carl Schiffner that translated Agricola into German emphasize that the issue of solutions and condensed products was also treated in his *De Natura Fossilium*. The Italian historian of geology Nicoletta Morello guesses that Agricola may have borrowed the term *succi* from Dioscorides' *Materia medica*.[25] Indeed, several authors of the early 17th century employ this term and refer often to Agricola and Dioscorides. In his work *Hoc Scrutinium Chimicum Vitrioli*, the German physician Johann Georgius Trumph explains *succi* to be a mineral fossil mentioned by Agricola in his *De Natura Fossilium*.[26]

In Agricola's work, the *succi concreti* are not clearly assigned to one aggregate state: 'However, *succi* are naturally or artificially made out of solids and of waters, that moistens *succi*, either to make liquid *succi* or mixed stones.'[27] The group of substances Agricola calls *succi* can manifest either in a liquid or in a solid form. Their most important characteristic seems to be that each material is composed of many substances. *Succus* does not designate a liquid, in contrast to some usages

24 Agricola, Schiffner, *De Re Metallica*, p. 466.

25 Nicoletta Morello, "Agricola and the Birth of the Mineralogical Sciences in Italy in the Sixteenth Century", in: *The Origins of Geology in Italy*, eds. Gian Battista Vai and W. Glen E. Caldwell (The Geological Society of America, Special Paper 411), Boulder, CO 2006, p. 26.

26 Johan Georgius Trumph, *Hoc Scrutinium Chimicum Vitrioli*, Jena 1666, ch. 3.

27 Agricola, *De re metallica*, p. 439. Original: 'Succi autem concreti conficiuntur uel ex aquis, quas natura, aut ars, succis infecit, uel ex ipsis succis liquidis, uel ex lapidibus mistis.'

of the term in medical writings of the period.[28] For Agricola, *succus* designates a mix of different substances of both aggregate states, in which solid substances are bound and can through chemical and technical processes be extracted. In their translation, Lou Henry and Herbert Hoover introduced a very early explanatory footnote, stating that they used the term 'juice' to translate *succus*. They considered any modern chemical terminology, such as solution or salt, inappropriate to 'the state of knowledge in Agricola's time'.[29] Schiffner and his colleagues translated this term as *Verdichtungsprodukt* (condensed products) in German.[30] They argued that Agricola described the interaction of solid substances and water, both in their solubility and in their resistant solidity, in an apparently contradictory manner, as *succi*. In both the German and the American translation, the main aspect was not the aggregate state, but the fact that these were mixed products bearing different chemical substances mixed together and soluble in added water.

In most cases, the metallurgist Agricola was interested in a specific substance that was obtained and extracted from the original *succus*.[31] In his description, a *succus* contains a proportion of water, or else water is an important means of dissolving and decomposing the *succus*. According to Agricola, one group of these *succi* includes natural bitumen or natural oils. The second group contains rock salts and soils that can be dissolved in water.[32]

Agricola's focus on mixed products relates directly to his conception of the relationship between nature and humans, because it highlights the separation between a natural world of mixing and an anthropogenic world of producing pure substances for economic use. If *succi* occur in nature, in which they can be either solid or liquid as mixed products, a transformation (or transmutation) into a pure substance is sought through a series of chemical and physical steps. The production of copper, silver and gold in their respective pure forms meant precisely this transformation, whereby in metallurgical practice the metallurgist, as an expert himself, produced new mixtures as intermediate products, so that separations could be carried out in a subsequent step.[33]

---

28 Johann Gottfried von Berger, *De succi nutricii per nervos transitu*, Vitemberga 1695; Galenus, *De cibis boni et mali succi Liber*, Rostock 1594.

29 Herbert Hoover and Lou Henry Hoover, *Georgius Agricola. De Re Metallica*, New York 1950, p. 1, n. 3.

30 Agricola, Schiffner, *Zwölf Bücher vom Berg- und Hüttenwesen*, p. 466.

31 Francesco Luzzini, "Harvesting Underground: (Re)generative Theories and Vegetal Analogies in the Early Modern Debate on Mineral Ores (I)", in: *Notes and Records: the Royal Society Journal of the History of Science* (2023), p. 10, https://dx.doi.org/10.1098/rsnr.2023.0032.

32 Agricola, Schiffner, *Zwölf Bücher vom Berg- und Hüttenwesen*, p. 466.

33 Ursula Klein, *Verbindung und Affinität. Die Grundlegung der neuzeitlichen Chemie an der Wende vom 17. zum 18. Jahrhundert*, Basel/Boston/Berlin 1994; Tara Nummedal, *Alchemy and Authority in the Holy Roman Empire*, Chicago/London 2007, p. 92; Helge Wendt, "Kontingenzbewältigung der Stoffvielfalt bei Agricola am Beispiel der Gruppe Gagat-Bitumen-Kohle", in: *Logbuch Wissensgeschichte*, eds. Mira Becker-Sawatzky et al. (Episteme in Bewegung 36), Wiesbaden 2024, pp. 241–257.

Thus, mineral water was in Agricola's understanding a *succus*. Once the miner had identified and tested the mineral content of a water spring, he could start to extract them through mechanical and chemical processes. In his aim of gaining as pure a substance as possible, Agricola relied in his texts on practices of extraction from earlier times and from other periods. In this sense, he created a new economy of mining knowledge that blended formerly separated areas of mining and metallurgical practice.

A practice of extracting salt dissolved in water that Agricola described was common on the Atlantic and Mediterranean coasts. In these so-called 'salt gardens', salt water from the sea was retained in low basins. Over several days or weeks, the heat of the sun evaporated the water and all that remained on the ground of a basin was relatively pure salt.

Terminology at this point is crucial again. Nicholas of Cusa, for instance, describes a process of hardening or solidification. The transformative process that occurred in the basins of the 'salt gardens' was understood as if the mineral-rich water solidified through the impact of the sun's heat and was transmuted into a solid substance that could be used.[34] The way Agricola understood this process was very similar. He too did not consider a loss of water through evaporation: this is the best explanation of the term *succi concreti* or (in the Hoover translation with reference to Agricola's *De Ortu*) 'solidified juice'.[35] In light of the definition of *succi* as a mixed product of either a liquid or a solid state, as discussed above, this interesting interpretation of the transformation of sea water into salt by Cusanus and Agricola becomes understandable. It is not that the water disappears, but that it becomes solid, so salt still contains water, but in a solidified state.[36] When the *succus* changed its appearance and its usability for the human sphere, the water remained a part of it. Only further human action could extract the water from that state of *succus*.

In his construction of a European economy of mining knowledge, Agricola also mentioned salt-extracting processes in other parts of Europe, where salty springs provided humans with this useful raw material. It could be acquired by heating the mineral water in large kettles on a fire, fueled by wood or charcoal. Agricola was not the first to consider both forms of gaining salt in a single text. Bernard Palissy dismissed this form of acquiring salt, as it consumed a high amount of fuel.[37] Agricola backed this process, however, as it meant that salt could be produced in a greater variety of European regions. Besides gaining salt from naturally salty

34 Nikolaus Cusanus, *Der Laie über Versuche mit der Waage (Idiota de staticis experimentis)*, ed. Hildegund Menzel-Rogner, Leipzig 1942, p. 31, URL: https://nbn-resolving.org/urn:nbn:de:bvb:355-ubr21737-8 (09.04.2025).

35 Agricola, *De re metallica*, p. 439; Hoover and Hoover, *Georgius Agricola*, p. 1; p. 49.

36 Cf. on the solidification and petrification of water, Robert Halleux, "La littérature géologique française de 1500 à 1650 dans son contexte européen", in: *Revue d'histoire des sciences* 35/2 (1982), p. 125, URL: https://www.persee.fr/doc/rhs_0151-4105_1982_num_35_2_1818 (09.04.2025).

37 Palissy, *Discours admirables*, pp. 189–192.

springs, even worthless material from the rock-salt mines could be exploited by dissolving the salty stones in water.[38]

Agricola also described how different types of vitriol could be acquired by the artificial heating method. Water containing vitriol could be collected in pots or kettles and heated by fire, or by being stored in low basins and exposed to the heat of the sun. By these processes, gray, black or red vitriol could be yielded.[39] If the liquid mixture was heated by a charcoal or wood fire, the air pollution and the pollution of the adjacent rivers must have been quite significant.[40]

Vitriol was a rather heterogeneous group of substances defined by medieval and early modern chemical knowledges. Besides gray, black and red, vitriol could be of green color, depending on the kind of oxidation the substance went through. Especially iron, zinc and copper were connected to the natural origin of vitriol.[41] In the human sphere, the various types of vitriol were turned into sought-after natural products and were employed in cloth dyeing, leather processing or in the production of tinctures and remedies, for instance.[42]

7 The Powerful Water: Aqua valens

In 16th-century mining, water could be enriched artificially by adding substances that were believed to influence other materials in a metallurgic process. After these were applied, the enriched water helped to extract the target substance, as gold or silver for instance. During the transformation of ore into pure gold or silver, a so-called separating water was employed. In his Latin version Agricola called this water *aqua valens*. The Hoover translation opts to leave this term untranslated, while Schiffner and his colleagues mostly employed the German term *Scheidewasser* (separating water):

> I will start with the gold: to disjoint silver from it or the other way around, because they were alloyed by nature or art, *aqua valens* or a similar powder composed with a similar aim, is employed. […] In order to observe the right order, I will first speak about the composition of the ingredients

38 Agricola, Schiffner, *Zwölf Bücher vom Berg- und Hüttenwesen*, pp. 466–471.

39 Agricola, Schiffner, *Zwölf Bücher vom Berg- und Hüttenwesen*, p. 489.

40 Arne Andersen, "'De re metallica' — ein Beitrag zu einer frühneuzeitlichen Umwelttechnologie?", in: *Georgius Agricola, 500 Jahre*, ed. F. Naumann, Basel 1994, p. 259, https://doi.org/10.1007/978-3-0348-7159-4_27.

41 Florian Neukirchen and Gunnar Ries, *Die Welt der Rohstoffe. Lagerstätten, Förderung und wirtschaftliche Aspekte*, Berlin/Heidelberg 2016, p. 218; Anna Marie Roos and Victor D. Boantza, "Mineral Waters Across the Channel: Matter Theory and natural History from Samuel Duclos's Minerallogenesis to Martin Lister's Chymical Magnetism, ca. 1666–86", in: *Notes and Records of the Royal Society of London* 69 (2015), pp. 373–394.

42 Klein, *Verbindung und Affinität*, p. 145; Wilhelm Sandermann, *Die Kulturgeschichte des Papiers*, Berlin et al. 1988, p. 89; Volkhard Wels, "Leonhard Thurneyssers Archidoxa (1569/75) und Quinta essentia (1570/74)", in: *Nach der Kulturgeschichte. Perspektiven einer neuen Ideen- und Sozialgeschichte der deutschen Literatur*, eds. Maximilian Benz and Gideon Stiening, Berlin 2022, pp. 249–289.

> of which this water is made: furthermore, of the ratios of its production: finally, on the mode how to gain gold from silver, and silver out of gold.[43]

Agricola was rather cautious in explaining the chemical processes when adding *aqua valens* to the crushed ores. However, he could distinguish four different groups of substances that acted as a kind of catalyst, as we would call them today, to enable the extraction of pure materials as gold or silver. *Aqua valens* was part of the second group of powerful substances, which were added to the ore mixture as "additives".[44] This *aqua valens* was supposed to bind certain substances present in the ore mixture that bore alloyed gold and silver. This new mixture, now a solution, became in the following step of the metallurgic process the material from which components must be extracted. This was a complex chemical working process and sometimes *aqua valens*, sometimes pure water helped to isolate ever purer gold or silver. *Aqua valens* could help to dissolve silver molecules from the compound with gold and absorb them into the solution. There, silver of a high degree of purity could be yielded, just as gold could be obtained from the already extracted substance.

> However, this composition, which has brought silver and copper in itself, will be dried after the water has been poured out and be ground with wood: mixed with lead and impoverished plumb, it will be melted in the first type of furnace – a mixture of silver and lead, or silver and copper and lead, that flows out will be roasted in a second furnace in order to separate lead and copper from silver: the latter step is repeated in a burning place, so that no or only a very little silver is lost.[45]

During the metallurgical process, *aqua valens* became a waste product, largely enriched with other substances extracted from the initial ore mixture. At that stage, the newly enriched artificial water contained several materials, such as silver, copper or lead, that could be recycled in a subsequent procedure. From that perspective of waste reuse, *aqua valens* was already a product gained from other waste substances: saltpeter was obtained from wine production, and diuretic wa-

43 Agricola, *De re metallica*, p. 354. German translation by Schiffner (Agricola, 1928, p. 381). Original: 'Sed ordiar ab auro: id ab argento, uel hoc etiam ab illo, seu natura, seu ars permiscuerit ea, separatur aqua ualenti, & puluere, [...] Verum, ut hic etiam ordinem conseruem, dicam primo de compositionibus rerum, ex quibus aqua illa conficitur: deinde de conficiendi ratione: tum de modo, quo aurum secernitur ab argento, uel argentum ab auro.' Cf. the slightly different translation by Hoover and Hoover, *Georgius Agricola. De Re Metallica*, 439.

44 Agricola, Schiffner, *Zwölf Bücher vom Berg- und Hüttenwesen*, pp. 199–200.

45 Agricola, *De re metallica*, pp. 366–367. Original: 'Sed res compositæ, quæ in se traxerunt argentum uel æs, aqua effusa siccentur, ligno terantur: cum molybdæna & plumbo, depauperato permistæ excoquantur in prima fornace mistura argenti & plumbi, uel argenti & æris & plumbi, quæ effluxit, denuo coquatur in secunda fornace, ut plumbum & æs ab argento separentur: hoc postremo in ustrina perpurgetur; quo sane modo argenti nulla, uel perexigua particula perit.'

ter to produce vitriol was acquired from urine.[46] Vitriol was dissolved with the aid of *aqua valens*, which could not be reused in turn, but evaporated while the mixture was heated, leaving behind the pure vitriol substance.[47]

8 Conclusion: Differentiating Uses of Water in Mining

The examples of legal disputes over water usage rights and draining obligations, as well as the legal privileges for the successful building of drainage infrastructures, indicate the diverse interests relating to water in early modern mining regions. Some actors wanted and needed more water, other felt disturbed by it. While water had the power to disrupt economic activities on the one hand, it enabled other human activities on the other. The competition for water is a sign of its versatility. Water as a means of propulsion, water for cleaning, water for transportation or as a source of raw materials – water had many uses in the sector of mining.

In the 16th century, water was an indispensable matter in many other social domains of everyday life and for a variety of economic activities. In many cases, one use did not exclude the other: Transportation water could also be fishing water that could further be used for textile processing. Still, some restrictions were applied, as water from textile and leather processing could often no longer be drunk. It was heavily contaminated and had become unusable even for irrigating fields and gardens. The same applied to water that had been used for metallurgical purposes. The proportion of heavy metals such as lead, mercury and copper was high and it was already known to the people of the 16th century that it could be harmful to the human body.

The usage of water in mining activities went hand in hand with a high technical input in order to construct technical infrastructure, mechanical devices and chemical processes. The many uses of water in that economic sector implied far-reaching interventions in natural water cycles through pollution, the diversion of watercourses and damming. In addition, through evaporation of water in metallurgical processes, humans removed water in its liquid state. These anthropogenic interventions changed natural watercourses and the local water ecology.

In his writings, Agricola shows his awareness of the wide range of possibilities that can be inherent in water. Unlike with minerals, rocks and metals, he did not attempt a typology. However, his work shows an effort to use different types of water in a way that is as appropriate as possible for each type. From this perspective, the use of water to wash out fine ores or to power waterwheels were both specific kinds of usage related to the specific features of that material, just as it was to extract substances through chemical processes.

46 Agricola, Schiffner, *Zwölf Bücher vom Berg- und Hüttenwesen*, pp. 484–485.
47 Agricola, Schiffner, *Zwölf Bücher vom Berg- und Hüttenwesen*, p. 490.

Reference Lists

Sources

Agricola, Georgius, *De re metallica*, Basel 1561.

Agricola, Georgius, *Zwölf Bücher vom Berg- und Hüttenwesen. In denen die Ämter, Instrumente, Maschinen und alle Dinge, die zum Berg- und Hüttenwesen gehören, nicht nur aufs deutlichste beschrieben, sondern auch durch Abbildungen … aufs klarste vor Augen gestellt werden (1556)*, transl. and ed. Carl Schiffner, Berlin 1928.

Berger, Johann Gottfried von, *De succi nutricii per nervos transitu*, Vitemberga 1695.

Cusanus, Nikolaus, *Der Laie über Versuche mit der Waage (Idiota de staticis experimentis)*, ed. Hildegund Menzel-Rogner, Leipzig 1942, URL: https://nbn-resolving.org/urn:nbn:de:bvb:355-ubr21737-8 (09.04.2025).

Galenus, *De cibis boni et mali succi Liber*, Rostock 1594.

Hoover, Herbert and Lou Henry Hoover, *Georgius Agricola. De Re Metallica*, New York 1950.

Palissy, Bernard, *Discours admirables, de la nature des eaux et fonteines, tant naturelles qu'artificielles, des metaux, des sels & salines, des pierres, des terres, du feu & des emaux. Avec plusieurs autres excellens secrets des choses naturelles. Plus un traité de la marne, fort utile & necessaire, pour ceux qui se mellent de l'agriculture. Le tout dressé par dialogues, esquels sont introduits la theorique & la practique. Par M. Bernard Palissy, inventeur des rustiques figulines du Roy, & de la Royne sa mere. A treshaut, et trespuissant sieur le sire Anthoine de Ponts, chevalier des ordres du Roy, capitaine des cents gentils-hommes, & conseiller tresfidele de Sa Majesté*, Paris 1580.

Schmid, Friedrich August, *Diplomatische Beiträge zur Sächsischen Geschichte*, vol. 1, Dresden/Leipzig 1839.

Trumph, Johan Georgius, *Hoc Scrutinium Chimicum Vitrioli*, Jena 1666.

Research Literature

Andersen, Arne, "'De re metallica' — ein Beitrag zu einer frühneuzeitlichen Umwelttechnologie?", in: *Georgius Agricola, 500 Jahre: Wissenschaftliche Konferenz vom 25.–27. März 1994 in Chemnitz, Freistaat Sachsen*, ed. Friedrich Naumann, Basel 1994, pp. 255–266, https://doi.org/10.1007/978-3-0348-7159-4_27.

Asmussen, Tina and Pamela O. Long, "Introduction: The Cultural and Material Worlds of Mining in Early Modern Europe", in: *Renaissance Studies* 34/1 (2020), pp. 8–30, https://doi.org/10.1111/rest.12581.

Brandl, Simon, Mystik und Magie im Frühparacelsismus: Erkundungen um Alexander von Suchtens Traktat ‚De tribus facultatibus', Berlin/Boston 2021.

Chang, Hasok, *Is Water H2O? Evidence, Realism and Pluralism*, Dordrecht et al. 2012.

Fessner, Michael and Christoph Bartels, "Von der Krise am Ende des 16. Jahrhunderts zum deutschen Bergbau im Zeitalter des Merktantilismus", in: *Geschichte des Deutschen Bergbaus. Band 1: Der alteuropäische Bergbau. Von den Anfängen bis zur Mitte des 18. Jahrhunderts*, ed. Wolfhard Weber, Münster 2012, pp. 453–590.

Halleux, Robert, "La littérature géologique française de 1500 à 1650 dans son contexte européen", in: *Revue d'histoire des sciences* 35/2 (1982), pp. 111–130, URL: https://www.persee.fr/doc/rhs_0151-4105_1982_num_35_2_1818 (09.04.2025).

Herrmann, Bernd, *Umweltgeschichte. Eine Einführung in Grundbegriffe*, Berlin/Heidelberg 2016.

Jaschik, Eva, ed., "Bergordnung für Schemnitz/ Banská Štiavnica von 1466", in: *Das Stadt- und Bergrecht von Banská Štiavnica, Schemnitz. Untersuchungen zum Frühneuhochdeutschen in der Slowakei*, Oulu (Veröffentlichungen des Germanistischen Instituts) 1986, pp. 3–9, URL: https://e-docs.geo-leo.de/bitstream/handle/11858/11345/Bergordnung%20Schemnitz%201466.pdf?sequence=1&isAllowed=y (09.04.2025).

Klein, Ursula, *Verbindung und Affinität. Die Grundlegung der neuzeitlichen Chemie an der Wende vom 17. zum 18. Jahrhundert*, Basel/Boston/Berlin 1994.

Krümmer, Heinz, "Bergbauurkunden der Markgrafen von Meißen aus der zweiten Hälfte des 14. Jahrhunderts und ihre Bedeutung bis zur Agricola-Zeit", in: *Georgius Agricola, 500 Jahre: Wissenschaftliche Konferenz vom 25.–27. März 1994 in Chemnitz, Freistaat Sachsen*, ed. Friedrich Naumann, Basel 1994, pp. 299–306, https://doi.org/10.1007/978-3-0348-7159-4_32.

Luzzini, Francesco, "Harvesting Underground: (Re)generative Theories and Vegetal Analogies in the Early Modern Debate on Mineral Ores (I)", in: *Notes and Records: the Royal Society Journal of the History of Science* (2023), https://doi.org/10.1098/rsnr.2023.0032.

Mathé, Gerhard, "Agricola und die Geologie", in: *NTM International Journal of History & Ethics of Natural Sciences, Technology & Medicine* 2/1 (1994), pp. 13–26, https://doi.org/10.1007/BF02914993.

Mauersberger, Klaus, "Maschinenwesen und Maschinenkunde im 16. und 17. Jahrhundert", in: *Georgius Agricola, 500 Jahre: Wissenschaftliche Konferenz vom 25.–27. März 1994 in Chemnitz, Freistaat Sachsen*, ed. Friedrich Naumann, Basel 1994, pp. 380–391, https://doi.org/10.1007/978-3-0348-7159-4_40.

Morello, Nicoletta, "Agricola and the Birth of the Mineralogical Sciences in Italy in the Sixteenth Century", in: *The Origins of Geology in Italy*, eds. Gian Battista Vai and W. Glen E. Caldwell (The Geological Society of America, Special Paper 411), Boulder, CO, 2006, pp. 23–30.

Neukirchen, Florian and Gunnar Ries, *Die Welt der Rohstoffe. Lagerstätten, Förderung und wirtschaftliche Aspekte*, Berlin/Heidelberg 2016.

Neumann, Franziska, *Die Ordnung des Berges: Formalisierung und Systemvertrauen in der sächsischen Bergverwaltung (1470–1600)*, Göttingen 2021.

Nummedal, Tara, *Alchemy and Authority in the Holy Roman Empire*, Chicago/London 2007.

Roos, Anna Marie and Victor D. Boantza, "Mineral Waters Across the Channel: Matter Theory and natural History from Samuel Duclos's Minerallogenesis to Martin Lister's Chymical Magnetism, ca. 1666–86", in: *Notes and Records of the Royal Society of London* 69 (2015), pp. 373–394.

Ruddiman, William, Steve Vavrus, John Kutzbach and Feng He, „Does Pre-Industrial Warming Double the Anthropogenic Total?", in: *The Anthropocene Review* 1/2 (2014), pp. 147–153, https://doi.org/10.1177/2053019614529263.

Sandermann, Wilhelm, *Die Kulturgeschichte des Papiers*, Berlin et al. 1988.

Wels, Volkhard, "Leonhard Thurneyssers Archidoxa (1569/75) und Quinta essentia (1570/74)", in: *Nach der Kulturgeschichte. Perspektiven einer neuen Ideen- und Sozialgeschichte der deutschen Literatur*, eds. Maximilian Benz and Gideon Stiening, Berlin 2022, pp. 249–289.

Wendt, Helge, "Kontingenzbewältigung der Stoffvielfalt bei Agricola am Beispiel der Gruppe Gagat-Bitumen-Kohle", in: *Logbuch Wissensgeschichte*, eds. Mira Becker-Sawatzky, Şirin Dadaş, Anne Eusterschulte, Kristiane Hasselmann, Andrew James

Johnston, Falk Quenstedt, Claudia Reufer, Hanna Zoe Trauer, Christian Vogel, Katrin Wächter and Helge Wendt, Wiesbaden 2024 (Episteme in Bewegung 36), pp. 241–257.

Wickman, Thomas, "Narrating Indigenous Histories of Climate Change in the Americas and Pacific", in: *The Palgrave Handbook of Climate History*, eds. Sam White, Christian Pfister and Franz Mauelshagen, London 2018, pp. 387–411.

The First and Proper Companion of Mines: Water and Ore Generation in Biringuccio's *De la Pirotechnia* (1540)

Francesco Luzzini

1 (Self-)caveat

To deal with the history of science – all of it – means to confront a tangle of contingency, individual talent, and economic, geographical, political, social, cultural, intellectual nuances that are at the same time causes and consequences of scientific and technological progress.

In delving into this issue the importance of contextualization can hardly be overrated. And yes, I am aware of how obvious this assertion sounds. But how essential it still is for us historians: for it is exactly in our assumed familiarity with the notion of *context* that our inveterate inclination to overlook it (and, therefore, our frequent failures to grasp its complexity) lies.

I deemed this statement necessary, as the subject I wish to discuss here is particularly tricky. The endeavor of exploring the relationship between natural philosophy and mining in the Renaissance offers plenty of reasons for caution, given the many different (often contradictory) interactions that linked the research of alchemists, physicians, academics, learned clergymen, and other *curious* savants with the practical traditions of technicians, engineers, artisans, and simple miners. This heterogeneous body of knowledge was influenced by a multitude of geographical and geological settings and by social, political, cultural, religious contexts which overlapped all over Europe and throughout the early modern period, a stratification of theories and practices that makes venturing into this maze no simple task. And yet, it is exactly on the complexity of this collective effort (which was both intellectual and practical) that we need to focus in order to understand how early modern inquiry fostered the development of the Earth sciences – and how, at the same time, it shaped the evolution of the human-environment system.

As I shall try to explain in the following, the debate on mineral generation (and, some argued, *re*generation) provides an excellent starting point for our attempt to understand such complexity. And more specifically, the work of the Sienese metallurgist Vannoccio Biringuccio (1480–1539) seems to offer an exemplary case study.

DOI: 10.13173/9783447123693.185

2 Whence All those Treasures?

Several studies in the past two decades[1] have shown how providing a coherent understanding of the subterranean growth of ores was not just a *philosophical* whim to early modern societies. Not only scholars, but workers, too, needed theory: to those who were bound to live a great (and quite uncomfortable, and dangerous) share of their existence in mines, rationalizing the underground presence of minerals and metals was a first necessary step to build the notions of *predictability, exploitability, exhaustibility* and *renewability* of these natural resources. And all these notions, in turn, formed the indispensable theoretical ground for the interests and hopes – economic, social, political – which propelled the growth of the mining industry during the Renaissance (when, not incidentally, many more-or-less independent models aiming to explain the origin of ores appeared and confronted each other).[2]

These explanations emerged from an intricate and fluctuating panorama which was made up of first-hand experience, practical, technical, alchemical and philosophical traditions, a good deal of bookish learning, and many, many doubts and reconsiderations. So intricate and fluctuating was this panorama in fact, that in most cases it would be more appropriate to speak of *concepts* or *ideas*, rather than *theories* or *systems*, of the formation of ores. Still, it is safe to say that

1 See Warren Alexander Dym, "Mineral fumes and mining spirits: Popular beliefs in the *Sarepta* of Johann Mathesius (1504–1565)", in: *Reformation & Renaissance Review* 8/2 (2006), pp. 161–185; idem, "Alchemy and mining: Metallogenesis and prospecting in early mining books", in: *Ambix* 55/3 (2008), pp. 232–254; Francesco Luzzini, "Sounding the depths of providence: Mineral (re)generation and human-environment interaction in the early modern period", in: *Earth Sciences History* 39/2 (2020), pp. 389–408; idem, "Harvesting Underground: (Re) generative theories and vegetal analogies in the early modern debate on mineral ores (I)", in: *Notes and Records: the Royal Society journal of the history of science*, Online First (2023), https://doi.org/10.1098/rsnr.2023.0032; Martin Lynch, *Mining in World History*, London 2002; John Norris, "The mineral exhalation theory of metallogenesis in pre-modern mineral science", in: *Ambix* 53/1 (2006), pp. 43–65; idem, "Early theories of aqueous mineral genesis in the sixteenth century", in: *Ambix* 54/1 (2007), pp. 69–86; Raffaello Vergani, "Miniere e minerali nella Pirotechnia di Biringuccio: natura, ricerca, sfruttamento", in: *L'ultimo secolo della Repubblica di Siena. Arti, cultura e società*, eds. Mario Ascheri, Gianni Mannozzi and Fabrizio Nevola, Siena 2008, pp. 467–475.

2 On the role played by economic, cultural, and social factors in the evolution of early modern mining, see Tina Asmussen, "Glück auf! Fortuna und risiko im frühneuzeitlichen Bergbau", in: *FKW // Zeitschrift für Geschlechterforschung und visuelle Kultur* 60 (2016), pp. 30–41; idem, "The Kux as a site of mediation: Economic practices and material desires in the early modern German mining industry", in: *Sites of Mediation: Connected Histories of Places, Processes, and Objects in Europe and Beyond, 1450–1650*, eds. Susanna Burghartz, Lucas Burkart and Christine Göttler, Leiden 2016, pp. 159–182; idem, "Wild men in Braunschweig: Economies of hope and fear in early modern mining", in: *Renaissance Studies* 34/1 (2019), pp. 31–56; idem, "Spirited metals and the oeconomy of resources in early modern European mining", in: *Earth Sciences History* 39/2 (2020), pp. 371–388; Tina Asmussen and Pamela Long, "The cultural and material worlds of mining in early modern Europe", in: *Renaissance Studies* 34/1 (2020), pp. 8–30; Sebastian Felten, "Managing Mineral Growth in Early Modern Mining", in: *Isis* 114/3 (2023), pp. 626–630.

well-defined and pervasive theories arose and significantly influenced the development of the natural-philosophical debate on the subject. Notably, some of these models were circulating in Europe already in the Middle Ages, when the works produced by Islamic alchemists and physicians like Jabir ibn Hayyan (721–813), Rhazes (Muhammad ibn Zakariya al-Razi, 854–925), Avicenna (Ibn Sina, 980–1037), the members of the esoteric Brethren of Purity (or Ikhwān Al-Ṣafā), and by other Arabic and Persian scholars began influencing the Latin West.[3]

A key role in the success of these notions across the Continent was played by Albertus Magnus (circa 1200–1280) and the synthesis of Islamic science, alchemy, and classical (especially Aristotelian) knowledge that he provided in his *De mineralibus* (circa 1260, first printed in 1476).[4] In his treatise, Albertus did not restrict himself to an uncritical transmission of preexisting theories. Rather, in combining Aristotelian and Islamic concepts he introduced an interpretive model of mineral generation which – no matter how variously accepted, interpreted or modified in the following years – served as the matrix for a flourishing of opinions that would endure well into the eighteenth century.

Albertus' general model describes ore veins as resulting from subterranean vapors, the so-called *mineral exhalations*. These vapors, in turn, are formed by two *essential constituents* (also known as *compositional principles*): a male and a female seed (sulphur and quicksilver, respectively) which combine and condense under the effect of solar heat. The different levels of moisture in the exhalations, the variable warmth of the sun's rays, and the relative proportions of the two essential constituents determine the qualitative and quantitative differences in the seven known main metals: gold, silver, mercury, copper, iron, tin, and lead, each corresponding to a specific celestial body.[5]

Depending on the authors who accepted this theory, in part or completely, a number of additional causes were believed to influence the final result. Among other frequently mentioned factors we find the prevailing influence of one or more of the seven classical planets (Sun, Moon, Mercury, Venus, Mars, Jupiter, Saturn), the variable qualities of the earth where the ore veins lay, or the latitude of mining sites which affected the angle of incidence of solar rays – and, therefore, the heat they generated. Even the agreement on the traditional seven-metal scheme was far from unanimous. This became especially true as the debate on ore generation evolved following the development of mining industry, and new species like zinc, cobalt, bismuth, antimony, etc. were identified and their metallic nature (and, consequently, their status as new members of the original group)

3 See Norris, "The mineral exhalation theory of metallogenesis", pp. 46–49; idem, "Early theories of aqueous mineral genesis", pp. 70–72.
4 Albertus Magnus, *Alberti Magni philosophorum maximi de mineralibus liber*, Patavium 1476.
5 See Norris, "The mineral exhalation theory of metallogenesis", pp. 53–55; Dorothy Wyckoff, "Albertus Magnus on Ore Deposits", in: *Isis* 49/2 (1958), pp. 109–122.

was discussed.[6] Already in 1530, for instance, Agricola (who in any case rejected the *sulphur-mercury* model) observed in his treatise *Bermannus* that bismuth fully belonged to the group of metals ('metallorum in numero est') despite it being 'unknown to the ancients' ('sed veteribus [...] incognitum').[7]

In light of its many variants and in spite of the many disagreements, the *Aristotelian-Arabic* interpretive model proved to be clear and versatile enough to explain a wide spectrum of locations and compositions of ores that were (and would be) found across Europe – and, more generally, the Old World – from the Mediterranean shores and the Middle East, up to the northernmost regions of the Holy Roman Empire and beyond. Thanks to this interpretive flexibility, the notion of mineral exhalations in association with that of *sulphur-mercury* remained important elements of the debate on ore generation throughout the early modern period.[8] And indeed, these concepts continued to be an unavoidable benchmark even when, in the early sixteenth century, someone began to question and even openly criticize the general validity of the *Aristotelian-Arabic* model. In fact, although many of these contesters had strong technical and practical backgrounds and claimed that experience had taught them that mineral vapors and the *sulphur-mercury* seminal principles were inconsistent with what they had observed in mines, there were many other (and equally trustworthy) practitioners who still considered the *sulphur-mercury* model to be not only possible, but also *more* in line with their observations.

A good example of this, so to speak, traditionalist inclination comes from the Lutheran pastor Johann Mathesius (1504–1565). In his collection of mining-themed sermons, the *Sarepta* (1562),[9] this author upheld a providential interpretation of the occurrence of mineral resources in the rich silver mines of Joachimstal (now Jáchymov, a town in the Czech Republic) which understood the formation of ores essentially in terms of *sulphur-mercury* combination: and this theory, as Mathesius himself attested, seemed to be far from unpopular in the mining community where he lived and worked as a preacher.[10]

Such prolonged coexistence of conflicting interpretations should not surprise us, especially if we consider what said in the incipit about contextualization. In a

6 See John Norris, "Mining and metallogenesis in Bohemia during the sixteenth century", in: *Alchemy and Rudolf II: Exploring the Secrets of Nature in Central Europe in the 16th and 17th Centuries*, eds. Ivo Purš and Vladimír Karpenko, Prague 2016, pp. 657–670, p. 662.

7 Georgius Agricola, *Bermannus sive de re metallica*, Basileae 1530, p. 75.

8 See Dym, "Mineral fumes and mining spirits"; idem, "Alchemy and mining"; Norris, "The mineral exhalation theory of metallogenesis".

9 Johann Mathesius, *Sarepta oder Bergpostill, sampt der Jochimssthalischen kurtzen Chroniken*, Nuremberg 1562.

10 See John Norris, "Auß Quecksilber und Schwefel Rein: Johann Mathesius and sulfur-mercurius in the silver mines of Joachimstal", in: *Osiris* 29/1 (2014), pp. 35–48. On Mathesius, see also Dym, "Mineral fumes and mining spirits"; John Norris, "The providence of mineral generation in the sermons of Johann Mathesius (1504–1565)", in: *Geology and Religion: A History of Harmony and Hostility*, ed. Martina Kölbl-Ebert, London 2009, pp. 37–40.

geographically, geologically, climatically, and culturally diverse context like that of early modern Europe, it was certainly not unreasonable that the notions of *sulphur-mercury* and mineral exhalations were found to be more consistent with empirical evidence in some places than in others, and vice versa. In the case of Mathesius, just to make an example, John Norris reminds us that 'Joachimstal in [those years] was a place where the generation of metals seemed evident and ongoing, and where *sulfur* and *mercurius* seemed physically present in the *realia* of mining and smelting'.[11]

It is undeniable, however, that in many cases the persistence of conflicting opinions and reports coming from different mining sites all over Europe did not prevent these opinions and reports from resembling each other in terms of style. In fact, in those years a growing number of *practicians* (but also many university-trained humanists) wrote treatises and pamphlets which focused on the issue of mineral (re)generation. And in these works, the *empirical remarks* of the authors turned out to be more and more frequently expressed through assertive narratives which stressed the contrast between the *vain speculations* of philosophers, natural magicians, and alchemists – the latter two categories being usually depicted as fraudulent, unnecessarily and suspiciously obscure – and the concrete, reliable, and accessible knowledge of practitioners and miners.[12]

And yet, this contrast between theory and practice was often more rhetorical than real. For – as we said – practitioners, too, needed theory; and even the work of the proudest advocates of empiricism was not devoid of philosophical strands, as the case of Biringuccio clearly shows.

3 Mixing Backgrounds

Undoubtedly, when it came to practice Biringuccio could boast plenty of solid credentials. His posthumous book *De la Pirotechnia* ('On Pyrotechnics', figure 1),[13] considered as the first printed work on metallurgy ever published in Europe (1540), is also regarded as a cornerstone of Renaissance technical literature – and deservedly so. The mass of information made available in this treatise was the

11 Norris, "Auß Quecksilber und Schwefel Rein", p. 37.

12 On this topic, see the works by Pamela Long, "The openness of knowledge: An ideal and its context in 16th-century writings on mining and metallurgy", in: *Technology and Culture* 32/2 (1991), pp. 318–355; idem, *Openness, Secrecy, Authorship: Technical Arts and the Culture of Knowledge from Antiquity to the Renaissance*, Baltimore 2001; idem, *Artisan/Practitioners and the Rise of the New Sciences, 1400–1600*, Corvallis, OR 2011. See also Hiro Hirai, *Le concept de semence dans les théories de la matière à la Renaissance. De Marsile Ficin à Pierre Gassendi*, Thournout 2005, pp. 327–349; Francesco Luzzini, "Through dark and mysterious paths. Early modern science and the search for the origin of springs from the 16th to the 18th centuries", in: *Earth Sciences History* 34/2 (2015), pp. 169–189, pp. 176–177; Norris, "Early theories of aqueous mineral genesis", pp. 80–83.

13 Vannoccio Biringuccio, *De la Pirotechnia*, Venezia 1540. All passages reported here refer to the English edition: *The Pirotechnia of Vannoccio Biringuccio*, eds. Cyril Stanley Smith and Martha Teach Guidi, New York 1959.

product of decades of field experience spent by the author working as engineer, *Bergmeister* and metallurgist in German and Italian mines and foundries.

In a time when unprecedented technological developments in metallurgy and warfare had spurred a seemingly insatiable demand for mineral resources all over Europe (just think of the introduction of gunpowder artillery and firearms),[14] Biringuccio's uncommon expertise and skills could not pass unnoticed. In fact, these led to his appointment as head of the Papal foundry and arsenal in 1538 (although, unfortunately, this happened just one year before his death). And according to the recurrent claims about the superiority of practice over speculation featured in the *Pirotechnia,* there is little doubt that Biringuccio was quite proud of his practical background. At the same time, however, many passages from the book suggest an uncommon acquaintance of the author with philosophical and alchemical knowledge, an acquaintance – one might suspect – far greater than he would have been willing to admit.

Despite the lack of documentary evidence on the subject, the historian and philosopher of science Andrea Bernardoni has traced in painstaking detail the educational, professional, and scholarly influences that shaped Biringuccio's work and thought.[15] As the son of Paolo, a prominent technician close to the ruling class of the Republic of Siena, in all probability Vannoccio received his early education attending the abacus school (where, arguably, he was assisted by a well-learned private tutor). In the following years, he began his *practical* apprenticeship under the direct guidance of his father. Later on, he continued working in close connection with the large group of engineers, miners, metallurgists, architects, and other experts gathered under the banner of the Sienese patron (and tyrant) Pandolfo Petrucci (1452–1512), whose aggressive military and political ambitions had promoted the production of artillery and – wherever possible – the exploitation of ores in the territory of the Republic since the late fifteenth century.[16]

As noted by Bernardoni,[17] the fact that during the Renaissance engineers and other technicians lacked a proper academic training often makes it difficult to identify the classical and medieval sources and references on which an unculti-

14 On this topic, see Long, *Openness, Secrecy, Authorship,* pp. 175–209.

15 Andrea Bernardoni, "Il recupero del pensiero tecnico-scientifico antico e il problema dell'accesso alle fonti nel *De la Pirotechnia* di Vannoccio Biringuccio", in: *Automata* 2/1 (2007), pp. 93–103; idem, "Biringuccio, l'arte dei metalli e la mineralogia", in: *Il Rinascimento italiano e l'Europa.* Vol. V, eds. Antonio Clericuzio, Germana Ernst and Maria Conforti, Treviso 2008, pp. 497–511; idem, *La conoscenza del fare: Ingegneria, arte, scienza nel* De la Pirotechnia *di Vannoccio Biringuccio,* Roma 2011, pp. 71–114.

16 See Bernardoni, "Biringuccio, l'arte dei metalli e la mineralogia", pp. 501–502; Roberto Farinelli and Marco Merlo, "La Camera del Comune: miniere, metallurgia, armi", in: *L'età di Pandolfo Petrucci. Cultura e tecnologia a Siena nel Rinascimento,* ed. Petra Pertici, Siena 2017, pp. 189–226; Long, "The openness of knowledge", p. 331; idem, *Openness, Secrecy, Authorship,* p. 178.

17 Bernardoni, "Il recupero del pensiero tecnico-scientifico antico"; idem, "Biringuccio, l'arte dei metalli e la mineralogia".

VENE TIA

DE LA PIRO
TECHNIA.
LIBRI. X. DOVE AMPIAMEN
te ſi tratta non ſolo di ogni ſorte & di
uerſità di Minere, ma anchora quan
to ſi ricerca intorno à la prattica di
quelle coſe di quel che ſi appartiene
a l'arte de la fuſione ouer gitto de me
talli come d'ogni altra coſa ſimile à
queſta. Compoſti per il. S. Vanoc
cio Biringuccio Senneſe.

Con Priuilegio Apoſtolico & de la
Ceſarea Maeſta & del Illuſtriſs. Sena
to Veneto. M D XL.

FORTITVDINE

Fig. 1. Frontispiece of Vannoccio Biringuccio, *De la pirotechnia*, Venice 1540.
Courtesy of Science History Institute.

vated and self-taught author relied. And even more so, since these practitioners seemed rarely to feel hindered by their academic illiteracy: by the late decades of the fifteenth century, in fact, many *practical* traditions (including not only engineering and architecture, but also the arts and crafts) had undergone a cultural and social evolution that emancipated them from the intellectual authority of the learned scholars.

On the one hand, this radical change was triggered by a strong corporate and empirical pride and the fostering of an exceptional variety of intellectual environments in many Italian cities (especially, but not exclusively, in Tuscany). On the other hand, however, it was also the result of the emergence of new theoretical frameworks – humanism, above all – which encouraged 'the worlds of artisanal practice and the worlds of learning' to move 'closer together',[18] thus providing epistemological legitimacy to the knowledge of technicians and allowing them to define rigorous methodologies based on calculations and measurements.[19]

The complex process of discovery, re-evaluation, and critical analysis of the great technical authors of the past (like Vitruvius, Archimedes, Euclid, and many others) had played an essential role in this 'new attitude toward technical knowledge' which was typical of the Renaissance spirit.[20] Not a few high-profile practitioners – Leonardo is perhaps the most famous, although certainly not the only one – strove to understand and make use of these new theoretical tools. In some cases, these pioneers learned Latin in the attempt to achieve an unmediated knowledge of the ancient sources, and some of them even translated these sources into the vernacular language. A notable example is the artist, architect and engineer Francesco Di Giorgio Martini (1439–1502) who produced a celebrated Italian translation of Vitruvius' *De architectura*.[21]

Nor did the interest of many of these authors remain confined to *technics:* for, as we know, curiosity grows as knowledge deepens. Soon enough, even the works of classical philosophers and natural historians (such as Pliny the Elder, Aristotle, Plato, Democritus, just to mention a few) became subject of study and of great, often heated, debate. Workshops, art studios, construction sites, foundries, mines, quarries: first in Italy, and then all over Europe, these and other *technical* places became hotspots of encounters between artisans, scholars, artists, engineers, minters, alchemists, physicians, and many other characters from both the

18 Long, *Artisan/Practitioners and the Rise of the New Sciences*, p. 30. On this topic, see also the work by Pamela Smith, *The Body of the Artisan: Art and Science in the Scientific Revolution*, Chicago 2004.

19 Long, *Artisan/Practitioners and the Rise of the New Sciences*, pp. 30–61. On this topic, see also Florestano Evangelisti, *The Concept of Matter: A Journey from Antiquity to Quantum Physics*, Cham 2023, pp. 17–19; Paolo Galluzzi, *The Italian Renaissance of Machines*, Cambridge (MA) 2020.

20 Robert Friedel, *A Culture of Improvement: Technology and the Western Millennium*, Cambridge, MA 2007, p. 133. On this topic, see also Paolo Galluzzi, *Gli ingegneri del Rinascimento da Brunelleschi a Leonardo da Vinci*, Florence 1996; idem, *The Italian Renaissance of Machines;* Vasco La Salvia, "*De la Pirotechnia* of Biringuccio. A Key to the Craftsman Production: Technical Questions and Aspects of the Organization of Production", in: *Technology and Engineering*, eds. Michel Lette and Michel Oris, Turnhout 2000, pp. 13–25; Long, *Artisan/Practitioners and the Rise of the New Sciences*, pp. 62–93; Sally Newcomb, *The World in a Crucible: Laboratory Practice and Geological Theory at the Beginning of Geology*, Boulder, CO 2009.

21 Bernardoni, "Biringuccio, l'arte dei metalli e la mineralogia", pp. 500–502; Long, *Artisan/Practitioners and the Rise of the New Sciences*, pp. 62–93.

Fig. 2. A table from the *Pirotechnia* (Book I, Introduction, fifth page, not numbered) depicting scenes of mining and metal working. Courtesy of The History of Science Collections, University of Oklahoma Libraries.

(mainly) practical and (mainly) theoretical factions. It comes not as a surprise, then, that these factions turned out to be quite permeable to reciprocal influences and learning.

It was from such a vibrant and complex environment that Biringuccio's work, ideas, and also his passionate defense of mining as an accessible and collective form of expertise (he was an enthusiastic 'advocate of openness', as Pamela Long called him)[22] took shape and developed. And indeed, *De la Pirotechnia* is a fine expression of its author's eclectic and original approach to knowledge, the word in the title itself – *Pirotechnia* – being a neologism in the Italian vernacular of the time.[23] Thus, from the pages of this book we can see that Biringuccio's opinions were grounded on a solid empirical basis; and yet this basis, although unquestionably predominant, was not exclusive. Biringuccio was also well acquainted with authors like Pliny, Aristotle, Albertus Magnus, whose thoughts and writings he had probably learned from his Sienese contacts (like the already mentioned Francesco Di Giorgio Martini, the painter and architect Baldassarre Peruzzi (1481–1536), the scholar and clergyman Claudio Tolomei (1492–1556), and the foundry specialist Paolo Salvetti (14?–15?), who was also a renowned expert in minerals and mining). Nor was he unfamiliar with many alchemical concepts and procedures which, most likely, he had learned more in detail (if not *de novo*) during his encounters with the Florentine historian and natural philosopher Benedetto Varchi (1503–1565).[24]

22 Long, "The openness of knowledge", p. 330.

23 Bernardoni, "Biringuccio, l'arte dei metalli e la mineralogia", pp. 498–499.

24 Bernardoni, "Il recupero del pensiero tecnico-scientifico antico", p. 95; idem, "Biringuccio, l'arte dei metalli e la mineralogia", pp. 502–504; idem, *La conoscenza del fare*, pp. 83–86.

Of course, learning and agreeing are not the same thing. In the *Pirotechnia,* carefully selected elements of philosophical and alchemical knowledge are discussed and often appreciated. But many other passages in the book sharply critizise the arguments of the *theorists.* Among these, we find especially those *bad* ('sophistic') alchemists whom the author blames for their vain claim that it is possible to exactly replicate the complexity of natural processes in laboratory, as well as for the habit they have of shrouding in secrecy their operations and discoveries. Indeed, Biringuccio uses terrible words for those who indulge in this art:

> Usually, only criminals and practicers of fraud exercise it. It is an art founded only on appearance and show, one which corrupts the substances of metallic bodies with various poisonous mixtures and transforms them so greatly that it easily makes them appear at first sight to be what they are not. [...] it contains only vice, fraud, loss, fear, and shameful infamy. Thus, since its result is mean and poor, this art is followed only by persons of a like nature.[25]

At the same time, however, Biringuccio – who for this reason has been described by Martin Lynch as a 'grudging supporter'[26] of alchemy – praises the *good* ('philosophic') adepts of this discipline. Thanks to their hard work and study, they act as 'imitators and assistants to nature': they are 'manipulators and true physicians of mineral bodies', purge these bodies 'of superfluities', and assist them 'by augmenting their virtue and freeing them from their defects'.[27] And according to the *Pirotechnia,* the true value of this art lies not so much in its goal (which many deem as 'emptiness'), as in a most commendable side effect that is perfectly in line with the ideal of practical usefulness of knowledge promoted by the author:

> Besides the sweetness offered by the hope of one day possessing the rich goal that this art promises [...], it is surely a fine occupation, since in addition to being very useful to human need and convenience, it gives birth every day to new and splendid effects such as the extraction of medicinal substances, colors, and perfumes, and an infinite number of compositions of things.[28]

---

25 Biringuccio, *The Pirotechnia,* pp. 337–338. On this topic, see also Andrea Bernardoni, "La *quaestio de alchimia* nel *De la Pirotechnia* di Vannoccio Biringuccio", in: *Rendiconti della Accademia Nazionale delle Scienze detta dei XL,* Memorie di Scienze Fisiche e Naturali 31/2 (2007), pp. 261–276; idem, "Biringuccio, l'arte dei metalli e la mineralogia", pp. 502–504; Long, "The openness of knowledge", pp. 333–334; Alfredo Perifano, "L'alchimie dans *De la pirotechnia* de Vannoccio Biringuccio", in: *Revue des Études italiennes* 42 (1996), pp. 189–202.

26 Lynch, *Mining in World History,* p. 20.

27 Biringuccio, *The Pirotechnia,* p. 336.

28 Ibid., pp. 336–337. On Biringuccio's relationship with alchemical knowledge, see also Bernardoni, "La *quaestio de alchimia* nel *De la Pirotechnia*"; idem, "Biringuccio, l'arte dei metalli e la mineralogia", pp. 502–504; idem, *La conoscenza del fare,* pp. 71–114; Dym, "Mineral fumes and mining spirits", p. 183; idem, "Alchemy and mining", pp. 234–235; Smith, *The Body of the Artisan,* pp. 143–144. On the role played by alchemy in the development of natural philosophy,

This dichotomy between 'sophistic' and 'philosophic' (i.e. between fraudulent and honest) alchemists echoes a well-established theme in medieval and Renaissance Europe, a topos whose early traces date back to the twelfth century.[29] But in the *Pirotechnia*, a similar ambivalence also pervades Biringuccio's remarks on the opinions of philosophers. Even frequently mentioned and frequently praised authors like Plato, Aristotle ('that most divine scrutator of all the sciences and of every other secret of Nature'), and even Pliny and Albertus Magnus ('both of whom, like eager hunting dogs, [...] journeyed throughout all the regions and shores of the world, seeking [...] to understand the wonders and powers of Nature'),[30] are not immune from criticism when their theories are contradicted by experience or 'become more confused in explanation'.[31] And like alchemists, philosophers are approved when their theories are tested on the field (or in laboratory), whereas they are censured (although less harshly than the 'sophistic' alchemists) when they indulge too much in speculation.

In short, in the *Pirotechnia* there seems to be no trace of a biased dislike or distrust of theoretical explanations, as long as these explanations – no matter their proponent – agree with empirical evidence. And in fact, Biringuccio himself was not afraid to make use of well-selected philosophical and alchemical notions. He assembled them into an original theory of matter which, he argued, could also explain the origin of minerals more convincingly (or less unconvincingly) than the *sulphur-mercury* model did.

4 As Every Miner Knew

It is reasonable to assert that the understanding of water as an essential agent for the generation of mineral ores resulted – in part, at least – from the new impulse that the empirical fervor of practitioners had given to natural philosophy during the late fifteenth and early sixteenth centuries. As noted by John Norris, the new *aqueous* theories which appeared in that period shared a 'stronger empirical basis' than those relying exclusively on the concepts of mineral exhalations and *sulphur-mercury*, a *solid* approach that in many cases had deep roots in the mining industry (where the link between water and the formation of certain minerals – alum, vitriol, saltpetre, and other salts – had been a fact of common knowledge since the ancient times).[32] And in fact, Biringuccio was not alone in his criticism of the *sulphur-mercury* theory. Already in 1505, the German engineer and physician

see Lawrence M. Principe, "Evidence for Transmutation in Seventeenth Century Alchemy", in: *Scientific Evidence: Philosophical Theories and Applications*, ed. Peter Achinstein, Baltimore 2005, pp. 151–164; idem, *Chymists and Chymistry: Studies in the History of Alchemy and Early Modern Chemistry*, New York 2007.

29 See Tara Nummedal, *Alchemy and Authority in the Holy Roman Empire*, Chicago 2007; Alfredo Perifano, "L'alchimista senza alchimia tra Medioevo e Rinascimento: il volto di una 'passione'", in: *Studi dellaportiani* 1 (2022), pp. 39–60.

30 Biringuccio, *The Pirotechnia*, pp. 36–37.

31 Ibid., p. 387.

32 Norris, "Early theories of aqueous mineral genesis", pp. 70, 75–76, 86.

Ulrich Rülein von Kalbe (1465–1523) had observed in his *Bergbüchlein* that not a few experts disagreed with this well-known model;[33] and also Agricola's descriptions of ores formed after the passage of 'mineral juices' ('humores') through underground 'fissures' ('canales') left little or no room for Albertus' vapors.[34] Similar remarks would appear in the next decades, when seminal authors like Paracelsus (1493–1541) and Bernard Palissy (1510–1589) would join in with new opinions which – although different in many respects – agreed in stressing the importance of the relationship between water and the growth of ores.[35]

In any case, at a rhetorical level all these authors insisted on the contrast between theory and practice as well as on another crucial point: theoretical interpretation *served* empirical evidence, and not vice versa. And so did Biringuccio, whose remarks 'against the opinion of philosophers' relied on years of experience during which, he wrote, he had never 'seen sulphur found in any metal mine, or metal [grow] near any sulphur or mercury ore'.[36] For the same empirical reasons, he could not believe (and in doing so he dissented significantly from many ancient philosophers, the revered Aristotle first and foremost) that the interaction of the two couples of opposite qualities used by many supporters of the *sulphur-mercury* theory to explain the formation of metal ores – that is, heat and cold, moisture and dryness – could occur:

> Indeed, thinking of this just now another question to be solved has occurred to me; that is, how heat and cold, moisture and dryness, can be generated in the same place at the same time, and, once generated, how they can unite in such an elemental mixture that one is almost converted into the other, as they say necessarily happens when metals are generated from mercury and sulphur. To this is added the moisture of the water and the coldness of the earth that are in the same place; and it seems that the warmth of the fire element has little power because of its great distance. Hence it seems to me that these things far surpass the dry and hot, although the sun when it is hot can be called upon to intervene.[37]

But experience had taught him more. In describing a mining district 'in the Duchy of Austria between Innsbruck and Halle' where he had worked years before, Biringuccio reported how he entered 'a large valley surrounded by many moun-

33 Ulrich von Kalbe, *Das Bergbüchlein,* Augsburg 1505, p. 4.

34 Georgius Agricola, *De ortu et causis subterraneorum*, Basileae 1546, pp. 5–13, 35–38, 43, 48–50, 63–82. On this topic, see Norris, "Early theories of aqueous mineral genesis", pp. 73–76. See also Dym, "Alchemy and mining", pp. 234–235, 237–238, 248.

35 Bernard Palissy, *Discours admirables de la nature des eaux et fonteines,* Paris 1580; Paracelsus, *Congeries Paracelsicae Chemiae de Transmutationibus Metallorum, ex Omnibus quae de His ab Ipso scripta reperire licuit hactenus. Accessit Genealogia Mineralium, atque Metallorum Omnium, eiusdem Autoris,* Francofurti 1581. On this topic, see Luzzini, "Sounding the depths of providence", pp. 395–396; Norris, "Early theories of aqueous mineral genesis", pp. 71–86.

36 Biringuccio, *The Pirotechnia,* p. 87.

37 Ibid.

tains, between which passed a river with much water'; and in 'almost all the neighboring mountains some kind of an ore was mined' (principally 'copper and lead', although – he noted – 'in almost all [the mines] some silver was found'). In these places, water seemed to be ubiquitous: and in the middle of one of the largest mines, the author saw 'a channel which collected all the' rills that 'fell continuously from the various openings', and this water was 'issued in such quantities' that 'it would have satisfied every demand of a large mill'.[38] To the point that, he wrote,

> In going in and out of the mine I remember that because of water above and water below I was soaked as if I had passed through a heavy rain, but this did not surprise me since I had always understood that water was the primary and peculiar companion of minerals, indeed that it was perhaps the very reason for the generation of their substance. For this reason, as I have already said, experts in speaking of this give it as a universal rule that all mountains from which abundant waters spring also abound in minerals.[39]

So, the 'experts' (a category into which many philosophers and alchemists did not seem to fall, according to Biringuccio) placed great importance on water, considered as the 'first and proper companion' ('prima et propria compagna') of mines – and, therefore, a key factor for understanding the formation, quality, productivity, and location of ores. Accordingly, the presence of water was also to be considered as a 'general sign' that 'mountains and other places' were rich in mines, for in such places 'large quantities of fresh water' invariably sprang up – and this water was usually 'clear', although it had 'some mineral taste' and changed 'its quality with every season, becoming warm in the winter and very cold in the summer'.[40]

Taking the hint from this well-known fact, some practitioners had gone even further in their research. In the attempt to grasp some signs of subterranean treasures, they had defined a set of tests to be performed on water samples, a series of (comparatively) standardised practices which the American geochemist Erbert E. Hawkes (1913–1996) has described as 'probably the first written record of the use of chemical analyses in prospecting':[41]

> There are some who praise highly as a good sign certain residues that waters make where they are still, and after having stood for several days, frequently warmed by the rays of the sun, they show in some parts of their residues various tinctures of metallic substances. There are others who usually take this water and cause it to evaporate or dry up entirely by boiling it in a vessel of earthenware, glass, or some other material, and they test the gross earthy substance that remains at the bottom by tasting, by the ordinary fire assay, or in some other way that pleases them. In this

38 Ibid., p. 20.
39 Ibid., pp. 20–21.
40 Ibid., p. 15.
41 Herbert Edwin Hawkes, *Principles of Geochemical Prospecting*, Washington, DC 1957, p. 313.

> way (although they do not have an exact proof) they approach some sort of knowledge of the thing.[42]

It is easy to see here (and important studies have already highlighted this fact)[43] how the *new science* that appeared and flourished in Europe in the next decades owed much, both epistemologically and methodologically, to these empirical traditions. And Biringuccio, with his insistence on practical knowledge, could be described as a worthy champion of this legacy. Still, his intellectual ambition seemed to stretch beyond the (however proud) community of practitioners. By attempting to make sense of what he had witnessed in mines and foundries, he aimed to engage even the restricted and lofty circle of natural philosophers. And in fact, he merged these experiences in a consistent theoretical system which also made room for a new interpretation of the origin and transformations of minerals and metals.

The theory of matter expressed in the *Pirotechnia*[44] is an original and complex synthesis of Aristotelian and atomistic/corpuscular motifs. According to this system, the structure of every substance results from the mixture of the four elements of classical Greek philosophy: earth, air, fire, and water. These elements are present in nature as microscopic ('elemental') particles ('particelle') and join together in various proportions and ways, thus forming different kinds of microstructures which, in turn, are responsible for different kinds of substances.

In the specific case of metals, this *Aristotelian-corpuscular* concept proved to be particularly apt to explain not only the individual characteristics of every metal and alloy, but also the different effects that smelting, calcination, distillation, sublimation (figure 3), and other basic operations performed by practitioners and alchemists had on these substances. Thus – for example – exposing a metallic sample to fire caused the evaporation of water, the expulsion of air, a change in the degree of humidity, and a consequent change in the relative proportions of the four essential elements (which in most cases led to the transformation of a substance into another). Only gold, the most noble of all metals, was composed of such a well-balanced, 'perfect and uniform elemental mixture' of 'finely purified' corpuscles that it was (almost) impossible to change its structure (that is, despite the vain claims of many 'sophistic' alchemists):

42 Biringuccio, *The Pirotechnia*, p. 15. This passage is also mentioned and commented in Tony E. Edmonds, "An indicator of its time: two millennia of the iron–gall-nut test", in: *Analyst* 123 (1998), pp. 2909–2914, p. 2911; Hawkes, *Principles of Geochemical Prospecting*, p. 313.

43 For example: Galluzzi, *Gli ingegneri del Rinascimento da Brunelleschi a Leonardo da Vinci*; idem, *The Italian Renaissance of Machines*; Long, "The openness of knowledge"; idem, *Openness, Secrecy, Authorship*; idem, *Artisan/Practitioners and the Rise of the New Sciences*.

44 See, in particular, Bernardoni, *La conoscenza del fare*, pp. 71–114. See also Evangelisti, *The Concept of Matter*, p. 26.

Fig. 3. *De la Pirotechnia* (Book IX, 130, *verso*). Sublimation devices. Courtesy of The History of Science Collections, University of Oklahoma Libraries.

> I tell you that [gold's] original and peculiar materials are none other than elemental substances, with the quantity and quality of each proportioned equally one to the other and very finely purified. From this union of elements which are of equal force there is born a pleasing and perfect elemental mixture, and then after fermentation and decoction the elements finally become fixed, permanent, and joined together in such a union that they are almost inseparable […].[45]

In a sense, in this understanding of metals as products of different mixtures and proportions of elemental particles, the role of water was no different from that of the other main classical elements (earth, air, and fire). Still, this very contextualization allowed Biringuccio to explain coherently why – as every miner knew – the presence of water was to be considered a typical feature in mining sites: and, therefore, this could also explain why the analysis of the water in a specific place could reveal important details on the resources that lay underground. Accordingly, this model also served to make reasonable sense of another commonly observed phenomenon: the seemingly 'watery' composition of certain 'semiminerals' ('mezzi minerali') such as quicksilver, 'the salts, vitriol, rock alum, and saltpeter'. For all these substances were 'fairly dense', and yet they dissolved in water; and by means of water they could be 'obtained and reduced to their perfection'.[46]

In brief, Biringuccio's interpretation had been built from, and stood the test of, practice. Experience – the final touchstone of theory – seemed to confirm his *Aristotelian-corpuscular* model, much to the pleasure of both the practitioner and the natural philosopher.

Or at least, this seemed to happen in most cases.

45 Biringuccio, *The Pirotechnia*, pp. 26–27. On this passage, see also Bernardoni, *La conoscenza del fare*, pp. 80–81.

46 Biringuccio, *The Pirotechnia*, p. 77.

5 Water in the Dark

As noted, the empirical remarks featured in the *Pirotechnia* were not an exception in the cultural landscape of Renaissance mining. Nor did they claim to be so: actually, this is the very reason why Biringuccio's encyclopedic knowledge of the 'ideas circulating at that time' (together with his discussion of these ideas, of course) makes his book so useful to us, it being a most 'convenient barometer'[47] for the different streams of theory and practice that met, clashed, merged, and shaped the study of the mineral world in the first decades of the sixteenth century.

In the following years, new *aqueous* theories where water gained an even more central role in the understanding of the generation of ores were formulated independently by important authors like (among the others) Agricola, Paracelsus, and Bernard Palissy, paving the way for various opinions which in many cases rejected the traditional concepts of mineral exhalations and *sulphur-mercury*.[48] As we have seen, in these new systems empiricism and field research played a pivotal role. But the *old* theoretical frameworks, no matter how reduced their influence, continued to be important actors in the effort to understand natural processes. True, the interpretations suggested by many technicians were unequivocally and predominantly grounded on fieldwork and empirical evidence; but it is also undeniable that inductive reasoning, analogies, assumptions, and a great deal of classical, philosophical, and alchemical reading remained essential ingredients in these authors' attempts to make sense of their experiences.

It was not just a matter of intellectual ambition. In many cases, practice simply could not explain or prove *everything* (not yet or not immediately at least), and theory inevitably jumped in to fill the gap between the observable and the understandable. And once again, the *Pirotechnia* offers good examples of this epistemological and methodological tension. In fact, Biringuccio's *watery theories* were not confined to metals and semiminerals: even the composition of minerals, 'rock crystals, and all important gems in general'[49] was understood by this author as essentially or predominantly aqueous.[50] In these objects, however, the presence of water could not be proved directly – not on the field, nor in the laboratory. Hence

47 Norris, "Early theories of aqueous mineral genesis", p. 71.

48 Though, as a matter of fact, still in the seventeenth and early eighteenth centuries important authors continued to uphold the mineral exhalation theory. See Luzzini, "Sounding the depths of providence", pp. 392–394; Norris, "The mineral exhalation theory of metallogenesis".

49 Biringuccio, *The Pirotechnia*, p. 119.

50 This interpretation is in line with the view of many scholars – both Arabic and European – who understood rocks and crystals as produced by generative processes occurring in an aqueous medium. Differently from these *stony* objects, however, metals were generally believed to result from the interaction of moist and dry exhalations (whereas Biringuccio extended the *aqueous* theory to metals and minerals alike). See Dym, "Alchemy and mining", pp. 238, 247; Norris, "The mineral exhalation theory of metallogenesis", pp. 44–45, 52–53; idem, "Early theories of aqueous mineral genesis", pp. 69–71; David R. Oldroyd, "Some Neo-Platonic and Stoic influences on mineralogy in the sixteenth and seventeenth centuries", in: *Ambix* 21 (1974), pp. 128–156, pp. 145–146.

the need for a solid theoretical framework that would rely on analogies and conjectures to explain what could not be seen:

> Believing firmly that every white thing is watery or airy, I shall say that crystal is of a watery substance with subtle earthiness and with much air and little fire; and that therefore it is cold and it floats in water, if this be true. The same must be said of the other gems since they are too watery, but their natures vary as there is more or less of the mixture of the elemental substances, although their particular material, as that of the metals, is watery. Yet these stones do not melt like those metals nor does crystal dissolve in fire as ice does into water, but this would happen if the elemental mixture of the other substances did not impede it. However, let it be enough of this subject that you take this universal and deduce from it another more limited universal which contains a composition of materials of much greater perfection.[51]

'Believing firmly', 'this would happen if': when empirical evidence was unavailable or dubious, even Biringuccio had no other choice than to venture onto speculative ground. But this was not a contradiction: not in a cultural context like that of premodern Europe, a context where the natural world *had* to make sense and *had* to maintain structure and coherence in all its parts – and where, therefore, resorting to theoretical speculation and to apt metaphors was a far from unacceptable (though perhaps not optimal) option even to the minds of many *practicians*.[52] From this point of view, the *Pirotechnia* is another powerful testimony of how permeable the boundaries between theoretical construction and first-hand experience were in the Renaissance, and of how essential this permeability was (and, in many senses, still is) for promoting the study of nature in all its complexity and, therefore, the evolution of scientific knowledge. Far from being outdated, this lesson remains valid for us today – at a time when interdisciplinarity is much more preached than actually practiced, and hyperspecialization and academic sectarianism seem to hinder dialogue not only between the humanities and the sciences, but even among scientific disciplines.

---

51 Biringuccio, *The Pirotechnia*, p. 120. On this topic, see also Sven Dupré, "The Art of Glassmaking and the Nature of Stones. The Role of Imitation in Anselm De Boodt's Classification of Stones", in: *Steinformen: Materialität, Qualität, Imitation*, eds. Isabella Augart, Maurice Sas and Iris Wenderholm, Berlin 2019, pp. 207–220, p. 214.

52 On the epistemological and methodological tension between theory and practice in Biringuccio's work, see also Bernardoni, *La conoscenza del fare*, p. 86. On the importance of this issue in general, and how the relationship between theory and practice affected science and field research during the Renaissance and the early modern period, see also Luzzini, "Harvesting Underground", pp. 11–14; Pietro Daniel Omodeo, "Practices and theories of contingency in Renaissance approaches to nature", in: *Contingency and Natural Order in Early Modern Science*, eds. Pietro Daniel Omodeo and Rodolfo Garau, Cham 2019, pp. 93–114; and – especially with respect to alchemy – Principe, "Evidence for Transmutation in Seventeenth Century Alchemy"; idem, *Chymists and Chymistry*.

In the debate that followed in the early modern period and shaped the development of natural philosophy as well as mining industry, the mediating role of water in the generation of ores became an increasingly popular and influential notion. And again, the overlapping and interaction of different forms of knowledge (from and through professional, social, intellectual, cultural contexts) proved crucial in fostering this conceptual change. More and more frequently, the study of nature turned mines into field laboratories which helped to understand not only the origin of minerals, but also the origin of water itself. When, shortly thereafter, natural philosophers began investigating the complex dynamics of the hydrologic cycle, they found many of the answers they were seeking in the bowels of the Earth.[53] And in that darkness, once again, savants and practitioners met, discussed, argued, and influenced each other, enriching the beautiful picture of early modern science with new strokes of theory and practice.

We like to think that Biringuccio would have been proud of them.

Acknowledgements

I am much indebted to Lawrence Principe for reading and commenting on the manuscript of this paper and for improving the overall quality of my work during my stay at Johns Hopkins University. My sincere thanks also go to Pietro Daniel Omodeo and Helge Wendt for inviting me to contribute to this volume. Last but not least, I am grateful to THE NEW INSTITUTE Centre for Environmental Humanities (NICHE) at Ca' Foscari University of Venice and its director, Francesca Tarocco, for generously supporting me during the completion of this paper.

This work was supported by the European Union's Horizon 2020 research and innovation programme under the Marie Skłodowska-Curie project SOUNDEPTH [grant agreement No. 101019781].

Reference Lists

Sources

Agricola, Georgius (Bauer, Georg), *Bermannus sive de re metallica,* Basileae 1530.

Agricola, Georgius, *De ortu et causis subterraneorum,* Basileae 1546.

Albertus Magnus, *Alberti Magni philosophorum maximi de mineralibus liber,* Patavium 1476.

Biringuccio, Vannoccio, *De la Pirotechnia,* Venezia 1540.

Biringuccio, Vannoccio, *The Pirotechnia of Vannoccio Biringuccio,* eds. Cyril Stanley Smith and Martha Teach Guidi, New York 1959.

Kalbe (von), Ulrich, *Das Bergbüchlein,* Augsburg 1505.

Mathesius, Johann, *Sarepta oder Bergpostill, sampt der Jochimssthalischen kurtzen Chroniken,* Nuremberg 1562.

Palissy, Bernard, *Discours admirables de la nature des eaux et fonteines,* Paris 1580.

Paracelsus (von Hohenheim, Philippus Aureolus Theophrastus Bombastus), *Congeries Paracelsicae Chemiae de Transmutationibus Metallorum, ex Omnibus quae de His ab Ipso*

53 Luzzini, "Through dark and mysterious paths".

scripta reperire licuit hactenus. Accessit Genealogia Mineralium, atque Metallorum Omnium, eiusdem Autoris, Francofurti 1581.

Research Literature

Asmussen, Tina, "Glück auf! Fortuna und risiko im frühneuzeitlichen Bergbau", in: *FKW // Zeitschrift für Geschlechterforschung und visuelle Kultur* 60 (2016), pp. 30–41.

Asmussen, Tina, "The Kux as a site of mediation: Economic practices and material desires in the early modern German mining industry", in: *Sites of Mediation: Connected Histories of Places, Processes, and Objects in Europe and Beyond, 1450–1650,* eds. Susanna Burghartz, Lucas Burkart, and Christine Göttler, Leiden 2016, pp. 159–182.

Asmussen, Tina, "Wild men in Braunschweig: Economies of hope and fear in early modern mining", in: *Renaissance Studies* 34/1 (2019), pp. 31–56.

Asmussen, Tina, "Spirited metals and the oeconomy of resources in early modern European mining", in: *Earth Sciences History* 39/2 (2020), pp. 371–388.

Asmussen, Tina and Pamela Long, "The cultural and material worlds of mining in early modern Europe", in: *Renaissance Studies* 34/1 (2020), pp. 8–30.

Bernardoni, Andrea, "Il recupero del pensiero tecnico-scientifico antico e il problema dell'accesso alle fonti nel *De la Pirotechnia* di Vannoccio Biringuccio", in: *Automata* 2/1 (2007), pp. 93–103.

Bernardoni, Andrea, "La *quaestio de alchimia* nel *De la Pirotechnia* di Vannoccio Biringuccio", in: *Rendiconti della Accademia Nazionale delle Scienze detta dei XL,* Memorie di Scienze Fisiche e Naturali 31/2 (2007), pp. 261–276.

Bernardoni, Andrea, "Biringuccio, l'arte dei metalli e la mineralogia", in: *Il Rinascimento italiano e l'Europa.* Vol. V, eds. Antonio Clericuzio, Germana Ernst and Maria Conforti, Treviso 2008, pp. 497–511.

Bernardoni, Andrea, *La conoscenza del fare: Ingegneria, arte, scienza nel* De la Pirotechnia *di Vannoccio Biringuccio,* Roma 2011.

Dupré, Sven, "The Art of Glassmaking and the Nature of Stones. The Role of Imitation in Anselm De Boodt's Classification of Stones", in: *Steinformen: Materialität, Qualität, Imitation,* eds. Isabella Augart, Maurice Sas and Iris Wenderholm, Berlin 2019, pp. 207–220.

Dym, Warren Alexander, "Mineral fumes and mining spirits: Popular beliefs in the *Sarepta* of Johann Mathesius (1504–1565)", in: *Reformation & Renaissance Review* 8/2 (2006), pp. 161–185.

Dym, Warren Alexander, "Alchemy and mining: Metallogenesis and prospecting in early mining books", in: *Ambix* 55/3 (2008), pp. 232–254.

Edmonds, Tony E., "An indicator of its time: two millennia of the iron-gall-nut test", in: *Analyst* 123 (1998), pp. 2909–2914.

Evangelisti, Florestano, *The Concept of Matter: A Journey from Antiquity to Quantum Physics,* Cham 2023.

Farinelli, Roberto and Marco Merlo, "La Camera del Comune: miniere, metallurgia, armi", in: *L'età di Pandolfo Petrucci. Cultura e tecnologia a Siena nel Rinascimento,* ed. Petra Pertici, Siena 2017, pp. 189–226.

Felten, Sebastian, "Managing Mineral Growth in Early Modern Mining", in: *Isis* 114/3 (2023), pp. 626–630.

Friedel, Robert, *A Culture of Improvement: Technology and the Western Millennium,* Cambridge, MA 2007.

Galluzzi, Paolo, *Gli ingegneri del Rinascimento da Brunelleschi a Leonardo da Vinci,* Florence 1996.

Galluzzi, Paolo, *The Italian Renaissance of Machines,* Cambridge, MA 2020.

Hawkes, Herbert Edwin, *Principles of Geochemical Prospecting,* Washington, DC 1957.

Hirai, Hiro, *Le concept de semence dans les théories de la matière à la Renaissance. De Marsile Ficin à Pierre Gassendi,* Thournout 2005.

La Salvia, Vasco, "*De la Pirotechnia* of Biringuccio. A Key to the Craftsman Production: Technical Questions and Aspects of the Organization of Production", in: *Technology and Engineering,* eds. Michel Lette and Michel Oris, Turnhout 2000, pp. 13–25.

Long, Pamela, "The openness of knowledge: An ideal and its context in 16th-century writings on mining and metallurgy", in: *Technology and Culture* 32/2 (1991), pp. 318–355.

Long, Pamela, *Openness, Secrecy, Authorship: Technical Arts and the Culture of Knowledge from Antiquity to the Renaissance,* Baltimore 2001.

Long, Pamela, *Artisan/Practitioners and the Rise of the New Sciences, 1400–1600,* Corvallis (OR) 2011.

Luzzini, Francesco, "Through dark and mysterious paths. Early modern science and the search for the origin of springs from the 16th to the 18th centuries", in: *Earth Sciences History* 34/2 (2015), pp. 169–189.

Luzzini, Francesco, "Sounding the depths of providence: Mineral (re)generation and human-environment interaction in the early modern period", in: *Earth Sciences History* 39/2 (2020), pp. 389–408.

Luzzini, Francesco, "Harvesting Underground: (Re)generative theories and vegetal analogies in the early modern debate on mineral ores (I)", in: *Notes and Records: the Royal Society journal of the history of science,* Online First (2023), https://doi.org/10.1098/rsnr.2023.0032.

Lynch, Martin, *Mining in World History,* London 2002.

Newcomb, Sally, *The World in a Crucible: Laboratory Practice and Geological Theory at the Beginning of Geology,* Boulder, CO 2009.

Norris, John, "The mineral exhalation theory of metallogenesis in pre-modern mineral science", in: *Ambix* 53/1 (2006), pp. 43–65.

Norris, John, "Early theories of aqueous mineral genesis in the sixteenth century", in: Ambix 54/1 (2007), pp. 69–86.

Norris, John, "The providence of mineral generation in the sermons of Johann Mathesius (1504–1565)", in: *Geology and Religion: A History of Harmony and Hostility,* ed. Martina Kölbl-Ebert, London 2009, pp. 37–40.

Norris, John, "Auß Quecksilber und Schwefel Rein: Johann Mathesius and sulfurmercurius in the silver mines of Joachimstal", in: *Osiris* 29/1 (2014), pp. 35–48.

Norris, John, "Mining and metallogenesis in Bohemia during the sixteenth century", in: *Alchemy and Rudolf II: Exploring the Secrets of Nature in Central Europe in the 16th and 17th Centuries,* eds. Ivo Purš and Vladimír Karpenko, Prague 2016, pp. 657–670.

Nummedal, Tara, *Alchemy and Authority in the Holy Roman Empire,* Chicago 2007.

Oldroyd, David R., "Some Neo-Platonic and Stoic influences on mineralogy in the sixteenth and seventeenth centuries", in: *Ambix* 21 (1974), pp. 128–156.

Omodeo, Pietro Daniel, "Practices and theories of contingency in Renaissance approaches to nature", in: *Contingency and Natural Order in Early Modern Science,* eds. Pietro Daniel Omodeo and Rodolfo Garau, Cham 2019, pp. 93–114.

Perifano, Alfredo, "L'alchimie dans *De la pirotechnia* de Vannoccio Biringuccio", in: *Revue des Études italiennes* 42 (1996), pp. 189–202.
Perifano, Alfredo, "L'alchimista senza alchimia tra Medioevo e Rinascimento: il volto di una 'passione'", in: *Studi dellaportiani* 1 (2022), pp. 39–60.
Principe, Lawrence M., "Evidence for Transmutation in Seventeenth Century Alchemy", in: *Scientific Evidence: Philosophical Theories and Applications,* ed. Peter Achinstein, Baltimore 2005, pp. 151–164.
Principe, Lawrence M., *Chymists and Chymistry: Studies in the History of Alchemy and Early Modern Chemistry,* New York 2007.
Smith, Pamela, *The Body of the Artisan: Art and Science in the Scientific Revolution,* Chicago 2004.
Vergani, Raffaello, "Miniere e minerali nella *Pirotechnia* di Biringuccio: natura, ricerca, sfruttamento", in: *L'ultimo secolo della Repubblica di Siena. Arti, cultura e società,* eds. Mario Ascheri, Gianni Mannozzi and Fabrizio Nevola, Siena 2008, pp. 467–475.
Wyckoff, Dorothy, "Albertus Magnus on Ore Deposits", in: *Isis* 49/2 (1958), pp. 109–122.

Metals and Mining in the Knowledge Economy of the Royal Society of London

Joshua Hillman

In 1666, Robert Boyle published in the *Philosophical Transactions* his 'Articles of Inquiries touching Mines', a list of one hundred substantive queries about mines and mining that he hoped the other Fellows of the Royal Society would use as 'Instructions, to direct them, what Particulars to Inquire after upon this Subject'.[1] It is fair to say that this text has failed to excite many historians. Most accounts of the Restoration sciences of the earth ignore Boyle's mining queries entirely, focusing instead on debates about the Earth's history.[2] Moreover, when the queries do feature in the existing literature, they are usually interpreted as either unimportant or unsuccessful. Unimportant (it is suggested) because they were simply a 'sequel' or 'continuation' of Boyle's earlier 'General Heads for a Natural History of a Countrey, Great or Small' and thus there was nothing special about mines in Boyle's thought – they were merely a constituent part of topographical natural history;[3] unsuccessful (it is argued) because though they were 'learned and pertinent' they were 'tainted by Renaissance cosmology', amounted to a 'random accumulation rather than an inquiry directed to a particular end', and the answers they received 'threw little immediate light on the Earth's structure and history'.[4]

I contend that both of these interpretations have problems. The former is right to see the mining queries as being designed to contribute to a larger natural-historical enterprise but, as we shall see, this was not topographical natural history. And the latter interpretation – which is Roy Porter's – is right to see Boyle's queries as failing to contribute to knowledge about the Earth's history but is misguided in expecting them to do so in the first place. For Boyle's queries were not designed to discover Earth's deep history, nor to supplement topographical natural history: they were designed as a set of instructions for conducting a project

1 Robert Boyle, "Articles of Inquiries touching Mines" (1666) in: *The Works of Robert Boyle*, eds. Michael Hunter and Edward Davis, 14 vols., London 1999–2000, 5:529. Unless otherwise stated, all references to Boyle's writings are to this edition. Technically there are 101 queries, but one is actually a statement.

2 See, e.g.: Ivano Dal Prete, *On the Edge of Eternity. The Antiquity of the Earth in Medieval and Early Modern Europe*, New York 2022.

3 Michael Hunter, "Robert Boyle and the Early Royal Society: A Reciprocal Exchange in the Making of Baconian Science", in: *British Journal for the History of Science* 40 (2007), pp. 1–23, p. 19; Peter Anstey, "Locke, Bacon and Natural History", in: *Early Science and Medicine* 7 (2002), pp. 65–92, pp. 75–76.

4 Roy Porter, *The Making of Geology. Earth Science in Britain, 1660–1815*, Cambridge 1977, pp. 18, 56.

DOI: 10.13173/9783447123693.207

that can be characterized as 'the natural history of mines', itself a part of a larger project known as 'the history of the trades'. These two projects are important both in their own right and for our wider understanding of early modern economies of knowledge in relation to natural resources. Specifically, I shall argue that the natural history of mines constituted a seventeenth-century science of the earth that was rooted, first and foremost, in the practical knowledge economies of mine and metal workers.

1 Baconian Natural Histories and the History of the Trades Programme

The English philosopher and statesman Francis Bacon's early-seventeenth-century programmatic writings on natural-historical method, and the influence these had on Restoration naturalists, are familiar topics in the history of science – we therefore have no need to stay with Bacon long.[5] However, two salient features of Bacon's approach to natural history are worth recapitulating. The first is that – drawing especially on Georgius Agricola – Bacon frequently used mining as a metaphor for the pursuit of natural philosophy.[6] The second is that Bacon considered the natural history of the 'arts' to be the most useful branch of natural history: 'the history of Arts is of most use, because it exhibits things in motion, and leads more directly to practice'.[7]

The Royal Society's proposed history of the trades programme was essentially a response to Bacon's call for natural histories of the arts, comprising a series of detailed descriptions of the different trades in an attempt to benefit industry and to reveal nature's secrets.[8] At one of the first meetings of the society, in January 1661, John Evelyn and William Petty each presented their own list of trades that they thought the society should study. It was decided that Christopher Merret would then compare their lists and compile a master copy. This was not completed until 1664, but research on twenty-one different trades had already begun by this point. The history of the trades programme was vigorously conducted

5 On Bacon's influence on Restoration science, see, e.g.: Charles Webster, *The Great Instauration. Science, Medicine and Reform, 1626–1660*, London 1975; Michael Hunter and Paul Wood, "Towards Solomon's House: Rival Strategies for Reforming the Early Royal Society", in: *History of Science* 24 (1986), pp. 49–108.

6 See: Paolo Rossi, *Francis Bacon: From Magic to Science*, transl. Sacha Rabinovitch, London 1968, ch. 1; Brian Vickers, *Francis Bacon and Renaissance Prose*, Cambridge 1968, pp. 177, 292; Carolyn Merchant, *The Death of Nature: Women, Ecology and the Scientific Revolution*, New York 1980, ch. 7; Lauren Klein, "To Mine for Truth: The Metaphor of Mining in Francis Bacon's The Great Instauration", in: *Origins of Scientific Learning: Essays on Culture and Knowledge in Early Modern Europe*, eds. Sarah French and Kay Etheridge, New York 2007, pp. 117–137; Cesare Pastorino, "The Mine and the Furnace: Francis Bacon, Thomas Russell and Early Stuart Mining Culture", in: *Early Science and Medicine* 14 (2009), pp. 630–660.

7 Francis Bacon, *Preparative towards a natural and experimental history* (1620), in: *The Works of Francis Bacon*, eds. James Spedding et al, 7 vols., London 1857–1859, 4:257.

8 Kathleen Ochs, "The Royal Society of London's History of the Trades Programme: An Early Episode in Applied Science", in: *Notes and Records of the Royal Society of London* 39 (1985), pp. 129–158, p. 129.

until the mid-1680s, at which point the Fellows' interest in the project, for unknown reasons, began to decline. Only two original book-length histories were completed, Merret's *The Art of Glass* (1667) and Walter Charleton's *The Mystery of the Vinters* (1667), but John Pettus published a translation of an important German mining text by Lazarus Ercker in 1684, and sections of Evelyn's books on sculpting and forests dealt with the history of related trades. The society also promoted foreign trade histories on silk production and dyeing, and many articles in the *Philosophical Transactions* dealt with individual trades.[9]

Mining was an ideal subject for the history of the trades programme, and was widely supported: Evelyn recommended writing the histories of the 'Tin-man' and the 'Collyer', amongst other mineworkers;[10] Petty favored the histories 'Of finding, digging, smelting, refining, separating, compounding of metalls, and working the same into several uses';[11] and Robert Hooke later advocated 'The History of Miners, their ways of finding the Mineral; of digging, clearing, and breaking through Rocks and Rivers in their Passage, of the various Earths they meet with, as also of their Damps, and other Exhalations'.[12] There was thus a clear philosophical and institutional precedent for Boyle's mining queries, which no doubt goes a long way in explaining the rise of the natural history of mines. But it is also worth considering if the Fellows had any personal, pecuniary reasons for studying mines, a question that has not been addressed in any detail before.

2 A Royal Relationship

It is well known that the British mining industries expanded during the seventeenth century: the annual coal output increased over tenfold between 1560 and 1700 to around three million tons;[13] the annual lead output in England and Wales increased from around 12,500 tons in the 1630s to around 28,000 tons in 1705;[14] and the annual tin output more than doubled between 1603 and 1687.[15] Less well known, however, is the extent to which the earliest Fellows of the Royal Society were involved in these industries. Of the twelve founder members of the Royal Society, seven were involved in mining ventures: William Ball, Robert Boyle, William Brouncker, Alexander Bruce, Robert Moray, John Wilkins, and Christopher Wren. Some were involved through investment in mines for lead, silver, or coal

9 Ibid., pp. 132–138.

10 A. Forbes Sieveking, "Evelyn's 'Circle of Mechanical Trades'", in: *Transactions of the Newcomen Society* 4 (1923), pp. 40–47.

11 William Petty, "History of Trades", in: *The Petty Papers: Some unpublished writings of Sir William Petty*, ed. the Marquis of Lansdowne, 2 vols., London 1927, 1:205.

12 Robert Hooke, "The Method of Improving Natural Philosophy" (c. 1666), in: *The Posthumous Works of Robert Hooke*, ed. Richard Waller, London 1705, p. 24.

13 John Hatcher, *The History of the British Coal Industry. Volume 1. Before 1700*, Oxford 1993, p. 1.

14 Ian Blanchard, *Russia's 'Age of Silver': Precious Metal Production and Economic Growth in the Eighteenth* Century, New York 1989, pp. 43–49; Roger Burt, "Lead Production in England and Wales, 1700–1770", in: *The Economic History Review* 22 (1969), pp. 249–268, p. 265.

15 George Lewis, *The Stanneries*, Boston 1908, Appendix J.

(Ball, Bruce, Moray), others (Wilkins and Wren) by making inventions for drainage or extraction.[16] Furthermore, four of them – Boyle, Brouncker, Moray, and Wren – became members of the Society of Mines Royal.

'Mines Royal' were the mines of the metals required for coinage – gold, silver, quicksilver, copper, and tin – from which the Crown claimed a proportion of the profits. In 1568, the courts determined only if the precious metal had value over the cost of refining it, and only if the loss to the owner of the base metal was not too severe, would a mine be considered one of the mines royal.[17] Elizabeth I granted the so-called Society of Mines Royal the exclusive right to search for, extract, and smelt ores of copper, gold, silver, and quicksilver throughout eight English counties and most of Wales.[18] The Society of Mines Royal soon became associated with a Society of Mineral and Battery Works, which was established to find and smelt calamine alongside copper to make brass in the parts of England, Wales, and Ireland that laid outside the jurisdiction of the Society of Mines Royal.[19] Both societies were granted a royal charter in 1568, and thereafter they were often referred to collectively as the 'Societies of Mines and Mineral Works'.[20]

By the 1660s, four of the founder members of the Royal Society had joined the Society of Mines Royal; and the extant minutes of the latter reveal that the naturalists and philosophers Thomas Henshaw, John Harris, Martin Lister, and Isaac Newton were all members at various times.[21] Further, the two chief governors of the Society of Mines, Prince Rupert of the Rhine and Anthony Ashley Cooper, Chancellor of the Exchequer, were both Fellows of the Royal Society, as were five of the eight deputy chief governors: Brouncker, Thomas Foley, Moray, Edward Smith, and John Pettus. This overlapping membership was not coincidental. In his *Fodinae Regales* (1670), which served as the first official history of the Society of Mines Royal and the Society of Mineral and Battery Works, Pettus praised the Royal Society and also the Royal Company, before observing that 'these two Soci-

16 On Ball, see Michael Hunter's editorial note in Robert Boyle, *New Experiments Physico-Mechanical* (1660), 1:283–284. On Boyle, see Rachel Laudan, *From Mineralogy to Geology. The Foundations of a Science, 1650–1830,* Chicago 1987, p. 231; Robert Maddison, *The Life of the Honourable Robert Boyle, F.R.S.,* London 1969, pp. 112; 262–263. On Brouncker, see William Rees, *Industry Before the Industrial Revolution: Incorporating a study of the Chartered Companies of the Society of Mines Royal and of Mineral and Battery Works,* 2 vols., Cardiff 1968, vol. 2, p. 653. On Bruce, see David Stevenson, "Introduction", in: *Letters of Sir Robert Moray to the Earl of Kincardine, 1657–73,* ed. David Stevenson, London 2007, p. 18; Robert Moray, "Letter to Alexander Bruce, 15 August 1665", in: *Letters,* ed. Stevenson, pp. 252–253. On Moray, see Stevenson, "Introduction", p. 47. On Wilkins, see John Wilkins, *Mathematical Magick,* London 1648, 'To the Reader'. On Wren, see R.T. Gunther, *Early Science in Oxford,* 14 vols., Oxford 1923–1945, 6:365.

17 Rees, *Industry,* 2:367–369; Eric H. Ash, "Queen *v.* Northumberland, and the Control of Technical Expertise", in: *History of Science* 39 (2001), pp. 215–240.

18 Rees, *Industry,* 2:373–374.

19 Ibid., 2:386–387.

20 Ibid., 2:396.

21 See: Mines Royal and Mineral and Battery Records, Volume 3, (n.d.), The British Library, Loan MS 16/3.

eties of the *Mines Royale* and *Mineral Works* have been so prudent, as to make several of both the other Societies Members also of theirs, for the better entercourse between them in such publick concerns'.[22]

Pettus's remark about 'publick concerns' was an obvious appeal to the Baconian programme, but it should not be dismissed as mere rhetoric. Two pieces of evidence from the archives of the Royal Society serve to illustrate the close connections between the two societies on an institutional, rather than an individual, basis. The first is a draft of a petition to Charles II from the president, council, and Fellows of the Royal Society for the rights, for thirty-one years, 'for the sole power of digging allum mines'.[23] The draft is undated, but, since the president at the time clearly had an active interest in mining, it was probably written during Brouncker's tenure. We do not know if the petition was ever sent to the king, but the Royal Society was never given the sole power to dig alum mines. Nevertheless, the petition shows that the Fellows were confident enough to try to initiate their own mining venture, and it is a reasonable assumption that this confidence came in part from their close association with the Society of Mines Royal.

The second piece of evidence, a series of guidelines 'Concerning the Corporation for the Royall Mines', was written by Oldenburg, the first secretary of the Royal Society. Oldenburg's guidelines concerned the day-to-day operations of the Society of Mines Royal, including how many members the society should have, and how the shares should be allocated.[24] These were not inconsequential points. That the secretary of the Royal Society was in a position to draft a set of rules for the governing of the Society of Mines Royal surely suggests that there must have been closer ties between the two societies than those that their respective minutes reveal.

3 Robert Boyle: Natural Historian of Mines

For eighty years, a minor biographical error about Robert Boyle has persisted. In his 1944 biography of Boyle, Louis Trenchard More claimed that Boyle joined the Society of Mines Royal in 1664, a date that was later repeated by Marie Boas Hall.[25] However, although Boyle applied to be a member of the society in 1664, an entry in the minute book of the Society for Mines Royal dated June 1667 shows that he was not accepted – and thus not able to attend meetings – until that year:

> A proposition being heretofore made [in] July 1664 for the admittance of Robert Boyle Esq into the Society of this Corporation wch forwant of a full

22 John Pettus, *Fodinæ Regales*, London 1670, pp. 26–27.

23 Anon. 'Petition to the King for the sole power of digging Allum Mines' (n.d.), Royal Society of London, DM/5/37.

24 Henry Oldenburg, 'Guidelines Concerning the Corporation for the Royall Mines' (n.d.), Royal Society of London, CLP/24/65.

25 Louis Trenchard More, *The Life and Works of the Honourable Robert Boyle: Theologian, Alchemist, Chemist*, London 1944, p. 117; Marie Boas Hall, *Robert Boyle on Natural Philosophy: An Essay, with Selections from His Writings*, Bloomington 1965, p. 26.

> number of members [...] was referred to a full [council] when there might be eleven members. [This has now been] taken into consideration & by the generall consent of this [council] it is ordered that the said Mr Boyle be admitted a member of this Corporation.[26]

This is a minor clarification, but it is a significant one in the context of our present subject. Since 'Inquiries touching Mines' was published before Boyle began inspecting mines for the Society of Mines Royal we cannot interpret his queries as being developed in the context of his work as a mines inspector (which, incidentally, was the initial hypothesis of the present author). Perhaps he wrote the queries in an effort to expedite his election to the Mines Royal, but this is just conjecture. We can, however, be more confident in presuming that he wrote the queries to guide his friends who were already involved in mining, since, on 2 June 1666 (five months before his queries were published in the *Philosophical Transactions*), Boyle sent his queries to John Locke along with a letter explaining that he had drawn up the queries 'for the use of some freinds & partly for my owne'.[27] But what were his own purposes? To truly understand Boyle's queries, we need to situate them in the context of the excursions he personally conducted in mines before writing them. When and why did Boyle become interested in mines?

The 'when' is easier to answer. Boyle probably became interested in mines during his years in London and Oxford in the 1650s, when he first made the acquaintance of the naturalists who comprised the so-called Hartlib Circle. Given that these naturalists were amongst the first to be influenced by Bacon, it is no surprise that several of them, such as Petty, Wilkins, Gerard Boate, and Gabriel Plattes had natural-philosophical interests in mining. Boate and Plattes in particular had clearly conducted first-hand observations in mines, and Boyle was soon to follow their example.[28] As we shall see, though none of Boyle's earliest writings were expressly about mines, he frequently drew upon his own first-hand fieldwork in them to support his natural-philosophical arguments.

Consider his first natural-philosophical book, *New Experiments Physico-Mechanical, Touching the Spring of the Air and its Effects* (1660). Here, Boyle described forty-three experiments that he, Hooke, and his assistants had conducted on airs and gases. After recounting his eighteenth experiment, which involved observing the variable height of mercury in a glass tube by a window over several weeks, Boyle argued that there 'may be strange Ebbings and Flowings [...] in the Atmosphere [...] that it may admit great and sudden Mutations, either as to its Altitude or to its Density'. He then brought in some complementary evidence from a mine excursion: 'when we have visited those places that abound with

26 Mines Royal and Mineral and Battery Records, Volume 3, (n.d.), British Library, Loan MS 16/3, p. 40.
27 Hunter, "Robert Boyle", p. 19.
28 Webster, *Great Instauration*, pp. 47, 393–395, 430.

Mines, we have several times been told by the Diggers, that even when the Sky seem'd clear, there would not seldom suddenly arise [...] a certain Steam (which they usually call a damp)'.[29] Similarly, in defending one of the arguments from his forty-first experiment, that 'Air too much thicken'd [...] with Steams is unfit for Respiration', Boyle claimed that he had been 'inform'd by more than one credible Person' involved in lead mining in Devonshire that mineworkers struggled to breathe when damps arose, adding that he knew this to be true for other mines too.[30] Clearly, despite their lowly social status, Boyle had no qualms in using the testimony of mineworkers to defend his arguments. Sometimes he obtained this testimony first-hand, as with the diggers, and sometimes he obtained it via an intermediary, as with his credible witnesses.

Further, several passages from Boyle's *Certain Physiological Essays* (1661), a wide-ranging collection of discourses, suggest that he personally trusted the knowledge claims of mineworkers because he respected their practical, experiential knowledge. 'Having upon occasion had the Curiosity not long since to visit some Mines of Lead, and other Metals', Boyle noted in the first essay, 'I find, that there is a great difference, and discernible even to the eye, betwixt the several Oars'. He went on to distinguish between four different kinds of lead ore using the mineworkers' nomenclature – 'common Lead-Oar', 'Steel-Oar', 'Firm-Oar', and 'Pottern-Oar'. The mineworkers apparently made their distinctions based on the properties of the ores themselves, such as their hardness, color, and fusibility, as well as the different uses they were suited to and the price they could fetch. Boyle, for his part, was impressed that the mineworkers could judge the quality of different lead ores, and lamented that naturalists so often discussed lead as if it were a homogenous entity.[31] In so doing, Boyle validated their taxonomy and exemplified Thomas Sprat's claim that the early Fellows of the Royal Society '[preferred] the language of Artizans, Countrymen, and Merchants, before that of Wits, or Scholars'.[32]

In another physiological essay, Boyle again demonstrated his esteem for the knowledge of mineworkers in a discussion of the signs of mines and the divining rod. After comparing contradictory authors on the effectiveness of the divining rod to detect metallic veins, Boyle revealed that 'one Gentleman who [lived] near the Lead-mines in *Somersetshire*' toured the mining districts with him and attempted to demonstrate the effectiveness of the divining rod. Boyle was unconvinced. So, like a true historian of the trades, and taking the advice he would later give to other naturalists not to be afraid to trust the knowledge claims of workers, he consulted the mineworkers. 'Among the Miners themselves', he reported,

29 Boyle, *New Experiments*, 1:203–204.
30 Ibid., 1:283–284.
31 Robert Boyle, *Certain Physiological Essays* (1661), 2:43.
32 Thomas Sprat, *The History of the Royal-Society of London, For the Improving of Natural Knowledge*, London 1667, p. 113.

'I found some made use of this Wand, and others laughed at it'.[33] Ultimately, Boyle remained neutral on the question of the divining rod's usefulness. Nevertheless, his *Certain Physiological Essays* underlines two important points. Firstly, that by 1661 Boyle saw mines and metals as topics worthy of study in their own right, and probably as part of the history of trades programme – not merely as a means to explore his interest in pneumatic chemistry. And secondly, that he valued the natural knowledge of mineworkers.

These points are also evident in his *The Sceptical Chymist* (1661), the main purpose of which was to refute the matter theories of Aristotle and Paracelsus and advance Boyle's theory that matter consisted of moving corpuscles. Boyle structured *The Sceptical Chymist* as a dialogue between Carneades (representing his own views) and the personifications of Aristotelianism and Paracelsianism. In the sixth part of the book, Boyle provided observations on 'the growth or increment of Minerals' to advance his corpuscular philosophy.[34] Two of these observations came from German mining authors: the 'Industrious Chymist' Johannes Valehius, and 'That great Traveller and Laborious Chymist' Johannes Agricola. Now, both of these authors were closer to the Paracelsian position than Boyle's, so it is somewhat odd that he – via Carneades – described them with such flattering adjectives. He did not mention that they were adherents to a philosophy he was attacking. Because he borrowed their observations we can reasonably assume that Boyle found them epistemically trustworthy, and, given that Valehius's and Agricola's respective observations comprised the testimony of a 'Workman' and 'Mine-Men', this was consistent with his *New Experiments* and *Physiological Essays*.[35] This time, the intermediary that provided Boyle with mining expertise was textual, but he still nevertheless used the testimony of mineworkers to support his arguments.

A similar approach can be found in *New Experiments and Observations Touching Cold* (1665), written after Boyle had applied to be a member of the Society of Mines Royal but had not yet been accepted. Clearly, Boyle had personally visited several more mines in the four years since the publication of the *Physiological Essays*. A key theme in *Observations Touching Cold* was the internal heat of the Earth, but Boyle chose not to engage at length with the philosophical writings of the chemists and Cartesians who believed that the Earth had a 'Central fire'. Nor did he refer to the Renaissance physicians who had published well-known texts that dealt with the Earth's heat in the context of their balneological work.[36] Instead, Boyle turned to humble mineworkers. He insisted that it was not 'improper' to recount some of his observations of, and conversations with, 'men that have been either diggers of (or conversant in) Mines' – again demonstrating the trust he

33 Boyle, *Physiological Essays*, 2:68–69.
34 Robert Boyle, *The Sceptical Chymist* (1661), 2:347.
35 Ibid., 2:349–350.
36 Rienk Vermij, "Subterranean Fire. Changing Theories of the Earth During the Renaissance", in: *Early Science and Medicine* 3 (1998), pp. 323–347.

had in their experiential knowledge.[37] But there was one author that Boyle did quote at length on this topic: a comparably unknown Frenchman, Jean-Baptiste Morin. And, more surprising still, Boyle acknowledged that his reading of Morin had persuaded him that he had previously been wrong in believing that miners only sweated underground because the air there was damp and ill-suited to respiration – they sweated, in fact, because of the very real existence of a general 'Subterraneal heat or warmth'.

Boyle was no stranger to mines, and an expert on airs. So why did he revise his conclusions in light of Morin? A large part of the answer appears to be that Boyle had a lot of faith in Morin's method, which, it just so happened, was remarkably like his own. Like Boyle, Morin had visited several mines and asked 'all the Masters of them' questions. But Morin also had the advantage of having gone into mines much deeper than Boyle had, descending as far as 'three or four hundred' fathoms underground.[38] This convinced Boyle that Morin's claims were reliable enough to ensure that he (Boyle) had to reconsider his previous conclusions.

To sum up: Boyle took seriously the natural knowledge of mineworkers; he engaged with them face-to-face and interviewed them wherever possible; and his conversations with them were extended and involved a back and forth. He found such conversations – or reports of conversations – beneficial for a range of his natural-philosophical interests. In *Observations Touching Cold* he was interested in subterranean heat, an issue related to the mine damps that had interested him in *New Experiments*. In *Physiological Essays* he had been interested in the metallic veins, broadly construed, including how to identify them from the surface and how to judge the quality of the different ores they produced. And in *The Sceptical Chymist* he showed an interest in the natural resources that were found in the bowels of the earth. It is thus unsurprising that when Boyle came to write 'Articles of Inquiries touching Mines' he prioritized the knowledge of miners – he had by that point long since drawn upon the experiences and testimony of miners for his wider natural-philosophical purposes.

4 'Articles of Inquiries touching Mines'

Boyle's queries were divided under seven headings: 'The neighbouring Country where the Mines are' (6 queries), 'The Soyl where the Mines are' (1), 'The Signs of Mines' (22), 'The Structure and other particulars belonging to the Mines themselves' (18), 'The Nature and Circumstances of the Ore' (17), 'The Reduction of the Ore into Metal' (25), and 'Promiscuous Inquiries about Mines' (11).

Some of Boyle's queries were easier to answer than others. The queries under the first heading, for instance, could easily be answered without going into a mine. They asked broad, topographical questions, and while most of them seem to have been informed by what Boyle *observed* in mining districts, the third and

37 Robert Boyle, *New Experiments and Observations Touching Cold* (1665) 4:366.
38 Ibid., 4:368.

fourth queries appear to have been informed by what he *read*. The third asked about the cattle found in close proximity to mines, perhaps motivated by Plattes who had argued that healthy cattle indicated the presence of coal, while the fourth asked about the health of the 'Inhabitants' of the mining districts, a recurring topic in the German mining literature.[39] To answer these queries some conversation with the locals might have been necessary, but the other four, such as 'Whether the Country be Mountainous, Plain, or distinguish'd with Vales?' could be answered by observation. So too could the only query under the second heading, which asked about 'the *Soyle* that [was] neer the Surface of the Earth'.[40]

However, given that Boyle asked 'By what *Signs* they know or guess, that there is a mine in such a place?' he clearly expected naturalists to answer the queries under the third heading by consulting mineworkers. Indeed, only someone with prolonged practical experience searching for metals and minerals could answer queries like 'Whether the Waters of the place proposed, do by their tast, smell, ponderousness, &c. disclose themselves to contain Minerals?' or 'Whether Mists use to rise from Grounds stored with Minerals?'. And, likewise, only someone with prolonged experience in the bowels of the earth could answer queries like 'Whether there be any Signs of the depth of the Vein beneath the surface of the Earth; and what they are?'.[41] As for the queries under the fourth heading, those that asked about the infrastructure of the mine, such as 'What Air-shaft belongs to the Mine?' could be answered single-handedly by naturalists who were willing to go underground themselves. But because most of these queries concerned the methods of the mineworkers – 'What methods the Mine-men use in following the vein […]?' and 'How the Miners deal with the Rocks and Sparrs, they often meet with, before they come at the Ore?' are representative – it is probable that Boyle expected naturalists to answer them, too, by observing and conversing with mineworkers.[42]

Boyle's fifth heading, 'The Nature and Circumstances of the Ore', was somewhat vague. Some of the queries – such as 'Whether all the Ore, contained in the Mine, be of the self-same nature and goodness; and, if not, what are the differing kinds; and how to be discriminated and estimated?' – again betray Boyle's interest in the color, value, and quality of different kinds of metal. However, other queries under this heading asked about the *veins* of ore visible underground. Boyle asked, for example: 'Whether the Vein have or have not any particular Concomitants, or Coats (if I may so call them;) and, if any, what they are, and in what order they lie?'; 'Whether the Vein be every way of an uniform breadth, and thickness; and, if it be, what these Dimensions are; and, if not, in what place it varies and in what measures?'; and 'How wide the Interruptions are? what Signs, whereby

39 Gabriel Plattes, *A Discovery of Subterraneall Treasure*, London 1639, p. 48.
40 Robert Boyle, "Articles of Inquiries touching Mines" (1666), 5:529–530.
41 Ibid., 5:529–530.
42 Ibid., 5:533.

to find the Vein again? whether the ulterior part or division of the Vein be of the same Nature, and hold on in the same Course, as to its tendency upwards or downwards, or Horizontally, Norward, Southward, *&c.* with the Vein, from which it is cut off?'.[43]

Porter's claim that Boyle's queries about mines did not concern their history is vindicated by these queries, but his claim that they did not concern their structure seems to be exaggerated. Indeed, certain features of these queries will even be *vaguely* familiar to modern geologists. Expressed in modern terminology, they clearly concern the succession of strata and the faults they contained – though Boyle, of course, did not use these terms. Instead of 'strata' he spoke of 'layers' or 'Coats; instead of their succession he spoke of their 'Concomitants'; and instead of their faults he spoke of 'Interruptions'. But we must not get ahead of ourselves. Boyle was not a pioneer of stratigraphy. He was only interested in the layers of the earth insofar as they related to a given mine and the natural resources the mine yielded. He was not interested – as Nicolaus Steno had been in his *Prodromus* (1669), and as John Woodward would later be in his *Essay Toward a Natural History of the Earth* (1695) – in the continuity and succession of strata over larger geographical spaces.[44] This is a comment not a criticism. For, as I have been arguing, Boyle was not doing stratigraphy badly, but doing the natural history of mines effectively

Finally, consider the queries under Boyle's sixth heading, 'The Reduction of the Ore into Metal'. In the seventeenth century, most assay and smelting houses were located in close proximity to the mines, and it was often – especially with tin and lead – the same mineworkers who performed the assay and refining operations. Some of the queries asked about the equipment found in assay houses. For example, one query asked 'What kind of Furnaces they use, to melt the Ore in? Whether they be all of one sort and bigness, or of differing?'. Another asked: 'What Clay, Sand, or Mould they let run or pour [the ore] through? And after what manner they refrigerate it?'. However, Boyle's priority, as it had been with the mineworkers, was to codify the practical knowledge of the refiners and smelters, both generally and more particularly as regards the way they judged the quality and value of different metals. Boyle knew that different metals required different operations – such as 'Beating, Grinding, Washing, *&c*' – and he knew that different varieties of the same metal were of different qualities. Several of his queries were therefore about 'the Wayes of distinguishing them, and estimating their goodness'. One query asked about how the different metals were priced, and one of them was about the methods that refiners used to improve the quality of a given ore. Throughout the queries, we see Boyle making reference to what he had observed in assay houses, or been reliably informed of. A case in point

43 Ibid., 5:534–536.

44 See: Nicolaus Steno, *De Solido intra Solidum naturaliter Contento Dissertationis Prodromus*, Florentiae 1669; John Woodward, *An Essay Toward a Natural History of the Earth*, London 1695.

was his remark that 'in some places 'tis usual, to mingle poor and rich Ore; and at *Mendip* they mix two or more of those differing kinds of *Lead-ore* that they call *Frim-ore, Steel-ore, Potern-ore,* &c'.[45]

Boyle's eleven promiscuous inquiries were exactly that – ranging from asking about the presence of 'subterraneous *Dæmons*' to asking 'What are the Laws, Constitutions, and Customs, *Oeconomical, Political, Ethical,* that are receiv'd and practis'd among the Mine-Men?'.[46] The other eight, however, asked strictly about terrestrial phenomena: about whether or not different metals and minerals could be found in the same mine, about the airs, stones, 'Mineral Gelly', damps, and fossils in mines, and the trees and springs around them. In quoting only the query about demons to evidence his claim about Renaissance cosmology, Porter exaggerates (in my view) the randomness of Boyle's queries. Boyle did have a particular end in mind when writing his queries, though it was not stratigraphic or geological. It was to describe mines and their immediate surroundings in as much detail as possible, drawing on natural-historical observations as well as the knowledge of mineworkers.

5 The Natural History of Mines: An Overview

So, how influential were Boyle's queries in establishing the natural history of mines? Considerably. That is not to say that Restoration naturalists only became interested in mines after reading 'Inquiries touching Mines'. As noted earlier, most Restoration naturalists would have recognized the significance of mining for the Baconian programme. Moreover, two articles on mines that only appeared in the *Philosophical Transactions* after the publication of Boyle's queries actually predated them.[47] Boyle's contribution was therefore not to initiate the study of mines in Restoration Britain but to promote it. His queries provided a comprehensive remit and suggested a structure for inquiry into mines, and his reputation ensured that his queries were taken seriously. Thus, his queries exerted a noticeable influence on all work connected to mines produced by Fellows of the Royal Society for around thirty years.[48] (The Cornish philosopher Frank Nicholls even wrote two papers on the 'Natural History of Mines and Metals' as late as 1728.[49])

45 Ibid., 5:536–538.

46 Ibid., 5:539.

47 Christopher Merret, Manuscript "An Account of the Tyn-mines, and working of Tyn in the County of Cornwall" (n. d.), Royal Society of London, MS/215/49; and Edward Cotton, Manuscript "An Account concerning the Tin mines in Devonshire" (n.d.) Royal Society of London, CLP/9i/14/1.

48 After about 1695, John Woodward's new approach to conducting natural-historical fieldwork gradually began to supersede and replace Boyle's approach. See: Joshua Hillman, 'From Coallery to the Natural History of Strata: Mining and the Spatial Sciences of the Earth in Britain, 1600–1800' (University of Leeds, Unpublished PhD Thesis, 2024).

49 Frank Nicholls, "Some Observations towards composing a Natural History of Mines and Metals", in: *Philosophical Transactions* 35 (1728), pp. 402–407; Frank Nicholls, "farther Observations towards composing a Natural History of Mines and Metals", in: *Philosophical Transac-*

If Boyle's list of queries was the most influential contribution to the natural history of mines, then two books, Pettus's *Fodinæ Regales* (1670) and John Webster's *Metallographia* (1671), come in second and third place. Both books served to further outline the subject-matter and promote the natural history of mines. As mentioned before, *Fodinæ Regales* was the first official history of the Society of Mines Royal, but Pettus also included several natural-historical reflections on mines. *Metallographia* was mainly a compilation of German mining authors, but Webster's own observations in the northern counties of England were scattered throughout the text. And, as indicated by *Metallographia*'s full title, Webster's subject-matter was essentially the same as Boyle's. It was: 'an History of Metals. Wherein is declared the signs of Ores and Minerals both before and after digging, the causes and manner of their generations, their kinds, sorts, and differences; with descriptions of sundry new Metals, or Semi Metals, and many other things pertaining to Mineral knowledge'.[50] Both books also emphasized the Baconian nature of mining. For example, Pettus claimed that: 'From [the] *Metals* and *Minerals* digged out of the *Subterranean world*, may be studied the greatest part of NATURE, all *Arts* imployed, *Labours* encouraged, and the chiefest *Sciences* demonstrated'.[51]

Other naturalists responded to Boyle's queries in one of two forms: *Philosophical Transactions* articles and topographical writings. *Philosophical Transactions* articles were more voluminous. Usually, these focused on a single mine and addressed all of the topics that Boyle outlined. The queries were occasionally mentioned explicitly but were often not – though the structure of these articles always made clear Boyle's influence. Some authors answered Boyle's queries sequentially, like Joseph Glanvill, and others focused only on a specific heading. Topographical writings like Edward Browne's *A Brief Account of Some Travels in Hungaria* (1673) and John Ray's *Observations Topographical … Made in a Journey to through part of the Low-countries* (1673) largely followed Boyle's 'General Heads for a Natural History of a Countrey, Great or Small', but some of the most detailed passages of these books were the sections on mining which were clearly responses to 'Inquiries touching Mines'. Thus, they were no 'mere sequel' – they had their own rationale and approach.

In the remainder of this section, I sketch a big picture of the natural history of mines as it materialized in these two media. My aim is not to offer a comprehensive account of any singular contributor, so I proceed by illustrating each of Boyle's six main headings with some representative examples.

tions 35 (1728), pp. 480–485. It is from Nicholls that I have borrowed the term 'natural history of mines'.

50 See the title-page of John Webster, *Metallographia*, London 1671.

51 Pettus, *Fodinæ Regales*, 6.

[1] *The neighbouring Country where the Mines are.* The most detailed descriptions here can often be found in the topographical books. Browne prefaced all of the Central European mines he discussed with a description of their surroundings in his *Brief Account*, and, in his *Observations Topographical*, Ray similarly described the most pertinent topographical features in each mining district he visited.[52] Necessarily briefer descriptions can be found in the *Philosophical Transactions* articles. Several authors chose to dedicate just a sentence or two to Boyle's first heading; 'The Cole-work at *Moslyn* in *Flint shire* lies in a large parcel of Wood-land', sufficed for Roger Moslyn.[53] (Conversely, Henry Powle introduced his account of the iron-works in the Forest of Dean by providing greater detail: 'The Country if full of Hills, but so you may rather call it Uneven, than Mountainous, they being no where high, and rarely of a steep ascent. Betwixt them run great store of little Springs, of a more brownish colour than ordinary Waters, and often leaving in their passage tinctures of Rust. The Ground is naturally inclined to Wood, especially Hasle and Oak […]'.[54]

[2] *The Soyl where the Mines are.* Powle also provides us with a characteristic example of how naturalists answered Boyle's single query about the soil above mines: 'The Forest of *Dean* […] consists generally of a stiff Clay: which, according to the nature of those Soyls, is very deep and miry in the Winter, and in the Summer as dry and parched'.[55] For another example, we can turn to Glanvill's account of the soil near the Mendip lead mines: 'That the *Soyle* near the surface of the Earth is red and stony; and the stones that are drawn out thence, are either of the nature of *Fire-stones*, or *Lime-stones*, but no way *Clayie Marly* or *Chalky*'.[56] To give a final example, a number of brief descriptions of several different coloured soils are found in the anonymously authored article 'A Description of the Diamond Mines'.[57]

[3] *The Signs of Mines.* Soils and rocks of a certain color or texture; the presence of particular plants or minerals; and streams and springs of a particular color, smell, or taste – these were the potential signs of mines that Boyle had listed under his

52 Edward Browne, *A Brief Account of Some Travels in Hungaria* […] *and Friuli*, London 1673, passim; John Ray, *Observations Topographical, Moral and Physiological: Made in a Journey Through Part of the Low-countries, Germany, Italy, and France*, 2 vols., London 1673, 1:56, 204–205.

53 Roger Moslyn, "A Relation of Some Strange Phaenomena, Accompanied with Mischievous Effects in a Cole Work in Flint Shire", in: *Philosophical Transactions* 12 (1677), pp. 895–899, p. 895.

54 Henry Powle, "An Account of Iron-Works in the Forest of Dean", in: *Philosophical Transactions* 12 (1678), pp. 931–935, p. 931.

55 Ibid., 931.

56 Joseph Glanvill, "Answers to Some of the Inquiries Formerly Publish'd Concerning Mines", in: *Philosophical Transactions* 2 (1667), pp. 525–526, p. 526.

57 Anon., "A Description of the Diamond-Mines, as It was Presented by the Right Honourable, the Earl Marshal of England", in: *Philosophical Transactions* 12 (1677), pp. 907–917.

third heading, and that his fellow naturalists asked mineworkers about. Pettus provided a concise summary in *Fodinæ Regales*:

> *Gold, Silver, Tin, Copper, Lead, Iron and Quick*-silver [...] are often found lying upon the cliffs or chincks of Rocks, known by their *colour, brightness*, or other marks; or by such other *Minerals* as the Workmen call *Leaders*, because they usually accompany the *Metallick oar*, and lead to it. Or they are discovered to us either by the nature of *Plants* which grow over them by the *Plough*, by *Moles* which cast up their *shade* or glittering earth; (and therefore in *Derby-shire* and other places where *Lead* abounds, they rarely kill them) or by Springs and Streams of water, or by their use of an Hazel stick (if credit may be given to it:) But by some or one of these the *Miners* are encouraged and directed to dig.[58]

As this passage suggests, Restoration naturalists trusted the natural knowledge of the mineworkers and therefore trusted the accuracy of these signs.[59] Few naturalists boasted about their own knowledge of the signs of mines without emphasizing that they were relaying the knowledge of mineworkers. Webster was typical here: 'The signs to discover where Metals are that the expert Miners have informed me of, and that I have observed in these Northern parts [...] are these [...]'.[60] On the other hand, when the calamine miners that Giles Pooley interviewed told him – after he had listed several of Boyle's potential signs – that there were no certain signs of calamine on the surface, he assumed they were correct.[61] This serves to illustrate both the prevalent role that Boyle's queries played in practice, and the faith that naturalists had in the mineworkers' expertise. To give a final example, such was John Beaumont's faith in the mineworkers' ability to detect '*Lead-oar*' by its 'Oily-smell' that he hoped that the Royal Society would one day develop a method by which 'we may discover a smell at great distance'.[62] Like Boyle, those who followed in his footsteps and contributed to the natural history of mines were especially interested in the signs mineworkers used to guide them.

[4] *The Structure and other particulars belonging to the Mines themselves*. So too were they interested in the methods the mineworkers employed and the infrastructure of the mine – the two topics Boyle's fourth set of queries asked about. Samuel Colepresse, Edward Cotton, and Christopher Merret provided equally detailed

58 Pettus, *Fodinæ Regales*, 3.

59 The exception was Samuel Colepresse, who was more cautious than most naturalists, writing that he would neither deny nor insist on any of the mineworkers' particular signs: Samuel Colepresse, "An Accompt of Some Mineral Observations Touching the Mines of Cornwal and Devon", in: *Philosophical Transactions* 6 (1671), pp. 2096–2113, pp. 2101–2102.

60 Webster, *Metallographia*, 102.

61 Giles Pooley, "An Account of Digging and Preparing the Lapis Calaminaris", in: *Philosophical Transactions* 17 (1693), pp. 672–677, p. 673.

62 John Beaumont, "Two Letters [...] Concerning Rock-Plants and their Growth", in: *Philosophical Transactions* 11 (1676), pp. 724–742, p. 741.

accounts of how, once below the surface, the tin miners of Cornwall and Devon traced veins of tin, and how they knew the tin was 'Ripe'.[63] Beaumont and Glanvill described the tools and techniques the lead miners of Somerset used to extract the lead.[64] Browne and Walter Pope were among those who provided similar descriptions of the methods employed by the European mineworkers they encountered.[65] Such descriptions were clearly answers to queries like 'What Instruments they use to break the Rock *&c*?' and 'How Veins are follow'd, lost, and recover'd?'.[66] As for the infrastructure of the mine, nearly every contribution to the natural history of mines described the materials that the mine shaft and supports were made from. The anonymous author of an article 'Concerning the Sal-Gemme Mines in Poland' was characteristic when he described how the Polish mine-shafts were 'five square, four or five foot long, and as broad, lined downwards thorough with Timber', as was Glanvill when he wrote 'The *Groove* is 4 foot long, 2 ½ foot broad [...]'.[67]

[5] *The Nature and Circumstance of the Ore*. Recall that there were two kinds of queries under this heading: those about the 'goodness' and quality of the ore or mineral and those about the veins and their spatial relationship to other rocks. Most contributors to the natural history of mines focused more on the first kind, relaying the information they had obtained from the mineworkers about the 'colour', 'goodness', 'thickness', and 'softness' of the ores and minerals they sought after. Thus, in the pages of the *Philosophical Transactions*, we find that: 'gravelly *Tinn* they distinguish from that which is gathered from the Stones, calling it *Pyran Tinn* [...] Another sort of Ore they have, call'd *Mundick Ore* [...] Being mixed together, the *Mundick* may be easily known by its glittering, yet sad brownness, wherewith it will soon colour your fingers';[68] 'The Iron-Ore [...] is found in great abundance in most parts of the Forest [of Dean]: differing both in colour, weight, and goodness [...] The best, which they call their Brush-Ore, is of a Blewish colour; very ponderous, and full of little shining Specks like grains of Silver';[69] and

63 Colepresse, "An Accompt"; Cotton, "An Account"; Christopher Merret, "A Relation of the Tinn-Mines, and Working of Tinn in the County of Cornwal", in: *Philosophical Transactions* 12 (1677), pp. 949–952.

64 John Beaumont, "A Letter [...] concerning a New Way of Cleaving Rocks", in: *Philosophical Transactions* 15 (1685), pp. 854–855; Joseph Glanvill, "Additional Answers to the Queries of Mines", in: *Philosophical Transactions* 3 (1668), pp. 767–771.

65 Edward Browne, "Some Directions and Inquiries with Their Answers, Concerning the Mines, Minerals, Baths, &c. of Hungary, Transylvania, Austria, and Other Countries Neighbouring to Those", in: *Philosophical Transactions* 5 (1670), pp. 1189–1196; Walter Pope, "Extract of a letter [...] Concerning the Mines of Mercury in Friuli [...]", in: *Philosophical Transactions* 1 (1665), pp. 21–26.

66 Boyle, 'Inquiries touching Mines', 5:534.

67 Anon., "A Relation Concerning the Sal-Gemme-Mines in Poland", in: *Philosophical Transactions* 5 (1670), pp. 1099–2002 (2000); Glanvill, "Additional Answers", 768.

68 Merret, "A Relation", p. 950.

69 Powle, "An Account", p. 932

that '*Calamine* it self is of several Colours, some white, some reddish, some greyish, some blackish, which is counted the best [...]'.[70] Similar accounts of the differing qualities of ores, grounded in their sensible properties, were common in most contributions to the natural history of mines project.

Descriptions of veins were rarer, but these, too, were primarily derived from the testimony of miners. Merret's description is characteristic:

> The Stones from which *Tinn* is wrought are sometimes found a foot or two below the surface of the Earth, but most usually betwixt two walls of Rocks (which are commonly of an Iron-colour, of little or no affinity with the *Tinn*) in a Vein or Load (as the Miners call it) betwixt 4 and 18 Inches broad, or thereabout. Some say, the Load runs North and South: but in truth it runs East and West, and all other ways with very great variety.[71]

[6] *The Reduction of the Ore into Metal*. Finally, we come to Boyle's sixth heading. As noted already, the refinery or workshop was often an extension of the copper, tin, iron, and lead mines of seventeenth-century Britain, and many *Philosophical Transactions* articles focused entirely on Boyle's sixth heading. Pettus and Webster also provided lengthy descriptions of the assaying and refining processes of the various different ores, and the topographical books were scattered with detailed descriptions of the processes carried out at the specific workshops their authors visited. For a representative example, let us turn to Glanvill's account of the Mendip lead mines. He relayed how the mineworkers 'beat the Ore with an Iron flat piece', and how they washed it using a 'Wire-sive'. Then he described the 'Hearth' the ore was placed in, how they managed the 'Fire', and, finally, how they distinguished the best melted ore – by measuring its weight.[72] Similar descriptions of iron working, copper and tin smelting, and the making of copperas were provided by Powle, Colepresse, Cotton, Merret, and Daniel Colwall, respectively.[73]

6 Conclusion

Long overlooked, the emergence of the natural history of mines project as a distinct branch of the history of trades programme in the decades after 1660 offers important lessons for historians of science and historians of natural resources.

More generally, it reminds us of the centrality of mining in the thought of the seventeenth-century natural philosopher. The famous works of Agricola and other German authors; the vast development of the late Tudor and early Stuart

70 Pooley, "An Account", p. 674.

71 Merret, "A Relation", p. 949.

72 Glanvill, "Additional Answers", p. 770–771.

73 Powle, "An Account"; Colepresse, "An Accompt"; Cotton, "An Account"; Merret; "A Relation"; Christopher Merret, "The Art of Refining", in: *Philosophical Transactions* 12 (1678), pp. 1046–1052; Daniel Colwall, "An Account of the Way of Making English Green-Copperas", in: *Philosophical Transactions* 12 (1677), pp. 1677–1678.

mining industries; the frequent connotations made between mining and natural inquiry in Bacon's writings; the early studies of mines produced by the members of the Hartlib Circle; and the allure of the Society of Mines Royal: all of this was likely on Boyle's mind when he began taking excursions in mines and writing the queries that to defined and promoted the natural history of mines. Porter's claim that mining and the economic reward it promised did not significantly impact the development of the British sciences of the earth before 1830 no longer seems as convincing when we turn away from the 'incoherent jumble of cosmogony, fossil-collecting, Biblical theorizing, topography, and so on' that he saw as characterizing the seventeenth-century British sciences of the earth, and towards the natural history of mines.[74]

The natural history of mines project also suggests that we should rethink our approach to the *practice* of the sciences of the earth in this period. When the contributions to the natural history of mines are carefully read, it becomes clear that Restoration naturalists depended in no small measure on the mineworkers they encountered on their excursions. The categories the naturalists used, such as 'goodness' and 'thickness', were borrowed from the mineworkers, whose testimony on matters pertaining to the structure of the subterranean world naturalists (usually) accepted without comment. And importantly, these mineworkers were not 'invisible' in the same way as the technicians that assisted experimenters.[75] Recent work has tended to see mineworkers as being important to naturalists only insofar as they could provide them specimens of fossils.[76] Yet the foregoing analysis suggests that naturalists were often happy to repeat the knowledge of mineworkers, and that they rarely tried to conceal their debts. The practice of the natural history of mines thus involved direct observation and the management of testimonial knowledge. In Restoration England, natural-philosophical knowledge about metallic and mineral resources relied on the knowledge economy of mining.

Reference Lists

Sources

Anon., *Petition to the King for the sole power of digging Allum Mines.* (n.d.), Royal Society of London, DM/5/37.

Anon., "A Description of the Diamond-Mines, as It was Presented by the Right Honourable, the Earl Marshal of England", in: *Philosophical Transactions* 12 (1677), pp. 907–917.

74 Roy Porter, "The Industrial Revolution and the Rise of the Science of Geology", in: *Changing Perspectives in the History of Science. Essays in Honour of Joseph Needham*, eds. Mikulás Teich and Robert Young, Cambridge 1973, pp. 320–343, pp. 320–321.

75 Steven Shapin, "The Invisible Technician", in: *American Scientist* 77 (1989), pp. 554–563.

76 Martin Rudwick, *Bursting the Limits of Time: The Reconstruction of Geohistory in the Age of Revolution*, Chicago 2005, p. 33; Lydia Barnett, "Showing and hiding: The flickering visibility of earth workers in the archives of earth science", in: *History of Science* 58 (2020), pp. 245–274.

Anon., "A Relation Concerning the Sal-Gemme-Mines in Poland", in: *Philosophical Transactions* 5 (1670), pp. 1099–2002.

Bacon, Francis, "Preparative towards a natural and experimental history (1620)", in: *The Works of Francis Bacon*, eds. James Spedding et al., 7 vols., London 1857–1859, 4, pp. 249–271.

Beaumont, John, "A Letter [...] concerning a New Way of Cleaving Rocks", in: *Philosophical Transactions* 15 (1685), pp. 854–855.

Beaumont, John, "Two Letters [...] Concerning Rock-Plants and their Growth", in: *Philosophical Transactions* 11 (1676), pp. 724–742.

Boyle, Robert, "Articles of Inquiries touching Mines" (1666)", in: *The Works of Robert Boyle*, eds. Michael Hunter and Edward Davis, 14 vols., London 1999–2000, 5, pp. 529–540.

Boyle, Robert, "Certain Physiological Essays (1661)", in: *The Works of Robert Boyle*, eds. Michael Hunter and Edward Davis, 14 vols., London 1999–2000, 2, pp. 3–203.

Boyle, Robert, "New Experiments and Observations Touching Cold (1665)", in: *The Works of Robert Boyle*, eds. Michael Hunter and Edward Davis, 14 vols., London 1999–2000, 4, pp. 203–523.

Boyle, Robert, "New Experiments Physico-Mechanical (1660)," in: *The Works of Robert Boyle*, eds. Michael Hunter and Edward Davis, 14 vols, London 1999–2000, 1, pp. 141–303.

Boyle, Robert, "The Sceptical Chymist (1661)", in: *The Works of Robert Boyle*, eds. Michael Hunter and Edward Davis, 14 vols., London 1999–2000, 2, pp. 205–378.

Browne, Edward, "Some Directions and Inquiries with Their Answers, Concerning the Mines, Minerals, Baths, &c. of Hungary, Transylvania, Austria, and Other Countries Neighbouring to Those", in: *Philosophical Transactions* 5 (1670), pp. 1189–1196.

Browne, Edward, *A Brief Account of Some Travels in Hungaria [...] and Friuli*, London 1673.

Colepresse, Samuel, "An Accompt of Some Mineral Observations Touching the Mines of Cornwal and Devon", in: *Philosophical Transactions* 6 (1671), pp. 2096–2113.

Colwall, Daniel, "An Account of the Way of Making English Green-Copperas", in: *Philosophical Transactions* 12 (1677), pp. 1677–1678.

Cotton, Edward, Manuscript "An Account concerning the Tin mines in Devonshire" (n.d.) Royal Society of London, CLP/9i/14/1.

Glanvill, Joseph, "Additional Answers to the Queries of Mines", in: *Philosophical Transactions* 3 (1668), pp. 767–771.

Glanvill, Joseph, "Answers to Some of the Inquiries Formerly Publish'd Concerning Mines", in: *Philosophical Transactions* 2 (1667), pp. 525–526.

Hooke, Robert, "The Method of Improving Natural Philosophy" (c. 1666)", in: *The Posthumous Works of Robert Hooke*, ed. Richard Waller, London 1705, pp. 7–80.

Merret, Christopher, "A Relation of the Tinn-Mines, and Working of Tinn in the County of Cornwal", in: *Philosophical Transactions* 12 (1677), pp. 949–952.

Merret, Christopher, "The Art of Refining", in: *Philosophical Transactions* 12 (1678), pp. 1046–1052.

Merret, Christopher, Manuscript "An Account of the Tyn-mines, and working of Tyn in the County of Cornwall" (n.d.). Royal Society of London, MS/215/49.

Moray, Robert, "Letter to Alexander Bruce, 15 August 1665", in: *Letters of Sir Robert Moray to the Earl of Kincardine, 1657–73*, ed. David Stevenson, London 2007, pp. 252–253.

Moslyn, Roger, "A Relation of Some Strange Phaenomena, Accompanied with Mischievous Effects in a Cole Work in Flint Shire", in: *Philosophical Transactions* 12 (1677), pp. 895–899.

Nicholls, Frank, "farther Observations towards composing a Natural History of Mines and Metals", in: *Philosophical Transactions* 35 (1728), pp. 480–485.

Nicholls, Frank, "Some Observations towards composing a Natural History of Mines and Metals", in: *Philosophical Transactions* 35 (1728), pp. 402–407.

Oldenburg, Henry, "Guidelines Concerning the Corporation for the Royall Mines" (n.d.). Royal Society of London, CLP/24/65.

Pettus, John, *Fodinæ Regales*, London 1670.

Petty, William, "History of Trades", in: *The Petty Papers: Some unpublished writings of Sir William Petty*, ed. the Marquis of Lansdowne, 2 vols., London 1927, 1, pp. 205–207.

Plattes, Gabriel, *A Discovery of Subterraneall Treasure*, London 1639.

Pooley, Giles, "An Account of Digging and Preparing the Lapis Calaminaris", in: *Philosophical Transactions* 17 (1693), pp. 672–677.

Pope, Walter, "Extract of a letter [...] Concerning the Mines of Mercury in Friuli [...]", in: *Philosophical Transactions* 1 (1665), pp. 21–26.

Powle, Henry, "An Account of Iron-Works in the Forest of Dean", in: *Philosophical Transactions* 12 (1678), pp. 931–935.

Ray, John, *Observations Topographical, Moral and Physiological: Made in a Journey Through Part of the Low-countries, Germany, Italy, and France*, 2 vols., London 1673.

Sprat, Thomas, *The History of the Royal-Society of London, For the Improving of Natural Knowledge*, London 1667.

Steno, Nicolaus, *De Solido intra Solidum naturaliter Contento Dissertationis Prodromus*, Florentiae 1669.

Various, Mines Royal and Mineral and Battery Records, Volume 3, (n.d.). The British Library, Loan MS 16/3.

Webster, John, *Metallographia*, London 1671.

Wilkins, John, *Mathematical Magick*, London 1648.

Woodward, John, *An Essay Toward a Natural History of the Earth*, London 1695.

Research Literature

Anstey, Peter, "Locke, Bacon and Natural History", in: *Early Science and Medicine* 7 (2002), pp. 65–92.

Ash, Eric H., "Queen *v.* Northumberland, and the Control of Technical Expertise", in: *History of Science* 39 (2001), pp. 215–240.

Barnett, Lydia, "Showing and hiding: The flickering visibility of earth workers in the archives of earth science", in: *History of Science* 58 (2020), pp. 245–274.

Blanchard, Ian, *Russia's 'Age of Silver': Precious Metal Production and Economic Growth in the Eighteenth* Century, New York 1989.

Boas Hall, Marie, *Robert Boyle on Natural Philosophy: An Essay, with Selections from His Writings*, Bloomington 1965.

Burt, Roger, "Lead Production in England and Wales, 1700–1770", in: *The Economic History Review* 22 (1969), pp. 249–268.

Dal Prete, Ivano, *On the Edge of Eternity. The Antiquity of the Earth in Medieval and Early Modern Europe*, New York 2022.

Gunther, R. T., *Early Science in Oxford*, 14 vols., Oxford 1923–1945.

Hatcher, John, *The History of the British Coal Industry. Volume 1. Before 1700*, Oxford 1993.
Hillman, Joshua, From Coallery to the Natural History of Strata: Mining and the Spatial Sciences of the Earth in Britain, 1600–1800, University of Leeds, Unpublished PhD Thesis, 2024.
Hunter, Michael and Paul Wood, "Towards Solomon's House: Rival Strategies for Reforming the Early Royal Society", in: *History of Science* 24 (1986), pp. 49–108.
Hunter, Michael, "Robert Boyle and the early Royal Society: a reciprocal exchange in the making of Baconian science", in: *British Journal for the History of Science* 40 (2007), pp. 1–23.
Klein, Lauren, "To Mine for Truth: The Metaphor of Mining in Francis Bacon's The Great Instauration", in: *Origins of Scientific Learning: Essays on Culture and Knowledge in Early Modern Europe*, eds. Sarah French and Kay Etheridge, New York 2007, pp. 117–138.
Laudan, Rachel, *From Mineralogy to Geology. The Foundations of a Science, 1650–1830*, Chicago 1987.
Lewis, Georg, *The Stanneries*, Boston 1908.
Maddison, Robert, *The Life of the Honourable Robert Boyle, F.R.S.*, London 1969.
Merchant, Carolyn, *The Death of Nature: Women, Ecology and the Scientific Revolution*, New York 1980.
More, Louis Trenchard, *The Life and Works of the Honourable Robert Boyle: Theologian, Alchemist, Chemist*, London 1944.
Ochs, Kathleen, "The Royal Society of London's History of the Trades Programme: An Early Episode in Applied Science", in: *Notes and Records of the Royal Society of London* 39 (1985), pp. 129–158.
Pastorino, Cesare, "The Mine and the Furnace: Francis Bacon, Thomas Russell and Early Stuart Mining Culture", in: *Early Science and Medicine* 14 (2009), pp. 630–660.
Porter, Roy, "The Industrial Revolution and the Rise of the Science of Geology", in: *Changing Perspectives in the History of Science. Essays in Honour of Joseph Needham*, eds. Mikulás Teich and Robert Young, Cambridge 1973, pp. 320–343.
Porter, Roy, *The Making of Geology. Earth Science in Britain, 1660–1815*, Cambridge 1977.
Rees, William, *Industry Before the Industrial Revolution: Incorporating a study of the Chartered Companies of the Society of Mines Royal and of Mineral and Battery Works*, 2 vols., Cardiff 1968.
Rossi, Paolo, *Francis Bacon: From Magic to Science*, transl. Sacha Rabinovitch, London 1968.
Rudwick, Martin, *Bursting the Limits of Time: The Reconstruction of Geohistory in the Age of Revolution*, Chicago 2005.
Shapin, Steven, "The Invisible Technician", in: *American Scientist* 77 (1989), pp. 554–563.
Sieveking, A. Forbes, "Evelyn's 'Circle of Mechanical Trades'", in: *Transactions of the Newcomen Society* 4 (1923), pp. 40–47.
Stevenson, David, "Introduction", in: *Letters of Sir Robert Moray to the Earl of Kincardine, 1657–73*, ed. David Stevenson, London 2007.
Vermij, Rienk, "Subterranean Fire. Changing Theories of the Earth During the Renaissance", in: *Early Science and Medicine* 3 (1998), pp. 323–347.
Vickers, Brian, *Francis Bacon and Renaissance Prose*, Cambridge 1968.
Webster, Charles, *The Great Instauration. Science, Medicine and Reform, 1626–1660*, London 1975.

Authors

Ovanes Akopyan is a Marie Skłodowska-Curie fellow at Ca' Foscari University of Venice (Italy). He is the author of *Debating the Stars in the Italian Renaissance: Giovanni Pico della Mirandola's Disputationes adversus astrologiam divinatricem and Its Reception* (Brill, 2021) and editor or co-editor of four collections of essays. His second monograph, provisionally entitled *Explaining Natural Disasters in Early Modern Europe: Science, Politics, Rhetoric,* is under contract with Johns Hopkins University Press.

Florike Egmond is a researcher of early modern natural history based in Rome (Italy), but long affiliated with Leiden university. She is the author of many books and articles, among them *Conrad Gessners Thierbuch. Die Originalzeichnungen* (WBG Edition 2018), *Eye for Detail: Images of Plants and Animals in Art and Science, 1500–1630* (Reaktion Books, London 2017), and *The World of Carolus Clusius. Natural History in the Making, 1550–1610* (Pickering and Chatto, London, 2010). She co-edited (with Paul Hoftijzer and Robert Visser) of *Carolus Clusius. Towards a cultural history of a Renaissance naturalist* (KNAW 2007), and (with Francisco Bethencourt), *Correspondence and Cultural Exchange in Early Modern Europe 1400–1700* (Cambridge UP, 2007).

Joshua Hillman is currently a Teaching Fellow in History of Science at the University of Leeds (United Kingdom). He obtained his PhD at Leeds University with a thesis entitled *From coallery to the natural history of strata: mining and the spatial sciences of the earth in Britain, 1600–1800.*

Francesco Luzzini is Assistant Professor of History of Science at the University of East Piedmont (Vercelli, Italy) and Research Associate at the Max Planck Institute of Geoanthropology in Jena (Germany). His research focuses on the Earth and environmental sciences, natural philosophy, and medicine in early modern Europe, with important forays into modern and contemporary contexts. Formerly a Marie Skłodowska-Curie Global Fellow (Ca' Foscari University of Venice – Johns Hopkins University), he is Italian Editor for the *Isis Bibliography of the History of Science* and member of the Nominating Committee of the History of Earth Sciences Society (HESS). His recent books include: *Quando il mondo scalò il Sublime* (MuSe 2022); *Theory, Practice, and Nature In-between* (Edition Open Sources 2018).

DOI: 10.13173/9783447123693.229

Pietro Daniel Omodeo is professor of historical epistemology at Ca' Foscari University of Venice (Italy) and the director of the UNESCO Chair in *Water Heritage and Sustainable Development* at the NICHE Centre for Environmental Humanities. Moreover, he is affiliated to the Max Planck Institute of Geoanthropology in Jena and is head of the Max Planck Partner Group *The Water City* (Berlin–Jena–Venice). He has published widely across the fields of early modern science, political epistemology and critical science studies. His current research explores the political epistemology of the Anthropocene and historical hydrosociology. He is the author, among others, of *Political Epistemology: The Problem of Ideology in Science Studies* (2019), (with J. Renn) *Science in Court Society: Giovanni Battista Benedetti's* Diversarum speculationum mathematicarum et physicarum liber *(Turin, 1585)* (2019), and *Defending Descartes in Brandenburg-Prussia: The University of Frankfurt an der Oder in the Seventeenth Century* (2022). He is the director of the series *Knowledge Hegemonies in the Early Modern World: Sources and Interpretations* and a co-director of the series *Political Epistemology* (Springer Verlag).

Barbara Orland is Senior Researcher of the Pharmarcy Museum at Basel (Switzerland) and Lecturer of Early Modern History of Science at Basel University. Her research focuses are history of pharmacy and nutritional sciences, gender history, and body history. She is the co-edtor (with Kijan Espahangizi) of *Stoffe in Bewegung – Beiträge zur Wissensgeschichte der materiellen Welt* (Diaphanes 2014) and (with Byron Dowse and Evelyn Grassi) of *Materialwissen: Experimentelle Geschichte im Pharmaziemuseum* (Aether 7, 2023).

Justas Patkauskas is currently a Marie Sklodowska-Curie Postdoctoral Fellow at Ca' Foscari University of Venice (Italy). He works on geoanthropology, biopolitics, and knowledge-making in modernity. His recent publications include "Anthropocene Metabolisms" (in *Geoanthropology and Waterscapes,* Max Planck Institute of Geoanthropology 2025) and "Reflexive Biopolitics and the Structure of Experimental Knowledge" (in *Philosophy & Social Criticism* 2021).

Omar Rodríguez is a cultural historian and philosopher of science and technology, particularly interested in the particularities of knowledge and practices in the multicultural Ibero-American world, and theirimplications for their environments. Currently, he is doing a postdoctoral fellowship on *The Dispute for the Environment in the Valley of Mexico* at the Ca' Foscari University of Venice. Where he collaborates with the UNESCO Chair on "Water Heritageand Sustainable Development", and with the New Institute Centre for Environmental Humanities (NICHE). In Mexico, he is part of the project "Critique of Epistemocracy, Cognitive Pluralism, Epistemic Equity and Democracy" at UNAM.

Alexander Schunka is Professor of Early Modern History at the Freie Universität Berlin (Germany). He is the author of *Die Hugenotten* (C.H. Beck 2019), *Ein neuer Blick nach Westen* (Harrassowitz 2019), *Gäste, die bleiben* (Lit 2006) and *Soziales Wis-*

sen und dörfliche Welt (Lang 2000). He is also the co-editor of several books and has authored numerous articles on topics such as migration, religion, and natural resources in the early modern era.

Aina Trias Verbeeck is currently a postdoctoral researcher at Institució Milà i Fontanals de Recerca en Humanitats (IMF) – CSIC, Barcelona (Spain). Her PhD thesis deals with Catalan and French writings about fishing and sea fauna, based on Catalan and French writings of the early 18th century with the title *The sea in a cabinet. The fishing manuscript of Joan Salvador, 1722: contexts of production and reception.*

Helge Wendt is currently research coordinator of the Decision Agora project at Friedrich-Schiller-Universität Jena (Germany) and lecturer of Modern History at the Freie Universität Berlin. He is associated researcher at the Center for Advanced Latin American Studies (CALAS) and at the Max Planck Institute for Geoanthropology. He has worked on global and colonial history, as well as in the field of history of knowledge and science. He is the author of *Kohlezeit. Eine Global- und Wissensgeschichte, 1500–1900* (Campus 2022), *Geschichte des mestizischen Europas* (Springer 2019) and *Die missionarische Gesellschaft* (Franz Steiner 2011). His most recent publications include *Logbuch Wissensgeschichte* (Harrassowitz 2024).